For John Dolman

Although I was not privileged to know the late Professor Dolman, we became friends during my study of his text. His knowledge, understanding,
and love for the theatre have earned my undying respect. I hope that his
high standards of production continue to show through my efforts on this
book, which will continue to be his.

CONTENTS

vii

xiii

xv

Photographs on pages 33, 125, 153, and 250 by Amnon Ben Nomis. Photograph on page 57 by Richard A. Bull, University of South Dakota Theatre. Photographs on pages 84, 111, 166, 198, 216, 241, 271, and 411 by Nammi Lee. Photograph on page 311 supplied by Weiss, University of Virginia. Photograph on page 333 by Ritterson, Theatre 300. Photograph on page 436 courtesy of the University of Colorado Publications Service.

This book is for the beginner, but not for the dabbler. It does not presuppose any previous experience in play production, but it does presuppose a realization that the art of good play production is not to be learned in a day; that it is, in fact, a lifetime study, to be approached with humility and patience.

In the eighteen years since the book was first published, the standards of excellence in school, college, and community theatre production have risen considerably. It is true that the films have largely replaced the professional "road" theatres as popular entertainment outside of the larger cities—so much so that our wartime camp shows gave many servicemen their first glimpse of "round actors." But for that very reason the people in the smaller communities who crave real theatre, and who still prefer round actors to pictures, have given increasing support to amateur, educational, and semiprofessional theatre groups. Many thousands of such groups are now operating in this country—more than all the professional road companies in their palmiest days; hundreds of them are strongly organized and highly expert, and most people know that their expertness is achieved only by study, experience, and hard work.

It has therefore seemed even less necessary than before to address this book to the well-meaning but half-hearted beginner who would like to stage a play for the firemen's carnival or the mothers' club social, and wants somebody to tell him briefly in words of one syllable just how to turn the trick. It is addressed, rather—even more seriously than before—to the ambitious amateur who wants to learn how to work with, or to build up, a permanent and artistic producing group; to the student with professional aims who wishes to approach his life work thoughtfully as well as practically; to the student of liberal arts, in or out of school, who would like to enhance his appreciation of the theatre in relation to other arts; and to the teacher at any school level who is called upon to teach theatre or produce plays.

It is addressed to the amateur rather than the professional solely because it is the amateur who is most often the beginner and who needs the most help; but there is no implication that amateur production is necessarily inferior to professional, or that it is essentially different in its artistic aims. Good theatre is good theatre, whether the actors act for

xix

a living or for love of the work. That even the professional player may gain by a modest approach is attested by the fact that more and more of the best younger players now reach their profession by way of college or community theatre experience.

The previous paragraphs are from Mr. Dolman's Preface to the revision of this work done in 1945. I should like to add only that it has been my aim to retain that part of the original which continues to be meaningful and pertinent. New movements in the theatre must be reckoned with, yet the basic idea of what theatre is and how one must function within it have not changed.

In order to make this volume more helpful to those who produce plays, he technical aspects of production have been stressed to match the material on directing. With only this book in hand the beginner can struggle through all phases of putting on a play. He is encouraged, however, to consult the bibliography for those sources most oriented to his special problems of production.

All illustrations are new and have been chosen from the large number made available to me by the many brilliant designers at work today in the educational and regional theatres.

A special thanks to my wife and daughter, whose work in the preparation of the manuscript was invaluable; to my colleagues Gary Schattschneider, W. Joseph Zender, and Thom Schmunk for their charts and drawings; and to Eloise Pearson, whose typing and editing have made my work much easier.

Richard K. Knaub
University of Colorado

The theatre of today embraces so many forms of activity that an exact definition of the director's problems and responsibilities is hardly possible. There are many different kinds of plays and many different methods of producing them. There are literary plays, escapist plays, and plays of "social significance" – sometimes more concerned with propaganda than with art; there are operas, pantomimes, musical comedies, reviews, ballets, and variety shows, all of which belong to the theatre in its broadest sense; there are motion pictures, radio plays, and television plays, all calling for differences of technique. There are realistic plays, in which the theatre tries desperately to compete with the expensive realism of the movies; there are stylistic and imaginative plays; and there are experiments in theatrical abstraction and absurdism, as well as experiments involving the direct participation of the audience. The theatre of today has few limits or formulas, save that there be live actors performing for an audience. Every kind of theatre form and every kind of audience relationship is currently being tested. The theatre of the 1970s is the most varied and flexible the world has ever known. Elaborate costume dramas exist next to nudity, and the theatre of confrontation and audience involvement exists next to the theatre of illusion.

In the years immediately following World War I, a great deal was heard about "the new movement in the theatre," or "the theatre of tomorrow," as if a definite change were taking place, with definite objectives. It is now clear that there is no such thing as "the" new movement in the theatre. The theatre, like most other aspects of life, has entered into an experimental age – an age of restless inquiry, provocative criticism, and inventive ingenuity in both art and mechanics. Never in history have there been so many kinds of theatre, good and bad; never in history have theatre-goers been so uncertain in their minds as to what constitutes good theatre. Never has commercialism been carried to such fantastic extremes as in modern "show business" – yet never have there been as many successful and well-organized noncommercial theatres in the world. Never, in other words, was the theatre as heterogeneous as it is today.

Nevertheless, it is fair to say that the continuing tendency of the twentieth-century theatre is to place more emphasis on the work of the director than at almost any previous period of theatre history.

the director as artist

In the art of play production, to use the narrower sense of the word "play," it is the author who supplies the principal idea, determines the purpose, and functions in general as the original creative artist. But it is very generally agreed that a play is not a play until it is realized upon the stage, however important it may be as pure literature. From the standpoint of the theatre the written or printed text is merely a set of instructions telling the director, the actors, and the technical staff how to go about the task of giving life to the play. The art of the theatre is not an individual art; it is essentially a group art, in which the author, the director, the designers, the actors, the musicians, the stage crew, and even the audience all contribute to a common creative effort. It is the director, therefore, rather than the author, who is responsible for the finished product. The author, even when he is his own director, can hardly foresee all the conditions and problems that may arise in the course of production. What he does as author is suggestive but not necessarily conclusive, and it remains for the whole group, working under the director's guidance, to carry the creative effort to its full realization.

In this sense, then, the director is as much a creative artist as the author himself, and he must share the author's creative attitude. No amount of technical knowledge of facile craftsmanship will take the place of a true grasp of the author's purpose. Not infrequently a new play is half rewritten at rehearsals, and even though the director may do none of the actual rewriting, it is often his feeling for the play as a whole that serves to bring out the need of revision and to suggest the manner. No director can be expected to make a good play out of an idea that is, in its inception, hopelessly bad, but he can be, and often is, expected to make a finished play out of a very rough and unfinished text. Often, too, he is expected to take a play that was written for other times and conditions and adapt it for a new type of production and a new audience. If not a dramatist, he must at least be a competent "play doctor."

From the creative point of view it becomes evident that the first business of the stage director is to understand the nature and purpose of the drama

Practical trees take varied forms. *Above,* The University of Illinois production of *Summertree,* designed by Don Llewellyn. *Opposite,* The University of Colorado's *Grass Harp* by Aubrey Wilson.

as an art; to understand this clearly he must know something of the fine arts in general — especially of their purpose.

the nature of the fine arts

The fine arts may be described as activities that exist primarily for the purpose of giving aesthetic pleasure — that is, pleasure dependent upon the

appreciation of beauty. There are, of course, many notions as to what constitutes beauty; one person may find his conception of it in a vivid sunset,
another in a tragic poem, and another in a particularly smooth-running
gasoline engine. Some enjoy beauty only in connection with utility or with
social purpose; others prefer it alone and for its own sake. But the power to
appreciate some sort of beauty is almost universal—hence the wide appeal
of the fine arts and the wide variety of different arts to satisfy different
natures.

For a proper understanding of the fine arts, then, one must keep in mind their common aesthetic purpose. But that alone is not enough. One must also be able to discern, through all the variations of subject matter, method, and technique, a single common principle governing the relationship of the arts to life: the principle of conventionalization. The fine arts, despite their differences, are all alike in what they offer us—not life itself, but a representation of life in terms of artistic conventions. Perhaps "representation" is too narrow a word; some artists insist that art should be a presentation rather than a representation; others feel that it should be a reading or interpretation of life, a criticism of life, or a direct expression of the artist's thought or feeling. It is not necessary to settle this question or to insist upon an exact definition of the term *convention*. Obviously, the conventions are different for different arts, both in kind and in degree. It is, however, the principle of conventionalization that distinguishes art from reality.

Thus, the fine art of painting aims to give aesthetic pleasure by representing or expressing life through the convention of line, mass, and color on a flat surface; there is no actual movement and no actual depth, though both, of course, are suggested. The fine art of sculpture usually leaves out color, or reduces it to a conventional monotone; it leaves out movement also, but it retains depth. Photography ordinarily leaves out depth and movement but is so accurate in other respects that the artistic photographer usually finds it necessary to use some screening or defocusing process to eliminate unessential detail; if he follows the trend toward sharp definition, he offsets it by the use of odd lighting or queer angle shots. With brush or crayon it is hard to imitate nature accurately, but with the camera the difficulty is to avoid being too natural. It is significant that whenever artistic representation becomes too natural, it ceases to be artistic. Thus, we find that natural color photography has not proved popular as a fine art. It is very useful for giving us a truer vision of unfamiliar scenes, as in the *National Geographic Magazine*, or for treasuring the memory of beautiful things like last summer's garden or a colorful stage setting, but it is not in itself an effective means of creating beauty artistically. It is too much like life. So, as a rule, is colored statuary, especially when the coloring is natural and the statue life-size.[1] In the imitation of reality there must always be some element of unreality—not untruth, but exaggeration, understatement, or simplification—or the result, no matter how beautiful as life, does not appeal to us as art.

It will be noted that all of the arts mentioned conventionalize by retaining some of the elements of life as naturally as possible and boldly rejecting others as unessential. Their technique is based upon the simple principle of selection. The art of literature, in general, and the art of the drama, as generally understood, belong in the same class.

abstraction in the fine arts

Some arts, however, go farther in the direction of conventionalization; they reject all of the concrete elements of life itself and translate the thought or feeling into a language of abstractions—of pure form. Music, the most popular and universal of all the arts, is one of these. It expresses moods or feelings in terms of musical tones and rhythms, abstract things that have no specific or rational meaning in themselves but gain their effects directly through their power to stir up emotions. We accept and enjoy this convention because our senses tell us that it is a beautiful one, because it enables us to assume an aesthetic attitude; and the more accustomed we become to such abstraction the more we resent any attempt to rerationalize music by injecting elements of the concrete. So-called descriptive music is quite generally displeasing to persons of cultivated taste, except perhaps when it is frankly humorous, or associated with child's play, as in the case of Haydn's *Children's Symphony*.

the nature of the sense of beauty

The Ancients thought of beauty almost exclusively in connection with the fine arts, making very little mention of the beauties of nature as such. Yet with apparent inconsistency many of them emphasized the element of imitation in the fine arts, alleging that beauty lay in the subject matter imitated, and that the measure of the artist's achievement was his ability to reproduce beautiful subject matter accurately. Some even went so far as to maintain that there could be no beauty, no aesthetic pleasure, in the artistic representation of what was not in itself beautiful.

Plato and Aristotle were among the first to modify this idea, Aristotle recognizing that under some conditions the representation of actual ugliness must give aesthetic pleasure. Neither, however, was fully able to explain the phenomenon. Aristotle seemed to think that admiration of the skill with which the imitation was accomplished was the source of the pleasure, a theory that has found much support in modern times among certain schools of realists. He also developed the well-known theory of *catharsis*, the theory of beauty in tragedy based upon the idea of a cleansing or purging of the spirit of the observer. Plato tried to explain beauty by emphasizing the pleasure to be drawn from unity in variety. This became, and still is, one of the leading thoughts in aesthetic philosophy, but it explains the method of the fine arts rather than the aesthetic purpose. The Greeks thought the pleasure of unity a sensuous one, and their insistence upon the idea is partly responsible not only for the widespread exaltation of the unities in later times, especially in France, but also for the common notion that all art is sensuous.

Modern writers in general have ridiculed the idea that imitation or representation is the key to beauty. They have pointed out that if this were so there would be no excuse for art at all, since the beautiful object in nature would always be more beautiful than any possible imitation of it; whereas it is well known that we often take more pleasure in the representation than in the reality. They have pointed out also, following Aristotle, that we often take the very greatest pleasure in the representation of the tragic — of that which, in reality, would give us the greatest pain. In other words, they have denied that aesthetic pleasure in the fine arts is based either upon the intrinsic beauty of the object imitated or upon the fidelity of the imitation.

But that is about all they agree upon. When it comes to offering a substitute explanation, they differ widely. One says that beauty lies in the symbolism of the imitation; another that it lies in the revelation of the artist's own soul, in his interpretation of what he sees; another that it lies in the extent to which the creative impulse is exercised by the observer through his imagination. Some confuse their aesthetic with their ethical theories and assert that beauty is truth and truth beauty, or that beauty is an approach to goodness or perfection; others adopt a religious point of view and say that beauty lies in the approach to God. But possibly the largest number, following the Greek idea, believe that the sense of beauty rests on a more or less sensuous appreciation of form.

In recent years there has been a marked tendency in some quarters toward a great degree of abstraction in all the fine arts. Cubism, futurism, and surrealism in painting, mysticism in poetry, and expressionism and absurdism in the theatre are familiar examples of this—though in all these, as in other radical reforms, the principles involved have been much beclouded by opportunists seeking easy notoriety and by psychoneurotics seeking to satisfy their craving for the abnormal. An exhaustive discussion of abstraction in art would be out of place in this book; but the existence of the tendency cannot be ignored by anyone who would understand modern stage directing. A play like van Itallie's *America Hurrah* or Beckett's *Waiting for Godot* calls for a very different style of directing from that appropriate to a realistic comedy of family life. There is a great deal to be said for the enrichment of our opportunities to enjoy beauty in its more abstract forms; yet one can have little sympathy with those extremists who would abolish all art not highly abstract. It is true that many of our finest aesthetic feelings spring from such arts as music and the dance, but there is no need on that account to abolish representational painting, or the realistic novel, or the drama. These things give pleasure too. As new and beautiful abstractions are developed in the theatre, through which real messages of the spirit can artistically be conveyed, let us accept them by all means. But let us also cherish the more traditional art of the theatre—an art that is in some respects more concrete than any other because it retains actual life, speech, and movement, as well as color and form; but that is second only to music in the permanency and universality of its appeal.

is beauty sensuous?

The latter view finds considerable support in the teachings of modern psychology, and appeals especially to those who have started with a philosophical concept and are seeking to justify it on psychological grounds. But it raises a difficulty. If appreciation of beauty is purely a matter of the effect of form on our senses, what about the thought content of so many fine arts—literature and the drama, for instance? Is that merely incidental and of no consequence? Or, if we find pleasure in thought, must we regard that pleasure as nonaesthetic?

There are some who do not hesitate to go so far. Ethel Puffer,[2] for instance, seems to take such a position with respect to the fine arts in general, freely admitting the value of intellectual pleasure but denying that it is aesthetic. Gordon Craig certainly took it with respect to the theatre, demanding such unity of sensuous appeal as the Greeks themselves hardly dreamed of, and lamenting bitterly the intellectual distractions that are always getting in the way.

To complain that this theory would exclude from aesthetic consideration such plays as those of Shaw would be to invite the criticism that Shaw was a propagandist anyhow. Let us consider, then, not Shaw but Shakespeare. Although there is some sensuous appeal in the poetry of Shakespeare, it is not so much beauty of form or sound as beauty of thought that has made him the world's greatest poet; and it is not so much the appeal to the senses through sound and spectacle as the appeal to the understanding through revelation of human character and motive that has made him the world's greatest dramatist. Yet surely the pleasure he gives us is aesthetic in the highest sense. If not, then aesthetic pleasure is too narrow and trivial to bother about, and is not the sole or principal aim of the fine arts—as, indeed, many critics are now asserting, especially the devotees of propagandist or "socially significant" art. Some of us prefer to keep the term and make the interpretation broad enough to cover the kinds of pleasure we really do take in the fine arts.

What, then, is aesthetic pleasure in the broad sense? To formulate any sort of helpful answer we must take into consideration certain elements that play no direct part in ancient philosophy. A few modern writers, combining philosophical thought with scientific investigation, have clarified the problem considerably, and have given us some principles of aesthetic appreciation that are not only of great interest, but of great practical value to the stage director as well. A notable contribution of this sort in English was made by Herbert Sidney Langfeld in his book *The Aesthetic Attitude,* a book that every stage director should read.

the psychology of appreciation

It is quite usual for artists and aesthetes to scoff at psychology — except, perhaps, abnormal psychology — and to insist that art is on a higher plane than science and altogether independent of it. To some extent one must share this view, for too much science breeds self-consciousness and self-consciousness destroys ease and naturalness in art. But there is no profit in ignoring facts, and there are some facts about human behavior that so vitally affect our concept of beauty and our reaction to it that the creative artist cannot escape them. He may ignore them, or he may confirm them unconsciously; he may succeed in his art through accident or inspiration. But play production, being a group art, is of necessity a more conscious art than some others. The director's task, being largely that of criticizing and harmonizing the work of others, must be performed more consciously than those of some other artists, and he must thoroughly understand what he is doing.

Psychology is still, of course, an experimental science, and psychologists differ widely in their fundamental explanations of human behavior. Most of them, however, concede the importance of what is called motor response in relation to our emotional sensibilities, including our reaction to beauty. Motor response may be explained very simply in terms made familiar through elementary physiology as taught in the schools. Everybody knows that the human organism is controlled through a nervous system, of which the brain itself is the apex, and that the main portion of the system consists of two sets of nerves: sensory nerves, which report the experiences of the sense organs, and motor nerves, which control the movements of the muscles. Nearly everybody is familiar with what is commonly called *reflex action*, whereby certain sense impressions are received and corresponding motor impulses discharged without conscious realization.[3] Some schoolbooks assert that this function is carried on by the spinal cord, and some appear to treat it as exceptional. In point of fact it is quite normal; indeed it takes care of most of the impressions we receive. Only a few of the most striking impressions ever reach the brain – or at any rate the consciousness. In walking through a mile of familiar streets one may step up and down a score of curbs, turn corners, and avoid obstructions without ever being conscious of the sense impressions that have made him do these things, or of the motor activities involved in them. Only when an impression is unusual, contrasting, or vivid does enough of it reach the brain to engage attention; and perhaps even then a part of it finds its way into motor response automatically and in advance of the resulting thought process.

There is nothing new in the mere observation of motor response, or in the fact that most of our responses are unconscious. Long before the nervous system itself was discovered, men had observed that certain perceptions caused certain muscular reactions; and even the Ancients knew that some of these reactions had something to do with the appreciation of beauty. What is comparatively new is the scientific recognition of a general law – simple, but universal – governing the relation of motor response to sense impression.

the law of motor response

The law is this: For every stimulus impressed upon the human organism there is a direct motor response, the nature of which depends upon two factors, (1) the nature of the stimulus, and (2) the nature of the past experience of the organism.

By a *stimulus* is meant primarily an impression received through one of the senses and conveyed to the brain, or toward the brain, by the sensory nerves; but a remembered or imagined stimulus is also capable of inducing a motor response.

By a *motor response* is meant an impulse to activity, carried to the muscles of the body through the motor nerves. When the impulse is strong enough and is not inhibited or suppressed in any way, it results in a clearly defined muscular action, and we are all familiar enough with such manifestations. But many of our motor impulses are too feeble to result in any outwardly visible action, and many more are inhibited either consciously or unconsciously by reason of the restraints imposed upon us by civilization and education. That is why the operation of the law so often escapes notice, and why we get into the habit of supposing that perceptions sometimes result merely in thought or feeling, and not in action. What really happens is that every time we see, hear, touch, taste, or smell something, we experience almost instantly a corresponding motor response, even though it be limited to a mere *action pattern* or *motor set,* imperceptible to the eye. The existence of such a concealed response, when no outward response is discernible, can be proved in the laboratory through the use of delicate instruments that record changes in blood pressure, muscle tensions, and the chemical reactions in the body. A witness may be detected in a lie by this method; no matter how skillful he may be in concealing his inner reactions from an ordinary observer he is helpless to prevent the occurrence of automatic responses easily recorded by the so-called lie detector.

motor attitudes
in aesthetic
appreciation

The observation of a work of art takes place through the senses, particularly those of sight and hearing. According to the law, there must be certain motor responses induced by such observation and it seems reasonable to suppose that the nature of these responses may have something to do with whether or not we derive pleasure from the observation. As a matter of fact, it can be shown that our aesthetic enjoyment is chiefly dependent upon our motor attitudes – is actually felt in terms of those attitudes.

This is a strong statement, and at first glance may seem inconsistent with my previous contention that there is an intellectual as well as a sensuous element in beauty. But it must be remembered that the motor attitudes are dependent upon two factors: the observer's previous preparation and the stimulus itself. It is in the observer's previous preparation that the intellectual element is to be found. Into that preparation enter not only all the sights and sounds that have ever fallen upon his senses, but also all the thoughts and emotions that have resulted from them, either directly or indirectly. Sense stimuli are in themselves meaningless; it is only as they take on meaning in terms of the individual's experience that they become significant. A newborn infant, though his senses function, fails to notice even very obvious sights and sounds. It is not until he has grown familiar with certain impressions and begun to make associations and draw inferences that he begins to show appreciative response. If beauty were a matter of pure form, without meaning, and appreciation nothing but an automatic effect of form on sense, the youngest infant not blind or deaf would have as keen an appreciation of the fine arts as the most experienced connoisseur. Perhaps he has, but the evidence does not seem to show it. It seems to show, rather, that the highest aesthetic appreciation must be learned through experience; or in other words, that one's power to assume a pleasurable motor attitude toward the finest works of art must be acquired through familiarity with the stimuli involved, and understanding of their significance in relation to the whole experience of life.

The artist's problem, then, is largely the problem of producing the right motor attitude in his audience. To do so he must take into consideration both of the governing factors—the nature of the stimuli and the previous experience of his audience. Since the stimuli with which he is to make his appeal are themselves intelligible to his audience only in terms of previous experience, the two factors cannot be separated, but must be studied together. For the stage director such a study is especially important because he cannot escape the responsibility of appealing to his audience as a whole, regardless of their individual differences.

A painter or a poet can express himself on canvas or paper with the feeling that the public can take his work or leave it; he expects appreciation from some and not from others, and he knows that the unappreciative ones will not interfere with the others. But the stage director cannot afford to neglect any of his audience, for if he fails to reach some of them their indifference or hostility will soon affect the rest. The painter may concern himself with *ex*pression, leaving the matter of *im*pression to accident; the stage director must think in terms of *im*pression. To do so he must understand this matter of response as well as it can be understood.

An exhaustive study of the psychology of response would be impossible here. There are, however, two major principles on the aesthetic side of the study that are of such direct importance to the stage director as to call for careful consideration. The first of these is the principle of *empathy* or imitative response as an element of appreciation, and the second is the principle of artistic detachment or *aesthetic distance.*

notes and references

1. It is true that the Greeks colored their statues — probably more for decoration than for realism.
2. Ethel Puffer, *The Psychology of Beauty* (Boston: Houghton Mifflin, 1905).
3. Some modern psychologists define a reflex as an inherited response, but as the whole question of heredity is still in dispute, the definition is of no use to us. I am using the term in the popular meaning of unconscious response, though, to be sure, no one has yet successfully defined consciousness.

A great many of our motor responses are in some way imitative. Of that we can be sure, though the exact part played by imitation in our behavior, and especially in our learning processes, is another subject of dispute among the psychologists. Children certainly employ imitation in learning, if only to strengthen impressions already received, and most of their play is imitative. If older people seem less imitative than children, it is partly because their behavior is more complex and therefore less easily analyzed, and partly because they have learned to suppress many of their motor responses as a matter of good manners. But the impulses are there, and those that are not outwardly visible are often of great importance in relation to artistic appreciation.

If a man with a very peculiar walk passes a group of children at play, they are very likely to fall in behind and follow him, imitating his walk and exaggerating it. Perhaps this impulse is not so very far from the basic impulse of acting. But we do not always recognize the fact that older people feel the impulse just as strongly as children, and that they suppress it only because civilization has taught them to do so. They may be unconscious of the impulse, but that is because the lesson of inhibition has been so well learned that it operates instantly, and suppresses the impulse before it gets started.

In contemplating an object of interest we commonly assume an imitative attitude toward it, feeling out the lines of the object in our own bodies. Thus when we behold the ocean or the mountains we involuntarily throw back our shoulders and expand our lungs, seeming to feel in ourselves the vastness and grandeur of the scene. When we watch a ballet dancer in motion we follow vicariously her every movement, feeling the grace and lightness as if it were our own. When we watch a high jumper at a track meet, we relate so closely to him that we raise our own feet into the air when he takes off as if we were jumping in his place or that by our efforts we could help him over the bar. When we listen to music we instinctively seek out the rhythm and follow it with bodily pulsations of some sort, even beating time with feet or hands. And when we see a human being in a perilous or painful situation—a steeplejack in danger of falling from a high building, for instance—we experience much of the sensation of pain or danger in ourselves. When the stimuli are strong and the restraints weak we show these imitative responses in visible action; more often we feel and conceal them, and more often still we experience them only as motor sets, or patterns, and are not even conscious of their nature.

The importance of these imitative motor responses in relation to the sense of beauty has been pointed out by numerous writers,[1] but the most helpful discussion from the standpoint of stage direction is to be found in Langfeld's book, *The Aesthetic Attitude.* Following Titchener, he calls such responses *empathic,* and the term "empathy" is now generally accepted by students of the arts and especially stage directors.

Not all empathic response—not even all pleasant empathic response—is aesthetic; but it is probable that all aesthetic pleasure is empathic. Obviously we can experience pleasant empathy only in what is itself pleasant; the empathic response to pain cannot be pleasant since it consists in feeling the pain in our own attitude. This suggests an important limitation of the fine arts that some extreme realists disregard. However, a painful empathy with respect to a part of something may not be inconsistent with a keen enjoyment of the whole—as, for instance, when dissonances are properly employed in music, or when sorrow plays a part in drama. In such cases the unpleasant empathies may serve to season the pleasant ones by contrast—as red pepper and garlic season the soup—provided, of course, that the pleasant empathies dominate; and this has led some philosophers to believe that the highest form of aesthetic enjoyment lies in a reconcilement or fusion of varied empathies. One version of the theory is that complete aesthetic pleasure is to be found only in perfect repose,[2] and that such repose is to be found only in a perfect balance of empathic responses, a balance equivalent to neutralization. This theory has the advantage of seeming to explain the well-known principles of balance and proportion in design, and is not inconsistent with the rules of harmony in music and the principle of poetic justice in literature. Moreover, it seems to fit in perfectly with another principle of extreme importance, the principle of aesthetic distance—of which more later.

Impressionism, but with strong emotional overtones, is created by careful lighting
and the choice of elements used in the skeleton of the building. Especially effective
is the use of twisted branches, all of which direct the eye into the set. Menotti's *The
Medium*, designed by J. Wendell Johnson, San Jose State.

empathy in the theatre

Empathic responses play an equally vital part in all the fine arts, but in some arts they are obscure and difficult to study. Just how, for example, does one empathize in a Gothic cathedral? Unquestionably there is an imitative impulse of some sort, possibly a stretching upward in imitation of the vertical lines, but there can be no exact imitation because living muscles cannot take the form of a stone building. The very impossibility of exact imitation limits the response to a motor pattern, even if there are no inhibiting influences. Similarly, in contemplating a landscape or a piece of furniture or any inanimate object of beauty, one can but feel the lines in a rough sort of way; he cannot counterfeit the object as a whole.

But the art of the theatre is in terms of human beings—live ones, moving and speaking and showing emotions; and in these one can empathize more vividly and completely than in any other conceivable medium. Herein, I believe, lies the deep and universal appeal of the theatre: deep, because we can go so much farther in our empathic responses; universal, because all kinds of people can respond to it. To empathize properly in an etching, a beautiful building, or a symphonic poem, one must have had some artistic experience, some training, some cultivation; but anybody can feel an imitative response to a human being and anybody can take pleasure in it.

Nearly everybody likes to share the experiences of other human beings. That is the gregarious nature of man. Also, nearly everybody nurses certain suppressed longings for human experience that he has not himself had, and never expects to have, and perhaps in his better judgment does not really wish to have. In the theatre he is enabled to satisfy these longings vicariously, without entangling himself in the obligations and embarrassments that may be incidental to the real experience—just as the spectator at a football game feels in his own muscle tensions the thrill of heroic endeavor without actually suffering the hard knocks. This is a large part of the appeal of sport; it is also a large part of the appeal of fiction, and the theatre is the most vivid form of fiction.

This being so, the stage director can ill afford to ignore or neglect the principle of empathy, and its specific application to the art of the theatre. Bearing in mind the two factors that govern every response—the nature of the stimulus and the nature of the observer's previous preparation—he must ask himself what imitative responses each character, each scene, each piece of action will evoke, and whether they will be pleasant. There are other considerations, of course, but if he can cultivate the ability to foresee empathic effects, he will find that many of the most serious problems of play production become easier to solve.

empathy in casting

Many a play has been spoiled by errors in casting, quite apart from the abilities of the actors as actors. The leading lady may be a beautiful and capable actress, yet fail to win the kind of sympathetic interest that is essential to the play. The critics will say that she lacks personality or that her personality is not suited to the part. But "personality" is a vague word. It is more accurate to say that she lacks the power of inducing the proper empathic responses in the audience.

Generally speaking, the women in the audience empathize most strongly in the heroine, while the men empathize most strongly in the hero. Nothing could be more wholehearted than the response the women give to an actress who can make them feel the experiences of the heroine imaginatively in their own bodies. On the other hand, the reader will no doubt recall many actresses—beautiful, accomplished, and perhaps pleasing to the men—who have seemed always to leave the women in the audience cold and unresponsive.

Similarly, there are actors who antagonize the men, actors who seem capable enough and look their parts, who are popular, perhaps, with the women, but who produce only savage disgust in the men. The movies are particularly afflicted with such actors. There is the actor with deep dark eyes and curly hair and the build of a Greek god; the women say: "How handsome he is! What soulful eyes! How well his clothes fit him!" But the men are very likely saying: "Good Lord! What a ladylike voice! And look how he holds a baseball bat! If I talked and acted that way I'd feel a fool or a

Two interpretations for Eugene O'Neill's *Long Day's Journey Into Night*. Note the similarity of floorplans. *Above*, From Washington State University, directed by Paul Wadleigh and designed by Richard Slabaugh. *Opposite*, From Indiana University, directed and designed by William Kinzer.

---

sissy." The trouble is, they *are* feeling it—empathically—and the sensation is painful.

In choosing a cast, therefore, the director should consider two things: the direct effect of each player upon those who are to empathize most strongly in the character he represents, and the indirect effect upon those who are to empathize in the opposite character. The actress who is to play a sympathetic part must be able to appeal to the women by making them feel the experiences of the character in their own bodies, and she must be able to fit in properly with the empathic responses that the men are giving to the male characters. In other words, if she is to play the heroine, she must be capable of making every woman feel like the heroine herself, and of making every man in the audience fall in love with her vicariously. Every man must feel that it would be no hardship to embrace her, else when the hero does so there will be revulsion of feeling.

On the other hand, if the player is to do an unsympathetic part, it is just as necessary that he should not induce too warm an empathic response. A

sweet-faced, young ingenue was cast in the part of an adventuress who philanders with the hero's son because she has always loved the father. She played it so sincerely and sympathetically that the effect was very moving—and ruined the evening by killing the farce. It was not her fault; it was a plain case of miscasting through failure to foresee empathic response.

The physical characteristics of actors are important empathically and must be considered in casting—beauty, grace, stature, voice, and the rest. But the imagination is even more important, for it is the actor with a lively and flexible imagination who is most apt to create the proper empathic effects. Of the physical characteristics, voice seems most closely associated with imagination, at least when adequately controlled. The late Mrs. Fiske always insisted upon voice as the most important concern of the actor—a vehicle of the imagination, but to be considered before it because a voice is more susceptible to training and more generally in need of it. It is precisely because of its great empathic power that voice is so significant; and it is not only a vehicle of the imagination but to some extent an index of it. The director choosing a cast must look both for imagination and physical means of inducing empathic response, and the voice will tell him much about both.

naturalism and empathy

Most actors strive, by countless little tricks of stage business or pantomime, to create an impression of naturalness. Whenever a little touch of naturalness heightens the illusion it is the empathic response that is at work; we are feeling the reality of the character because he is doing things that, in terms of our past experience, we can easily imagine ourselves doing.

The function of stage business is largely empathic. There are those, of course, who would do away with stage business, especially in poetic drama, on the ground that it is cheapening and that great beauty of emotion can best be revealed through the play of voice and imagination in speech. Perhaps it can, if the artist is equal to the task – pure reading being undoubtedly a higher and more difficult art than acting. But we are considering acting, and not reading. Too much stage business is, of course, distracting, even in the most realistic drama, and stage business for its own sake is never justifiable. But as a means of creating the proper empathies, stage business not only is justifiable but is sometimes more effective than the voice itself, for the reason that it is less difficult to manage. The voice is subtle, even treacherous, and but few actors have it under perfect control, whereas stage business can be invented by the director and performed by the actor with a certain assurance of accuracy and stability.

The dramatist sometimes feels this, and so plans to have important or significant scenes played in pantomime; and the director can often point up or intensify scenes in this way. Many of Bernhardt's most telling scenes were silent ones, turning perhaps upon a single expressive gesture, rightly chosen to begin with, and then played with absolute precision at every performance – this despite her possession of a truly great voice.

There are times when silent action is empathically more eloquent than voice. To say this is not to deny the power of voice or to discourage its use when well controlled; but if in a silent scene there is no vibrant sympathetic voice to stir the proper emotions, at least there is no poorly controlled, disillusioning voice to interfere with them and create unpleasant empathies; and if the director has planned the movements and business effectively and the actor has imagination, the empathic response will be strong. It is an unfortunate fact that not one actress in ten can weep vocally and be convincing, and that not one in twenty can laugh convincingly. Yet a false cry or a false laugh is empathically one of the most unpleasant experiences anybody can have in the theatre. Very few directors seem to realize this, or if they do they are at a loss how to correct the trouble. Sometimes, it cannot be corrected at all so far as the voice is concerned, but pantomime can often be substituted effectively. An actress whose audible cry would make one's blood run cold can achieve a very satisfactory suggestion of grief simply by turning away from the audience, covering her face, and heaving her shoulders as if she were sobbing.

In general, if the dramatist has done his work well, the big scene of a play will have been prepared for, and the empathies of the audience will carry it with but the simplest suggestions from the actors.

It has often been remarked that some actors act only with their voices or their faces or their hands, whereas others act with their whole bodies. As a general rule the latter are immeasurably more effective, because they evoke more empathic response. A deaf person should be able to watch good actors and grasp their characters from their postures and movements. Helen Hayes, in *Victoria Regina*, told us more about certain moods of the Queen by the way she walked than by her words. As Marie in *Liliom*, years ago, Hortense Alden achieved an exit that was a masterpiece; ordered away by the bossy Mrs. Muskat, she had to go clear across the stage with never a word to say, but she did it with such an impudent expression and such a baffling mixture of shamble and skip that she left the audience literally tingling with her mood. There are many stage people of both sexes who fall short of the ideal in coordination of bodily movement, failing to stir up adequate empathic response because they do not seem to be feeling things down to their toes; and there are some who, failing to use their extremities expressively, use them distractingly, making all sorts of meaningless and irrelevant movements that stir up no empathies except those of uncertainty and self-consciousness. It should be the aim of every actor to make his whole body responsive to his imagination, and it should be the director's aim to choose actors and actresses who have succeeded in doing so.

the empathy of thrills

With an understanding of empathic response we are in a position to appreciate the tremendous effect of thrilling situations in the theatre.

The drama is built out of contrasts and conflicts, out of obstacles and dangers, and their overcoming. The greater the danger or obstacle, the greater the empathic satisfaction in seeing it overcome. It is the director's business, therefore, to see that the dangers are so presented that the audience will feel them keenly in their own imaginative experiences.

Some years ago we had a deluge of thrilling mystery plays, and the phenomenal popularity of many of these was largely due to the skill with which empathic effects were handled. Despite the impact of mass murder in two wars, the vogue of such plays has not completely died down; new ones appear from time to time, and old ones are revived in stock and community theatres—especially *Seven Keys to Baldpate* and *The Bat*. Mysterious banging of doors and rattling of chains, hairy arms reaching in through windows or out through panels in the walls, lights going out suddenly, trap doors opening in the floor, threats of vivisection or sudden death—by such means are audiences made to feel danger through identifying themselves with the imperiled character. In *The Ghost Breaker*, one of the earliest plays of this type, there was a scene in which the hero, after a fruitless search for the disturbers in a haunted house, stood near a huge suit of armor. Suddenly the latter came to life, raising a prodigious sword, prepared to bring it down on the hero's unsuspecting head. Audience after audience screamed in horror at the scene; they felt that sword descending on their own heads.

It is remarkable what nonsense audiences will accept if the empathy is only made strong enough. Most of the popular thrillers make no pretense of being anything but claptrap, but they often play to packed houses, and audiences squeal with expectancy when the lights go out, even before the rise of the curtain. However, equally thrilling effects can be achieved in drama of higher type and greater sincerity; in a good production of *Hamlet* or *Macbeth,* for example, the empathies are as powerful as in *The Bat,* though without the element of spoofing that leads to hysterical giggles.

In the movies abundant use is made of the empathic thrill, particularly in comedy; in fact, the film farce is largely based upon it, with wild rides on motorcycles, trains, or automobiles, with runaway baby carriages, narrowly avoided collisions, and daredevil stunts of all kinds. A favorite situation is one in which the comic character is seen slipping and falling on a narrow ledge ten stories above the street; when the window molding to which he is clinging suddenly gives way, one's stomach seems literally to turn over. It is almost too harrowing as a theatrical experience, but audiences seem to like such things. The movie director has a peculiar opportunity to intensify the empathic sensations by first showing the character in a precarious position and then moving the camera to that position and showing the danger just exactly as the character sees it. This is the strongest possible aid to complete empathy — but perhaps it is a blessing that stage directors cannot do likewise.

Another favorite situation in comedy is that of embarrassment. Nearly everybody has imagined — or dreamed — how it would feel to be caught out in public inadequately clothed, or to be called upon for a speech when unprepared, or to forget one's lines in a play; and when a character in a story or play gets into a similar situation one feels his experience with vivid empathy. The predicament of the young man in *To The Ladies* who finds his memorized speech preempted by another speaker, strikes a response in almost everyone; and that of the man who innocently loses his trousers is so universally startling that it has been worked to death, especially in the motion pictures.

empathy in poetic justice

One of the most intense empathic effects in the theatre, and one of the most truly dramatic, is that which one feels in the satisfaction of poetic justice. The concept of poetic justice may be an intellectual one, depending upon a nice balance of aesthetic and ethical ideals; but the actual sensation in seeing the concept realized is as physical as that of scratching a mosquito bite, or—better—of killing the mosquito.

When, to take a very simple and obvious case, the villain in a melodrama takes mean advantage of a defenseless female and for a time goes unpunished, there is gradually built up in the audience an intense itch to see that villain get what is coming to him. That itch must be satisfied or the play is no play. When it is satisfied—when in the last scene the hero, his patience exhausted, rises in just wrath and smites the villain—the empathic ecstasy is so keen that only a child with his freedom from inhibitions can do justice to it. Pick out a melodramatic movie—one with a cowboy or soldier hero, if possible—and go to the matinee when the house is full of children. See how quickly and instinctively they identify themselves with the hero, how they hiss and hate the villain, how they groan each time he escapes, how they fall into dismayed silence as he captures the heroine; and then how they burst into frantic cheering as the hero rides to the rescue, and scream with delight as poetic justice is finally achieved. Here is empathy in its simplest but most vigorous form. One may laugh at it for its childish crudity, but no one is likely to make a good stage director who does not realize that the most cultivated artistic appreciation is a development and refinement of the same thing.

The desire to see the villain vanquished can hardly be separated from the equally cogent desire to see the hero win out. The latter desire is particularly strong when the hero is not merely the protagonist but a heroic or admirable character as well. Hero worship is a powerful element in drama as it is in life, and we all recognize its claim upon us; but we do not always realize that it is largely empathic.

When Sherlock Holmes, in the Conan Doyle stories, or in one of the many stage, film, or television plays based on them, walks calmly into danger with a quiet reassuring mastery of the situation, we enjoy feeling that we are like that ourselves. We are not, of course—most of us, at any rate—but the very fact that he makes us feel a bravery and an efficiency greater than our own accounts for the pleasure he gives us. The small boy perhaps prefers a big, rough, two-fisted, quick-shooting, hard-riding hero who can make him feel like a stronger and braver animal. The small girl used to prefer Nancy Drew; perhaps nowadays she prefers a television heroine who qualifies as a test pilot or a lady mayor. It is the older man with a somewhat studious turn of mind, believing in the mastery of intellect over brute strength, who empathizes best in Sherlock Holmes; and it is the calmness and the master-ful intelligence even more than the bravery of the great detective that give such a man his greatest thrill.

There was a remarkably satisfying effect of poetic justice in a silent movie produced many years ago called *One Glorious Day*—one of the best comedy films ever turned out, and one that is still revived occasionally in some of the studio art theatres that make a specialty of reviving old films. The story is that of a particularly vigorous and bellicose spirit named Ek, who, escap-ing from the land of unborn souls, visits the earth ahead of time. Seeking a ready-made body to inhabit, he finds that of a certain professor of psy-chology; it is not just what he is looking for, but it is the only one he can find unoccupied, the professor being just then engaged in a psychic demonstra-tion that requires the presence of his disengaged spirit at a seance some distance away. Ek occupies the body and spends "one glorious day" on earth. The point is that the professor (delightfully played by the late Will Rogers) is an honest, inoffensive soul, much imposed upon by his neigh-bors, including a set of grafting politicians who are making him their inno-cent tool. We are just itching to see the scoundrels get what they deserve— but with little hope because of the professor's mildness and innocence— when Ek takes possession of the body. The transformation is electrifying; the professor (with the soul of Ek) tears into his enemies like the god of wrath. We have been wanting action and we get it, with a rapidity and thoroughness that makes us whoop for joy.

beauty in the theatre

The empathies of the theatre are varied in the extreme because the art of the theatre is complex. Many of them are not pleasurable or suggestive of beauty in themselves; the beauty in such cases lies in the effect of the whole, in the harmony and balance of empathies as the conclusion of the drama is reached. But normally it is the pleasant empathic effects that we expect in the theatre and that give us our sensation of beauty. There is room in the theatre for all the beauties of pure form that belong to painting, sculpture, music, literature, and the dance. The director must study and apply all these. In addition there are empathic effects of great beauty belonging to the theatre in its own right — like the thrill of Judy Garland's singing voice, the rhythm of the ant scene in *The World We Live In*, the crescendo of light and music at the end of Act Two of *Sound of Music*, and the Bali Hai sunset in *South Pacific*. The best thing about the present age of experiment in the theatre is that through it we are finding more and larger opportunities for such effects — opportunities to enjoy beauty in the means as well as the end of play production.

The theatre of confrontation has attempted another kind of experiment to create empathy through audience participation. Although the technique has enjoyed some success, there is opposition to it, which Walter Kerr sums up neatly as he reports his own first-hand experience.

What is the best way to total empathy? Through actual hand-to-hand contact, shoulders brushed against the actor, direct muscular participation — with the mind lulled to sleep? Or is it best sought — as Euripides sought and did find it — in the awful penetration of the words?

As things stood, the full contact did not work, had no cumulative possibilities short of rape, no staying power. We were intrigued but not truly involved. Those spectators who did join the dance danced feebly and were plainly glad to retire; one who submitted himself, at evening's end, to being pawed by a covey of Dionysiacs simply submitted himself, returning nothing.

It is only the actors who are liberated in this sort of meeting and there is something arrogant, condescending, and self-indulgent about that. Clearly these actors enjoyed the unleashing of their own inhibitions. During an impromptu aside on opening night, an actress was asked by another performer how she felt about dancing on the night of Senator Kennedy's death. She thought intensely for a moment, then answered, "I have to. It's my statement."

But it was her statement, not ours. She and her colleagues were in control of the master plan. They were free to do what they wished to do. We were free to do only what *they* wished us to do or invited us to do. That is not engagement. That is surrender.[3]

The danger is only that the means may be allowed to eclipse the end; that in our enjoyment of form we may forget all about purpose.

detrimental empathy

Not all empathic responses are helpful to the aesthetic purpose of a play. At the same time that the director is striving to build up the pleasing ones he must be on his guard against unnecessarily displeasing ones that hinder or distract or annoy.

When Romeo climbs a rickety latticework in the balcony scene, threatening to pull Juliet and the balcony down on top of him, there is a strong empathic effect, but it is unpleasant, distracting, and ruinous to the play. A few modern producers are to be thanked for sparing their audiences that customary agony. Every piece of flimsy scenery or rickety stage furniture is a possible source of detrimental empathy, especially if an actor must risk his weight on it in some way.

When Laertes jumps into Ophelia's open grave — sometimes followed by Hamlet — the effect is nearly always bad. It is traditional for him to do so, and of course one can explain away the difficulty by supposing that there is room enough in the grave for him to stand beside her; but it always looks as if he had jumped right on her stomach! The more one empathizes in him, the more revolting the sensation. Yet actors and directors go right on perpetuating that unpleasant bit of business.

A situation that often occurs, especially in amateur production, is that of the hero who is called upon to carry another character on or off stage and is hardly equal to the task. So great is the distracting empathy that some gallery wit is sure to shout "Oof!" and put the house in an uproar. The director should try to choose his cast with foresight in such matters, and to train his actors to simulate ease even when they do not feel it. There is a knack about carrying people, and even a strong actor will seem to labor heavily in carrying a lightly-built girl unless the scene has been carefully rehearsed; almost as much depends upon the skill of the person carried as upon that of the carrier.

Unpleasant and detrimental empathies may be stirred up by badly placed furniture, unnecessary business, clumsy movements, ill-fitting costumes, excessive makeup, and a thousand and one little things that escape the notice of many directors. If directors knew how to avoid unpleasant empathies as well as they are able to create dramatic ones, productions would be much more uniformly satisfying than they are. Hollywood directors learned about the detrimental empathies evoked by the *close-up* in the movies and they have revised their methods considerably. It is in avoiding detrimental empathies that the director's skill is put to the severest test. The dramatist may foresee and suggest the positive empathic effects that are needed in order to carry the meaning of the play; but he cannot foresee the distracting influences that may arise in the course of rehearsals. Neither can the director foresee them; he must be extremely alert during rehearsals in order to check them as they arise.

Examples of empathy, good and bad, could be multiplied indefinitely, but perhaps I have already given more than enough to illustrate the principle. It is the director's problem to apply it. He may learn much about empathic motor responses by observing people and their reactions, by analyzing the most common dreams—for they reveal the experiences, motives, and desires of men, their fears and inhibitions—and especially by studying the behavior of children. But in noting these things and in trying to apply them in such a manner as to strengthen the pleasurable empathies he must be constantly on his guard lest he destroy another factor essential to aesthetic appreciation—the factor of artistic detachment or, as Langfeld calls it, aesthetic distance.

notes and references

1. Lipps, Groos, Puffer, Bosanquet, Santayana, and others. The idea is well known among aesthetic philosophers as the *Einfühlungstheorie* of Lipps.
2. See Ethel Puffer, *The Psychology of Beauty* (Boston: Houghton Mifflin, 1905).
3. Walter Kerr, *Thirty Plays Hath November* (New York: Simon & Schuster, 1968), p. 78. These comments are about a performance of *Dionysus in '69* developed by Richard Schechner.

Motor impulses may be classified roughly in two groups: those that are participative and those that are nonparticipative. An impulse to dodge an approaching automobile is participative, as is an impulse to ward off a blow, greet a friend, catch a ball, hiss the villain in a play, or shout a warning to the heroine. In a response of this type one feels himself involved with the subject matter, not merely in imagination but in reality; he is himself a part of the situation to which he is responding. But an impulse to feel out the lines of a painting imitatively, or to beat time to the music of a band, or to follow the movements of a character in a play with one's own muscle patterns is quite different; one experiences a certain attitude of detachment, participating in imagination, perhaps, but not in actuality.

It is this attitude of detachment that Langfeld calls "aesthetic distance" and that seems to him essential to the appreciation of beauty. He points out, for example, that one may stand on the deck of a ship enjoying the beauty of a stormy sea just as long as he can feel that it does not concern him personally; but the moment an extra large wave threatens to sweep the deck and engulf him, he loses his detachment and with it his aesthetic appreciation. Similarly, one may take keen pleasure in watching the beauty of an electrical storm—until the lightning strikes too close. In the contemplation of the fine arts a detached attitude is normal and essential, and every conceivable device is employed by the artist to maintain it. The painter encloses his picture in a frame, that it may be set apart from the reality of its surroundings; the sculptor places his statue on a pedestal for the same reason. Each strives to preserve whatever suggestion of reality is necessary to the truth of his message and to the production of the proper empathic response, but no more. All superfluous elements of reality he tries to eliminate, lest they remind the observer too forcibly of his own affairs, and thus destroy his sense of detachment. For the same reason the illustrator uses a soft pencil or a pen instead of a camera; the dramatic poet makes his characters speak in blank verse; the musician employs abstract sounds. Each, in other words, conventionalizes life in some way, and it seems clear that at least one of the functions of such conventionalization is the preservation of aesthetic distance.

In the first chapter it was pointed out that naturally colored photographs and statues are not aesthetically satisfying in the highest sense. This is because, by bringing reality too close, they destroy aesthetic distance. They may give us great pleasure of a kind — we may like them for what they represent, for good composition and color balance, or for the skill displayed in their making — but they do not appeal to a cultivated sense of beauty in the same way as a drawing or painting. Sometimes they give positive displeasure. Nothing could be more painful, for example, than the hideously "lifelike" plaster figures that are so often used for the display of clothing and millinery in our shop windows. For the most part they are characterless in attitude and feature, yet so natural in physical detail as to suggest nothing less than remarkably well-preserved corpses. The best undertakers discovered long ago that lifelike makeup on a corpse only makes it look more deathlike; but some window decorators have not yet profited by their experience. Fortunately, however, there are signs of improvement, and in recent years more and more shops have been displaying millinery upon grotesquely comic heads, with sharp angular lines, and crude, though soft, colors — caricatures, of course, but interesting and amusing, and much more artistic than the old manikins because they can be viewed with aesthetic detachment.

the play instinct

The significance of the detached attitude may be a little clearer, and the conditions under which it is most likely to break down may be better understood, if we think of it in terms of the difference between work and play, between necessity and pleasure.

Two basic traits are universally essential to the survival of any species in any environment: the instinct of self-preservation and the instinct of perpetuation of the species. It happens that the great majority of living creatures are so constituted in relation to their environments that the business of satisfying these two instincts occupies nearly all their time and energy. Even such comparatively high orders of animals as cows and chickens spend most of their waking hours eking out a living, and if they seem at times to do nothing, it is probably only because their bodies are fatigued and need rest. They cannot be said to have an actual surplus of time in which to play, or to develop their social or artistic interests.

The luxury of surplus time is given only to a few species, and only in the highest of these does it seem to have resulted in the development of a well-marked play instinct. The goldfish has plenty of time on his hands, but he does not appear to do much with it. The dog, on the other hand, learns to play—to romp and gambol, to do all sorts of unnecessary things, and to experience a very obvious pleasure in doing them. His play is no doubt physically beneficial—certainly it is not unfavorable to survival, or playful dogs would long since have become extinct—and in that sense may be only a particularly unconscious manifestation of the instinct to survive. But the point is that the play instinct, from its earliest inception, is based upon leisure time, and upon freedom from any immediate concern about self-preservation.

In its simplest form play is little more than pleasant exercise—exercise not inconsistent with bodily health, yet not consciously related to it. But as intellect increases and life grows more complex, there is a need for mental as well as physical exercise. At the same time it becomes increasingly difficult to escape the bitter necessities of existence, because the memory and imagination have been developed, and even though there is plenty of surplus time the worries of life linger in the thoughts. In order to play, man, like any other animal, must have surplus time; but he must also have some means of escaping the pursuing sense of reality. With bodily play this is easy, for the shock of concrete sense impressions demands his attention; and doubtless that is one reason for the great popularity of athletic games. But with mental play man must have something more than an assurance that his life is not immediately at stake; he must have sufficient detachment to take him out of the maze of associated thoughts that are always there to drag him back into reality. In the most cultivated kind of mental play that we know—the fine arts—he must have the highest and most effective sense of detachment possible. In other words he must have a sense of aesthetic distance.

It may well be asked why the term "distance" is used. The meaning is figurative, of course, referring more to an idea than to a physical measurement; yet physical distance, or the suggestion of it, is not infrequently the means of maintaining an attitude of detachment. We often back off from an object in order to view it aesthetically, and sometimes we squint at it and try to see it through a kind of haze. We seldom appreciate the full beauty of a valley until we can view it from a distant hilltop, and we are proverbially indifferent to the beauty that may be found at home; "the far-off hills are green." Almost anything beautiful is spoiled for us if we get too close to it, much more so than if we get too far away. There is, of course, no exact distance that is always right; a painting might seem too distant at twenty feet and a mountain too close at a mile. The question is purely relative, the point being that for aesthetic appreciation the distance must be sufficient for the maintenance of a detached attitude.

In one sense the whole matter of a detached attitude is relative. The attitude of a football player is highly detached by comparison with that of a soldier in battle; but that of a spectator at a football game is detached by comparison with that of the player. The fine arts call for more detachment than any other form of play—for such detachment is possible only to a highly developed imagination. They call, in other words, for the highest type of play attitude. But because, in attitude, they still belong to play rather than to the business of living, less violence is done to the aesthetic attitude when it slips to a lower form of play than when it slips out of the play attitude altogether and into actuality. That point is worth remembering, for it sometimes marks the difference between crude art and a morbid realism that is not art at all.

aesthetic distance in the theatre

In the modern theatre the sense of aesthetic distance may be very strong and very definite. The elevated stage serves not only to embrace visibility but also to set the play apart from the audience as a statue is set apart on its pedestal. The *proscenium arch,* or *picture frame,* serves the same function. Usually the stage is brightly lighted while the auditorium is darkened, and there is a curtain that is raised or drawn aside only during the actual

Two interpretations of John Osborne's *Look Back in Anger. Top*, From Indiana University and designed for touring by Richard L. Scammon, who also directed. *Bottom*, University of Illinois, designed by Don Llewellyn.

performance of a scene. All these things put together tend to offset the effect of reality created by the use of living actors, and to maintain a sense of
detachment on the part of the audience. Although the majority of plays presented today strive for the illusion of reality and use aesthetic distance as
a means to effect detachment on the part of the audience, some theatre
artists are attempting to eliminate these "artificial" elements in efforts to
find total involvement between the play and the audience. Actors mingle
with audiences before, during, and after the performance. The play may be
interrupted while actors engage the audience in discussion of current moral
or political issues. In some productions (I hesitate to call them "plays") the
audience is urged to participate actively in the action. The whole idea of
audience detachment, of vicarious participation and identification with the
hero or heroine, is discarded. There is no division between audience and
stage, no raised platform, no proscenium arch, no darkened house and
lighted stage. Such performances are exciting – often shocking and unnerv-
ing. We react to these productions with no detachment. There is apparently
no separate stage reality to retreat from. We are ourselves, the time is now,
and we are there taking part. Aesthetic distance is almost totally destroyed.
Yet the audience is still the audience reacting according to their own personalities and degrees of objectivity.

The means are different in the theatre of confrontation, yet the end is the
same, for the purpose of theatre is enjoyment of the experience; whether
one does this by active participation or through the passive participation
allowed by aesthetic distance, it is still a total involvement.

During the 1930s, when *Waiting for Lefty* was first presented, the company that presented the play was overwhelmed by the audiences that so
identified with the situation that they rose and shouted to "strike" when
a vote was called for. We laugh at the naïveté of the rustic who shouts a
warning to the hero about to be attacked from behind by the villain, but in
both of these cases the involvement of the audience was due to their identification with the play and the actors and their loss of personal identity. In
the theatre of confrontation the involvement comes, if it does, because of
intellectual reaction and conscious desire to participate as oneself.

Different forms of writing will require different styles of presentation.
There is the actor on the one hand who is part of the play, and very much on

exhibition—not in his own identity, but in that of the character he represents. His own personality is suppressed or discarded; there is no sense of direct communication between him and his audience, for they are in the world of reality and he is in the world of imagination. The aesthetic distance is between the audience and the play; and the actor is in the play end of it. For the actor to "step out of the picture" in any way, or to establish any sort of direct communication with his audience is to break down the basic convention of modern acting. Yet the actor who does these things deliberately, who can improvise in order to involve his audience, who can be himself one moment and a character the next is, perhaps, now establishing a new convention for modern acting. Or what is more likely, he is establishing the idea that the modern convention is that there are no conventions! Distinctions in style and form have changed a number of times over the years. In the public theatre of Elizabethan times, for example, there was no proscenium arch, and there were no footlights to throw a glamor of unreality about the actors. In the private theatres the actors did not have the stage all to themselves, for young men of wealth and fashion insisted upon platform seats. Elizabethan audiences, especially in the public theatres, were boisterous and unruly, voicing disapproval as readily as approval, and laughing loudly at the obscenities and the buffoonery. They did not hesitate to exchange remarks with the actors, and to interrupt a play if they did not like it. Under such circumstances it is doubtful whether the sense of illusion was developed very highly. What there was must have been the result of good drama and powerful individual acting.

Conditions in the seventeenth and eighteenth centuries were even less conducive to a sincere aesthetic attitude in the theatre. The custom of seating the young gallants on the stage persisted even in the public theatres, and when women began to be employed to play the female parts the behavior of the audiences grew even more disorderly. The plays were as licentious as the times; few of the actresses were of good repute, and they flirted openly with the gallants on the stage and in the boxes. Interruptions were frequent, and riotous disturbances in the audience not at all uncommon.

Of course the behavior was not all disorderly. There were good plays and there was good acting, and there was plenty of hearty appreciation of both. But few people seemed to have such a sense of obligation to artistic sincerity and consistency as is taken for granted in our better theatres today. One of the first to feel it was Thomas Betterton; but he was ahead of his time. Not until David Garrick became a power in the English theatre did things begin to change.

It was Garrick who first succeeded in driving the London audience off the stage—inspired, perhaps, by Voltaire, who had instituted a similar reform in France. In so doing he recreated that psychological barrier between actor and audience that is the basis of modern theatrical convention. Like Betterton he abandoned the Elizabethan custom of entering out of character and only beginning to act at the center of the stage, and of dropping out of character between speeches. He forbade his actors and actresses to carry on flirtations or conversations with members of the audience, or to establish communication with them in any way. He insisted that they know their parts perfectly. He even required them to dress in such a way as to suggest the characters they portrayed, instead of to display their own charms to advantage—although he made no attempt at historical accuracy in costuming, and himself played Macbeth in the contemporary uniform of a British general. His technique of production was not like ours, but he was almost the first to set consistency and sincerity of imagination above mere histrionics, and to approximate a modern sense of aesthetic distance in the theatre.

Most people who love the theatre today—the "legitimate" theatre at any rate—value the artistic sincerity that dates from Garrick. Those who go to the theatre for rough animal play can get all they want in boisterous musical reviews or extravaganzas, especially those that follow the *Hellzapoppin* and the *Laugh-In* traditions. Those who go to draw aesthetic pleasure from an artistic representation—or presentation—of life appreciate a sincere, consistent, imaginative effort on the part of the artists, and an orderly sympathetic attitude on the part of the audience. There are many who have ruthlessly condemned the modern theatre for its illusion, its peephole realism, its picture-frame stage, and who have clamored for the greater freedom and spontaneity, the greater intimacy, the more direct theatricalism of the Elizabethan platform or the eighteenth-century forestage.

Most of the new theatres built since 1950 have incorporated the *thrust stage* and so give the director the opportunity to "bring the play to the audience." Perhaps the theatre building that has the flexibility to allow either proscenium realism or the theatricalism of the forestage will provide the bridge to the conventionless theatre of the late twentieth century. We should be free to adopt any convention that allows us the necessary artistic freedom for a particular play. To attempt to push all plays into a common mold is to limit creativity. There is only one permanent convention, that of good taste.

the proscenium and the fourth wall

Some years ago theatre practitioners were either strongly for or against the proscenium and fourth-wall realism. Arguing on either side categorically seems not only foolish, but a lost cause. There is a place for both the illusionistic theatre of the proscenium arch and the presentational theatre that the thrust stage allows. The argument should not be about the use of these forms but about the misuse of them for the wrong plays. To present *Hamlet* or *Macbeth* behind a proscenium and with many full realistic settings is a travesty but no more so than presenting *Ghosts* or *Glass Menagerie* on a platform stage with no setting at all. The problem is one of taste, judgment, compatibility. Neither form is the entire answer.

The proscenium arch is not, and never has been, conventionally representative of a fourth wall removed. The producer who attempts to make it so is guilty of false reasoning and ignorance of theatrical history and psychology, to say nothing of very bad taste. Fortunately this notion is rare, but unfortunately we sometimes find it in high places. When the Moscow Art Theatre, in Act Three of *The Three Sisters*, attempted to suggest the invisible fourth wall by arranging the furniture against the curtain as if it were backed up against that wall, the device was positively and seriously wrong. The effect was unreal, distracting, and inartistic. Happily, it was not repeated in other Moscow Art Theatre plays. A still worse effect is usually produced when a house or room is shown on the stage with ceiling and walls broken as if the front had been torn away, and with the surrounding landscape shown realistically at either side and above the roof.

In Eugene O'Neill's *Desire Under the Elms*, no less a person than Robert

Edmond Jones lent himself to that enormity by putting a whole house on the stage with a landscape background, and then removing various parts of the front wall to expose first one room and then another, and sometimes two or three at a time; as a result some members of the audience gave much of their attention to wondering which section would come out next, and how they were fastened on, and whether the frail-looking house would be able to stand the strain. There was, of course, some excuse for a divided setting in that play to convey the essential irony of certain scenes, but it need not have been so obtrusive. Jo Mielziner solved the problem successfully in *Death of a Salesman* and *Ethan Frome*.

Another obtrusive example was furnished by George Jenkins' setting for *I Remember Mama*, by John Van Druten, as produced by Rogers and Hammerstein. It centered about an open-front house representing an exceedingly vague period in the history of San Francisco. On either side of the broken walls were street spaces through which characters approached the house, stepping up onto a platform that was too obviously a wagon stage; above could be seen the edge of the roof, and above that a soaring backdrop, elaborately and beautifully painted with trees and houses or rocky promontories, and subjected to very interesting lighting effects. The whole setting presented an unusual and fascinating spectacle; but the outer half of it was irrelevant, unnecessary, and fearfully distracting. To add to the distraction, the actress playing Katrin (who doubles as narrator and as a character in the play) kept running in and out of the setting through the missing front wall, while the other characters were required to use the door in the side wall. A well-known director and writer on theatre arts who saw this play with me leaned over after a few moments and whispered, "Did you ever see so much distraction in one set?"

Something of the same distracting effect occurs every time a two-room scene is shown on the stage with the edge of a division wall staring the audience in the face—no matter how necessary to the action of the play. In the original *Anna Christie* there was a particularly bad arrangement of this kind. The division wall was not brought forward to the curtainline; it was stopped halfway, doubtless for visibility at the sides of the house. But it was evident that the actors on one side could see those on the other, and that when they passed from one room to the other through the door in the partition, they were taking the longest route. One worried a little about that, and about the missing portion of the wall, and wondered whether it had gone with the fourth wall, wherever the latter had gone. This sensation is always intensified when a divided setting is made to show realistically broken walls, jagged bricks, incomplete roof trusses, and other suggestions of catastrophe. Divided settings are not uncommon, for they lend themselves to many humorous effects and some dramatic ones; but it is doubtful if they can ever be entirely guiltless of distraction and artistically satisfying.

It should be understood that these remarks refer mainly to divided or broken settings that are essentially realistic. There are other kinds of unfinished settings in which the incompleteness is frankly conventional and the method frankly suggestive rather than representational. The simplest is that of the spotlighted area on a dark stage. More elaborate, but equally conventional, is the type of unit setting seen against black or neutral draperies, with a mere suggestion of back and side walls, and no ceiling. The walls may be frankly decorative or they may be simple flats with unfinished edges deemphasized by control of light. In either case they are more analogous to the soft-edge sketches used by illustrators than to photographs of half-built or badly "blitzed" houses.

Settings of this type make no logical challenge to our sense of realism and offer no suggestion that an actual fourth wall has been removed. In good theatrical technique there is simply no implication of a fourth wall. The fact that indoor and outdoor scenes are shown through the same proscenium arch should be enough to allay the myth; if the proscenium represents a missing wall in a room scene, what does it represent in a woodland setting? Uprooted trees? A missing fence? A large window in a house on the edge of the woods? Nonsense! Who would think of such a thing? Some critics have been strangely troubled by the fact that in the interior setting we see only three sides of the room. But whoever saw more at one time? A human being does not have eyes in the back of his head; his field of vision is always limited to some three-fourths of a circumference. The convention of the interior setting is not the convention of an imaginary fourth wall, but that of a very real limitation of the field of vision. The raising of the curtain is not the lifting of a wall but the beginning of a chapter of fiction—a measure of time rather than space.

Heartbreak House by George Bernard Shaw done through the abstraction of certain
nautical elements and careful lighting. Spectacular in its simplicity and its scale.
Designed for the University of California, Berkeley, by Henry May (*Photo:* Dennis
Galloway).

The function of the proscenium arch is merely to define the limits of the
composition, to set it off by separating the fiction of the play from the reality
of its surroundings, to prevent the eye from wandering to irrelevant things
—in short, to maintain the aesthetic distance. A painting is framed for the
same reason. To say that a picture is too flat, that the perspective is bad, that
the frame is too large, too ornate, or too conspicuous, is legitimate criticism
in either art. But to say that the proscenium arch should be abolished for

any of those reasons is just as foolish as to say that we should hang our pictures without frames; to demand that the arch be replaced—in every case—by a platform stage is just as ridiculous as to insist that all painting be replaced by sculpture.

There is a place for sculpture, and there is a place for the platform stage. The latter existed before the proscenium arch and gave way to it only because the arch lent itself best to the more realistic plays of the nineteenth century. Many types of plays can be more effectively presented without any loss of aesthetic distance on platform stages; Shakespearean plays are well suited to such a technique, as are most poetic or symbolic plays. Some experimental theatres have achieved very satisfactory results with *circus* or *arena* stages, or with acting areas on the floor level surrounded by spectators, as in the highly successful Penthouse Theatre at the University of Washington. With simplicity, restraint, and good taste, such methods can be as artistic as those of the proscenium stage. They do not necessarily destroy aesthetic distance; they merely change the methods by which it must be maintained.

The play is still the thing and the decision as to style of presentation should not be an arbitrary one but, rather, should grow out of a thorough analysis of the play. The director or producer must constantly keep in mind his responsibility to the play.

aesthetic distance and the sense of communication

The arrangements of the stage and setting are after all only incidental elements in the establishment and maintenance of aesthetic distance. The chief element is psychological, and depends upon the actor. To maintain the proper attitude on the part of the audience in a realistic play, the actor must consistently and rigidly refrain from any direct communication with them. Even in a presentational piece the actor who addresses the audience does so in a general way and does not establish individual contact with any one of its members.

To be sure, this principle does not apply to all theatrical entertainment. It seldom applies to the comic scenes of vaudeville and musical extravaganza, or to the humorous monologue.

An actor must, of course, convey the author's meaning to his audience. He must do more. He must convey a very subtle suggestion of appreciation of that meaning; that is his service as an interpretative artist. He must not appear visibly to enjoy the play as a spectator, yet he must somehow suggest an attitude of enjoyment to the observer. At the same time he must seem to be, not himself, but the character he represents, and as such he must seem to belong to another world, the world of fiction, of imagination. The instant he allows a bond of communication to become established between him and his audience, the imaginative spell is broken.

I once sat very far from the stage at a production of *The Devil's Disciple.* When Dick Dudgeon swaggered in and dominated the scene I found it very delightful. It was as if he were saying, "Here I am, folks of the play, Dick Dudgeon, a whale of a character." But certain friends of mine who sat near the stage told me later that the effect was spoiled for them by the actor's habit of *mugging*—that is, of looking directly at the audience with a communicative expression. To them it had seemed as if he were saying, "Here I am, ladies and gentlemen of the audience, a whale of an actor." For them aesthetic distance had been destroyed.

In a production of Mary Chases's *Harvey,* the leading actor was a well-known comedian who had a number of tricks that were his trademarks. His insertion of those gimmicks into the play got laughs and applause from his audience who accepted him as himself instead of the charming drunk Elwood P. Dowd. The play suffered accordingly.

Yet there is a difference between this kind of personal contact and the contact that Brecht continually makes with his audience through a set of conventions designed to break aesthetic distance. He works within the context of the play, as does Joseph Heller in *We Bombed in New Haven.* Heller has the characters make constant reference to themselves as actors playing parts, yet there is a kind of aesthetic distance established through the consistency of Heller's approach that we accept.

"When I go to the theatre," one critic wrote, "I go to sit in the audience, I do not care to be mixed up in the play." An audience can act and react about the play, with the play, and on the play, but participation is the real destroyer of aesthetic distance.

Advocates of the plastic stage have pointed triumphantly to the achievements of the late Max Reinhardt in bringing the action into the audience. In his *Theatre of the Five Thousand* in Berlin, he staged vast tumult scenes with the stage in the center of the auditorium and with actors and supernumeraries mingling with the audience and coming and going in all directions. I never had the pleasure of seeing those productions; but in Reinhardt's New York production of *The Miracle* aesthetic distance was perfectly maintained. There were 700 actors, and many of them came and went through the aisles, but they ignored the audience completely and established no sense of communication with them. Because of the mystic character of the play and the remarkable atmosphere of the theatre—remodeled to create the illusion of a cathedral—one could feel himself present in spirit only, or imagine that he was dreaming the whole thing. It was this atmosphere that served the purpose, ordinarily served by the picture frame, of maintaining aesthetic distance. The success of central arena productions like those of the Penthouse Theatre depends largely upon the maintenance of a similar psychological aloofness balanced against the intimate effect of proximity. Good control of lighting helps, but the essential atmosphere depends chiefly on the actor.

illusion in the theatre

The question of illusion in the theatre seems to be a very confusing one. The abstractionists are constantly berating the realists for attempting to create an illusion of real life on the stage, yet they seem to approve of productions like *The Miracle* in which there was a more powerful illusion than there is in most realistic plays.

The truth is that the word illusion is ambiguous: There are really two kinds of illusion. There is the illusion of deception, and there is the illusion of art, and the difference between them is precisely that between the liar and the actor. The illusion of deception is inartistic and has no place in the theatre, but the illusion of art is the life of the theatre.

The illusion of art is a thing of the imagination. In it there is pretense but no deception. The child expresses it perfectly when he says, "Let's pretend." He has no intention of deceiving anybody, not even himself. It is all a game, with nobody really fooled, but for good sport one must play the game consistently and wholeheartedly, allowing no interference with the imaginative concept. So in the theatre. Nothing is real; nothing is supposed to be. Children of a larger growth are pretending, that is all; but the more completely and sincerely they carry out the pretense—short of actual deception—the more pleasure they get out of it.

Langfeld, as usual, sees the matter clearly:

> The question of realism in art has caused much difficulty because it involves ideas that have appeared hard to reconcile. The dramatic critic asks for "real" situations and "real" incidents. He objects to a play that seems artificial, that does not correspond to life, yet we have said that a truly aesthetic enjoyment demands a sense of unreality. The seeming contradiction is readily explained by the fact that the object may be as real, in the sense of true to life, as is consistent with the intent of the artist, but the attitude of the observer should be different from that generally assumed toward the world. If we are able to maintain an aesthetic attitude, the most stirringly real play will continue to be a play for us, and the most ultra-realistic picture will continue to be a work of art, and the most lifelike statue will remain for us a series of graceful lines in marble; that is, we shall have maintained our distance, and the object will have remained an object of beauty.[1]

In other words, what is bad in art is not illusion—or the lack of it—*per se,* but loss of aesthetic attitude on the part of the observer. Such illusion as is consistent with aesthetic distance is generally desirable. At the same time it must be borne in mind that imaginative illusion can be very powerfully induced by means other than realism of detail.

how much illusion?

An aesthetic attitude in the theatre can be destroyed either by too much or too little illusion. When the scenery is tawdry and unconvincing, when the costumes are too palpably makeshifts, when the acting is feeble, there is

The use of nontheatrical materials to achieve highly theatrical results is illustrated in these settings, which incorporate scaffolding, pipe, and platforms for basic structure. *Above*, Aubrey Wilson loads his set for *Camino Real* with a multitude of screens, signs, and blinds while controlling the chaos with light. Designed for California State Polytechnic at Pomona. *Below*, The San Jose State production of *The Bacchae* eliminates all but the barest essentials. Designer Don Childs relied on lighting and dance to create a moving environment by covering figures with a parachute. *Opposite*, Paul Brady, University of Illinois, provides a variety of steps and levels while keeping a light and open setting. Light patterns, created by making the upper platforms of openwork, give added depth and interest to the production of *The Rimers of Eldritch.*

too little illusion, and one finds it impossible to maintain an aesthetic attitude. When, on the other hand, the scenery is so unnecessarily realistic as to distract attention from the play itself, or when the acting is so vividly real that one forgets it is acting and takes it for truth, there is too much illusion; the illusion of art has been replaced by deception, and the effect is again unaesthetic.

Actors, directors, and scenic artists not infrequently overdo the attempt to create illusion. Because the only measure of success in the theatre is the response of the audience, they very naturally and properly play for such response; but sometimes they forget that not all response is aesthetic. It may, for example, seem like a triumph of art when some member of the audience is so carried away that he forgets himself and laughs or cries aloud, cheers the hero, warms him of the villain's approach with a cry— "Look out! Here he comes"—or otherwise feels himself a participant in the play. Some would say this: It is not a triumph of art, but a triumph of hollow deception at the expense of art, for art stops short when the observer loses his sense of detachment.

Yet to define art in these terms is to ignore the wide levels of sophistication among audiences. The showboat *Majestic* run by Indiana University on the Ohio River plays to audiences of all types from the backwoods mountain folk to the city sophisticates. What reduced the hill folk to tears convulsed the city people. Yet the play was presented the same way from one day to the next.

At the same time we must not require all good theatre to exist at the level of detachment discussed above. Productions that do seek audience participation (*Viet Rock* and *Paradise Now*, for example) simply have other techniques and other goals and they would fail if they did not generate personal involvement. If the problem lies in determining how much or how little illusion is necessary, certainly these plays require little illusion. If a sense of reality is sought, then the degree to which this sense of reality is achieved should be the determining factor in evaluating the success of the production, and hence its aesthetic or artistic merit. We cannot impose one set of criteria on new forms of theatre but must develop new criteria to judge these forms.

There is a story that one of the famous actresses of England—Mrs. Kendal, if I remember correctly—in playing a scene very like that of the death of her own child so gave way to emotion herself that the audience could not stand the realism of it, and a woman stood up and cried, "No more! No more!" Highly emotional scenes always involve some risk of thus destroying distance and creating a sense of reality.

Joseph Heller, in his play *We Bombed in New Haven,* wrote two sets of lines so that the desired result could be obtained whichever reaction an audience responded with.

I have yet to hear anyone object to Peter Pan asking us to clap our hands to save Tinker Bell's life, nor have I heard the play labeled an artistic failure because we did.

Degree is the important word. As long as our audiences react as we wish them to the amount of illusion is correct. No one has found a way to measure the amount as yet.

The more abstract or the more conventional the type of presentation, the greater the sense of unreality, and the easier it is to maintain aesthetic distance. Sometimes there seems to be actual pleasure in an illusion of unreality about something one knows to be real. The Parade of the Wooden Soldiers in the famous *Chauve Souris,* for example, seemed to please people of all ages and all degrees of culture. One knew, of course, that the soldiers were real men, but the illusion of woodenness was so perfect that one became a child again, with a child's delight in a toy. However, I recall a distinct loss of aesthetic distance and aesthetic pleasure upon one occasion when a member of the wooden army lost his balance slightly, and for the instant became quite human in the effort to regain it; for me the illusion was spoiled, and I felt an unpleasant shock in being suddenly reminded that the soldier was not really unreal.

The highest form of art is in its essence very close to child's play; the difference lies in its being carried out with a skill and consistency sufficient to satisfy the more critical imaginations of adults.

In a somewhat similar way, *The Yellow Jacket,* by Hazleton and Benrimo, makes use of the highly naïve "let's pretend" attitude of the Chinese theatre, and, in spite of the distractions created by the Property Man, gives keen aesthetic pleasure even to a sophisticated American audience. It is a fact often lost sight of by modern producers, that a simple technique not only proves more stimulating to the imagination and more productive of illusion than an elaborate one, but renders the task of maintaining aesthetic distance vastly easier.

Illusion is, as has been said, a relative matter, and no definite technique can be specified for maintaining it in all cases. But it may safely be said that whatever tends to distract the attention from the main idea or to disrupt the imaginative concept, tends to destroy illusion and to spoil the aesthetic attitude. It is remarkable how much the imagination can do with the barest suggestion, provided only that there is no distracting influence to recall reality or otherwise disturb the attitude of detachment. It may even be said that the stimulation of the imagination is the easy part of play production, while the hard part is the suppression of the many distracting influences that are potential enemies of aesthetic distance.

the actor as a source of distraction

One of the worst sources of distraction in the theatre is too much emphasis on the identity of the individual actor. When the audience recognizes an actor not as the character he represents but as a favorite actor—as Richard Burton, or Elizabeth Taylor, or Ethel Merman—there is an obvious interference with the illusion. Up to a certain point this may be beneficial, as a defense of aesthetic distance against too much illusion of reality. But in the modern commercial theatre it is often carried so far that it interferes seriously with the imaginative concept. In discussing a play one finds himself using the actor's name instead of the character's name; often he cannot even recall the latter. The greater the emphasis upon the star and the more unchanging his or her personality in different parts, the greater the strain on imaginative illusion.

The screen is even worse than the stage in exploiting actors instead of characters. Bette Davis is a hard-working and versatile actress, but she is always Bette Davis to her admirers; nobody remembers her as Elizabeth, or Mildred, or Caroline, or Miss Moffat. John Wayne is always John Wayne to every small boy; why bother one's head with his various fictitious names?

Perhaps it does not matter so much in comedy, especially low comedy; perhaps it is right that Ed Wynn should always be Ed Wynn, and Jimmy Durante always Jimmy Durante. But in a serious play it does matter that the audience should be utterly unable to think of a character as such. Some of the more artistic producers have come to realize this, and some movies are released with no stars featured and with no mention of the actors except in the list at the beginning; and in some instances the names of the actors are even omitted altogether in order to concentrate attention on the characters. Less emphasis has been placed on stars in recent years, for producers have found that stars alone will not draw an audience. Many well-made, low-budget movies using unknown actors have achieved great success.

There are a number of theatre groups that are attempting to re-create the form and philosophy of the repertory company. No actor receives star billing, and casting requires top performers in the group to play walk-ons and bits in productions in which they are not leads. Such a scheme will not only improve greatly the playing of small parts but help deemphasize the audience adulation of "stars." If performers are expected to develop characterizations and not just play themselves, there will be more illusion, less actor personality, and acting will be more important than actors. The identity of the actor separate from that of the character will be of less concern.

The repertory system, whether amateur or professional, is always open to the objection that the more often one sees and recognizes an actor in different roles, the harder it becomes to accept the illusion of each new role; what the star system does to destroy illusion with respect to one actor, the repertory system tends to do with respect to all. Perhaps it is to overcome this tendency that the Moscow Art Theatre company traditionally takes such pains with makeup, costume, and all details of characterization, and refuses to tolerate applause during the play, or anything else likely to destroy illusion. The fine work of this organization proves that the repertory system, with proper care, can be made consistent with the highest degree of aesthetic distance; nevertheless, the use of the same actors in successive plays, or in two or more parts in the same play, is essentially a disadvantage and must be compensated for in other ways if the proper illusion is to be maintained.

the artistic balance

Hardly anything is to be gained in art by going to extremes, for art is essentially a matter of balance. It has often been observed that we take the greatest pleasure in a combination of the real and the imaginary, the familiar and the strange, the true to life and the true to art. That which is totally unfamiliar is uninteresting because it is meaningless; it gives us no basis of comparison. That which is totally familiar is uninteresting because it is monotonous and humdrum. Interest lies always in a balance of the extremes. It may be that such a balance is pleasurable because it permits us to empathize without losing aesthetic distance. The familiar element, besides giving us the thrill of recognition, stirs our empathic responses, while the unfamiliar preserves the consciousness of detachment.

I do not insist that empathy and aesthetic distance offer a complete explanation of our pleasure in the fine arts, but it seems probable that they are essential elements of such pleasure. Certainly they strike a balance. In the theatre it is the director's business to see that this balance is maintained, and that neither element is allowed to exclude the other.

In that simple statement lies the solution to nine tenths of the major problems involved in effective and artistic stage direction.

notes and references

1. Herbert S. Langfeld, *The Aesthetic Attitude* (New York: Harcourt Brace Jovanovich, 1920).

So far we have been considering, somewhat abstractly, the nature of the aesthetic appeal in the theatre, and artistic ideals and purposes as they relate to play production. We have now to consider the matter of translating these into actuality through plan and execution.

Creative planning or composition in the fine arts is generally spoken of as *design,* and in the schools of fine arts it is treated as a separate study with its own body of principles and precepts. These principles and precepts hold good for every fine art, no matter what the medium; and one of the most valuable lessons an artist can learn is that good design is good design, whether the object is a poem, a temple, or a woman's hat.

In the theatre the problem of design is especially complex because of the composite nature of the art and the large number of elements that have to be considered and put in order. The black-and-white artist designs in line and mass; the painter in line, mass, and color; the musician in melody, harmony, and rhythm; the poet in words and meter; the dancer in bodily movement and posture. But the stage director must often design in all these elements at once. It is inconceivable—and unnecessary—that he should be so expert in all arts as to compete with specialists, but it would seem particularly essential that he know the underlying principles of good design common to all of them. Without such knowledge he can hardly hope to achieve a consistently unified and pleasing effect.

the origins of design

The best way to study the principles of design is to consider the origin and growth of primitive art. It is a matter of common observation that primitive art is nearly always good art. But art is generally a product of insincerity, and insincerity flourishes best in a sophisticated civilization. There is, for example, almost no parallel in the art of primitive peoples for the meaningless gingerbread architecture of 1850 to 1890.

If the reader doubts this, let him spend an afternoon in some good museum of archaeology, one containing a large collection of implements, pottery, clothing, and the like, representing the culture of a comparatively simple race—the American Indian, for example. He will observe that whereas many of the implements are crude, judged by modern standards of manufacture, they are well and effectively made to serve their original purposes; also that they are ornamented in a simple but attractive way, suggesting that their makers took real pleasure in the work and in the product, aiming to satisfy their sense of beauty as well as their sense of utility. But he will seldom, if ever, find an instance in which the primitive designer allowed his sense of ornament to run away with his sense of utility, or allowed himself to indulge in orgies of meaningless elaboration. Grotesqueries he will find, of course, wild flights of imagination and fancy, but almost invariably subordinated to the purpose for which the object was intended, or to the ideas of magic potency associated with that purpose.

When primitive man made a bow and arrow, for instance, he wanted first of all a bow and arrow that would work, for he knew that his life might depend on it. He chose the kind of wood that gave the strongest spring, but if there were several kinds equally good, he chose the kind that also looked best and pleased him most. If he needed something to keep the dampness out, he looked about him for some resinous substance that would serve as a varnish, the best he could find for the purpose. But if there were several substances equally effective he chose the kind that best lent itself to ornamentation—the most highly colored kind, for instance; or perhaps he used several kinds, of different colors, working them out into a design. Finding that his bow could be improved by wrapping certain parts of it with rawhide or reeds, he chose the best materials for the purpose, but when several colors would do equally well, he alternated them or interwove them into a design. The purpose of the design might be to give pleasure or to invoke the powers of magic; doubtless the latter purpose came first. The more dependent the craftsman was upon his bow as a weapon, the more affection he lavished upon its construction, and the more pains he took to give it magical power and beauty. The small boy today does very similar things to his hockey stick or baseball bat, and from about the same motives.

While the warrior was engaged in making his bow the woman was busy, perhaps, in making baskets or pottery. She also aimed first at utility and only secondarily at beauty. She also used the materials at hand—reeds for the basket, clay for the pottery—and she developed the ornament out of the same materials. The earliest potters in all parts of the world worked their designs out of different colored clays; it was only in a later, more sophisticated, and less honest age that they learned to paint imitations of those designs on the surface.

In the development of ornament, primitive peoples drew naturally on their observation of things about them, and particularly upon nature. Human life furnished some of the motifs, but most of them were drawn from flowers, birds, animals, trees, mountains, rivers, the sun, the moon, or the stars. It is noteworthy, however, that these motifs were conventionalized almost from the first. Since the ornamentation was usually associated with religion or magic, there was no serious attempt at pictorial realism. When primitive men sought to portray actuality, it was usually to convey a message of some kind; in their arts they were content with the crudest suggestion, and concerned chiefly with fitting the ornament into some general scheme. If they wanted to decorate a bow with the figure of an alligator, they did not distort the bow to portray the alligator correctly; they distorted the alligator to decorate the bow. It is possible that this is the origin of conventionalization in the arts; certainly it is the origin of many conventional motifs familiar in historic ornament.

The subject of primitive art is a fascinating one and will repay a great deal of study. The more one sees of the work done by the earliest designers in all parts of the world, the more respect he feels for their simplicity, sincerity, and good taste, and the more he begins to realize that the problem of good design today is how to achieve a similar quality in the face of the complexities and perplexities of modern life.

Two facts about primitive design stand out above all others; first, the artist's fidelity to his utilitarian purpose, and second, his fidelity to his materials. The opinion appears to be unanimous among writers on design that these two elements are natural and basic in the history and psychology of art, and that no sound achievement in design is possible without them.

the utilitarian basis

To say that all good design is founded upon a basis of utility is seemingly to contradict the opinion previously maintained concerning artistic detachment and the purely aesthetic purpose of the fine arts. The contradiction, however, can be reconciled.

It must be remembered that design did not begin with the fine arts. It began long before the fine arts, in the days when men were still too preoccupied with the struggle for existence to indulge in art for art's sake. There was a strong play impulse among primitive men, but it existed for a long time as applied to the useful arts before it resulted in the development of separate arts entirely given to the purposes of aesthetic pleasure. The early artists whose work we so much admire were thus not artists at all in the narrower sense of that word; they were craftsmen, men who worked with their hands to produce useful articles and to satisfy their actual needs, but who also took pleasure in doing their work well and beautifully.

We still have the craftsmen; we still make useful articles and endeavor to beautify them at the same time. Good design in the crafts still means, above all, fidelity to the structural purpose of the object, whether a building, a piece of furniture, or an evening gown. Refinement and enrichment we expect, but they must be kept subordinate to utility.

At the same time we have given freer rein to our play impulses by establishing certain special arts such as music, painting, and the drama, which have no other purpose than to give pleasure. All of them began as useful arts with some ulterior application—a religious one in many cases—but by a process of evolution they have become independent and aesthetic. All of them, however, still make use of design, and good design in the fine arts is identical in principle with good design in the useful arts. Fidelity to the utilitarian purpose means, in the fine arts, fidelity to the *main* purpose, whatever that happens to be—to the central idea or emotion that is the aim of the artist to convey. It is just as essential for the fine artist to know what he is trying to do as it is for the craftsman; and it is just as essential that he subordinate his love of elaboration and ornament to the main or fundamental idea.

This, then, is the first lesson that the stage director can learn from the primitive craftsman. How often does one find in a theatrical performance anything like the rugged simplicity and directness, the sheer beauty of form, the sincerity of method, that are so easy to find in the glass cases of any good archaeological museum? How often can he feel that at no point in the play has the director or the actor forgotten the chief message of the play? There can be no question that many stage directors, amateur and professional, are seriously in need of just this simple lesson.

In the theatre the utilitarian purpose is simply the purpose of the play: the telling of a given story, or the expounding of a given theme. Good design in play production is design in which the director shows the same regard for his main business that the primitive man showed in making his bow, and the same unwillingness to sacrifice the main business to ornament in even the slightest degree.

fidelity to materials

The second lesson that the stage director may learn from the primitive craftsman is that of fidelity to the natural limitations of means, methods, and materials; and it is a lesson even more urgently needed in our theatres than the first one.

The primitive craftsman used the materials that were at hand, the kinds of wood, clay, or stone that were natural to the soil he lived upon. He used them not only for the structural elements but also for ornamentation, because he built his ornamentation out of the structural elements.

In modern art the ornamentation is too often but a vestigial remnant of the more organic ornament of earlier times, and sometimes it is not even that. Sometimes it is purely extraneous decoration plastered on from the outside and composed of cheap and unrelated materials. Almost everything today is an imitation of something else; even the most substantial-looking stone buildings are built first of steel, with the stone hung on afterwards. Some years ago we began imitating stone with terra cotta and plaster; later we imitated even the plaster with sheet iron or copper and then plastic. The point is not that we used sheet iron or copper, but that in using a new material we tried to pretend that it was something else; and instead of developing a structural and ornamental design appropriate to the new material, we borrowed lamely from the design belonging to the old.

It is a sign of real progress that the architects and industrial designers, at least, are beginning to get away from this and to develop new designs appropriate to the new materials.

Of course it will never be possible to return completely to the rigid simplicity of primitive times, nor is it, perhaps, desirable. It is not necessary to confine ourselves to materials accidentally at hand when better materials may be obtained. Indeed, with improved methods of transportation everything is, in a sense, at hand. It is not necessary, and not possible, to reject the suggestions that come to us from other arts, or other races, or other ages, in order to build up an honest and sincere art of our own. We need not and cannot follow the methods of primitive craftsmen with literal accuracy.

What we can do is realize that there are natural limitations connected with every art, and that the sincere artist recognizes these limitations, whatever they are, and abides by them. He does not struggle uselessly to transcend them, but seeks rather to turn them to account, to make conventions of them, and to find actual beauty in them.

This is a lesson that some would-be artists never learn. They sputter and storm at all limitations and conventions, and strive ceaselessly for some sort of "new freedom" – which means, more often than not, freedom from the obligations of hard work and painstaking study. In their efforts to attain the new freedom they often give us merely incoherence, tawdry imitation, and bad craftsmanship, and call it – quite accurately, perhaps – self-expression. They seem to miss the obvious fact that the greatest artists have never needed much of that sort of freedom; that they have always found true freedom, not in servile unoriginality, but in a sane and honest recognition of natural limitations. It would not be too much to say that the limitations make the freedom, for they relieve the artists of the necessity to attempt the impossible.

The true artist, like the true craftsman, first considers his purpose; secondly he considers the medium in which he is to work, choosing it in accordance with his purpose; and lastly he considers the possibilities and limitations of the medium. If his medium is the pencil, he does not try to make it do what only the brush can do; if it is the brush, he does not try to make it imitate the work of the camera. If his medium is the motion picture, he does not make it a clumsy imitation of the stage play; he develops

Highly theatrical design deriving its style from the play's title, *Life Is a Backyard Circus*, by David Shaffer, designed by Charles Thompson, University of Northern Colorado.

it according to its own capabilities, recognizing that though it may lack some elements of appeal to be found in the stage play, it can do many things that the stage cannot. Workers in the field of television will do well to learn the same lesson and develop their own art instead of treating it as radiated motion pictures or illustrated radio.

The stage director, working in an art that is a combination of many others, is constantly tempted to borrow indiscriminately from those others—to use beautiful settings, beautiful costumes, beautiful lighting effects, beautiful music, simply because they are beautiful, and without regard to their effect on the development of the central idea. He, almost more than any other artist, is in need of the lessons to be drawn from a study of primitive design. Fidelity to the natural limitations of material—this is the fundamental upon which he must build if he is to achieve an art that is honest.

But there is much more to the study of design than this fundamental. The experience of several thousand years has naturally enabled those engaged in creative art to observe some of the possibilities and limitations of the human mind, and some of the peculiarities of human response, and, as a result of such observation, to formulate certain working principles of good composition.

Among the best known and most universal are those of *unity, emphasis, rhythm, balance, proportion, harmony,* and *grace.* All these are broad enough to find equal application in all the arts, and psychologically sound enough to be beyond question. It goes without saying that the stage director should understand them.

unity

The principle of unity, as the name indicates, is the principle of oneness or singleness of thought; it is perhaps the most widely recognized of the principles of composition.

That the mind naturally seeks unity doubtless everyone will agree; the Ancients observed the fact and modern psychologists have rediscovered it and proved it by laboratory tests. It would seem that singleness of effect is, if not essential, at least conducive to understanding, to interest, and to aesthetic pleasure.

In the matter of understanding it is evident that, all other things being equal, the mind can more readily grasp a single idea than several ideas at the same time. Many people, while admitting this, still neglect the principle because the observance of it involves some effort, and because it seems to them that, after all, one can think of several things at once if necessity demands it.

Laboratory tests do not seem fully to support this theory. They seem rather to show that the mind is extraordinarily limited in the perception of even the simplest sort of multiplicity — the multiplicity of elementary units in a group, for instance. Most people can distinguish between a two-spot and a three-spot at cards or dice by what seems to be a single act of perception; but few, if any, can distinguish a nine from a ten except by some analytical or associative process — by counting, or by mental division into fours and a one, or by recognition of a familiar pattern. The Braille system of reading for the blind is based upon the belief that direct perception is limited to groups of four or five elements, or six at the outside limit. In other words, in the effort to grasp several things at once, the mind finds itself limited to very small groups of the simplest units.

As for the more complex ideas, it has been pretty clearly shown that the mind can give attention to but one at a time, and that whenever it appears to carry two simultaneously it is really alternating between them, very rapidly perhaps, but nonetheless distinctly. It is obvious that the result of such alternation must be some loss of efficiency, however slight, accompanied by some mental strain. For clarity of understanding, therefore, unity is desirable.

For interest it is equally desirable because interest depends upon attention and lack of unity represents diffusion of attention. The greatest enemy of attention is distraction, and lack of unity is distracting because it is constantly calling the attention away from one thing to consider another. The mind quickly tires of this and loses interest.

But while a lack of unity is injurious to interest, a unity that is too simple and obvious is no less injurious in another way. We all know the effect of monotony: Any attempt to give constant attention to that which does not change results either in mind wandering or in hypnotic sleep. Singleness in itself, though an aid to clarity, is not conducive to sustained interest. Sustained interest lies rather in the discovery of singleness in multiplicity, of unity in variety. This is the reason why a symphony is more permanently interesting than a popular song. The latter may seem more interesting on first hearing or tenth hearing, but we soon master all there is of it and it ceases to give us fresh stimuli. The symphony, however, contains many elements, and after fifty hearings we still find our interest engaged by the problem of discerning the unity in the variety. Of course the unity must be there, but it must not be too simple or obvious. It is commonly said that one's interest in a composite idea is proportional to the number and variety of elements that are disciplined into a single effect.

There is still another way in which the need of unity is felt in the fine arts, and that is with respect to aesthetic pleasure as we have tried to define it. If our sense of beauty is largely dependent upon empathic response, it will be apparent that a lack of unity is likely to be unpleasant in that it will provoke responses that are not unified. It has been demonstrated in the laboratory that conflicting empathies create physical shocks and strains.

Langfeld reports an experiment in which an observer was asked to admire a picture, which after a time was suddenly removed and replaced by another just like it but symmetrically reversed. The result was a distinct physical shock. We all know the empathetic effect of a discord in sound or color. Whenever there is lack of unity there is danger of unpleasant empathy, and unpleasant empathy is what, in the fine arts, we are for the most part striving to avoid.

In the theatre our pleasure is often lessened by disunity. One of the most interesting and unusual plays of the modern theatre, Thornton Wilder's *Our Town,* fell short of greatness chiefly because the third act — excellent in itself — was badly out of key with the first two in style and theme, and destroyed the unity of the whole.

It is not necessary to accept the Greek notion that all aesthetic pleasure is based upon the discovery of unity in variety in order to appreciate the fact that unity of effect does play a considerable part in enabling us to enjoy the fine arts, including the art of the theatre.

emphasis

The principle of emphasis is most often met with, by name at least, in the study of rhetoric; but it is really quite as universal in the arts as any other. It is the principle of appeal to attention through intensification of sense impressions. Important elements of compositions are to be given conspicuous inflections to appeal to the ear; they are to be *pointed up* so that they may not escape attention.

In written discourse emphasis is largely attained through the placing of important words at the beginning or the end of each sentence or paragraph, those being the positions most likely to catch the eye. The dramatist, assisted by the director, is carrying out the same principle when he tries to provide an effective opening scene and a strong "curtain" for each act of the play. The painter finds his points of emphasis in the highlights, the contrasts, or the effects of converging lines — the spots that naturally claim the attention of the observer — and into those spots he puts the important elements of the pictorial idea. The emphatic position in any type of composition is the position that makes the greatest claim upon the senses and provides the strongest stimulus to renewed attention.

In the theatre well-balanced emphasis is a constant need and a difficult problem. Here a story is told briefly—much more so than in a novel, for instance—under conditions that are not always favorable to steady attention. If the play is to convey its message in the short time allotted, the important elements of the story must be so pointed up that nobody could possibly miss them, and in this the dramatist needs every bit of help the director can give him.

The dramatist, as a rule, employs the methods of the writer to gain emphasis, including such rhetorical devices as the exclamation, the periodic sentence, the suspended climax, and the leading question. He likewise provides, or suggests, most of the major dramatic emphasis by his arrangement of situations, character contrasts, and conflicts of motive.

The actor points up important lines or scenes by means of vocal emphasis, gesture, pause, and all the devices of the orator, as well as by action and stage business, and the importance of his work in this respect can hardly be exaggerated.

But the director must oversee and coordinate all these, and at the same time provide other means of emphasis when these are not sufficient. There are endless possibilities of emphasis in the theatre through control of line, mass, color, light, force, tempo, movement, and music; and many of these escape the attention of the dramatist because he cannot visualize everything in advance, and of the actor because his attention is too deeply concentrated on his own part. It is in the adjustment of emphasis that the director performs one of his most valuable functions, one that can only be performed in actual rehearsal. Some of his problems in this connection will be analyzed in later chapters, especially in Chapter Nine, Control of Attention.

rhythm

A third principle of composition is that of rhythm. Rhythm is usually defined as periodicity or pulsation, or the more or less regular recurrence of emphasis. Whenever stress or accent recurs periodically, whenever there is a discernible alternation of strong and weak, high and low, positive and negative, light and dark, fast and slow, or of any other contrasting elements, we have a form of rhythm.

The appeal of rhythm is explained easily by the fact that we ourselves are rhythmic creatures. The pulsations of the blood are rhythmic, respiration is rhythmic, and most of our bodily activities, such as walking, running, swimming, rowing, hammering, sawing, sweeping, and so on, tend to be rhythmic. In other words, our habitual motor activities are trained, tuned, and accustomed to rhythm.

When we contemplate an object of beauty we experience imitatively the motor responses suggested by it. If those responses are rhythmic, they tend to fit in with the natural experience of the body, and it is not difficult to see that they are more likely to be pleasing than if they fail to fit in. Everyone is familiar with the manifestation of this principle in our ready appreciation of music, especially martial music or dance music. The more obvious the rhythm, the better we like it on first hearing; less obvious rhythms are baffling at first because we have difficulty in adjusting our bodily responses to them, though once mastered they may give us quite as much pleasure as the simpler ones with the added delight of unity discovered in variety. But nothing is more distressing from an aesthetic point of view than a rhythm that is so imperfect or so difficult as ultimately to defy adjustment—a point that some ultramodern composers seem to have missed.

Many people, though quite accustomed to the idea of rhythm in poetry, music, and dancing, seem unaware that the same principle is involved in every sort of composition, in every arrangement of line, mass, and color, in every inflection of pitch, force, and tempo, in every variation of movement or position. The empathic responses to painting or sculpture are, as we have already seen, less conscious than those in music or dancing, and we are less aware of any rhythmic element in them. But the effect is there, and is no less important because it happens to be subconscious.

In highly conventional art, like music or cubistic painting, the rhythms may be very obvious and direct, and similar elements may be repeated frequently in the same medium. In representative art, however, they must be in some measure concealed, else they tend to distract attention from the subject matter. The painter achieves this concealment by avoiding direct repetition of line or mass in the same medium, and by contriving instead to echo a line of one medium by a line of another – similar, but not the same. The line of a woman's arm may be echoed by a mass of pink or orange, or a dark shade of one color may be echoed by a dark shade of another. On the stage a group of characters may be so arranged that the lines of the setting echo the lines of the group. In plot-building a lesser plot may be made to echo a greater one, as the love of Gratiano and Nerissa echoes that of Bassanio and Portia in Shakespeare's *Merchant of Venice*.

The most obvious use of rhythm in the theatre, apart from music and dancing, is of course that of metrical dialogue. While this departs from naturalism and is more generally suited to abstract or symbolic drama than to realistic, it has a deep and universal appeal; and the success of modern plays like *J. B.* shows that it may be effectively used even in this prosaic age. The liltingly rhythmic prose of W. B. Yeats and J. M. Synge is no small part of the charm to be found in the Abbey Theatre plays.

The art of the theatre, being so highly complex, affords a greater variety of possible rhythms than almost any other; at the same time it is so concretely representative that it will not bear rhythms which are too obvious. This spells opportunity for the director who would achieve good design, but it also spells danger, for the temptation to play with rhythms at the expense of meaning is great. In this as in other matters of design, surprisingly good things may be accomplished by purely negative methods – by avoiding bad rhythms, and by so arranging the different elements that their natural rhythms may not clash with each other or with our bodily rhythms – in other words, by not doing the wrong things as much as by doing the right.

Much of our twentieth-century experimental drama provides opportunity for more pronounced rhythms than the older drama without sacrifice of meaning. In Eugene O'Neill's play *Emperor Jones*, for instance, there is a persistent rhythm furnished by the beating of a tom-tom, a rhythm that functions, one might almost say, as the nemesis of the play. In Max Reinhardt's spectacle *The Miracle*, there was much rhythm of light and movement in addition to that of the music. Examples may be found in the ballet-like procession of umbrellas in *Our Town*, and the questions and responses in *Interview*, the first play in *America Hurrah*, which beat so consistently that they heavily underscore the impersonality of modern life.

Even in the simplest and most direct art there are infinite possibilities of rhythmic effect but with corresponding possibilities of disaster. If the rhythm is made too obvious, it may distract attention from the main thought to be conveyed, and the technique of the art may become unpleasantly mechanical. On the other hand, if there is not enough rhythm, or if the rhythms are too confused, our motor responses are baffled and we experience a sense of restless futility and dissatisfaction.

Perhaps Walter Kerr is using rhythm in its broader sense, but in either case his point, "When a production that is mainly dependent upon a performance rhythm vanishes, we are left with nothing. When a production built firmly on a text closes, we are left with a playwright,"[1] summarizes the matter well.

balance

Balance, proportion, and harmony are all closely associated with each other and with the principle of unity because all involve the same problem of empathic adjustment. The principle of balance has to do, of course, with the maintenance of stability through equalization of contending forces.

The simplest form of balance is the form we call symmetry, which consists of exactly equal grouping on both sides of a central line or plane, each side the reverse of the other (A, B, Figure 1). It is chiefly useful in conventional design, the freer forms requiring balance of a more subtle kind.

In the theatre symmetry is often employed in the designing of formal settings for operas, spectacles, and symbolic plays, and in the grouping of characters and choruses in such productions. In the seventeenth and eighteenth centuries it was much more generally employed, even for comparatively realistic plays, than it is today; the normal stage group was triangular, with the important character upstage center at the apex of the triangle and the minor characters equidistant down right and down left. The modern tendency, however, is away from pure symmetry, even in opera and musical comedy.

A more subtle form of balance than the symmetrical is achieved in design by a modification of the leverage principle. It is well known that a light

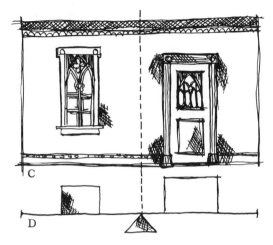

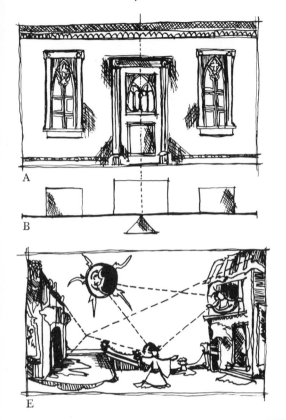

A

B

C

D

E

Figure 1. Forms of balance. A and B are symmetrical; C, D, and E are asymmetrical but balanced on the center line. E illustrates some of the problems of pictorial balance. The triangle connecting the two figures and the moon forms one balanced element; the two buildings with their lines of perspective form another. But note that after a moment the triangular balance becomes less satisfactory because the figures hold interest longer than the moon and begin to outweigh it.

weight may be made to balance a heavy one if placed proportionately farther from the fulcrum of a lever. Assuming that the center of a picture represents the fulcrum, the various elements may be grouped according to their apparent or suggested weight in such a way as to satisfy the sense of balance without even approximating exact symmetry (C, D, E, Figure 1).

Apparent weight in a picture is governed by such qualities as light and shade, color intensity, size, and suggested movement, as well as by association of ideas. In the theatre all of these must be considered and, in addition, we have real movement, speech, and the elements of memory and anticipation to affect our association of ideas. The latter elements are of great importance and are apt to be neglected by the director whose training has been largely visual; he may fail to realize that a character's importance in the minds of the audience is governed by what has gone before and by what is anticipated, and that a character who is important in the minds of the audience has greater apparent weight in the picture than a less important character of greater physical stature.

Here size does, of course, suggest weight, all other things being equal. So does a dark color by comparison with a light one, while, at the same time, we find that actual illumination weighs more heavily than shadow—at least it seems to demand a place nearer the center of the picture. A vista seems to suggest more weight than a cutoff view, and, generally, looks better near the center. Movement toward the center appears to outweigh movement away from the center. A group of characters ordinarily outweighs a single character; but this may be reversed when the single character is of great dramatic importance. Generally speaking, when the physical elements are equal, apparent weight is governed by intrinsic interest; hence our traditional custom of giving the dominating character the center of the stage.

The matter of balanced weight in design is psychological rather than physical, and the key to it is to be found in the relative strength of our empathic responses. Herein also lies the reason why balance is so very important aesthetically. We must balance our empathies for the same reason that we must unify them—that is, to avoid actual displeasure. The physical sensation of losing balance is unpleasant, even painful, to all normal people; and a picture that lacks balance makes us feel that sensation empathically.

The nature of the sense of balance itself is something of a mystery. The semicircular canals of the inner ear are supposed to have something to do with it; but be that as it may, there is no doubt that it exists as a very real thing, even in early childhood. The fear of falling is one of the earliest fears, and whenever one feels a loss of balance that fear seems to come upon him, even though there is no actual danger. In early childhood the sense of balance is imperfect, or at any rate the muscular response is imperfect; but as one grows older he becomes more sensitive and most skillful through practice, and those who are most sensitive and most skillful develop the keenest and most delicate sense of balance; in most cases they retain it empathically even after age and infirmity have begun to lessen the skill. From the standpoint of aesthetics it is not necessary to understand the nature of this sense, but it is quite necessary to realize its existence, its relation to pain and pleasure, and its effect upon our empathies.

proportion

Closely associated with the problem of balance is that of proportion, which involves all questions of quantitative relationship.

The first thing to learn about proportion is that it is everywhere – that all things are relative and therefore proportional. At the same time there is no such thing as an absolute basis of good proportion; even the basis is relative. You may draw the picture of a man and then put a hat on him, raising the question of whether the hat is too large or too small for the man. Or you may draw the hat first and then draw a man to fit the hat, as a small boy often does. Which method is used depends upon the circumstances; if you are making a poster for the window of a hat store, the boy's method may be the more logical one. The safest starting point for any problem in proportion would seem to be that which is most closely associated with the dominant thought or purpose of the work under consideration.

The psychology of proportion is a little more obscure than that of balance, and on one point seems a bit inconsistent with it. Balance implies equality, yet equality is a relatively uninteresting proportion. Balance is a matter of pivoting weights – or apparent weights – on a center, but if we make the center of balance the exact center of measurement, the effect is not entirely pleasing. We do not seem to like an equal division; it may be that our empathic responses in such a case are too evenly balanced, creating an impasse or dilemma that baffles the mind more than it rests the senses. The mind demands unity and there can be no unity where there is division without subordination (as in C and D, Figure 2). The effect is too much like walking a tightrope; the balance is good but too critical.

In respect to the proportion of length and breadth the same rule seems to hold; a square is generally less interesting than a rectangle, especially when its squareness is emphasized in some way (as by concentric squares in

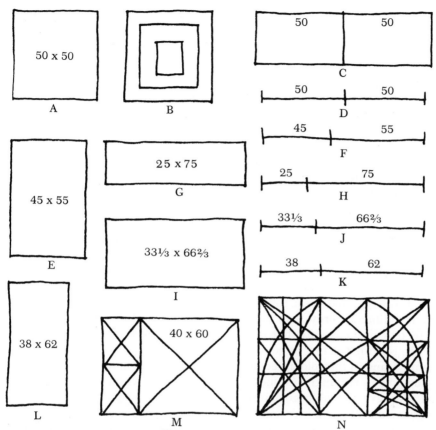

Figure 2. Studies in proportion. M represents the proportion of the "rhythmic half." K is (approximately) the "golden section," and L and N are golden rectangles. Note the repeated, or rhythmic, relations in the subdivisions of M and N.

B, Figure 2). The square is a very useful element in combination with others, but as an independent form it has the same baffling quality as the bisected line. One never knows whether it is right side up.

However, mere inequality is not in itself a sign of good proportion. A rectangle 45 × 55 (E, Figure 2) looks a bit dumpy by itself, whereas one that is 25 × 75 looks too long and narrow (G, Figure 2), though again it must be said that both are useful enough elements in composite design. A proportion of 33⅓ to 66⅔, or 1 to 2, is much better than either of these and may be contemplated separately without great violence to the aesthetic sense. The rectangle of 1 to 2 — a union of two squares — is not particularly interesting (I, Figure 2), but in the division of lengths a proportion of 1 to 2 is moderately pleasing (J, Figure 2).

It is this proportion that divides the length of the rectangle shown at M in Figure 2, the famous rectangle of the "rhythmic half," that some designers consider the most useful, if not the most beautiful, basic form. A square is extended by half a square so that the length is one large square and two small ones, which seem to echo it rhythmically. There is no doubt that the eye finds this proportion interesting and the fact that the diametric ratio is simple — 2 to 3 — makes it easy to use.

But there is one other proportion that for pure abstract beauty has been long regarded as the finest of all: the proportion of the so-called *golden section*. It is expressed in the formula x is to y as y is to $(x + y)$. Mathematically this is a difficult formula to handle, for the relationships involved are not perfectly commensurate, but for all practical purposes in design the ratio may be regarded as that of 38 to 62. The golden section is illustrated at K in Figure 2, and in the golden rectangle at L and N. The internal relationships of the golden rectangle are most interesting. Take a square from one end and you have a smaller golden rectangle left; take a square from that and you have a still smaller rectangle. Draw the diagonals of the squares and rectangles and you have a perfect deluge of little squares and rectangles, the latter all showing the golden ratio. If there is rhythm in the discovery of the repeated squares in the *rhythmic half*, there must be much more in the discovery of all these subtleties of repetition. Whether our appreciation of these forms really is rhythmic would be hard to say. The relationships are all so abstract that one wonders whether the mind can grasp them without conscious effort, and, of course, it is the unconscious response rather than the conscious that we must consider. Certainly there is general agreement that these two proportions are pleasing.

It must not be thought, however, that all the elements in a composite design should display the golden ratio, or even an approximation of it. That would be monotonous in the extreme. There is plenty of use for the less beautiful forms provided they are worked together harmoniously, counter-balancing each other's faults and producing a total effect of good proportion. A poorly proportioned actor may fit in with other actors to make a well-proportioned group; or a poorly proportioned group may join with furniture and setting to make a well-proportioned stage picture. When we hang a long narrow picture over a mantlepiece, we do so because that element, badly proportioned in itself, is just what is needed to complete an effect of good proportion for the whole scheme of decoration. The west front of Notre Dame Cathedral shows several long narrow rectangles and several short squatty ones, and the central element is a square enclosing a circle. Yet the proportions of the whole and the interrelations of the parts are excellent beyond description.

In the composite art of the theatre there are problems of proportion as between the theme and the plot, the ascending and descending action, the climax and subclimaxes, the play and its acts, the main character and subordinate characters, the lines and the business, the actors and the setting, the words and the music, the thought and the feeling; and there are problems of internal proportion in most of these elements, including those of visual proportion in the composition of the stage pictures.

The director cannot solve these problems by slide-rule methods. He cannot say for instance that in a play lasting 100 minutes the main climax should occur at the end of the sixty-second minute; or that the proscenium arch should always measure exactly 38 × 62 feet; or that the performance should consist of three parts words and two parts music. What he can do is to cultivate his own sensibilities in the matter of proportion by first making an intelligent study of the principles involved, and then forming a habit of observing proportions—not only in objects of art but in everything about him. After a time he will find that a bad proportion in any phase of his work will be as painful to him as a "sour" note is to a musician.

harmony

After what has been said about unity and empathy and their relationship, the principle of harmony may be understood easily. Each element in a com-

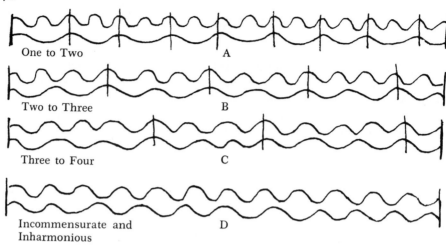

One to Two   A

Two to Three   B

Three to Four   C

Incommensurate and   D
Inharmonious

Figure 3. Harmonious and inharmonious frequencies

position provokes a corresponding empathic response, and in order that these responses may blend agreeably the elements themselves must be in physical harmony.

The laws underlying the principle are those of physics and physiology. Harmony of pitch, in music, for example, is a question of the frequency or rate of vibration of the sound waves. The audible frequencies range from about sixteen cycles per second to several thousand. Each octave in the ascending scale represents a doubling of the frequency. The frequency ratio between a note and its octave is thus one to two, a very simple ratio; every second beat of the higher note coincides with a beat of the lower (A, Figure 3), and the result is a harmonious blending of sound, empathically pleasant. Other combinations of notes, like the first and third or the first and fifth, have frequency ratios only a little less simple, and produce almost equally pleasant harmonies. But some notes have frequencies that do not bear a simple relation to each other, and such notes in combination produce dissonances because the beats almost never coincide (D, Figure 3).

In a similar way the slower rhythms of the tempo in music and dancing show problems of harmony that have a simple mathematical basis. A movement in two-four time, for example, blends readily with one in four-four or common time, while a movement in three-four or waltz time does not. Within reasonable limits we enjoy the effort to harmonize slightly different movements, just as we enjoy the effort of finding unity when it is not too obvious; and it is to give just such pleasure that some composers make use of displaced accents, triplets, grace notes, syncopation, and cadenzas. In general, however, the more easily the rhythms blend, the greater the sense of harmony and the more readily we derive empathic enjoyment.

The problem of color harmony is much more abstruse. Differences in color theoretically represent differences in the rate of vibration of light, but as the frequencies of light run to trillions of cycles per second, it is hopeless to look for any mathematical basis of empathic effect. Moreover, the visual sensation of color does not seem to bear an absolute relation to the mechanical theory of color, as the physiological laws are quite distinct from the physical ones. Theoretically there are vast numbers of pure colors between the lowest red and the highest violet of the visible spectrum, each having its own definite frequency. Actually the normal eye is capable of distinguishing only three primary colors, red, green, and blue, and all color sensation is but a varying combination of these three.

The point here is that there are underlying laws governing the relationships of all natural elements, and that when these laws clash the empathic effect is essentially unpleasant.

grace

Graceful motion has been defined as "motion that is affected with economy of force." A graceful line, figure, or picture is one that suggests, empathically, a similar economy of force.

Grace does not mean weakness or passivity. A graceful motion may be forceful, swift, and impetuous, if the result achieved is in proportion and there is no sense of futility or waste. It is in the suggestion of misapplied effort, or of effort impeded by hopeless incapacity or unsuitability, that we experience a sense of ungracefulness. To feel that a motion is graceful we must feel that there is no easier or pleasanter way of accomplishing the desired result.

Grace is pleasing for the obvious reason that normal human nature dislikes unnecessary effort, or the empathic suggestion thereof. It is not that we are all hopelessly lazy; indeed, most of us enjoy a sense of bodily activity, and gladly expend energy in a good cause. But we do not like to waste it in mere friction, and we do not like the baffling sense of futility when the results seem inadequate in proportion to the effort expended. We like to get the largest and freest sense of action from the least possible effort. This undoubtedly accounts—at least partially—for the great popularity of such sports as skating, skiing, and racing.

It also accounts for the fact that we prefer a smooth, sweet-running, eight-cylinder car to a rattling, wheezy "jalopy." We feel the labor and strain of the latter in our bodily responses and the sensation is distressing. The man who regularly drives his own car becomes extraordinarily sensitive to the slightest change or irregularity in its rhythms, and suffers bodily distress at any indication of loss of power. Objects in nature affect us in the same way. It is pleasant to watch the seemingly effortless flight of a sea gull, soaring into the wind on motionless wings; but a waddling duck is not as pleasing an object, especially to a fat man. The mere sight of a dachshund is painful—or would be but for the saving relief of humor. From the standpoint of unsatisfying effort, nothing, probably, is more distressing than the sensation we sometimes experience in a dream when our feet seem weighted with lead and the slightest movement seems to require almost superhuman effort.

When we empathize in the suggested movement of a picture or statue, or the real movement of a character on the stage, we normally prefer that movement to be graceful—that is, easy and economical of effort. There are exceptions, of course—movements and situations in which the meaning demands awkwardness. But gratuitous awkwardness we resent because we cannot help feeling it in ourselves. I have mentioned the effect produced when one actor has to carry another and seems to have great difficulty in doing so. Similarly, when an actor stands or moves awkwardly, or when the

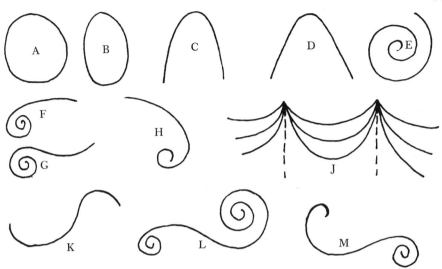

Figure 4. Studies in grace of line. Conic section curves: A, circle; B, ellipse; C, parabola; D, hyperbola. Higher degree curves: E, spiral of Archimedes; F, reciprocal, or hyperbolic, spiral; G, lituus; H, logarithmic spiral; J, catenary curve. Double curves: K, two circular arcs; L, a lituus and a spiral of Archimedes; M, an arithmetic spiral and a lituus.

setting displays ungraceful lines, we are bound to feel uncomfortable because our induced motor patterns are graceful.

But what lines are, as a matter of fact, ungraceful? What classes of lines suggest economy of force and what classes do not?

Offhand one might suppose that a straight line, being the shortest distance between two points, would represent the greatest possible economy of force in motion, and consequently, the finest grace. This, however, is not the case. What is gained by economy in distance is more than lost by the sense of effort in keeping the line straight. If one tries to walk a chalk line for 50 or 100 feet he is quite conscious of the effort required, and if he tries to draw a straight line on paper, he finds it much more difficult than to draw certain types of curves. The effort suggested by the straight line is the effort of self-conscious rigidity, of intentional resistance to contending forces, of artificial and precarious balance. This does not mean that the straight line is never useful in design, but it does mean that its usefulness is generally to be found in the achievement of effects other than grace.

So, too, for the perfect circle. It is useful, but not primarily graceful, at least with respect to the motion that it suggests. An arc of a circle is, like a straight line, artificially regular and self-conscious; its motion is maintained against the insistent pull of centrifugal force, and therefore implies considerable effort. The circle is most pleasing when used whole, with the emphasis upon its unity and centrality; it is least pleasing when the eye is led around its circumference.

Somewhat more grace may be found in the other comic section curves: ellipse, parabola, and hyperbola (B, C, D, Figure 4). They are not all perfectly graceful, especially if considered in their entirety, but they do show some variation of curvature at different points, and a portion of one side taken near the focus is sometimes fairly pleasing.

Still more graceful curves are to be found among the so-called higher plane curves—that is, curves whose mathematical formulas involve trigonometric functions or coefficients higher than the square. Most of the spirals belong to this class (E, F, G, H, Figure 4). Another curve, by some artists considered the most graceful of all, is the catenary curve, or festoon curve—the curve made by a perfectly flexible cable or chain supported at two points (J, Figure 4). This is often seen nowadays, slightly modified for engineering reasons, in suspension bridges, and is, of course, very common in draperies and decorations.

The trouble with straight lines and circles is that they imply a perfect balance of forces not often found in nature. Natural forces are unequal, and the confluence of unequal forces results in curves of more varied type and complex formula. Such curves are more graceful for the very reason that they seem more natural, less studied, less suggestive of conscious effort. It is precisely because the catenary curve is the natural position of flexible draperies that it suggests absence of effort.

Those so far mentioned are all single curves, but with other things equal, a double curve is ordinarily more graceful and more interesting than a single one. Its superior grace is doubtless due to the compensating effect suggested; the centrifugal force developed in the first part is absorbed or balanced by the opposite force in the second part. Even in double curves, however, an exact equality between the two parts is not pleasant; we prefer curves in which we can discern no studied ratio. It is economy of mental as well as physical effort that constitutes grace.

Perhaps that will do to suggest the principle. The application of this and other principles of design in the art of the theatre is obvious enough in a general way if one remembers the strength of empathic effects in the theatre; and of course it is obvious in relation to scenic art. No stage director can possibly know too much of the principles of design, or have his tastes and sensibilities too highly trained.

notes and references

1. Walter Kerr, *Thirty Plays Hath November,* New York, Simon & Schuster, 1968, p. 70.

We turn now to the more practical problems of play production; and for the sake of order and completeness I shall begin with some elementary matters that will seem to have little relation to the artistic principles so far discussed. The usefulness of the latter will, however, become gradually clearer as we proceed.

Most books on play production for amateurs devote considerable space to the problem of choosing a play, but this is so largely a matter of local conditions that no specific recipe appears to be very helpful. The professional producer chooses a play that he thinks will bring in a large profit; the amateur chooses one that he thinks is within the capabilities of his actors and his equipment, and that promises to please the particular audience to which he must appeal.

In the latter respect the amateur producer sometimes runs unwisely to extremes. When the audience is a popular one, not especially intellectual, he selects entertaining comedies and farces, and for a time all goes well. The audience enjoys an occasional evening of harmless laughter and the players have a good time. But neither the players nor the audience enjoy very much intellectual or artistic growth, and the work of staging and rehearsing seems more and more futile and irksome. The older members grow tired of doing all the hard work, and withdraw; very young people take their places, and the dramatic purpose gradually gives way to a social one. When, on the other hand, the audience is a bit "arty," the producer is apt to select only avant-garde plays with the result that after a time the company degenerates into a class in abnormal psychology and the audience dwindles until only the neurotics remain.

As a matter of general policy it would seem best to choose plays sufficiently varied in their appeal to keep the interest of the normal human animal, but at the same time, sufficiently good in a literary and artistic way to make the work spent on them worthwhile. The real test of a play is its effect upon the players. If they grow to like it better and better as they work with it—to see new meaning, new humor, new beauty in each repetition, even after five or six public performances—the play is a good play and is worth doing, both for its own sake and for its influence on the morale of the organization. But if, after a half dozen rehearsals, it seems to grow wearisome—if the sentiments begin to seem tawdry and the jokes stale—one may suspect that it is not really a good play; and even if it seems to entertain the audience, the long-range result will be bad. Professional actors can be hired to purvey trash for the entertainment of the customers; but an amateur group can thrive only when the actors enjoy their work enough to share their enjoyment with the audience, and to want to go on with it.

The production group should choose a script because it offers challenges for the director, actors, and technicians, and because it will be of interest to the potential audience. These must be the prime considerations. The director must assess the actors he will have to work with, the capabilities of the designers and technicians, as well as the physical facilities and the budgets available. It is the ambition of most amateurs to approach a professional standard of ease and smoothness, and their best chance of doing so is to start with a good play.

As to the choice of particular plays, there is little to be said. It is altogether a matter of what is wanted and what is available. In the bibliography of this book will be found some suggestions as to where to look for the best lists of plays; no actual lists are included for the reason that their usefulness would be merely temporary.

The matter of royalties is a serious one for amateurs. Authors cannot be blamed for wanting to be paid for their labors, and amateurs should regard the payment of royalty, when due, as their first obligation. But the prevailing royalty rates for good modern plays are undoubtedly too high and too rigid, and amateur groups in very small theatres cannot afford to pay them. They must either forego the use of desirable plays or steal them; and many, unfortunately, are dishonest enough to do the latter. Authors and agents take the position that good plays are valuable property and should not be rented for production at a low price; but the actual effect of high flat royalties is injury to the authors' interests. Honest, responsible amateurs in the little theatres, who would gladly pay a modest royalty for a good play, refrain from using that play if the royalty is too high; while the dishonest ones give it surreptitiously, often under a false title and without crediting the author.

Fifty dollars is not an excessive royalty for a recent popular success when it is to be given to an audience of 1,000 people at $1 per ticket; but when a little theatre group is playing to an audience of ninety-nine people—or even twice that number—at a subscription rate of $1.50 or $2.00 each, a $50 royalty is prohibitive. Major firms, such as Samuel French and Dramatists Play Service, are usually willing to negotiate royalties when the quoted rate is prohibitive. If one writes, quoting the size of the house and the admission price, an adjustment is often possible except for the most sought-after scripts.

There is great discrepancy from area to area and theatre to theatre for royalties charged for musicals. Since no flat rate is quoted, companies charge whatever the traffic will bear. The National Theatre Conference, the University Resident Theatre Association, and the American Theatre Association are working to secure an equitable royalty charge for all. In the meantime the astute producer should shop for the best deal. Time spent will be dollars saved that can better be spent for advertising, costumes, or scenery.

studying the play

It would seem natural after selecting a play—if not before—to study it carefully in order to discover the author's aim and purpose. Yet many directors, amateur and professional, are content to omit this and to plunge right into rehearsals with the idea of learning the play in the process. In a professional production the skill of the actors and their ability to cooperate quickly with the last-minute inspirations of the director sometimes save him from the consequence of this procedure; but the amateur director can count upon no such luck. If there is one supreme shortcoming of the inexperienced actor, it is his inability to unlearn something that he has once learned wrong; and if rehearsals are begun before the director knows what he is about, some things certainly will be learned wrong and will have to be unlearned. Moreover it is well to remember that the director who shows a thorough knowledge of the play at the first rehearsal commands the respect of his actors and gets better work out of them.

The wise director will therefore seek first to know the play, to understand its construction, its plot, theme, and characters, and to grasp the full significance of the author's message.

In construction, every play is basically a conflict between the main forces, one of which is more universal, abstract, and extensive than the other. The fortunes of the protagonist, his aims, ambitions, and desires, ordinarily constitute the more particular force; whereas the more universal consists of the law of God or man, the doctrine of chance, the established conventions, prejudices, and inhibitions of society, or the larger influences of heredity or environment. Another way of saying the same thing is to say that every play represents the struggle of a protagonist against forces greater than himself—or, as some put it, against Fate.

A play in which the protagonist, or "hero," triumphs over the universal forces is technically a comedy, and one in which he is defeated by the universal forces is technically a tragedy. These designations do not always correspond, of course, to the popular ones or the ones stated in the playbills. Some plays billed as comedies are in reality tragedies in that the characters fail to rise above their obstacles. Some of the broadest farces are technically tragedies for the same reason. On the other hand, many of the most intense dramas, *The Merchant of Venice*, for example, are technically comedies, because they end triumphantly, with the obstacles overcome.

If a director is to produce a play intelligently, he must know the nature of the conflict involved; he must know which is the universal and which the particular force, and whether the play is a comedy or tragedy. He must know what subordinate plots or counterplots there are and what relation they bear to the main plot. He must know the nature and position of the climax—the high point of action, the point at which the main plot turns and begins to resolve itself in the final direction. Without such knowledge he cannot hope to work up the proper dramatic foreshadowing, to point up the important scenes, and to maintain the proper balance and proportion.

But plot is not all. In nearly every play there is also a theme, an abstract idea of some sort, often more important than the plot. It is generally the theme, rather than the plot, that determines the spirit of the play and the mood in which it is to be played. In a satirical play, for example, the plot may be quite serious, and a group of actors who grasp the plot but miss the theme may perform the play as a romantic comedy or heroic tragedy, failing completely to carry the point. In Shaw's *Saint Joan* the plot is the tragic story of the life and death of Joan of Arc, but the theme is the cynically humorous one that, although the saints are good souls who mean well, they are hard to get along with in real life, and are much to be preferred in the dead and canonized state. In *Macbeth* and *Hamlet* the plots are concerned with murder and its avenging, but the theme in the first is the progressive entanglement of ambition and in the second, the weakening effect of indecision and procrastination. The whole flavor of any play depends upon the director's recognition of the theme.

One can always find the plot—if there is one—by reading the play, but the theme and spirit and mood are sometimes so subtle and elusive that they can be sensed only after considerable study. A knowledge of the author and of his other work is very helpful here, likewise a knowledge of dramatic history and the kinds and types of plays current in each period. When it is possible for the director to confer with the living author, the advantage gained is great. The ideal situation is of course that in which the director is himself the author. In the latter case he will not only be familiar with the text of the play, but will—presumably—know the author's intention throughout and will have visualized the scenes and characters in his imagination. When the director is not the author, his first step is to put himself imaginatively in the author's place.

The question of whether the director has the right to consider himself the author and to change or falsify the author's meaning is interesting, but it is a moral or legal question rather than an artistic one, and so a little out of our province. It is well within our province, however, to consider how the director may best modify, or alter, or adapt the written text in order to convey the author's message with the greatest artistic fidelity.

editing the text

When a new play is staged under the direction of the author, or in consultation with him, it ordinarily undergoes considerable last-minute alteration. Only a very egotistical author regards his text as final and inviolable, or supposes himself infallible in the matter of foresight. In the case of an older play, however, many directors consider the text too sacred for alteration. With respect to plays of high literary or poetic merit, there is some justification for this feeling; yet it is almost inconceivable that any play could be revived after a lapse of time and played by a different company, in a different theatre, with different costumes, settings, and properties, and to an audience of different training and environment, without at least some modification of text. It may well be that the greatest service the director can render the author is to adapt the text to the new situation in such a way that the message of the play may not be lost.

This does not necessarily mean a great deal of rewriting or addition to the text – the dangers of which are fairly obvious. It means, as a rule, intelligent cutting; judicious rearrangement of scenes; excision or alteration of passages that may have lost their original meaning through changes in language or through loss of allusive reference; alteration of phraseology to meet the unavoidable limitations of the actors; and modification of the action as necessitated by limitations of equipment.

The recognition and acceptance of limitations are among the director's first concerns, and their importance from an aesthetic point of view has already been emphasized. When the limitations are such as to make adequate production of a given play impossible, the only honest procedure is to choose another play. When they are such as not to interfere with the main thought of the play, it is far better not to struggle uselessly against them, but to accept them frankly and adapt the play to fit them.

For example, if the text calls for hearty laughter on the part of the heroine, and the leading lady, otherwise satisfactory, is unable to laugh convincingly on the stage, the question then arises: Is the laughter essential to the thought of the play? If so, there are only two possible solutions, a new leading lady or a new play. If not, why ruin the play by an unconvincing laugh? Would it not be better to revise the text, eliminating the laugh?

Or, suppose that the text specifies a practical staircase for entrances and exits in full view of the audience, and the limitations of the stage make such a thing impossible. Again the question: Is it essential to the meaning of the play? If so – another play, or another theatre. If not, the best plan is to do without the staircase and alter the text to suit. It is generally more satisfactory to eliminate the impracticable feature entirely, even at the cost of considerable change in the text, than to adopt a pretentious compromise. One group that I know of went to a great deal of trouble to solve just such a staircase problem on a very restricted stage by having an archway built out from the wall, with one or two steps leading up into it and a platform on which the actor might stand concealed after having supposedly gone upstairs. But the members of the audience – all regular subscribers – knew that there was a solid wall behind that archway and that the actor must be hiding just out of sight, and their attention was distracted accordingly; they were busy watching to catch a glimpse of his elbow or coattails instead of paying attention to the play. It would have been possible to have used an ordinary exit, right or left, with an imaginary stairway off stage, and to have suggested it by a line in the text and by having the actor look upwards at the proper angle when making his exit. The simpler solution will almost invariably prove the better, for the very good reason that the imagination requires only a little assistance in a creative way, whereas it is very easily distracted by any sort of unnecessary complication.

The amateur director has, of course, a great many more limitations to contend with than the professional. The latter usually works in a regular theatre with standard equipment, and almost anything called for in the text can be supplied in some fashion. In reviving an old play he can use the stage directions of the original production, placing entrances and exits as called for in the text, and depending upon the designer, stage manager, and stage crew to reproduce the original effects with reasonable accuracy. He cannot always choose an ideal cast, especially in a repertory company, but at least he can rely upon some experience and adaptability on the part of his actors and he can expect steady attendance at rehearsals and earnest work. The amateur director, on the other hand, must often put up with the most distressing obstacles in limitation of stage space and equipment, in lack of time and assistance, in paucity of financial resources, and in the inexperience of his actors. Under these circumstances, he will more often find himself required to modify the text.

It would be impossible to catalogue all the types of alteration and modification that are most apt to prove necessary, but the mention of one or two of the most common may suggest the sort of thing a trained director must be prepared to do.

cutting

The most common of all is, of course, cutting. Many long plays, especially five-act plays, are, in the original text, too long for modern production, especially by amateurs, and must be abridged considerably. Even a modern comedy arranged for professional production in two hours and a half will often require further cutting when produced by amateurs, partly because the waits are apt to be longer, and partly because the amateurs are apt to be slower in getting through the dialogue. Accurate timing of a play cannot, of course, be done until rehearsals are going smoothly, but the intelligent director can do the bulk of the necessary cutting in advance if he gives his mind to it, and in so doing, he can combine cutting for length with abridgment for clarity and consistency.

Most amateur directors, and a good many professional ones, put altogether too much confidence in the so-called standard *acting editions,* especially of Shakespeare's plays.

The modern director, amateur or professional, should make his own acting edition. In the case of Shakespeare he should start with a good standard edition based on the *First Folio* of 1623. By cutting out the portions least helpful in conveying the meaning to his particular audience, and by minor rearranging and adapting of the remainder, he will have something honest, effective, and appropriate for a contemporary audience. This is a dangerous and difficult job and should be undertaken only after long and careful study of the Folio text.

In the preparation of an English play for production in America it must be borne in mind that there are some language differences; that some words and phrases which are merely commonplace in England are unintelligible or misleading to an American audience. Where such elements are necessary to the English flavor, and the English flavor is necessary to the play, they should of course be left in, even at the expense of a footnote in the program explaining them. Where the play is more universal and not essentially English, it will often be found that an omission or substitution can be made with a gain in clearness and without loss of truth or spirit.

In the same way obscurities of meaning caused by lapse of time are best ironed out, unless there is some definite gain in archaic flavor to be had by leaving them in. A play twenty or twenty-five years old is not generally old enough to be worth treating as archaic; costumes, settings, properties, and dialogue may best be brought up to date, and the time specified as "the present." But a play 75 or 100 years old is usually beyond this process, and so better played in the spirit of its time. Even in the latter case there will be some passages in the text that, because of obsolete words or lost allusions, will do more to destroy clearness than to bear out the archaic flavor. The author intended them to be clear; if they are not, it may be falsifying his meaning more to leave them as they are than to change them.

But the most troublesome modifications of text are those made necessary by the limitations of the actors. For example, many dramatists make a habit of leaving lines of dialogue unfinished for the sake of naturalness, allowing the characters to interrupt each other as people do in real life. Professional actors are sometimes able to carry this out in a natural way, but inexperienced amateurs have great difficulty with it; either they interrupt too soon, destroying the meaning, or they interrupt too late, leaving an awkward pause. What is worse, the actor who is to be interrupted anticipates it in his tone, and stops with a suggestive coaxing inflection as if to say, "Come on now, interrupt me; that's the end of my line." In another chapter I shall try to suggest ways of correcting these tendencies when the meaning requires that the broken dialogue be retained. But when it does not, the director will often find it expedient to complete or curtail the interrupted lines, and to rely upon other means of achieving naturalness. There is no use in retaining a device that the author intended for naturalness if the effect with a particular actor is greater unnaturalness.

The language of many plays is literary rather than conversational, and only actors of some ability and experience can deliver such language convincingly and without artificiality. When the play is of high literary merit it may be better to put up with the artificiality for the sake of the beauty; but when the only effect of the artificiality is stiltedness — as is the case with many nineteenth-century plays — and when the actors are inexperienced, a certain amount of rewriting for naturalness is advisable. An actor who cannot say, "The carriage waits," without appearing a "stick" may be able to say, "The carriage is waiting, sir," with a reasonable degree of naturalness.

In the preparation of the text the director should always make sure that his scholarship is equal to the task, and that he is not merely working upon ignorance and guesswork. If he feels the need of revision and is not competent to do it himself, he should seek the help of someone who is.

the prompt book

All cuts and revisions should be carefully marked in the prompt book and in the individual parts to be given the actors, and care should be taken to see that all subsequent corrections are entered in both places.

If the play is in printed form and on small pages, the best way to prepare the prompt book is to cut up two copies and paste the pages in a strongly bound blank book, large enough to provide wide margins, so that all corrections, stage directions, calls, and warnings can be clearly entered. If the play is typewritten, it will usually have plenty of marginal space for this purpose. If it is rented and must be returned without disfiguration, it may be interleaved with blank sheets clipped to the pages and the notes entered on these.

It is also good practice to paste into the spare pages of the prompt book copies of the rehearsal schedule, the scene plot, light plot, property plot, and any other plot needed for the particular play; also any program notes, publicity releases, photographs, or other incidental material that might be useful and otherwise possibly would be mislaid.

It is an evident advantage for the director to have his prompt copy ready for annotation when he begins his study of the play so that he can enter all his notes and comments as he goes along. This usually results in so much marking-up that a new and simpler copy has to be prepared for the stage manager to use at actual performances; but aside from the cost of the additional copy this is usually wise, for his script must contain the warnings and cues for light changes, curtains, music, sound effects, telephone bells, doorbells, and so on; also calls for the actors if these are to be used. The additional notations of the director of the tempo, interpretation, and movement for actors will make any single script unintelligible in the half-light of backstage and speed of performance. Since the sharpness of the production depends on the efficiency of the stage manager, his script must be as simple and as clear as he can make it. A prompt book is essential for the director's preparation of the show and a stage manager's book is just as essential for a smooth, well-run production. An extra script or two is a small price to pay for this.

planning the setting

Having mastered the play and made the necessary cuts, the director must now concern himself with the settings. It is not unusual in the amateur theatre for the director to serve as his own scenic designer, but this is not ideal if a capable designer, skilled in his art, as the director must be in his, is available. A capable artist can become a skilled scenic designer by learning the requirements of the stage. There is far more to scenic design than drawing pretty pictures, however. A later chapter treats in some detail the problems the designer must consider.

Plays may be interpreted in many ways. Style may be changed; emphases may vary, depending on the director's approach, but it is the director's concept that governs what the design scheme will be. Some years ago a college theatre group was to present *A Doll's House.* When Ibsen wrote the play about 1890, women were not emancipated and the play was a controversial, exciting piece of theatre. Nowadays the problems Nora faced do not exist, and so the play is no longer meaningful in the same way it was for Ibsen's audiences. For this reason the designer suggested that the setting be a huge, gilded bird cage and that Nora be treated as a little bird kept there and shielded from the world by her husband. The allusions that Torvald makes to Nora as "my little thrush," and so forth, made the concept quite possible although highly unusual. Such a production would have provided a new kind of interest and meaning for its audience. Because the director disagreed completely with the idea and since the responsibility for setting the interpretation was his, the play was successfully presented as a museum piece within a carefully realistic set designed by the designer mentioned above. Any production must be a careful integration of all its parts, and making those parts match and complement each other in a single, coherent whole is the director's job.

The wise director will consult with his staff regarding the advantages and disadvantages of various schemes before he sets his approach. Updating a period play may not be his first wish, but when he learns from his costumer that the cost of the historical production would be doubled or tripled, he may quickly find the modern approach far less objectionable. A number of

Occasionally the director is versatile and can design as well as direct. This series of photos for *Prometheus Bound* is the result of the work of Richard L. Scammon, Indiana University, who designed, directed, costumed, and choreographed the work. Note how placement of actors serves not only as a dramatic statement, but as a design element as well.

trained heads will produce a worthier stew—or at least a more suitable recipe. Whatever the influences upon his decision, it is, in the last analysis, the director's to make.

Once the design concept has been established, the director must communicate to the designer the actual physical requirements that the set should have—how many doors and windows, stairs, fireplaces, and so on, as well as specific items of furniture, trees, rocks, or the like. If a director is planning to use a large grand piano on the set, the designer must know in order to incorporate it well. If an actor who cannot play must fake the playing to recorded sound, then the piano must be placed so that the keyboard does not show to the audience. Only after such determinations have been made can the designer begin the actual job of designing. He must provide a workable, appropriate setting for a particular stage within a given time at a set price. This is indeed a job for the specialist!

Yet many amateur theatres have no one with such skills, and this responsibility, too, falls on the director. A wise director and a growing theatre or-

Backing

Door C.

Door R.   Door L.

T.E.   A   T.E.

Backing

Door C.

Bookcase   Door L.

B   Curtain Line

Back Drop

Window

Door U.L.C.

Door R.

C

Up

R.   Hall L.

Window

Fireplace

D

ganization should recognize the need for capable technical people and begin training talented individuals in this field.

Whether design specialist or director-designer, a good designer must consider the needs of the director as he determines the ground plan, for his set must not only appear appropriate, but it must also work well for the movement and composition of actors. This involves many considerations.

entrances and exits

Insofar as there is any option in the matter, the designer should exercise the greatest care in the placing of entrances and exits, for they have much to do with the effectiveness of stage pictures and bits of action. What might

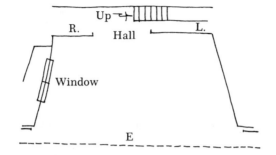

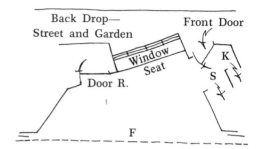

Figure 5. Arrangements of entrances and exits. A, B, and C are common arrangements in cottage interiors. D and E suggest city houses, and F a suburban house. G is the conventional wing-and-drop exterior setting, with old-fashioned numbered entrances.

be called the stock arrangement for interior settings provides three entrances, right, left, and center (A, Figure 5), the center door being often a double one or a large open doorway. The constant repetition of this same arrangement in a succession of plays is a bit monotonous, yet the plan is a good one—flexible, and adaptable to almost any play. It is certainly better to use the stock entrances than to be obliged to do without them when they are needed. One of the worst possible handicaps in the arrangement of stage pictures and movements is to be denied the use of an entrance where one ought to be placed for best effect.

In general the following suggestions will be found helpful in the planning of entrances and exits.

1. *Number.* Have enough of them to account for all comings and goings and to tell the story intelligibly.

2. *Need.* Do not have more than are needed. An unusual exit, visible to

the audience, is a source of constant distraction; people are busy wondering where it leads to or who is to come in by it when they should be paying attention to the play. If a stock set that has an extra door not needed in the play is used, it is better to make a window or an alcove of it or to conceal it with draperies or a piece of furniture. The number of exits should be as small as is consistent with clarity and convincingness. Ordinarily two or three will be enough; some plays, especially farces and melodramas, require more.

3. *Relation of exits to text*. Let each exit mean some particular place mentioned or implied in the text, and then see to it that it is always used by an actor supposed to be going to that place, or coming from it. Audiences are very quick to notice a discrepancy in this. It is sometimes possible, of course, to use one exit as indicating several places. For example, an upstairs sitting room may have only one doorway leading to the hall, used alike by persons going to another room or to the street. An open doorway may be made to suggest two exits, one right and the other left, according to which way the actor turns. In the setting shown at D, Figure 5, two archways give on a hall; the street door is imagined in the hall off stage left, and the rest of the house off right. At E, Figure 5, there is just one wide doorway to the room itself, but it shows three exits: a street exit off right, a back hall off left, and a stairway leading up. Such an arrangement was used with great effectiveness and apparent variety in *Life With Father*.

4. *The arrangement must be conceivable*. It should be possible in a real house—not necessarily an exact imitation of reality built to scale—but something bearing at least a slight resemblance to the arrangements familiar in real life, so that the audience is not unduly puzzled and distracted. The settings shown at A and B in Figure 5 are possible, though not particularly suggestive of reality. That at C is sufficiently convincing as suggesting a small cottage. Those at D and E suggest real city houses, and have been effectively used in many plays. The setting at F, representing a country house, is an elaborate attempt to be convincing; it shows a hallway and front door at stage left, with an exit to the kitchen at K, seen by only a small part of the audience, and one to the stairway at S, invisible to the audience, but suggested by the actor standing in the doorway and looking up; the situation is somewhat clarified by a broad window showing the outdoor approach through a front garden. The arrangement is fairly successful in

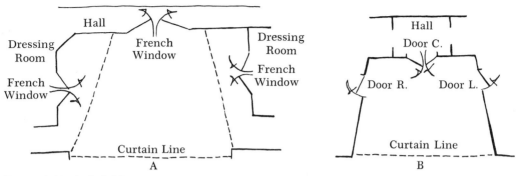

Figure 6. Typical clubhouse stages

suggesting a real house, but it is very one-sided and would tend to throw the action too constantly to the left; and in a feeble attempt to correct this the designer has added a most unconvincing door at the right, the effect of which is to puzzle the audience as to the construction of the house, and, thereby, distract them. After all, the problem is not so much how to create a positive illusion of reality as how to avoid destroying illusion by distracting attention. The trouble with a setting that is too unusual is that it does just that.

5. *Placement of entrances.* Let the entrances be so placed as to be seen easily by all the members of the audience. Nothing is more annoying to the spectator than an arrangement like that at A, Figure 6, which represents the stage of a certain clubhouse. The walls are solid and immovable, and the proscenium arch is narrower than the stage itself, so that the right door is always invisible to nearly half the audience, and the left door to the other half. Every actor entering right or left must walk about 6 feet in view of some of the audience before he is visible to all of them; and whenever during the action he goes near either side of the stage, some of the audience are left in doubt as to whether he has gone off or not. In arranging entrances and exits the director should have in mind the shape of the auditorium as well as that of the stage, and should take pity on those who are unfortunate enough to occupy the side seats.

6. *Let some of the entrances be placed downstage.* This is especially important in a long act that has much coming and going, and on a deep or narrow stage; it is less important on a wide, shallow stage. An arrangement

like that at B, Figure 6, representing another stupidly designed clubhouse, grows fearfully monotonous after a time. If the action is to be kept downstage, each entering character must walk straight toward the audience before he seems to be part of the play, and straight away from it before making his exit. The result of such an arrangement is either an arbitrary awkwardness, or an irresistible tendency for the actors to hang back upstage. In a formal play the artificial parade to the footlights is sometimes acceptable, especially if it is made a frank convention throughout; but in a realistic modern comedy it is destructive of illusion. Only the most skillful director can arrange natural stage movements for such a setting.

7. *Use of doors.* Let the doors be hung to swing downstage, as at A and C, Figure 5. The arrangement at A, with the doors swinging downstage and opening offstage, is the usual one; but that at C is fairly common, and is very useful when a character is to peep in and be seen doing so. Only very exceptional circumstances would justify a door placed to swing upstage, for the fairly obvious reason that the movement of an actor entering or leaving by such a door would almost inevitably be clumsy.

8. *Tormentor entrances.* Avoid the use of the so-called tormentor entrances; this term refers to the spaces between the proscenium arch and the *tormentors*, or false proscenium, as at T.E. in A or G, Figure 5. Usually they are not wide enough, but even if they are, the audience does not naturally think of them as doorways; the tormentors are part of the frame whose purpose is the maintenance of aesthetic distance, and the use of the spaces in front of them for entrance or exit is destructive of illusion.

9. *Use in exterior scenes with wing settings.* In such scenes, as at G in Figure 5, avoid indiscriminate use of the entrances and exits between the wings. Establish the meaning of each exit used, and stick to that exit for that meaning. If it seems confusing to leave some of them constantly unused, it may be possible to block them up from the stage by means of set pieces—trees, rocks, benches, bushes, or fences, or perhaps projecting bits of buildings. Never block up an entrance off stage, however, when it appears open from the stage. To do so is to invite some nervous or forgetful actor into a most embarrassing trap.

10. *Featuring of most important entrances.* Those entrances that are to figure most vividly in the essential action of the play should be placed so as to catch the eye easily; and if possible they should be designed to

create a sense of expectation. When an actor enters through an inconspicu-
ous doorway the effect is one of surprise; when he enters through a conspicuous or seemingly significant doorway it is rather one of inevitability
satisfied. Usually the latter is the more desirable effect.

windows

The placing of windows may be part of the problem in design and decoration, or it may be a matter of the essential action of the play. When the
dramatist requires a character to look in or out of a window, open or close
one, speak or signal from one, or when there is some significance in the
light coming through a window, the placing of that window is just as fundamental to the action of the play as the placing of entrances and exits.

A window through which the audience is expected to see something
should normally be placed upstage, either in the rear flat or in a sharply
slanting wall, and not in a side wall visible to only half of the audience. A
large window is best for this purpose, so that the backing to be seen by the
audience can be placed at a reasonable distance behind the window and still
be visible in all parts of the house. If the view is to include anything supposed to be below the level of the stage, the window must be set low; otherwise the people down front will be too conscious of looking uphill and seeing downhill.

When a character on the stage is to look out of a window and to show
some important reaction to what he sees outside, and it is necessary for the
audience to see for itself, the window is best placed in the side wall, fairly
well downstage. This enables the actor, as he looks out of the window, to
show at least his profile, and perhaps a three-quarter view of his face.

Important entrances can often be pointed up very effectively by the
judicious placing of windows. A character seen passing a window before
he enters takes on a heightened interest and makes as deep an impression
on the audience as if he had paused in tableau; at the same time there is
no suspension of the action of the play, and no sense of self-conscious
artificiality.

When a window figures significantly in the action, the whole setting must be designed about that window. It is just as important as any entrance or exit. Conversely, it must not be forgotten that a window is a natural point of interest, so that the placing of one in too conspicuous a position when it has little or no real significance in the play is sure to cause at least some distraction.

lighting

Since the advent of electricity, stage lighting has come to be an important part of scenic art. As a problem in design and in mechanics there will be more to say of it later. But even in the rough planning of his settings the director must take into consideration the major sources of light and their relation to the action of the play. Without knowing the sources from which the light is to come he cannot know which are the conspicuous places on the stage and how his groups should be placed for emphasis.

In interior scenes representing daytime the windows are thought of as the natural sources of light, and whenever possible the audience should be allowed to feel that the light actually comes from them. Of course it is very seldom that a stage can be adequately lighted from this source alone; something must be sacrificed to keep the actors' faces out of constant shadow. A consistent illusion must be created, and one can do this simply by justifying his sources of light and balancing levels of light in an acceptable proportion. Audiences do not expect light as bright as day, but the illusion of day must be suggested by a light level that is the brightest used. Conversely, dark can be suggested by a level that is lower than any other but still allows the audience to see.

In evening scenes indoors the windows will of course be dark or a dull blue, and the sources of effective light will be internal and frankly artificial. Care should be taken to place table lamps, floor lamps, and fireplaces so that the supposed light from them may seem to fall upon points of emphasis in the stage groupings. Each of these artificial sources should serve primarily as justification for the light that the designer will add to make the scene believable and properly bright for the actors to be seen. A visible chandelier may be used as a period furnishing, but the light sources in it should be dimmed to a warm glow so as not to blind the audience. Additional instruments can then be located to provide effective light with the chandelier as justification.

Symbolic scenes, or scenes intended to convey a single larger mood, can often be played in bold relief with a single source of light at one side or above, and with simple plastic effect. The posture of the character, the composition of the picture, the poetry of the lines, and the emotional effect of the light itself serve to convey the mood. But in scenes depicting subtleties of character, humor, dialogue, or repartee, or revelation of inner thought and feeling, the action must generally be placed in more general illumination and the lighting of the actor's face considered before either naturalism or abstract beauty.

A more detailed treatment of the topic of lighting may be found in Chapter Twenty.

furniture

As a rule it is best to fix the positions of the furniture as carefully in advance as those of the doors and windows, especially of those articles of furniture that are to be used by the actors—tables, chairs, sofas, and the like. Last-minute changes are, of course, more easily made than in the case of the doors and windows, but are to be avoided as far as possible.

The amateur who must work on a small stage is often at a great disadvantage in the arrangement of furniture. The small stage (say 16 × 10 feet) is crowded to the limit with a davenport, a table, and two chairs, and perhaps one or two wall pieces. Practically speaking, there is only one possible arrangement of these: the sofa on one side and the table and chairs on the other (as at A, Figure 7). This can be reversed (as at B), but the variation is slight, and after one has seen the two arrangements a few dozen times he begins to tire of them. If the sofa is placed in the center (as at C), there is a freshness of effect, but the spaces at the sides are too limited for freedom of action, and the general feeling is one of stiffness and formality. If it is placed approximately at right angles facing a fireplace (as at D), it looks out

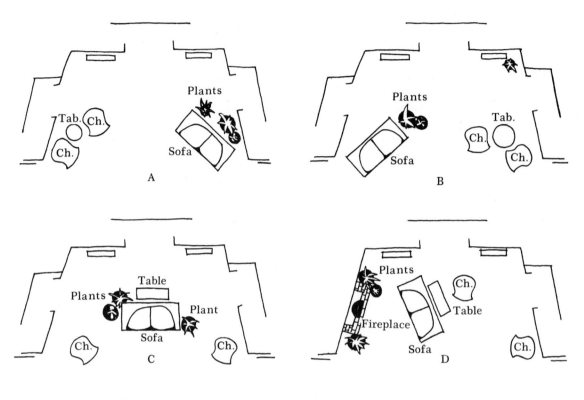

Figure 7. Arrangements of furniture on a small stage

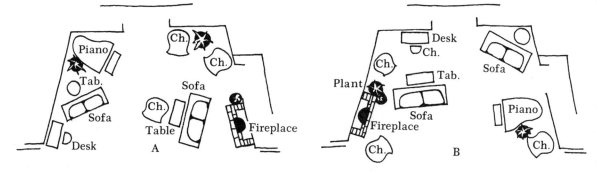

Figure 8. Arrangements of furniture on a large stage

of scale, and tends to split the room in two. If it is placed against the side wall (as at E), one side of the audience does not get a full view, and as soon as you move it out a little, you get back to the arrangement at A. If the sofa is left out and one or two chairs are substituted, there is a slight variation of effect, but the stage is apt to look spotty and disunified. Unless the character of the play is such as to admit of some very unusual arrangement, the director finds himself, therefore, constantly baffled in the attempt to get variety.

A great deal has been said and written about the superior intimacy of the small stage and the cold artificiality of the large one, but the large stage has a distinct advantage when it comes to arranging furniture. It holds more furniture without overcrowding and permits an infinite variety of different arrangements without detriment to the playing space and without unnaturalness. The arrangements shown in Figure 8 merely suggest what utterly different effects may be obtained on a moderately large stage (26×15 feet) by rearrangement of the same furniture. The average commercial theatre stage is still larger (perhaps 40×20 feet).

There are several important considerations in the placing of stage furniture.

1. Amount of furniture. Have enough to relieve the bareness of the stage, but not enough to overcrowd it. Either extreme is bad, not only in its direct power of distracting the audience, but also in its effect upon the actor. On a bare stage the actor finds it hard to seem natural. He feels the lack of support, becomes self-conscious, and takes refuge in declamation instead of acting; in a declamatory play this may do no harm, but in a realistic play it is bad. On an overcrowded stage he feels his movements hampered and is unable to develop the freedom necessary to dramatic contrasts. Of course some plays, and some scenes, call naturally for more furniture than others. A brief street scene may require no furniture at all, and a scene in a poor man's house may be appropriately played with very little; whereas a scene in the living room of a great mansion in which a number of guests are to be served with tea may require a great deal. But the best rule is always moderation.

2. *Type of furniture.* Except when there is some point in a stylistic production, avoid startling or conspicuous furniture. Furniture that is too interesting, either in its design or in its placing, is a common source of distraction.

3. *Level of furniture.* Avoid a dead level. If too many chairs, tables, and sofas are the same height, there is a persistent horizontal line across the stage that catches the eye and creates a distraction.

4. *Height.* Specify chairs and sofas at least 17 inches high, 18 if possible. Lower chairs may suggest ease and comfort when the actors are sitting down, but when it comes time for them to get up there is trouble. It is a real effort to rise from a low, soft chair, and it is impossible to rise from one with freedom, eagerness, and force. Boards or sheets of plywood can often be used under cushions to bolster up otherwise too large, too soft, overstuffed pieces.

Imagine seeing the action of a play temporarily suspended while several members of the cast assist the elderly matron to rise from a sofa – or worse, while she attempts to do so unassisted. In these years when short skirts are in fashion, low seats also create additional worries for the actresses and distractions for the audience.

5. *Arrangement.* Have the furniture arranged so as to suggest reality, though not necessarily to represent it. It is natural, for example, to place chairs near a table, and a lamp on the table, and to have a sofa near a fireplace. There is no need to imitate the conventional arrangements illustrated in the advertisements of the August furniture sales; but it is best to avoid any arrangement that is queer or outlandish, or that provokes a housewife in the audience to murmur, "If that was my room I'd move that sofa where someone could sit on it and feel like one of the family."

6. *Limitations of naturalism.* At the same time it is essential to remember that the stage is not life, but a conventionalization of life in terms of certain accepted limitations. If the furniture were arranged exactly as in an ordinary living room, too many of the actors would have to sit with their backs to the audience, and the latter would feel a sense of exclusion. The stage is not a room with one wall removed. It is a room, or other place, subjected to a peculiar convention, a kind of opening out toward the audience like the unfolding of a flower. One can only acquire a keen sense of this relationship through the study of many stage settings. The setting must give the observer 50 or 75 feet away as comprehensive a view of its essential features as one gets of a real room by standing just within it; and this can only be done by some sort of distortion. While distortion should be kept to a minimum, a surprising amount is permissible when it is carried out in accordance with the accepted conventions to which audiences are accustomed.

7. *Do not block the entrances and exits.* A clear sweep for characters entering or leaving adds much to the effectiveness of the dramatic action.

8. *Leave playing space for the actors who are not sitting down.* It is especially important that they have adequate space in which to cross from right to left or left to right, or diagonally up or down stage. A reasonable amount of freedom in arranging diagonal crosses is a great help to the director who is trying to break up a "talky" scene, or to maneuver his characters into the positions necessary for some later bit of action.

9. *Movement of chairs by actors.* In a long scene, and especially in a long play with only one setting, plan to have the actors move some of the chairs at appropriate points in the dialogue. In this way it is possible to get some variety of grouping with comparatively little furniture. But be careful not to have an actor move a chair, sit down on it, pop up again, and put the chair back, all in such a brief time as to make the device seem obvious and unconvincing. Even professional directors sin frequently in this respect. When a chair is moved there should be some apparent reason, as when two people draw their chairs closer together for secrecy in conversation, or when a gentleman places a more comfortable chair for a lady. A chair that has been moved out of place can often be replaced quite naturally a little later.

What has been said of furniture applies also to other large stage properties. Small properties need not be considered here; some of them have to do with the designing of the setting, and some of them, especially the *hand props,* have to do with the action of the play and the business of the characters. The placing of the latter is part of the problem of planning the action itself.

The comments about furniture placement are directed toward the proscenium stage, yet with a few qualifications, they may apply equally to the thrust or round playing area.

Naturalness, balance, and possibilities for variety of action must be considered no matter what the playing space. Yet a thrust stage with audience on three sides will require more openness and less orientation to the single audience side. Audience on four sides will require furniture placement far more like that of a conventional room.

Choice of furniture is critical for these kinds of stages, for items must be low enough not to block the view of audiences from any position, yet furniture must carry the entire load of visual identification without the help of conventional scenery. Benches, backless sofas, and stools judiciously placed can do much to simplify the director's blocking problems, but such units must be properly dressed and integrated into the period play.

How much of the action of the play, including stage movements and positions, and stage *business*, should be planned in advance of rehearsals?

This is a subject of perpetual controversy. Most experienced directors believe in careful preplanning in the matter of stage directions. They believe in fixing every movement, every stage position, every piece of stage business, as early as possible, and making only such changes as may be dictated by unforeseen necessity or discovery of error. At the same time there are a number of eminent theatre people who hold the opposite view, maintaining that to fix the details of stage movement and business in advance of rehearsals is to stifle the actor's freedom of interpretation and make the performance a soulless, mechanistic exercise.

The whole improvisational movement in the theatre of recent years is based on the premise that actors should "find" their feeling and actions through games that allow them to create spontaneously the blocking and interpretations necessary for a scene. In fact, a number of the plays of van Itallie are described as *devised* rather than written, for the Open Theatre actors created much of these plays from skeletal material provided by the author. At the same time it should be noted that the plays were directed and it was the director's job to sift and select, reinforce, and define from the many, many things the actors were trying. Such an approach to theatre is one that only experienced people can do well, and companies who employ such techniques must work closely together for long periods of time in order to achieve the kind of blend such improvisation requires.

Most plays profit greatly from careful thought and preparation on the part of the director. Occasional bursts of inspiration are wonderful but seldom spring from the imagination of the director who has not examined many, many possibilities. It is true that blocking and business supplied to the actor who does not understand them in relation to the character he is developing will find it difficult to make them his own. His attempt to do so, however, will help the understanding process, and a skillful director can use these opportunities to help his actors achieve characterization. The things that work can be kept, other things changed or discarded, but such blocking and business is only the outline upon which the good actor builds. In the end everything he does must appear to be his own. Anything else is wrong.

There is, of course, no real disagreement in the major premise: Whatever tends to destroy the actor's freedom of interpretation in such a way as to make his performance coldly mechanical certainly ought to be condemned. Whether or not the actor can be conscious of his technique without loss of art, the audience ought not to be conscious of it, ought not to feel the mechanism dominating the thought and emotion. The question at issue is whether adherence to specific stage directions helps or hinders the actor in the attainment of that sort of freedom that we all agree is desirable. Since our whole procedure in the planning of a production will depend upon how we answer this question, its importance is obvious.

unpremeditated art

There are those who go so far as to maintain that the action of a play should never be specifically defined, either before or after rehearsals have begun; that the actor should be free to come and go according to his inspiration and to invent his own business under pressure of emotion, and to do it differently at every performance. No one, to be sure, claims that a beginner can act well by this method; the theory presupposes at least an experienced actor, if not a great one. No one whose opinion is worth serious consideration denies that there are limitations imposed by the facts of the play and by the necessity of some slight cooperation with the other players. Granted that the actor ought to know his lines and speak them accurately, that he ought to give the proper cues to his colleagues, that he ought to make his entrances and exits on time and according to the meaning of the play, and that he ought to take his assigned part in the action essential to the plot of the play, the advocates of freedom still demand that he shall not be required to speak a given line from the same spot at every performance, or to light his cigarette on the same line, or to illustrate his emotions with the same piece of business. They demand more. They demand that he shall have as much freedom to reinterpret his part at each performance, and to express his interpretation spontaneously in action, as is possible without actually disrupting the play.

The motive back of this opinion is sound and praiseworthy. It is the feeling that what matters in a play is the context of thought and emotion, and not the technique of expressing it. This is the fundamental basis of good design – what I have called the utilitarian basis. Yet the opinion itself is unmistakably posited upon the notion that good art is necessarily unpremeditated.

A more absurd notion would be hard to find. The very phrase, "unpremeditated art," is a contradiction in terms. If art were unpremeditated, the greatest artists would all be babies, for babies are the only people who can be entirely guiltless of premeditation. The very fact that the greatest artists are people of mature experience in art, and that they grow greater through experience, is sufficient proof that premeditation of some sort is not inconsistent with the highest art. True art is sincere art, but a thing can be wholly sincere without being in the least unpremeditated.

acting in the palmy days

Advocates of interpretative freedom are constantly referring to the methods of the last century, when great actors traveled about the country playing with resident stock companies, often without rehearsal and usually with only one or two rehearsals in each place. We have no such acting nowadays, they tell us, and no such giants of the stage as Booth, or Barrett, or Forrest, or Charlotte Cushman, or Macready; or their predecessors, Kean, Mrs. Siddons, or Charles Kemble. These people could act anywhere, with anybody, and could dominate the stage and the audience by sheer force of passion and eloquence. No humdrum mechanical repetition in those days. Each performance was different; you could see the same actor in the same part a dozen times and never twice alike.

They neglect to add that of the dozen performances two might be stirringly good, four acceptable, two more dull and lifeless, one a complete artistic failure, and the other three broken up altogether by some disaster to the scenery, or the illness of the star, or a riot in the audience. Variety is the spice of life, and the palmy days were spicy.

As a matter of fact, a little reading in the biographical literature of those

times—there is plenty of it available, for every actor or actress of promi-
nence leaves at least one volume of biography or autobiography—will
quickly reveal a vast amount of discontent with conditions on the part of
the actors themselves. The sincere, painstaking actor of the late nineteenth
century complained bitterly of the slipshod methods of his time, of the lack
of time for adequate rehearsal, of the nerve-racking uncertainties of production, and the fact that success in a performance was so dependent upon
chance and the inspiration of the moment. Macready tells us that he was
thought very eccentric and amateurish because he insisted upon ten or
twelve days of study before performing a new role, and that he was much
ridiculed for acting at rehearsals. "It was the custom of the London actors,"
he says, "to do little more at rehearsals than to read or repeat the words of
their parts, marking in their entrances and exits, as settled by the stage
manager, and their respective places on the stage."[1] Of Charlotte Cushman
it is said that, "Beyond the due expression and feeling given to the words,
which she could never quite wholly omit even in study or at rehearsal, the
acting was left to the inspiration of the time and place."[2] The inference
seems to be that she tried to omit "the due expression and feeling," or that
her contemporaries expected her to. Whether Miss Cushman approved of
the system we are not told, but under it she shone at the expense of the play.
Surely Juliet is the most interesting figure in *Romeo and Juliet,* but when
Miss Cushman played Romeo, the critics praised her for two or three columns without mentioning Juliet. When she played Lady Macbeth, her name
appeared in very large type and that of the actor playing Macbeth in very
small type—even though he might have been the leading actor of a very
fine resident company. The whole system meant, inevitably, the exaltation
of the exceptional actor with the temperament and the emotional power to
thrive under it; but it meant also the subordination of the lesser actor, and
an emphasis on parts rather than plays, which is perhaps the chief reason
why the giants of the day before yesterday stood out so prominently.

Even so, it is well to realize that the giants did not have quite the freedom
they are sometimes supposed to have had. First, their activities, especially
on tour, were for the most part confined to a standard repertory of well-
known plays, and for these plays the essential movements and business
were already established by tradition, and familiar to experienced actors

everywhere. But for this the traveling star system could never have existed
at all. The star had, of course, the privilege of making changes, and the
chief purpose of rehearsals was to let the supporting actors know what
changes were to be made. Second, even the London actors, as we see by
Macready's remark just quoted, acknowledged the authority of the stage
manager to settle their exits and entrances and their respective places on
the stage, as all but the most childishly temperamental actors always have
done.

The chief reason why the matter so established was less elaborate and
more sketchy than it is in most modern plays was the fact that the standard
drama, especially the poetic drama, was less dependent for its effects upon
naturalistic movements and business, and more upon the declamation of
the lines. The taste of the time was for a style of acting that many of us
today would not call acting at all, a passionate, oratorical style that focused
attention upon the actor rather than the play, and compelled acceptance of
certain artificial conventions that may or may not have been more artistic
than our present conventions but were unquestionably different. It may be
doubted whether very many serious critics of the stage today really want
to see a return to the conditions of the last century, or would if they understood them.

the price of freedom

But we have not yet disposed of the contention that for freedom of interpretation the actor must be unhampered by specific stage directions. The
improvisational school apparently supports such a premise. Yet when one
examines the working methods of a group using these techniques, he finds
great freedom to experiment but he also finds, gradually, that movements
and business that work become fixed and a permanent part of the performance. There is great reliance on the inspiration of the moment, but these
moments are in rehearsal, not in performance. Even in some of the very
experimental groups, where several possibilities for a certain scene exist,
each possibility has been rehearsed and on-the-spot invention is not encouraged.

The surest way to chaos on stage is simply to turn the actors loose to wait for inspiration. A play depends upon balance, rhythm, harmony, pacing, and emphasis, among other things, but these five are ample evidence that planning is necessary to place actors on the stage, to establish and change relationships, and generally to create interest through movement. These elements are necessary if one plans to reinforce, not negate, the meaning of a play.

No actor, regardless of ability or experience, can instinctively place himself properly and do the right thing at all times, especially when he is working with other actors who are intent on instant creation also. The argument that an actor should not have his mind cluttered with business and blocking lest he be unable to concentrate on the play is patently false. There is only one way in which a good actor, in anything but a highly declamatory play, can avoid agitating his mind about physical movements at an actual performance, and that is by having them so well learned in advance that he can perform them without agitation; only thus can he purchase the freedom of mind necessary to real freedom of interpretation. Most sincere, painstaking actors are quite willing to admit that the business of a play does not come to them without thought; that, on the contrary, they must pay for their apparent freedom and spontaneity by weeks of intensive labor, by working out every detail of action, by articulating it with the lines, and by memorizing both lines and action so perfectly as to render them almost subconsciously.

are stage directions inhibitory?

Much of the opposition to specific stage directions lies in the notion that they inhibit the actor, render his performance mechanical, and check his creative impulses.

As a matter of fact they do nothing of the kind — not if they are good stage directions. On the contrary, they leave the actor perfectly free to interpret the part in his own way. Of course I refer to directions covering movement and business and not to coaching or instruction in the meaning of the part. The two things are quite separate. Now and then, it is true, a single specific action planned by the director may prove inconsistent with some later development of the actor's interpretation; in that case we have a legitimate and proper reason for a change. But the vast majority of stage directions have surprisingly little to do with the individual actor's interpretation of his part.

In illustration I may cite a production of Barrie's *The Admirable Crichton* that I staged many years ago for a college dramatic club. Partly to employ as many members as possible and partly to guard against disaster in case of illness, we used two separate casts, giving them identical stage directions and shifting them about at rehearsals until every player was accustomed to playing with every other. This play calls for some very intricate movements and a good deal of business; there are many properties, and in some of the scenes there are many people on the stage at once, all taking part in the action. Our stage was laid out to scale at rehearsals, and all the furniture placed exactly; and every movement was planned down to the most minute detail. There had to be some changes, of course, but all matters of doubt were settled early, and the play was rehearsed almost without change for about six weeks. The action was articulated with the lines, and each player knew exactly the position and attitude in which he was to deliver each word of his part; he knew exactly when to flick the ashes off his cigarette, when and from whom to receive a cup of tea, which hand to take it with, where to sit down, and when to get up. Because of the inexperience of the players and our special desire for smooth performance, we went to extremes, and indulged in much more exacting drill than is at all usual with amateurs or at all necessary with professionals.

Yet a surprising thing happened – surprising at least to those who could not see the use of so much precision, and who were afraid of a mechanical effect. We gave eight performances with the two casts alternating, and halfway through the second performance it became evident that we had two different plays! One cast gave us a romantic comedy, the other a cynical, ironical satire. When one cast played, the other was always in the audience. There was keen rivalry, and each cast, largely because it did not have to agitate its mind over entrances or exits or stage business, was free to seek new shades of meaning through comparison. Not a single important stage direction was changed during the week, but new inner meanings were brought out at every performance, and the difference between the two versions grew greater as the week progressed.

With identical stage directions you can have a good or a bad performance, according to the spirit and ability of the actors; or you can have two entirely different interpretations. You can even have two different interpretations by the same company, for there are many cases on record in which the mood or tone of a scene, or even of a whole play, has been changed without any change in the words or action. When students in a studio theatre presented Cameron's *The One Hundred and First*, it was a fast-paced, highly amusing farce on opening night, yet those who saw the second and final performance found it to be sick comedy. The lines and action remained the same, but the inexperienced actors began to take their characters and the play seriously. The pace slowed and the result was catastrophic!

On the whole, it seems quite as absurd to demand that the action of the play be left to the inspiration of the moment, as to demand that the words be improvised differently at each performance, as they were in the vagabond companies of medieval Italy. To the talented and experienced actor, the one thing is as likely to come naturally as the other; within certain limitations both are possible, but the result is not very apt to be the highest order of art.

the James-Lange theory

The idea that "the physical action of the play should not be defined while the thought and feeling that should prompt it are still unsure" makes a strong appeal on the ground of common sense and sincerity; but is it in accordance with scientific fact? It seems to me to run afoul of the so-called James-Lange Theory, now pretty generally accepted by students of psychology. According to this theory, feeling, or emotion, is not the cause but the result of action. To go back to the law of motor response: For every stimulus received by the organism there is an immediate and direct motor response, the nature of which depends partly upon the nature of the stimulus and partly upon the previous experience of the organism. Whether a given stimulus will produce a given action, or a given motor set, depends upon the thoughts and feelings in the subject's past experience, but not upon a preceding emotion in the given case. It is the motor response that is the primary reaction. What we call feeling or emotion is secondary; it is the realization in consciousness of the motor state.

Thus when we see an automobile bearing down upon us, or hear a warning signal, we do not jump out of the way because we are frightened; we jump out of the way because our experience has taught us to do so automatically, and if we are frightened it is because we have had to jump out of the way. Whether we do jump out of the way depends altogether upon our *conditioned* responses. City-bred people, accustomed to dodging traffic, jump promptly and in the right direction; or perhaps it would be more accurate to say that only those whose responses are conducive to survival have survived. What is often called "presence of mind" is not presence of mind at all·but, rather, absence of mind; it is neither intellectual nor emotional but is purely a matter of automatic response properly prepared for by previous training and sufficiently quick and accurate to function before there is time for thought.

Whether the James-Lange theory is sound or not is of course debatable, and the question is too abstruse for discussion here. But in view of its wide acceptance it would seem a little dangerous for a stage director to assume that the action of a play is necessarily or merely the result of the actor's emotions. It may, as a matter of fact, be the cause. At any rate the theory gives some hint of the importance of action in relation to emotion and suggests the danger of hastily devised and inappropriate action, whether planned early by the director or later by the actor.

It also suggests that the right actions, thoroughly rehearsed to recur automatically, may have some effect in calling up the desired emotions in the actor, and empathically in the audience.

technique and trickery

There is another sort of opposition to the careful planning of stage movement and business, a sort that comes less frequently from actors and

directors than from critics, authors, and professors of literature. It is based
on an exalted worship of sincerity and takes the form of a denunciation of
all conscious technique as a kind of trickery.

One of the best teachers of dramatic literature of our time takes somewhat this view. Whenever one mentions to him the manner in which certain
effects are achieved in the theatre through control of attention, creation of
suspense and anticipation, invention of business to naturalize movements,
and the like, he throws up his hands in deprecation. "Trickery! Trickery!"
he says. "All trickery!"

He is right, of course. It is trickery. But so in a sense is all art. The only
perfect absence of trickery is to be found in pure accident, and pure accident
is not art. Life itself may or may not be pure accident, but art is design — the
antithesis of accident.

One of the most eminent representatives of the "No Trickery" party was
John Galsworthy. His position in the matter was amusingly stated by William Archer, as follows: "Even the most innocent tricks of emphasis are to
him snares of the Evil One. He would sooner die than drop his curtain on a
particularly effective line. It is his chief ambition that you should never
discern any arrangement, any intention, in his work. As a rule, the only
reason you can see for his doing thus or thus is his desire that you should
see no reason for it." And Mr. Archer adds: "He does not carry this tendency,
as some do, to the point of eccentricity, but he certainly goes as far as any
one should be advised to follow. A little further, and you incur the danger
of becoming affectedly unaffected, artificially inartificial."[3]

Exactly. If you do not drop your curtain on an effective line, you must drop
it on an ineffective one; but why in the world should you? What artistic end
is achieved by choosing the greater of two evils? By Mr. Galsworthy's own
standard, a curtain on an ineffective line is a greater evil than the usual
curtain, because it calls attention more insistently to the author's technique.
The audience expects an effective curtain, and takes such a curtain as a
matter of course, without undue attention to the why and the wherefore.
But when the curtain descends on a commonplace line, the audience is left
wondering whether the stage manager blundered, or, if not, why the author
chose such a peculiar ending — wondering, in short, what particularly subtle
and elusive brand of trickery he had in mind.

It is a characteristic of enthusiasts that they seldom examine alternatives; they consider the frying pan but not the fire. When sincere artists revolt against the pettiness and crudity and obtrusiveness of much modern stage technique, they are abundantly justified by the facts; but they are not right in concluding that all stage technique is bad, nor are they right in substituting an obtrusive and distracting absence of technique—a technique of ostentatious inartificiality.

With respect to the movement and grouping of characters on the stage it is well to remember that the alternative is not between an effective grouping and no grouping. It is between an effective grouping and an ineffective one. If the characters are on the stage at all, they are making some kind of impression on the audience, and if the director does not see to it that the impression is helpful to the purpose of the play, it is pretty sure to be detrimental. A bad group or movement is just as distracting, just as inimical to sincerity, as a good one, and it is unpleasant in its own right besides. If the director does not control the empathic responses of his audience, the audience will empathize anyhow, and in all probability they will empathize in the wrong things. That is exactly what happens when an actor makes an awkward or amateurish movement or gesture, or stands in an awkward posture, or does not know what to do with his hands. Well-planned movement or business has at least this virtue, that it keeps the actor's body occupied and prevents him from doing all sorts of wrong things and thereby stirring up unwanted effects.

One cannot insist too strongly upon this negative side of stage technique. Good stage technique lies quite as much in knowing what to avoid as in knowing what to do, and one of the best reasons for trying consciously to do an effective thing is to guard against the likelihood of doing an ineffective or positively distracting thing unconsciously. It may seem illogical to emphasize the negative side of a creative art, but the point is that the artist must keep the imagination of the audience working on his side. So long as he can avoid doing the wrong thing, he need offer little more than suggestion, and the imagination of the audience will do the rest; but the moment he does something obtrusively ineffective, the imaginative concept is shattered.

dictatorship or democracy?

Whether much or little of the action is to be planned in advance, the question still remains: Who is to plan it? Shall the director work it out in advance of rehearsals and then dictate it ready-made to the actors; or shall the actors be allowed to work it out for themselves in rehearsals, with the director serving merely as critic?

Upon this question, also, expert opinion differs. Some directors, thinking first of the importance of unity in the production, insist upon the autocratic method. Gordon Craig, with his idea of the actors as *übermarionettes* and the director supreme, exemplified this view. Others, moved by a love of sincerity in realism, feel that action evolved "naturally" in rehearsal, with comparatively little interference from the director, is more likely to be right.

The history of Stanislavsky and the Moscow Art Theatre affords an interesting exposition of both points of view. At one time, as Stanislavsky himself tells us in his autobiography, it was his custom to plan every detail of the action before calling a rehearsal, and to require rigid adherence to it on the part of his actors. In later years he went to the other extreme and the method advocated in his later writings is to begin with round-table discussion of the play, followed by informal rehearsal, at which the actors try out various movements, offer suggestions, and continue the discussions until the finished play gradually evolves.

How much of the fine ensemble playing of the Moscow group was due to the latter method, and how much to the rigorous training that the older actors received under the earlier method, is a matter of speculation. In my own judgment most of it was not primarily due to either. I believe that the greatness of the Moscow Art Theatre could be attributed chiefly to the high character of the artists, to their painstaking sincerity, to the solidarity of the group, and to the long period of study and rehearsal given to each play before its first performance. Under such conditions either method might give good results.

The advantage of what may be called the democratic method lies in the greater opportunity for creative work on the part of the individual artist, and the greater stimulus to group imagination. But this advantage cannot be realized fully unless there is abundant time for careful study and rehearsal, and unless the players are experienced and able to lose themselves imaginatively in the parts. The original Moscow players, men and women of education and character, associated through long years of sincere creative effort, were able to realize it as few others could.

There is a middle course, analogous perhaps to government by responsible ministry, recognizing neither the divine right of autocracy nor the divine right of do-as-you-please. In a permanent theatre it may be wise to provide some form of appeal from arbitrary rulings of the stage director, but it is not wise to leave those matters that are largely matters of teamwork either to pure accident or to the whims of a dozen diverse and changeable temperaments.

After all, the real test is the test of results. I think I have seldom seen a production the faults of which could be in any way attributed to too much dictation of movement and position by the director; but I have seen scores of productions—amateur and professional—that were ragged and restless for the very obvious reason that the actors were moving pretty much as they pleased and very much at cross purposes. Rare indeed is the amateur production that could not be improved by more detailed, more skillful, and more unified direction of movement.

notes and references

1. William Charles Macready, *Macready's Reminiscences,* Sir Francis Pollock (ed.) (New York: Harper & Row, 1875). p. 109
2. Emma Stebbins, *Life and Letters of Charlotte Cushman* (Boston: Houghton Mifflin, 1899).
3. William Archer, *Playmaking; A Manual of Craftsmanship* (New York: Dover, 1960). p. 328.

Assuming that stage movement, stage groupings, and stage pictures are to be carefully planned, what principles and methods should govern the planning?

The problem is a problem in design and the principles that apply are the principles of design as we have already considered them. But they must be translated into the concrete terms of stage technique.

In plotting stage movements one must remember that the movements, and even the characters themselves, are but parts of a composite design of which the central element is the thought of the play; and that success will depend not only upon the director's grasp of the thought but upon his ability to visualize his characters against a background of setting and furnishing, of line, mass, and color, and upon his power to coordinate speech, action, and sometimes music, into a single harmonious composition.

To assist him in visualizing the movements he will sometimes find it expedient to employ some sort of mechanical aid — something to stimulate the imagination. Of course the designer will lay out the stage setting of each scene in the form of a plan on paper, and mark the positions of the entrances and of the furniture on the plan. Often the director will find it helpful to mount the plan on a soft drawing board and use push pins to represent the characters, moving them about as a means of studying the groupings. Some directors prefer to work on cardboard models of the settings, and even of the properties, and use little paper-doll figures to represent the characters. For decorative or symbolic plays, in which stage pictures, lighting effects, and color harmonies are of first importance, the latter method has special advantages. It is also helpful when the setting includes stairways, ramps, and various acting levels affecting the vertical aspects of the stage picture. For ordinary plays, and especially those with many characters in rapid motion, the horizontal plan is probably more helpful.

methods of notation

For setting downstage movements in the prompt book some method of notation is necessary. The terms *Right* (R.), *Left* (L.), and *Center* (C.) are

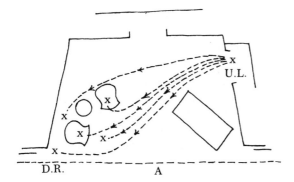

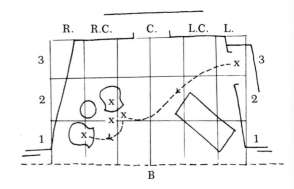

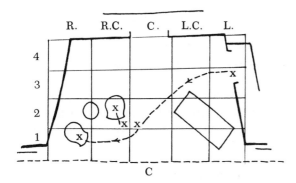

Figure 9. Methods of plotting stage movements

almost universally employed in this country to designate stage positions —
right meaning the actor's right as he faces the audience. Most directors also
use the terms *Right Center* (R.C.) and *Left Center* (L.C.) for the inter-
mediate positions. *Down*, or *downstage* (D.), means toward the audience,
and *Up*, or *upstage* (U.), away from the audience. The direction to proceed
from one side to the other is usually indicated by the word *cross* or the sign
X. In most professional prompt books these are about the only terms used
and directions are given only in a very rough way. The experienced actor

is supposed to perfect the details himself. Thus when he is told to *cross D.R.*
he is supposed to know instinctively which way and how far to go.

It sometimes happens, however, that a single direction may mean any
one of a half dozen things. In A, Figure 9, for example, an actor up left
(U.L.) told to cross D.R. might follow any one of the paths indicated. When,
because of the inexperience of the actors, or for any other reason, it becomes
desirable to specify movements in more detail, some more accurate system
must be found. The zoning system illustrated in B and C, Figure 9, serves
the purpose very effectively. It has the merit of retaining the usual designations of R., R.C., C., L.C., and L., and the lateral zones may correspond
roughly with the old-wing entrances, L.1.E., L.2.E., and so on.

In laying out a zoning plan it is important to know the exact dimensions
of the set and, consequently, of the zones and to place all articles of furniture accurately to scale. A sofa, for example, may be 6 to 7 feet long × 3 feet
wide; the largest chair is about 3 feet square. In B, Figure 9, the proscenium
opening is 25 feet, the depth 15 feet, and the zones 5 feet each way. In C,
the proscenium opening is 40 feet, the depth 20 feet, and the zones 8 feet
one way and 5 feet the other.

Such a system as this makes it possible to record stage directions with
reasonable precision. When an actor at L.3 in B or C is told to cross to R.C.2,
shake hands with Mr. Jones, and at his invitation sit down R.1, he knows
exactly what is required of him.

The commercial director and the inspirational director may laugh at a
scheme so mechanical; but when one is dealing with inexperienced players
and a fairly intricate play, it saves much time in the early rehearsals, and
that time can be very valuable later on for polishing.

no movement without a purpose

The first and most important principle in the designing of stage movements
is to avoid all purposeless movement.

The soundness of this principle is apparent, yet is constantly violated by
inexperienced actors and directors, and sometimes by experienced ones.

Nothing is more difficult to achieve than unaffected repose; the untrained actor fidgets and wanders whenever he is on the stage, unable to keep his hands or his feet still, yet having no conscious purpose in moving them. The director must teach him to suppress this tendency, or to divert it into purposeful movement.

To say that there should be no movement without a purpose is not to say that a play should be all talk, with the actors sitting or standing about like statues. There are plenty of legitimate reasons for stage movement, and whenever one of them is present and not inconsistent with the larger purpose of the scene, or of the play, it is possible to design an appropriate movement. But purposeless movement is never good design because movement attracts attention, and purposeless movement distracts it from the thought of the play. Every movement should have a purpose and the purpose should be associated, or at least consistent, with the main purpose of the scene and of the play. That is the fundamental principle of all design, the principle of the utilitarian basis.

types of stage movement

Understand that any set of general standards is dangerous because of the many exceptions that oppose them, but as long as one understands that these types of movement are not absolutes, but guides, they will provide a takeoff point for the budding director and actor. There are several important types of stage movement—among the many possible ones—that we have classified according to purpose.

1. Movement dictated by the plot. Such movement (or that kind prescribed by the dramatist as essential action) is, as a rule, the easiest to follow and the least likely to create distraction, as it is naturally part of the main interest of the play. The entrances and exits of characters ordinarily belong to this class, as do movements that are involved in fighting, dancing, hiding behind screens, serving stage meals, telephoning, and the like. Whereas this type of movement is not foolproof, it is less likely to be overlooked by the director or to lead him into difficulty than some of the other types.

2. *Movement to delineate character or state of mind.* For this purpose, stage business is more often useful than stage movement, but movement serves to convey some of the broader effects. A restless or excited character, for example, should be moved about the stage frequently and may sit down and jump up a half dozen times in a short scene; a calm or phlegmatic character must do nothing of the kind. A firm character may be given straightforward, decisive movements; a weak or bewildered character should be given little, aimless, abortive ones.

Because character is likely to be closely associated with the purpose of the play, this type of movement, like the first, is fairly easy to handle and to keep within the bounds of unity. The chief danger is that of overemphasis on unimportant but interesting minor characters.

3. *Movement for emphasis.* This is a little less obvious and not so generally understood. Some directors seem to think that emphasis is just a matter of having important lines spoken forcefully and that it is largely the business of the individual actor. However, the audience is watching not an actor, but a play—a complex phenomenon spread over a large stage, with many actors, and with a center of interest that shifts constantly. Out of this complexity it is the director's task to pick those elements that the dramatist would wish to have emphasized and make them stand out. The actor must, of course, point up the important line; but before he can do so the director must maneuver him into an effective position—often the center of the stage, but not always so—and must do it in such a way as to focus attention upon him at the right moment.

Moreover, there is a kind of emphasis in movement itself, and certain types of movement are more emphatic than others. A quick movement, for example, is normally more emphatic than a slow one; the emphasis, however, is in the contrast and on a stage where everybody else is moving, the one character who remains motionless may appear as the most emphatic. A movement toward stage center is ordinarily more emphatic than one toward offstage L. or R., and a movement toward the audience more emphatic than one away from the audience. When a movement accompanies a line, there is a gain in emphasis if the movement is started a little ahead of the line; a loss if it is started later. One may work out a whole system of normal contrasts in emphasis based in this way upon types of movement.

4. *Movement to control attention.* This, of course, includes movement for emphasis; but the general problem of controlling attention in the theatre is so important and so little understood by most amateurs as to demand separate consideration in a later chapter. Movement is only one means to such control, but skillfully handled it is a legitimate means.

5. *Movement for suspense and anticipation.* Half the force of a dramatic episode lies in the proper preparation for it, the proper creation of suspense and anticipation in the minds of the audience. The dramatist knows this, and provides for it by what is called *dramatic foreshadowing* — that is, by *planting* certain ideas in advance, and by anticipatory lines of dialogue. But at least a part of the problem still rests with the director, and proper control of stage movement may be one factor in the solution. The entrance of an important character, for example, may be made more effective if the characters already on the stage are so moved as to create a gap in the stage picture at the point where the character is to appear. In Act One of Drinkwater's *Abraham Lincoln,* in the original American production, the first entrance of Lincoln was skillfully anticipated. The scene was in Lincoln's home. Two of his neighbors, who had come to congratulate him on his nomination, were conversing by the fireplace at stage R. and waiting for him to appear, while the entire left side of the stage was vacant. The only door was at stage L. The unbalanced picture at once created an expectation of Lincoln's entrance. After a moment the door opened and in came — not Lincoln, but a pert serving maid who bustled about for a moment, more than filling the gap, and then went out, leaving, by contrast, a greater sense of emptiness than before. The emptiness was sustained for two or three minutes, during which one's desire to see Lincoln grew more and more insistent; then the door opened and in came — again, not Lincoln, but Mrs. Lincoln. She also filled the gap pictorially, yet one felt a restless impatience to have her out of the way, and a sense of relief when, after giving a hint that her husband would soon appear, she also went out. "Now," we thought, "we shall see Lincoln," and our anticipation had reached its highest pitch. A little too much delay at this point and the whole effect would have been spoiled; our impatience would have turned to annoyance and disgust. But the timing was perfect, and in just a few seconds more the door opened a third time and Lincoln appeared, becoming instantly the focus of attention.

Perhaps the chief gain through the use of this device was the fact that it permitted the quietest and most repressed sort of acting on the part of the actor playing Lincoln, without loss of emphasis; had there been no preparation he would have had to "act up" a little in order to dominate the scene.

6. *Movement for pictorial effect.* The desirability of good stage pictures is well known and, generally, appreciated by the amateur. Movement for the purpose of maneuvering characters into good pictorial groups and out of bad ones is clearly justified, and if not performed too suddenly or pointedly it is ordinarily quite satisfying to the audience.

The principles of composition in design we have already considered, and stage pictures should be good in composition. Some directors, however, fail to realize the extent to which good composition in stage pictures may differ from good composition in painting or sculpture. In painting there are but two dimensions with a suggestion of the third. In sculpture there are three; but in stage pictures there are four.

The fourth dimension is time. Stage life is not still life; it is moving, dynamic, and the composition of every picture, like that of every chord in music, is affected by memory of what preceded and anticipation of what is to follow. In music some very inharmonious chords can provide a transition to better ones; and, in the same way, it is possible to use some bad stage pictures in the course of a rapidly moving scene, provided only that the action is not allowed to rest on the bad ones. Whenever there is anything in the nature of a tableau on the stage, the picture should be good in composition.

In a painting, each element affects the composition almost at its face value; but in a stage picture—even a tableau lasting several minutes—each element has a value dependent upon association of ideas through other pictures in the series. Thus a very good stage picture might seem a very poor pictorial composition to a newcomer just entering the theatre; and a single exposure from a well-directed movie might make a very poor *still* picture of the scene. Indeed, the film director usually has a number of specially posed stills taken for advertising purposes because pictures clipped from the film are not good enough as separate pictures, and do not tell enough of the story. As parts of a moving composition they may be excellent, but as separate compositions, they are often dead and meaningless.

7. *Movement for rhythm.* The place of rhythm in the movement of ballet, opera, and musical comedy is obvious enough, but it is only in recent years that we have begun to realize the tremendous possibilities of rhythm in serious drama. The rhythm of poetic verse has long been established as an element of drama, and various forms of prose rhythm have been effectively used by such dramatists as Synge, O'Neill, Williams, and Ionesco. But rhythm of movement is to the modern producer of serious plays largely a new toy—or rather, an old one rediscovered since it was common enough in the festival drama of primitive times. Just as the poet and musician have used rhythm of sound for direct expression of mood, the modern producer is learning to use rhythm of movement. A little study of such plays as *The Emperor Jones, The World We Live In, R.U.R., The Skin of Our Teeth,* and more recent works like *America Hurrah, The Bald Soprano,* and *The Lesson,* will reveal some of the opportunities.

8. *Movement for tempo.* Most plays call for variations of pace, partly as a means to avoid monotony and partly as a means to express variations of mood and emphasis. Some scenes should proceed more rapidly than others —or seem to do so. The most obvious changes of tempo are, of course, those in the utterance of the lines, but these may be supplemented by variations in the rate and character of the movements.

9. *Movement for position.* Movements not in themselves clearly motivated are often necessary as a preliminary means of getting characters into position for later movements, or for business. Naturally, such preliminary movements should be as unobtrusive as possible; in the hands of an unskilled director they are very apt to seem arbitrary and mechanical.

10. *Movement for compensation.* When, for good reasons, a character must be moved from one place to another, it often happens that the balance of the group is upset and, to restore it, some sort of compensation on the part of another character becomes necessary. A good actor with years of training should make such compensating movements naturally and almost unconsciously; but some otherwise good actors are temperamentally insensitive to the stage picture and would not learn to "give" or "counter" in fifty years of experience. It is worth remembering that many of the best compensating movements actually precede the movements they are designed to balance.

11. Movement to illustrate change. This kind of movement concerns changes of thought or relationship. The grouping of characters on the stage should suggest their relationship; and changes of relationship should be symbolized by changes of grouping. When this is skillfully done, one can follow the meaning much more easily.

12. Movement for relief. In almost every play there are moments of monotony, of "talkiness," or of too sustained emotional strain, and the wise director will seek to provide some sort of relief from them by movement or otherwise. It should be remembered, however, that movement for relief means movement for the relief of the audience – not of the actor. The most awkward and fidgety movements of the rankest amateur are in the nature of relief for the actor – but hardly for the audience.

Other legitimate purposes of movement might be mentioned, but these are the most important and will serve to suggest the possibilities. A skillful director will contrive to design the movements in such a way as to accomplish the various purposes harmoniously and with the greatest economy of means; that is, he will make one movement serve several purposes at the same time. He will also take pains to articulate the movements with the lines and with the individual business of the actors.

traditional rules of stage movement

The professional stage abounds in traditions, technical as well as personal. Many of them have to do with particular plays, but there are some general rules of stage movement, business, and acting technique that have been handed down for generations and regarded, especially by those to the theatre born, as more or less sacred. The tendency in many theatres nowadays is to discard such rules along with the footlights and the proscenium arch and other mossbacked traditions, on the ground that they hamper the artist's freedom of expression. But it is just as stupid to cast them aside without analysis as to obey them blindly. The best way for the intelligent actor or director to treat them is to study them with a view to understanding the aesthetic or psychological principles involved and then to apply the principles rather than the rules.

Several important traditional rules may affect the designing of stage movement.

1. Facing the audience. The actor should always face the audience when speaking. This is a blanket rule inherited from the days when acting was declamation; under modern conditions it must often be modified. Lines may well be spoken away from the audience, but only for good reasons and with proper compensation of voice and attitude. The principle is reasonable enough—namely, that the play is for the audience and should, as a whole, be played toward them.

2. Handling of humor. Humorous or telling lines should be spoken straight front, with a sort of round-eyed frankness and with a slight lift toward the balcony. This rule, of course, can be overworked, but the psychology is sound and audiences are accustomed to the convention without realizing it. Many a good line is thrown away through needless disregard of the principle involved, which is simply that the actor must signal the author's intention to the audience without establishing direct communication with them. When he can think of a better way of doing so, no harm is done. The device is especially useful in conveying *dry* humor, which is apt, otherwise, to miss its laugh.

3. All important scenes should be played downstage. This is an inheritance from the apron stage of the eighteenth century and the platform stage of the sixteenth, and may be modified considerably in the modern theatre. The principle involved is simply that of emphasis, including audibility and visibility.

4. Movements should follow straight lines. This obviously admits of exceptions, and even the principle is open to dispute on the score of grace. The intention is to make the movements seem decisive and purposeful and this, in itself, is generally good.

5. Designing entrances. An entering character should come well onstage and not linger in the entrance—especially a side entrance. This is an excellent rule except when the action of the play calls for unmistakable exceptions.

6. Designing for dialogue. When two characters enter in conversation, the one speaking should come last. The idea is that otherwise the speaker would have to turn and address the person following, thereby blocking his entrance. Numerous exceptions suggest themselves at once as, for instance, when the speaker is a master or mistress and the other a servant.

7. Designing exits. An exit should always be made on a line; that is, a character should not go out while another is talking. If necessary, the line should be broken by a pause, so that the last few words may be spoken from the doorway as the character goes out. The reason underlying this rule is that a character going out when others are speaking distracts attention from them and, at the same time, renders his own exit ineffective; on the other hand, if he finishes speaking some distance from the exit and the others withhold their speeches until he is gone, there is an awkward stage wait. Of course, even the latter may sometimes be justified by the meaning.

8. Placement of characters in dialogue. When two characters in conversation are to sit on a sofa or davenport, the one who is to talk most, or whose words are most important, should be placed at the upstage end. This, of course, is merely a device to enable that character to face the audience.

9. Placement of a character's weight. When a character stands at stage right, his weight should rest on his right (or downstage) foot, and his left (or upstage) foot should be slightly advanced (A and B, Figure 10). For a character at stage left the directions should be reversed.

10. Designing a character's movements. When a character at stage right starts to walk toward the left, he should start by taking a half step with his left (or upstage) foot, and then a full step with his right (or downstage) foot. If he is to speak as he moves, or if the movement is to be leisurely, he should advance his left foot farther than his right to keep him facing partly toward the audience (A, Figure 10).

These two rules, if applied with literal precision, would carry acting back to the artificial declamatory technique of the last century. Yet they cannot be entirely ignored, for nothing is uglier than the movement by which a character, partly facing the audience at stage right, starts to walk left with the right foot, crossing it over the left (B, Figure 10). It makes him look pigeon-toed and, at the same time, swings him away from the audience in an awkward manner.

11. Shifting of weight by characters. When a character in a similar posi-

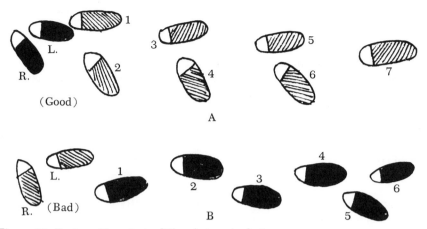

Figure 10. Foot positions in traditional stage technique

tion at stage R. is to back off a little farther to the right, he should shift his weight to the left foot without moving it and take his first backward step to the right with his right foot. This movement should be used very sparingly; most amateurs have to be cautioned not to walk backward at all except for very good reasons. A particularly bad trick of many amateurs in making a cross is to pivot before the cross is completed and then finish it, walking backward.

12. Executed turns toward the audience, not away from it. That is, an actor walking to stage L. and back should turn to his right, not to his left. This is an old rule that has been so rigidly applied by professionals (even in the movies) as to result in occasional absurdity. I have seen an actor execute a veritable pirouette through 270 degrees to avoid turning 90 degrees with his back to the audience.

13. Kneel on the downstage knee. That is, if a character must kneel on one knee, and he is kneeling at stage center, facing left, his right knee should be down and his left up.

14. Designing movement for embraces. When a man and woman embrace, the man's downstage arm should be below the woman's, his upstage arm above. The object, of course, is to let the woman's face, rather than the man's, swing toward the audience as they relax.

Some of these rules may seem very old-fashioned and arbitrary, yet there is a good deal of wisdom and experience packed into them. The director who will consider each of them in its relation to empathy, aesthetic distance, and the principles of design can hardly fail to learn something of value; at the least, he may learn when the rule can be safely violated.

suggestions and warnings

In designing stage movements, one must constantly remind himself that the stage is not real life, but a conventionalized representation of life; hence the warping of the stage setting, the opening out of the stage picture, the suppression of unnecessary detail – including all accidental or meaningless movements – the selection and emphasis of essentials. It is for the latter purpose that stage movements should ordinarily be free, bold, and decisive, as well as meaningful, like the lines of a crayon sketch or the color masses of a poster picture. They are to register on the audience suggestively with a minimum of distraction. The pest of amateur dramatics is the "stage wanderer" – the actor who edges and sidles about the stage, fidgets constantly, and is never still. His movements may be "natural," but there are so many of them and they are so indecisive and characterless that they mean nothing. Good movements do not complicate; they simplify and clarify.

Many directors think of stage movement entirely in terms of the grouping of characters. This is important, pictorially and psychologically, but less important than the main business of conveying the thought of the play. Movements designed for the sake of the picture alone are subject to some degree of alteration, because the full effect cannot be accurately determined until costumes, scenery, and lights have been tried out together. Inexperienced directors must be warned against:

1. Grouping characters for pictorial effect at the expense of meaning.

2. Designing an excellent stage picture in line and mass, only to have it turn out an atrocity in color.

3. "Dressing the stage" too carefully. That is, using too much symmetry or too even a distribution of characters. The latter makes for spottiness and works against unity, besides obscuring the meaning.

In regard to the psychology of grouping, it should be remembered that proximity of characters ordinarily suggests relationship, whereas distance suggests isolation, and that a downstage position, or a central position, denotes importance, at least with respect to the thought of the moment.

asides and soliloquies

One of the most troublesome problems in stage movement is the provision for *asides* and *soliloquies*. When a character in soliloquy has the stage to himself he may, of course, take the center; but when a character speaks apart while other characters are on the stage, it is ordinarily best to give him the extreme position D.R. or D.L. When two groups are to hold separate conversations, each unheard by the other, it is obviously well to separate them as far as possible right and left. More important than the location of the actors, however, is the prior determination of style that establishes the aside and the soliloquy as natural and appropriate actions for the play. Soliloquies and asides are perfectly acceptable in nonrealistic plays. It is necessary only to establish a convention that the audience can accept. The asides in an eighteenth-century play like *The School for Scandal* or *The Rivals* are such a part of the period atmosphere that they add as greatly to the flavor being established as do the wing and drop scenery and the posturing of the actors.

The problem arises when the director attempts to impose realistic techniques on the nonrealistic play. Soliloquies or asides seem totally impossible under these circumstances—and they are. Once again the point must be made that consistency and unity are necessary in directing any play. The presentational style in which the actor freely acknowledges his audience and is at all times an actor on the stage allows easy use of the soliloquy and the aside. The representational style in which the actor attempts to become the character, and ignores the audience in his efforts to appear "real" to them, makes his speaking of lines to the audience "unreal." This inconsistency is completely unacceptable to his audience.

Some realistic plays may require that certain lines be heard by the audience and not by others onstage. Some convention must be established to make this believable to the audience. The nonhearer must be distracted by something else. He may be in an earnest unheard conversation with another nonhearer. He may be interested in some other event taking place either on stage or off. Audiences will believe what they are asked to believe if some excuse is provided them. To fail to provide a means for this "willing suspension of disbelief" is to ruin the production.

grace in stage movement

As far as possible, stage movement should be designed to be graceful in plan; this is especially important to those of the audience who sit in the balcony. In other words, the path taken by the actor should be graceful as seen from above.

This may seem inconsistent with the traditional rule about moving in straight lines. A slightly curved line, especially a double curve, is more graceful and less studied than the straight line; and if there is much furniture on the stage it is often more practical. On the other hand, too much curve in the actor's path suggests too much concern about the movement itself and too little about the objective. A fair rule is to use straight movements for short distances and strong objectives, such as eager approach, determination, or haste (A, Figure 11), and to use slightly curved movements over longer distances, or for less urgent objectives (B, Figure 11), or for avoiding furniture (C, Figure 11). In any case, where a movement must necessarily be curved it is obviously better that a graceful rather than an ungraceful curve should be used. When a single movement cannot be made graceful in plan, it can often be broken into two shorter, more graceful movements, with a line or piece of business between them (D, Figure II).

Grace of plan is especially desirable in movements designed for a thrust stage because the third dimension plays a more important part on such a stage. The thrust stage creates many special problems for the director in that movement and groupings must be so designed as to be effective as seen from three different directions, and in the case of the central or arena stage, from all four directions. No matter which way the actor faces on a central stage, some members of his audience are always behind him. Deep

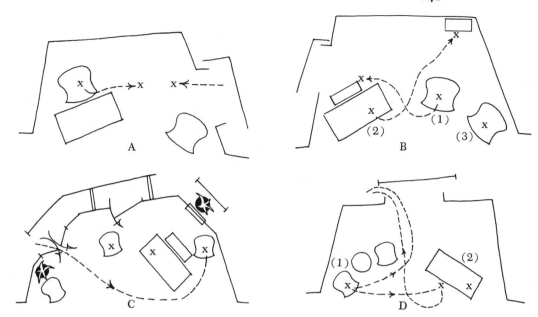

Figure 11. Grace of plan in stage movement

apron and platform stages suffer in a lesser degree from the same limitation. In designing movements for three-dimensional stages, the director must achieve great variety in the grouping, but he must not permit his actors to pivot constantly as they speak in a futile effort to reach all parts of the audience at all times. That is a trick of the orator and goes with the direct sense of communication. In the actor it kills illusion.

The director must, of course, have considerable experience before he can expect to design movements on paper and have them work out on the stage satisfactorily. He should study closely the way in which they do work out at each new attempt, and should not be too loath, at first, to make changes in rehearsal. The very best directors make plenty of mistakes and plenty of corrections. But if the beginner will digest the underlying principles suggested here, and especially the various purposes of stage movement, and will analyze carefully the movements in as many professional productions as possible, he will soon cultivate at least a little of the right sort of sensitivity.

With stage business, as with stage movement, the most important principle to observe is: None without a purpose.

types of stage business

Classifying stage business according to purpose, we find that many of the purposes are similar to those of stage movement, whereas some are slightly different. The following are only the most important types.

1. Business essential to the action of the play. This is ordinarily prescribed by the dramatist, and the director's task is not so much to invent it as to arrange and supervise it. As in the case of movement essential to the action, it is, comparatively, a simple problem. Juliet taking the sleeping potion, Hamlet's duel with Laertes, Androcles removing the thorn from the lion's paw, all these are examples, if examples are needed.

2. Business to delineate character or state of mind. This sort of business is especially rich in possibilities and so is often overworked. It is most legitimate when the delineation of character is essential to the action of the play.

In Neil Simon's play *The Odd Couple,* for instance, the plot turns on the meticulousness of Felix. Even during his most distraught times he is emptying ashtrays and putting coasters under glasses. This business is extremely funny as well, but its other purpose is to establish the character of Felix, which is essential to the plot. Oscar, the slob, is just as clearly defined and it is the contrast between the two characters that provides the real humor of the play.

When Penelope Sycamore, in *You Can't Take It With You,* stops pounding the typewriter and gets out her painting equipment, or when Mr. Day, in *Life With Father,* stamps on the floor to summon the cook, or when Shylock strops his knife on the sole of his boot, we have character delineation quite as important as the plot itself.

Business for delineation of a state of mind may be equally important. In Herman Wouk's *The Caine Mutiny Court Martial,* Captain Queeg's habit of rolling steel marbles in his hand when agitated is brought out in testimony. During the trial, when the Captain actually does this, the audience is made doubly aware of his mental state.

3. *Business for background, atmosphere, or local color.* Within reasonable limits this also may be made to enrich a play, but again, its appropriateness depends upon the extent to which the background is, in itself, important. The business of putting turf on the fire in plays of Irish peasant life is certainly legitimate and is often suggested by the dramatist. Sometimes it is the manner rather than the act that is significant. Europeans usually hold cigarettes between thumb and forefinger and they do not reverse the knife and fork as Americans do. In *The Inspector-General* the characters cross themselves frequently—not from left to right as in the Roman Catholic Church—but from right to left in Russian Orthodox fashion.

4. *Business for emphasis or illustration.* Whenever a line, or movement, or character needs pointing up in some way for greater importance or greater clarity, there is the possibility that a piece of business will do the trick. Pure gesture is the simplest form of business for this purpose, but more elaborate forms are common, as when Yank, in *The Hairy Ape*, emphasizes his curse by hurling a shovel at Mildred, or when Hamlet points up his lines about Yorick by handling the skull.

5. *Business for control of attention.* Of this, more in the next chapter.

6. *Business for dramatic foreshadowing.* The unobtrusive planting of ideas that are later to be built up dramatically is a device that every accomplished dramatist understands. Much of the foreshadowing is done in the lines; but, occasionally, either because the dramatist prefers it so, or because he has overlooked the matter, the director or the actor must invent business for the purpose. In *Dial "M" for Murder* a pair of scissors which has been left casually on a desk is the weapon that Margot grabs to defend herself against the would-be murderer. The amount of discussion about cutting and pasting clippings, seemingly so unimportant, prepares the audience to accept the sudden situation reversal. An audience often feels tricked if no preparation is made. For this reason it is fairly standard practice to "plant" ideas by having the actor check to see if the gun is loaded before it is used, that the safe is secure before it is robbed, and the like. In *Of Mice and Men* we hear about Lenny's tendency to squeeze things that struggle before we see him strangle the puppy and this, in turn, precedes

the strangling of the rancher's wife. The act seems more intelligible and inevitable because of the plant.

A bit of business is often a better plant than a line. It is generally less obtrusive for the reason that we accept the lines as representing the dramatist's conscious intention, while the business, if well done, seems casual; at the same time, it is less apt to escape the attention of the audience than a line would be, because in the theatre the eye ordinarily misses fewer things than the ear.

7. *Business for position.* It often happens that a certain stage movement is desirable but lacks apparent motivation because the real reason for it cannot at the moment be disclosed. When the director of *Abraham Lincoln* wanted to keep the left half of the stage clear for Lincoln's entrance, he had to find a reason for crowding the visiting neighbors at extreme stage R. He put the fireplace at stage R. and had them warming their hands before it. In *Bus Stop*, Bo Decker leaps behind the lunch counter to get to his ham and eggs, which not only shows his boisterous nature, but more specifically puts him in position to discover Cherie's suitcase, which she had hidden there.

8. *Business for rhythm.* What was said with respect to movement for rhythm also applies here.

9. *Business for humor.* Humor is one of the motives for much of the best stage business—one of the motives, in fact, for the theatre itself. But outside of pure farce, humor alone is a very risky purpose either for the dramatist or the director. Humorous business is artistic only when it combines the motive of humor with that of legitimate character delineation, or that of clarifying a line, situation, or state of mind—in other words, when it contributes to the main thought or feeling of the play without distracting the attention. Even the so-called *comic relief* in a serious play may be a source of distraction if it is forced or irrelevant. Humorous business is good theatre, but only when it is natural and appropriate to the meaning of the play. There are many instances of this in Murray Schisgal's *Luv*, but perhaps the funniest is when Milt rushes to push Harry off the bridge. Unsuspectingly, Harry leans on his cane, which slips, and he falls down just as Milt dives at him. Milt goes over and Harry straightens up wondering what the splash was all about. The screen and closet business in *The School for Scandal*, or Bottom's business of handing the dagger to Thisbe in *A Midsummer*

Night's Dream, are other good examples. The final scene of the latter play is perhaps the richest opportunity in theatrical history for legitimate comic business.

10. Business for naturalism or relief. Under the most favorable circumstances acting involves some measure of strain, rigidity, or self-consciousness. Inexperienced actors have a tendency to seek relief from this in movement or business of some sort. Left to themselves they are apt to take it out in mere fidgeting, relieving themselves but not the audience. It is futile for the director to attempt to suppress this tendency by merely instructing the actors to keep still; but if he can divert their energy into useful channels by suggesting little bits of business, unobtrusive in themselves, and seemingly unimportant, but natural to the situation, he will not only ease the strain but will actually improve the play at the same time. When, for instance, an actor enters ostensibly from outdoors, he may be kept busy taking off his gloves and hanging up his hat, and so will have no time to fidget.

combining purposes

With business, as with movement, it is well to combine the purposes as much as possible for economy of expression and unity of effect. It is also well to combine the purposes of the business with those of the movement, and both with the motives of the play itself. A piece of business that is necessary to the action enriches the delineation of character, is humorous, excuses a movement of the character to a position where he will soon be needed, and at the same time, improves the picture, is clearly an asset to the production.

The real importance of stage business, especially in modern plays, is not always fully understood. Properly managed, it adds verisimilitude, enriches the interest, and helps greatly in the rounding and polishing of the production. The less experienced the actors, the more important the latter point becomes. Only the most finished actors can declaim lines convincingly without business, but even beginners can often perform business convincingly under competent direction; and beginners who have difficulty in reading their lines usually find them easier to deliver when accompanied by appropriate business, well rehearsed. Ability to arrange good business will therefore count heavily when the director's problem is how to get a finished performance from unfinished actors.

At the same time it is obvious that stage business is interesting in its own right and, therefore, a potent source of distraction if poorly conceived or overelaborated. A good deal of nonsense has been written about the *art that conceals art*, but if there is any phase of art that needs such concealment, it is the designing of stage business. A stirring or impassioned reading of a line may—the point is debatable—just happen. But good business does not just happen; it is carefully and intelligently designed, with consistency of motive and economy of means, and nothing is more important than to keep it within bounds.

It is neither necessary nor possible to arrange all the business of a modern play before the first rehearsal, but if time is short, or if most of the players are inexperienced, it is wise to arrange as much as possible. Business that has to do with the larger movements and groupings of the characters and the major effects of the play can and should be arranged first. Business that calls for teamwork should be settled before the actors have had a chance to form very definite conceptions of their parts. Individual business connected with the enrichment of lines and character can be allowed to wait until rehearsals have begun, but even this should be fixed early enough to be learned with the lines. The director should not be expected to invent all of the individual business. He should encourage his actors to experiment and create for themselves whenever possible. He may suggest, refine, and integrate, but the director who expects his actors to contribute to the creative process will no doubt achieve better results, and the actors will profit far more from this kind of experience.

aids to invention

With all proper regard to the danger of excessive stage business it remains a fact that most amateur performances suffer from too little rather than too much, and that the amateur director often finds himself at a loss as to how to devise suitable business. The following suggestions may help him to cultivate a little more fertility of invention in such matters:

1. Study the period. This includes the manners and customs of the people in the time represented in the play. Remember, however, that the object is to produce a work of art, not a museum of antiquity. Art implies discrimination and selection.

2. Study the costumes and makeups in advance. Have the costumes (or adequate substitutes) on hand for trial as early in rehearsal as possible, especially costumes that differ essentially from modern street dress. A Roman toga, a Turkish veil, or a military uniform may suggest business that would otherwise not suggest itself. It may also reveal when and where business is needed, especially business for naturalism, for an actor may seem perfectly easy at rehearsal with his hands in his pockets, only to lose his poise when he finds himself in doublet and hose, without any pockets.

3. Study the placing and use of properties, including hand props. As with costumes, have the properties (or adequate substitutes) ready for use at an early rehearsal. The height or depth of a chair, the width of a davenport, the space available between a chair and a table, the length and weight of a cane, umbrella, or parasol, the position of a hat rack or telephone, the placing of a flower vase, ash tray, or matchbox—any of these considerations may suggest a piece of business or affect the character of one.

4. Make use of ordinary objects. This can be especially helpful in devising business for naturalism or relief. Consider the objects men carry or handle: cigars, pipes, matches, tobacco, pencils, watches, fountain pens, notebooks, wallets, briefcases, suitcases, keys, canes, pocketknives, guns, swords, revolvers, whips, monocles, snuffboxes, and what not. Or those women handle: fans, gloves, vanity cases, compacts, purses, handbags, parasols, shawls, scarves, furs, sewing bags, needles, thimbles, scissors, knitting needles, lorgnettes—any woman can extend the list. Or consider the objects in more general use by both sexes: books, papers, cigarettes, lighters, furniture (chairs to be moved, for instance), dishes, knives, forks, spoons, pen and ink, call bells, telephones, lamps, light switches, candles, pictures, hats, coats, wraps, handkerchiefs—and so on almost indefinitely.

5. Study real people in various locations. Watch them on trains and trolleys, in restaurants and stores, at church, in the theatre, at dances and parties, on the street, in their homes, and at their occupations. Note especially what they do with their hands, for an amateur actor needs more help on that point than almost any other.

6. *Study bits of business on the professional stage.* The best way to do this is to see the same play several times and to note the care with which certain bits of business are timed and the precision with which they are repeated. Note also the skillful articulation of business with lines. Never miss an opportunity to see two different companies do the same play, whether trained by the same director or not; the experience is highly instructive in either case, though in different ways.

7. *Watch the actors' natural movements in the early rehearsals.* In many instances these will not be appropriate, but when they are, make use of them. For example, if a member of the cast sits down without being told, decide at once whether the action is appropriate. If not, rule it out; if so, establish it as part of the play, note it in the prompt book, and insist upon it at subsequent rehearsals. If a real change of interpretation later requires a change in the business, well and good; but do not allow the actors to keep changing their incidental business at every rehearsal for no reason at all.

8. *Have a stage rehearsal as early as possible.* Also, try to have a few friends present to suggest an audience. The behavior of the actors on the stage with even a small audience before them is astonishingly different from their behavior at a private rehearsal in a bare room.

9. *Do not hesitate to experiment in the early rehearsals.* Try every possibility and see how it works out. But decide early, settle everything, and have the business learned with the lines. Make copious notes and study the problems of business between rehearsals; ideas do not come just when they are wanted, and it is futile to hold up a rehearsal while you seek inspiration.

One of the most difficult problems for the amateur director is the articulation of lines with business, or business with lines. The amateur actor wants to speak his line first and then carry out the business, or vice versa, and cannot seem to manage the two things at once. The problem can finally be solved only in rehearsal, but in planning the business the director should have regard to the timing and cadence, and should not ask the actor to do impossible things.

For example, it may be appropriate in a certain scene to have an actor light a pipe. The director should time the business so that it does not create an awkward interruption of the dialogue, and so that the dialogue does not

A

B

interfere with the business, causing the actor to bungle the latter. This piece of business is most effective when it seems to articulate with the line. The skillful actor fills his pipe as he talks, lights a match, finishes a sentence, lights the pipe, speaks another word or two while he throws the match away, and gets in a few more puffs in time to make the pipe draw. The green actor (perhaps a confirmed smoker offstage) creates an awkward stage wait, tangles his words, burns his finger, and lets the pipe go out. Audiences are quick to note such bungling and are not tolerant of it.

Even more troublesome is the task of articulating the lines and business of a scene at the dinner table. If the actor fails to eat a reasonable quantity of food, the audience notices it at once. If he eats continuously, he cannot speak his lines. If he takes a large mouthful, he is almost sure to hear his cue before he can swallow, and there is either a stage wait or a strangulation scene. Unless the actors are very old and capable hands at it, a scene of this kind must be carefully timed by the director, and each bite of food considered as a separate bit of business to be prescribed, memorized, and rehearsed.

the principle of balanced forces

In relation to the problem of stage position and posture there is one very important principle that ought to be mentioned here because it often calls for invention of stage business. It is the principle of balanced forces, some-

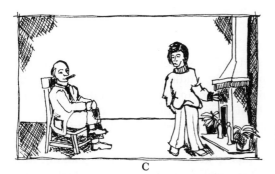

C

Figure 12.
Balanced forces in stage business

what akin to the principle of resultant forces in physics. Most experienced professional actors make constant use of it, sometimes without analyzing or understanding it; but amateurs are not apt to make use of it at all unless the director is prepared to teach it to them.

To illustrate the principle: Suppose a character at stage L. is to speak an important line following a cue from another character at stage R. If he faces the audience squarely (as in A, Figure 12), the line will be pointed up, but the effect will be mechanical and declamatory. If he faces the other character (as in B, Figure 12), the effect will be natural enough, but he will be seen only in profile, and his voice will travel across the stage instead of toward the audience. Sometimes this will do no harm, as when the character is rather loud-mouthed and the line a bald or blunt one. But suppose, in this case, it is important to have the actor's full face seen as he speaks the line, or that the line is of such a nature that it ought to go straight out to the audience, yet with no suggestion of declamation. The solution is to give the character a bit of business at stage left—flicking the ashes from his cigarette into the fireplace, for example—and to time it so that he is pulled left by the business at the very moment when he is pulled right by the cue from the other character. The result of these two forces is a force in the direction of the audience. In other words, with his body turned left to perform the business and his thoughts drawn right by the cue, his face is toward the audience (as in C, Figure 12), yet the effect is perfectly natural. A slight inclination of the head toward the right helps to suggest the direction of his thoughts without forcing him to turn his face too far.

Trickery? Of course. But a reasonably intelligent amateur can learn to do a trick of this kind in six weeks, and to do it so naturally and at so little cost to his freedom of interpretation that the audience will hardly notice the device; whereas it may take him ten years to learn how to declaim a line straight toward the audience without seeming stiff and unnatural.

Among the types of business most often useful for balancing forces in this way are:

Lighting cigarettes, cigars, or pipes; getting rid of ashes; looking in a mirror and adjusting hair, hat, or tie; opening or closing a door; looking out a window; moving a chair or other object; examining a book or photograph; warming the hands at a fire; smelling flowers or rearranging them; dusting or tidying; lighting lamps; pouring drinks; ringing for servants; reading books or newspapers; and writing letters.

simplicity in stage business

All this suggests, no doubt, a great deal of complication and a great danger of overemphasis. Simplicity is highly desirable in art, for complication is distraction. But simplicity does not mean sterility. The best simplicity is not that which results from a paucity of ideas, but that which is resolved by choice out of many possibilities; and one must often find his way through great complexities before he can simplify intelligently. The best stage business is simple, not because the director lacks experience or knowledge, but because — from a wealth of ideas — he has selected wisely.

The problem of controlling the attention of the audience is one that must be studied throughout the period of rehearsal and even after performances have begun; but as certain aspects of it affect the planning of stage movement and business, it may be best considered at this point. The problem is much more complex and much more important than the inexperienced director is apt to imagine.

the kinds of attention

Psychologists do not agree upon the nature of attention – or of consciousness – and they are hardly likely to agree as long as some believe the body to be a piece of soulless mechanism, responding automatically to stimuli, whereas others believe it to be controlled through consciousness by an immaterial mind or soul. They do agree, however, upon a practical distinction between two types of attention that they call *primary* and *secondary*.

Primary attention is the automatic or involuntary attention that we give to a strong external stimulus – a bright flash of light, for instance, or a loud noise, or a sudden slap on the back. The appeal is concrete; that is, it is more or less directly in terms of sense impressions, either real or suggested. Primary attention involves no sense of effort, no conscious intention, no exercise of will power.

Secondary attention is voluntary attention, the sort that one gives to a difficult problem through a sense of duty or by force of great concentration. Whether or not there is such a thing as real *will power* is, of course, the point in dispute, the mechanists holding that what we mistake for will power is but the reaction to the more remote stimuli in the past experience of the individual; but there is certainly a kind of attention in the giving of which we are aware of conscious effort.

attention in the theatre

In the theatre very little dependence should be placed upon secondary or voluntary attention. The teacher or the preacher may conceivably have a right to expect his audience to attend by an effort of the will, but the actor has no such right. The problem in the theatre is how to gain, hold, and control primary or involuntary attention.

The conditions under which most theatre is presented make the first part of this—and to a certain extent, the second part—easy. People come to the theatre expecting to be interested and entertained; they await eagerly the beginning of the play; the house lights go down, there is a sudden hush, the curtain rises, and out of the darkened auditorium they gaze in fascination upon the lighted stage. This is primary attention at its best, and if the circumstances are reasonably favorable, it is likely to continue simply because the concentration of sound and light on the stage acts as a powerful magnet and tends to hold the audience spellbound.

Yet in our do everything, try everything theatre of today, playwrights and producers are breaking all the rules in order to create new forms and new effects. Deliberate efforts have been made to distract and to bore audiences. A half-dozen points of emphasis may exist at the same time on a stage, requiring the audience to shift attention from one to another, or to ignore several in order to concentrate on one. Staged events may be repeated and repeated at carefully controlled rhythms in order to deliberately create monotony. Why? For what? Perhaps just to be different, or perhaps, as experiments, to find out how audiences can be moved and controlled. Such productions are interesting up to a point, but more as novelties than as significant theatrical events. Several years ago I watched Julien Beck and Judith Molina's Living Theatre Company present *Frankenstein*, in which actors representing police darted through the audience, seizing—one by one—actors representing political prisoners. The first was seized and interrogated and then placed in a cell. Then the second was arrested and the process was repeated. The first prisoner was moved to cell two and the second into cell one. Some fifteen cells on three levels were on the stage and as each was occupied it was lighted. The prisoners moved from cell to cell until all were occupied. The procedure was carefully repeated fifteen times with the same movements and the same rhythms so that my boredom grew and grew. One could hardly believe that a director would intentionally so treat his audience, yet there was something highly theatrical about the production, and the predominantly college-age audience indicated strong approval at the conclusion. They were obviously not affected as I was.

Attention must be controlled if the performance is to succeed. Although the above illustration cites an unusual example, we can generalize by saying that there are normally two possible enemies to sustained attention, and either of these may operate in the theatre, if not to destroy attention, at least to shift it or weaken it. One of them is distraction and the other is monotony.

overcoming distraction

Distraction may be described as primary attention gone wrong; it is the shifting of primary attention caused by some external and irrelevant demand upon the senses.

Most American theatre audiences of today suffer from comparatively little distraction, especially distraction external to the performance. This may seem a very rash statement if one has been annoyed recently by the coughers and sneezers, or the people who rattle programs, or carry on conversations, or push their feet into one's back, or the people who arrive late and depart early. But the word is "comparatively." Things used to be much worse. Only a few decades ago audiences in this country expressed themselves freely by shouting, stamping, applauding, hissing, heckling, and sometimes by throwing eggs or vegetables, by quarreling and rioting, and even (in a few notorious cases like the Forrest-Macready feuds) by violence and bloodshed. I remember seeing a performance by the Abbey Theatre Players of *The Playboy of the Western World* with dozens of policemen stationed in the aisles to eject angry Irish-Americans as fast as they raised disturbances. Not all performances were so interrupted, nor are all performances free from interruption today; but distractions that would be almost unbelievable today were common a few years ago. And even today the European theatres tolerate demonstrations of approval or disapproval— especially the latter—for which a theatregoer in the United States would be promptly put out and perhaps arrested.

Even so, there is more distraction than there ought to be. Perhaps conditions will continue to improve as we become more civilized—if we ever do.

Much of the responsibility for improvement in the theatre rests with the house manager, the theatre owner, or the theatre architect, rather than with the director. If audiences cannot be educated to come on time, they can certainly be refused admission while the curtain is up. Seats are being made more comfortable and spaced more generously, house lights and decorations are being made less distracting, and theatre walls more nearly soundproof. As for those distractions that arise from the bad manners of the audience, the only solution would seem to be a law defining the slaughter of their perpetrators as a trifling misdemeanor instead of a crime.

Very little of this concerns the director. What does concern him, vitally, is that quite as many distractions may be caused by the faults of the production itself as by the defects of the house or the misbehavior of the audience. Poorly built settings that waver with each closing of a door or the noisy shifting of scenery contribute to the problem.

Distractions may be caused by divided or broken scenes, unused exits, or misplaced empathic effects. A teaser hung too low or not low enough, a delay in the rise or fall of the curtain, a late entrance or other stage wait, an audible prompt, an uncovered light shining in the eyes of the audience, an actor *out of the picture,* an illogical entrance or exit, an unexplained movement, a gratuitous piece of business, a forced joke or gag, an awkward gesture, a line spoken too softly or otherwise unintelligibly, a piece of overacting, a too conspicuous costume or property, a mirror facing the audience, an unnecessary clock or unused telephone, an unintentional noise backstage, a spotlight badly managed, a shadow in the wrong place—these are just a few of the possible causes of distraction that may be blamed on the director, the production staff, or the actors. There is only one way to combat them, and that is by constant vigilance. There must be careful planning, thorough rehearsal of both cast and stage crew, and the most rigorous censorship of every single element that might catch the primary attention of the audience and lead it astray.

overcoming monotony

The effect of monotony is less obvious than that of distraction. There is seldom danger in the theatre of the droning humdrum that the word monotony ordinarily suggests (a notable exception being the Living Theatre production cited earlier), but there exists, in the theatre and elsewhere, a subtler sort of monotony which it is well for the director to understand.

The psychologists tell us, after due laboratory tests, that attention cannot be sustained for more than a few seconds at a time; that there is no such thing as continuous attention; that attention which seems continuous is really a succession of fresh perceptions, each the result of a fresh stimulus or a fresh effort of the will. They point out that fixation of attention is equivalent to destruction of attention; that complete concentration on a single, simple, unchanging element is the way to hypnosis or induced sleep. This very important fact is the explanation of why monotony is destructive of attention—not alone monotony of pitch, but monotony of force, tempo, rhythm, line, mass, color, or any other element of expression. If attention is to be held for any long period of time, it must be renewed by a constant succession of fresh appeals to interest.

The director must realize, therefore, that in the attempt to hold attention and keep it fresh, he is dealing with a psychological rather than a logical problem. He may know, for example, that a certain scene is of great intrinsic importance in the play, and may suppose therefore that it will prove interesting to the audience. But interest is not governed by intrinsic importance; it is governed by sense stimuli, and the most important scene in the play may fail utterly to hold attention if the effect upon the senses is either too weak or too continuous. There must be a succession of fresh appeals to the eye and ear, striking enough and varied enough to prevent either a relaxation or a too steady fixation of attention.

An audience that is familiar with a play, and fond of it, will contribute some measure of attention as a result of its previous knowledge—the sort of attention known to the psychologists as *derived primary* attention. An object that has little immediate sense appeal may, upon longer acquaintance, grow into the interests of the observer in such a way as to command what is virtually primary attention. A man who has made a hobby of science may take great interest in a formula that, to the rest of us, would prove quite unattractive. Similarly, an audience familiar with Shakespeare may be keyed up with anticipation the moment Hamlet begins his soliloquy, or

Mercutio his "Queen Mab" speech, and the task of holding attention may, at least for the moment, be easier.

There are many different ways of freshening the attention in the theatre, some depending upon the dramatist, some upon the director, and some upon the actors. The dramatist who knows his business is careful not to prolong a scene unduly, or to use too slow a method of development; when there is danger of monotony he brings in a new character or a new phase of the plot. The capable director supplements this by movements of the characters, variations of the stage pictures, changes of tempo, shifts of emphasis, and injection of stage business. The actor contributes variety in action and delivery as well as business of his own invention; and upon his power to gauge the attention of the audience and to strengthen his acting as needed depends much of the final success of each performance.

On the other hand many community and school groups have failed to hold the attention of popular audiences largely because they have not understood how to avoid monotony. Among such groups the commonest and worst form of this fault is simple talkiness.

When the Abbey Theatre players of Dublin first visited this country, they impressed two eminent teachers of dramatic literature in quite opposite ways. One praised highly their simplicity, naturalness, and freedom from artificiality; the other, while admitting the excellence of their diction, found them in other respects quite amateurish. The difference lay, no doubt, in the fact that the first, who was a specialist in Irish literature and already familiar with the plays, supplied not only a clearer understanding and a livelier imaginative interpretation, but also a keener derived primary attention. The second, a specialist in another field, had no such advance interest; he took the plays as actually presented, and was bored by the talkiness and uneventfulness of the performances. Fortunately the Abbey Players learned with experience, and their more recent visits have been anything but amateurish; if anything, they may have erred in the opposite direction.

The matter of audience interest and preparation is a major consideration in the control of attention. It is one thing to produce *Hamlet* before a well-established Shakespeare Society, which has seen the play many times before, and quite another to produce it before an audience of high school students who are seeing a Shakespearean play for the first time. Whenever a new or otherwise unfamiliar play is produced, the director can safely expect his audience to require constant freshening of interst. Neither the intrinsic interest of the play itself nor the intellectual curiosity of the audience will quite solve the problem in the absence of the necessary sense stimuli.

It hardly need be said that amateur directors and actors should go as often as possible to observe the work of the best professionals—not for slavish imitation but for intelligent study. Many professionals are extraordinarily clever in freshening interest. They do it by means of variations in the pitch, force, and tempo of the voice; by the skillful use of pauses; by unexpected yet expressive movements; by good coordination of lines and action; but most of all by the suggestion of a lively play of imagination. The actor who can keep his own attention awake by avoiding a perfunctory, unimaginative attitude can usually keep the attention of his audience awake also; and the director who can teach his actors to play imaginatively has most of what it takes to be a good director.

insuring the points of the play

Another problem of attention arises from the fact that in nearly every play there are certain lines or bits of action so important in conveying the meaning that the audience simply cannot be allowed to miss them. The dramatist points these things up as best he can, and when the plot permits he repeats important ideas several times to make sure that they are heard and understood. But sometimes the plot does not permit. An essential point may be of such a nature that it can be given only once, and the play may be spoiled for anybody who misses it. What sort of insurance will enable the director to guard against such contingencies?

The temptation, of course, is to have the actor shout the important line; but that is always painfully artificial and often leads to false accent. Sometimes a very slight increase of voice is allowable; at other times the situation may preclude even that, as when one character is supposed to speak the important line confidentially to another in fear of being overheard. A more

practicable plan is to arrange the business and movement, the stage picture, the lighting, and the contrasts of voice in such a way as to concentrate the maximum attention on the right character at the instant he is to
deliver the important line. This will not prevent external distraction, of
course; somebody may cough or sneeze just as the line is uttered. But the
more powerful the concentration of attention at the instant, the greater the
resistance to distraction, even on the part of the coughers and sneezers
themselves; and if a listener does miss the line that is so pointed up, he
realizes that he has missed something important and so tries harder to pick
up the context.

An essential line should always be expressed in easy familiar words with
strong vowel contrasts; such a line is less apt to be missed than a line
couched in unfamiliar words, or words not easily distinguishable in sound.
Unfamiliar proper nouns are the most troublesome of all, and more apt to
be misunderstood than any other class of words. While this is undoubtedly
the dramatist's business rather than the director's, a good director can often
repair some of the damage done by a dramatist unfamiliar with the realities
of production.

Clear enunciation is naturally a great asset in conveying the points of a
play to the audience—not only in its effect on the ear but in its effect on the
eye as well. Most people nowadays do a little lip reading, and those who are
at all hard of hearing do a great deal, so that if an actor faces front as he
speaks an important line and makes his lip movements distinct, many listeners will catch the line as much with the eye as with the ear. Gesture
helps in the same way; many dramatists and stage directors today are finding it safer to entrust important thoughts to pantomime than to express
them in words—partly because the public is predominantly visual-minded,
and partly because the eye is not so easily distracted as is the ear in a darkened auditorium. Safer still is a combination of both, for it is unusually violent distraction that causes one to miss an entire line and also the accompanying action; and if one gets a part of the thought and the contributing
conditions are helpful, he can often piece out the rest. The director's concern is to make the contributing conditions as helpful as possible without
obtrusive overemphasis.

All of this is ridiculously obvious when one stops to think of it. But how often does an amateur director sit down before the first rehearsal, check over the essential points of the play, and plan a constructive campaign to get those points across to the audience even at the sacrifice of minor effects? More often, perhaps, an otherwise good performance is ruined by the practical failure of one important line, when so trifling a thing as a well-planned movement or a well-timed pause might have saved it. The final line of Truman Capote's *The Grass Harp* requires Verena to say, "I would like to help—if you'll let me." The line must be read with just the right amount of hesitation and desire, and just as important, it must be followed by a pause and then Dolly's movement toward Verena as the lights fade. If the line delivery or the movement is off in the slightest, the play will be spoiled. The curtain line of *Bus Stop*, by William Inge, is just as critical and just as easily ruined. Virgil picks up his guitar, puts on his hat, looks around at the darkened, empty cafe and says with all of the loneliness of the world, "Well, that's the way it is for some people," and exits.

directing attention

The circumstances of a production often require that the attention of the audience be controlled and directed not merely to the stage, but to some particular spot on the stage, or that it be shifted at a given moment from one spot to another. To accomplish this, it is possible to devise a more or less complete technique, just a few points of which may be suggested here.

The first step is, naturally, to consider the various elements in play production and to study their relative effect in attracting or repelling attention. For example, it will be found that attention generally tends to fall on:

1. children or animals rather than people
2. any unusual element rather than the commonplace
3. people rather than inanimate things
4. speaking people rather than silent ones
5. moving people rather than still ones
6. light places rather than dark ones
7. bright colors rather than dull ones

8. converging lines rather than diverging ones
9. near objects rather than far ones
10. stage center rather than stage R. or L.
11. objects at which the characters seem to be looking rather than objects they seem to ignore
12. an advancing rather than a retreating character
13. a character in a state of emotion rather than one in a tranquil state of mind
14. a character framed in a doorway or holding a striking pose rather than one casually or inconspicuously placed
15. a character on a stairway or other high level rather than one on the ordinary stage level
16. a character who is being talked about by other characters
17. a thing that is being talked about, if visible

These are mere suggestions; the catalogue might be continued almost indefinitely. There will be plenty of exceptions, of course—as when a single silent character draws attention away from many talkative ones, or when a single dull costume stands out by contrast with many brilliant ones—but if one understands the principle of primary attention, these exceptions will explain themselves.

The extent to which it is possible to control and direct attention is perhaps best illustrated by the sleight-of-hand artist. Half the secret of his magic lies in his ability to direct the attention of the audience to the wrong place. By talking glibly and looking with great apparent interest at his right hand he practically compels his audience to look at that hand, whereas he performs the essential part of his trick with his left hand and nobody sees him do it. A good magician employs for this purpose not only the devices of the actor—speech, gesture, and facial expression—but those of the stage director as well, including position, movement, business, line, mass, scenic effect, light, and shadow. The student of stage directing who is not too sternly opposed to trickery may learn from such performers a great many facts about the psychology of attention that will prove valuable in actual play production.

Perhaps the most important trick for the ordinary stage director to know is the simple physical one of leading the eye to the right place at the right time. This is so common that almost any well-directed play will furnish an illus-

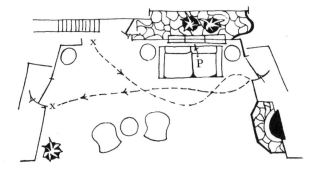

Figure 13.
A study in leading the eye

tration; but let us take a particularly striking one from Mary Roberts Rine-hart's *The Bat*. In one scene of that play—extremely popular in the 1920s and often revived by amateur groups—a bloody arm is thrust into view through a broken window pane and the hand unfastens the catch. For full effect it is necessary that every person in the audience be able to see that arm the instant it appears. The arrangement needs to be roughly that shown in Figure 13, with window U.L.C. and the broken pane at P. It is night, and pitch-dark outside, and a number of previous incidents have made every-body feel that some awful danger lurks in the garden, threatening the lives of the inmates. Miss Dale Ogden, the ingenue, has just been left alone, standing near the hall door upstage R., with the attention of the audience concentrated upon her. Should the mysterious arm appear just then not one person in twenty would see it, and the effect would be lost. But Miss Ogden, apparently fearing an attack from almost any direction, crosses tim-idly to the door U.L., listens there for an instant, then half reassured, crosses back as if to listen at the door D.R.—all this being natural enough under the circumstances. Of course all eyes follow her, and at the very instant when she passes the point P on the return trip, the arm comes through catching every eye in the house. Perhaps this one example is sufficient to illustrate the device. There is hardly a play in which some use cannot be made of it, and in some plays important scenes may miss fire completely unless it is skillfully employed.

Another device, equally useful in controlling and directing attention, is that of anticipation – a device employed by both the dramatist and the director in a great variety of ways, some of which have already been discussed in connection with stage movement. Whether the anticipation is created by the lines of the play, by an expectant vacancy in the stage picture, by the gestures or facial expressions of the actors, or by dramatic foreshadowing, it is one of the greatest possible incentives to attention; and properly understood, it is one of the easiest devices to manage. No more need be said of it here.

No amount of theorizing will teach the inexperienced director to control and direct attention unless it is backed by constant study and observation on his part. He should consider again and again the importance of the negative element in technique, and should beware of excessive and artificial straining for attention – which is itself a cause of distraction. He should control attention, but he should not get caught at it.

Before the play can be put into rehearsal it is necessary, of course, to choose the cast – tentatively, at least. Sometimes the director has no option in this matter, the cast being chosen before the play is put in his hands. More often he either aids in the choice or bears the entire responsibility himself.

The first question that arises is whether the choice is to be made solely in the interest of the particular production, or partly in the interest of the organization and its future welfare. In the commercial theatre a production is ordinarily an independent venture, and the producer endeavors to secure the best possible cast to fit the characters – or to shine as stars – regardless of any permanent organization. As a result what is known as *type casting* has come to be the general rule in the commercial theatre; an actor is chosen primarily because he is already identified with the type of part to be filled. But in an amateur or little-theatre group, or in a real repertory theatre, it is often necessary to consider the training of a permanent company and the building up of an organization as well as the needs of the particular play.

One thing should be emphasized from the beginning, however, and that is the utter futility of sacrificing the quality of the production for the sake of training the actors. Such a procedure defeats its own purpose, for nothing is more injurious to the training of an actor than a half-hearted production, or a feeling that the production does not matter very much as long as some other end is achieved; and nothing is more injurious to a sound *esprit de corps* than the toleration of inferiority. Considerations of permanent policy, therefore, should never be allowed to outweigh the needs of the particular play to the extent of spoiling the performance. If the demands of a later production preclude the choice of a good cast for an early one, the only sound procedure, artistically, is to omit the early one altogether, or to substitute a play that can be cast without prejudice to the later ones. If, to give the actors variety of experience, it is necessary to miscast them badly, the exercise should be confined to rehearsals or classroom practice, and both actors and audience should be spared the pain of an inferior public performance.

However, without serious detriment to the excellence of any one production, it is quite possible to establish certain general policies in casting that are permanently beneficial to the actors and to the organization; and a few of these may be mentioned.

type casting versus miscasting

The most important point is to steer a middle course between type casting and miscasting. To choose an actor to represent a character because he seems to be that character himself, or because he has specialized in that type of character, is perhaps to gain a temporary advantage in making the play convincing. But if this method of casting is continued as a permanent policy, the actors soon fall into ruts, become identified with their particular types, develop mannerisms, and fail to grow in imagination and sympathy. Meanwhile the audience, if a permanent one, learns to identify each actor by his mannerisms, to regard him always as the same character in a new situation, and to look upon each new play as a mere rearrangement of the old familiar types—very much as the small boy considers each new movie starring his favorite screen actor not a new story about new characters but a mere continuation of the adventures of his hero. Neighborhood audiences very quickly develop such an attitude toward the actors of a local theatre group, and while the result may be a fairly healthy spirit of play, it is not likely to encourage a very high order of art.

On the other hand, if actors are chosen arbitrarily and needlessly for parts totally beyond their range, the result may be ruinous to the quality of the performances and, eventually, to the morale of the group and the interest of the audience. It is a very good thing for the actor to try his skill at a variety of parts within reasonable limitations, but it should be obvious that some actors are physically or temperamentally unfit for some parts, and that if they are cast for such parts, they can meet only with failure and discouragement.

The Moscow Art Theatre has traditionally steered the middle course. In that theatre the actors are cast for varied roles, and several different actors are cast in rotation for the same role; yet no actor is assigned to a part for which he is seriously unfitted. The best feature of this system is that it educates the actors, but it is almost equally advantageous in its effect upon the audience as emphasizing the play and the character, rather than the personality of the actor.

Within limitations, the rotation of parts is one of the chief merits of the repertory system – of which the Moscow Art Theatre is neither the sole nor the first example. That system prevailed in most of the oldtime *stock companies* of the United States. In the famous Arch Street Theatre of Philadelphia, for example, between 1850 and 1860, a favorite billing was *Othello*, given on two successive nights with John Dolman (my grandfather) and E. L. Davenport alternating as Othello and Iago. Many people would come on both nights, for the audiences of that day loved to discuss the merits of differing interpretations. In such cases, however, it was generally assumed that both actors were good in both parts, if in different ways. This was neither miscasting nor type casting.

casting for teamwork

A second important point is that good teamwork has more to do with training the actors and building up a strong group than has emphasis on individual talent. From the standpoint of permanent policy, therefore, it is not always best to choose those who show the most obvious virtuosity. It is better to choose those who show the most intelligent sense of cooperation with the director and the other actors. As a matter of fact, this type of actor frequently gives the better performance in the end, even considered as an individual, though his superiority is not so noticeable in the early rehearsals.

In other words, if there are four candidates for two parts, it is better to take the pair who are not brilliant but who work well together than to take the brilliant ones who work at cross-purposes. In this connection physical fitness is a consideration, of course; one does not want a heroine who is a head and a half taller than the hero, even if they are individually the best actors. Compatibility is another consideration; experienced professionals may act smoothly together though sworn enemies in private life, but amateurs can seldom do so. It is better to sacrifice a little talent than to allow a constant element of friction to disrupt the teamwork.

An important element of teamwork is leadership, and in choosing the cast of a play it is wise to assign actors of experience and tried ability to those parts that involve leadership. However, it is not always the so-called leading

parts—those of the hero and the heroine—that carry the greatest responsibility. Often there are other parts, long and exacting, if less conspicuous or
attractive, that have more to do with sustaining the play. A thoroughly
dependable actor in such a part will do much to steady the performance, and
will exercise a most beneficial influence on the less experienced members
of the cast; an untrustworthy actor, on the other hand, even though talented,
will ruin the whole performance. Unfortunately, he may also carry off the
individual honors, for the audience will note his flashes of good acting and
at the same time fail to discern that it is he who is upsetting the others; and
they will blame the raggedness of the performance on almost anybody else
—which is most exasperating to the director and unfair to the other actors.

When the actors are all young, as in a school or college production, it is
usually much easier to cast the juvenile parts than those of old or middle-
aged persons. Occasionally a young man, aided by a broad character makeup,
can play very acceptably the part of an extremely old man; less often, but
for the same reasons, a young girl can play an old woman. But it is usually
the hardest thing in the world for a young person of either sex to play a
middle-aged part convincingly. The youngster's face, voice, and movements
are too youthful, yet he dare not indulge in elaborate makeup and he cannot
change his voice without becoming painfully unnatural. It is advisable,
therefore, to cast the middle-aged parts first, using the most capable actors
for the purpose, even though the younger parts suffer somewhat in consequence. It often happens, fortunately, that the middle-aged parts are also
the sustaining parts of the play, so that these last two problems merge
into one.

casting the small parts

While the most difficult and most responsible parts should always be given
to capable actors, the members of the group should never be allowed to
regard the small parts as unimportant—mere leftovers to be parceled out
among the defeated candidates as consolation. Such a feeling is bad for the
production as well as for the spirit of the organization.

Every actor should be made to feel that a brief part is just as essential to the play and just as worthy an object of study as a long one, and that it affords him just as fine an opportunity for good acting and good teamwork. One way of encouraging this feeling is to assign experienced players to small parts every now and then when they are not otherwise engaged, impressing upon them the dignity of doing a small thing well, and the importance of subordinating the individual to the ensemble effect. In the Moscow Art Theatre—if the reader will pardon another reference to that exemplary organization—even the smallest *bits* are carefully cast, and played with the utmost attention to detail. In *The Three Sisters* there is a serving woman who never speaks a word and does nothing but answer the doorbell; but even on tour in this country that part was played by a painstaking actress who made it a finished character study. Stanislavsky himself was not above playing a supernumerary part when he did not happen to be cast for a main one, and by so doing he encouraged the subordinate members of the company to sink their individual pride and consider only the good of the play. Many a little theatre in this country and elsewhere has framed upon its green room wall the memorable words of Stanislavsky: "There are no small parts; only small actors."

fairness in casting

The loyalty and good sportsmanship of a producing organization depend in no small measure upon the feeling that the casting is being done wisely and fairly.

It is a bad plan to give the impression that talent is being overlooked or neglected, but it is even worse to push the merely talented members forward too easily and too rapidly. Service, experience, and reliability should be considered first. When important parts are hastily assigned to comparatively inexperienced players because they have displayed some flash of brilliancy, jealousies are quick to arise among those who think themselves equally brilliant; at the same time less brilliant members are apt to feel the hopelessness of competition and lose heart. Nobody likes to be given a minor part in support of an irresponsible young upstart. On the other hand, most people who are at all seriously interested are glad to play in support of an experienced and reliable old-timer. They know they can depend upon him, that he has won his place by hard work, and that they can learn from him what is most likely to help them in their own efforts. The result of such casting is a spirit of loyalty and cooperation very desirable in a permanent organization.

the needs of the play

Granted that the needs and policies of the organization are taken care of, there still remains the problem of casting the particular play as effectively as possible.

The question most often asked in regard to casting is whether ability or suitability should be considered more important as determining the fitness of a candidate. The answer would seem to be fairly obvious: A certain degree of suitability is a necessary requirement, but beyond that requirement, ability rather than suitability should determine the choice.

The first test, then, to apply to a candidate for a part is that of minimum suitability. Is he physically possible in the part? In considering this question one naturally makes allowance for the possibilities of disguise, especially disguise of the face through makeup. There are some things, however, that even makeup cannot do. It can make an average face seem a bit narrow or a bit broad, but it cannot make a very broad face seem narrow, or vice versa. It cannot change greatly the facial angle so important in profile – not unless the part allows a copious application of whiskers. It can make a character face out of a straight juvenile, but it cannot make a straight juvenile face or a straight middle-aged face out of a character face. In a small theatre a heavy makeup is apt to be too obvious and so to weaken the illusion; and in a play calling for subtleties of facial expression a heavy makeup is a serious detriment anyhow. It is not well, therefore, to put too much dependence upon the possibilities of makeup, or to disregard in casting the facial characteristics of the candidate.

Another consideration is bodily physique. The six footer obviously cannot play Napoleon, the short fat man cannot play Abraham Lincoln, and the lady who weighs 400 pounds cannot play the heroine – historical precedents notwithstanding. Little can be done to disguise such physical extremes. Even lesser peculiarities of build, proportion, carriage, and gesture are difficult to disguise, especially in the case of the women. Modern styles may permit a woman to conceal the facts about her complexion, but not about her architectural idiosyncrasies. Time was when a bow-legged actress could play the lovely heroine, but not so today. A grasshopper build, pigeon-toes or knock-knees, even an absence of curves where the style of the moment says that the curves should be, will now disqualify an otherwise talented actress for anything but a character part; and if there is any part in the play that calls for a particular physique, a candidate must be found who can satisfy the requirement.

Even more important than face and figure for certain parts is a suitable voice. Some voices are flexible and adaptable to many different characterizations, but most voices, especially young voices, have definite limitations that make them totally unfit for some parts. Voices can be trained and flexibility can be cultivated, but the time required is a matter of months and years. For the sake of the play, therefore, the director must often reject at once the candidate whose voice is inappropriate and who cannot change it sufficiently in six weeks to make it right. Different vocal qualities are essential as well. If the hero and the villain sound alike, we may confuse them at a time when clarity is vital. Voices that are similar can cause even more problems than physical similarity, which can easily be changed.

problems of empathy

Given a candidate who has the physical equipment for a part, the next question is: Will he, or she, create the proper empathic effect upon the audience? This is not always easy to determine in advance, and sometimes the director is badly fooled. An actor who seems warmly human in real life may stiffen up on the stage, becoming cold and mechanical. On the other hand, a dowdy frump of a girl who would be described by a smart writer as having no sex appeal may sometimes make up to look positively alluring on the stage, and, conscious of the effect she is producing, develop a magnetic stage personality and a freedom in emotional acting that nobody could have supposed possible. I have seen this happen in startling fashion on several occasions. Stage personality is simply not the same thing as social personality. Many of the loveliest stage actresses are rather unimpressive, even mousy, persons offstage, and a few are actually homely. So the wise director will not judge empathic effect except in terms of actual projection over the footlights.

As pointed out in an earlier chapter, there are two questions of empathy to be considered in casting: the effect of the actor upon those who are to empathize in him directly—especially those of his own sex—and the effect upon those who may empathize in some other character with whom he is involved. Since it is almost impossible for a man to judge how the women in the audience will respond, or vice versa, it is a good plan for the director to consider the problem in consultation with somebody of the opposite sex. Two heads may or may not be better than one, but two sets of motor nerves are certainly better than one when the problem is to prophesy motor responses; and a half dozen sets may be better than two, especially if they represent both sexes and several different ages and temperaments. At best the prophecy is uncertain, and for this reason, as for many others, the director should avoid too hasty decisions in casting.

Another question is whether the candidate has the sympathy and imagination necessary to a full appreciation of the part. Possession of these qualities is, to be sure, no proof of a good actor, but absence of them is pretty good proof of a bad one. Without the power to put himself mentally in the character's place, to imagine his sensations and emotions, and to sympathize with them even though they are entirely different from his own, an actor can hardly expect to interpret a part successfully. Fortunately for the casting director, these qualities are not so difficult to judge, provided the method of trying out the candidate gives him opportunity to reveal them to the director. An intimate, informal talk about the character will usually afford such an opportunity. Pantomimes improvised by the actors at the request of the director and various games can quickly show the kind of freedom, spontaneity, and imagination the actors have. This technique coupled with reading and interviews will give the director a very good picture of the actor's potential.

Another qualification that some directors demand in a candidate is intelligence, a reasonable amount of which would seem to be at least desirable. Whether a very high order of intelligence properly belongs to the art of acting is a question long in dispute; there are those who believe that a good memory, a fine voice, a responsive body, and a strong emotional temperament are much more to the point, and the history of the stage bears them out in some measure. But the teamwork and cooperation required in a modern production, and the cooperative spirit of a modern producing organization, certainly call for intelligence. It is doubtless still true that the reaction of the audience is largely emotional rather than intellectual, but it is becoming increasingly necessary under modern conditions for the actor to have intelligence himself if he would create the right emotions in others. The more sophisticated our audiences become, the more intelligence the actor needs to enable him to penetrate their intellectual armor and touch their real emotions.

Perhaps the least important quality to look for in a new and inexperienced candidate, though one of the easiest to test, is technical excellence. Not that technique is unimportant in the finished production; but a new candidate should not be expected to have it ready-made. A candidate who professes to have had considerable experience should of course be judged a little more severely in the matter of technique. On the other hand, a player who shows a facile but superficial technical skill without much background of understanding, sympathy, and imagination is not usually a person of very good promise. The indications are that he has been overtrained and undereducated, or that he lacks balance. What the director must find out is not how well the candidate knows the traditional conventions, but how well he can adapt himself to whatever conventions may be called for by each new play. This of course *is* technique, in the broadest sense, but it is not what many old actors mean by technique.

the tryout system

Some sort of tryout system is often necessary to assist the director in choosing the cast, and is often desirable from the standpoint of competition and morale in the producing organization. It should be understood, however, that such a system is at best a mere makeshift, dictated by policy or necessity.

There is no director on earth who can really tell in one tryout, or half a dozen, what an actor has in him. Only test of actual performance – of many performances in many parts – can reveal that. It may be true that beginners have been cast in major roles and succeeded, but for every such case a dozen could be cited in which utter failure was the result. One has but to read the biographies of famous actors, past and present, to be impressed with the fact that many of them were themselves misjudged in youth and had to go through long years of apprenticeship and failure before their talents were recognized. There is only one thing harder to foretell than the future development of an actor and that is the success or failure of a play. And if commercial managers cannot judge correctly among actors who have had, as a rule, at least some experience, the director of amateurs should have little faith in any judgment he can form on the basis of two or three tryouts.

But to say that is not to solve the problem. When the director has a play to cast and most of the candidates are strangers to him, he cannot wait several years to find out what they can do. He must go ahead and choose, as wisely as possible, without hope of infallibility, but with the determination to reduce the probability of error to a minimum.

How, then, can a series of tryouts be planned so as to come as near the truth as possible in the time available? Among the many methods now in use, which are most genuinely helpful?

The commonest method – and the worst – is to have the candidates read at sight the parts for which they are competing and to pass judgment upon the reading alone. This is, to be sure, the quickest way to eliminate a large number of candidates. But the best sight reading, or at any rate the most spectacular, is usually done by the superficially clever elocutionist. With a facility born of much practice and some egotism, he – or she – can give almost any part a lively and *expressive* reading that may or may not be correct, but which positively shines by contrast with the more cautious reading of the careful, modest actor. It frequently happens that the person who puts a great deal of expression into the first reading of a part overacts it seriously at a later period, and because he forms his conceptions so quickly, he forms some misconceptions that are later hard to break. Many of the most capable and finished actors form their conceptions slowly and read very poorly at first, giving little evidence of interpretation until they have gone far enough to lay aside their books. To eliminate such persons at the first tryout would be most unfortunate. So deceptive, generally, is a judgment based upon a first reading that if I were compelled to choose a cast by that method, I should almost think it safer to reject the good readers and retain the poor ones.

A far better method is the one occasionally used in amateur casting, and sometimes in professional, by which each candidate is required to perform a scene from some play in which he has previously appeared, or a scene especially chosen in advance and rehearsed for the purpose. If the candidate has sufficient notice and some idea of the kind of play and the kind of part for which he is being considered, he can choose a scene that will demonstrate his abilities in an appropriate manner. Still better is an elaboration of this method by which the candidate appears in several scenes from several different types of plays.

It is possible, of course, to use actual scenes from the play to be produced, and a great many directors do this. But scenes so used are apt to become tiresome to the actors before the real rehearsals have begun and the total period of rehearsal is apt to seem painfully long and dragged out. Another difficulty is that some of the candidates will have learned these scenes without proper direction and will have to make too many readjustments in rehearsal.

On the whole, it is generally better to keep the tryouts separate from the play itself, giving out the parts only after the final cast has been chosen. When the competition is very keen, or when the candidates are serious-minded students eager for every scrap of coaching or instruction, it is possible to keep them working on the play for some time with no certainty of making the cast; but with the average group of amateurs it is easier to maintain the competitive spirit through a series of tests distinct from rehearsals. Most young candidates will work hard enough on preliminary tryouts, but they have a strange aversion to doing any real work on the play until they are sure of their parts.

The problem, then, is not so much how to conduct a series of trial rehearsals as how to devise a series of independent tests that will make possible the tentative choice of a cast, or at least the elimination of impossible candidates. Obviously no single recipe will do for all productions; plays and parts are so different in their requirements that the director must be prepared to meet each new occasion, changing his plan much or little, according to circumstances.

tryout methods

By way of illustration, suppose we are to produce a play of Noel Coward, *Private Lives,* for example. Here is a play about two English couples. It has the humor and wit of Coward, plenty of comedy, a little romance, and a great deal of *satirical kick.* Clearly, we shall have to eliminate those candidates who are too uncouth in speech or manners to suggest English society, even satirically; or too persistently American in speech to play English parts; or too naïve to appreciate the value in satire. We shall need some, or all, of the following tests:

1. a reading test for pronunciation and enunciation
2. a conversation test to supplement the reading test
3. an improvisation test for diction, manners, poise, and imagination
4. a pantomime test for poise, carriage, technique, and imagination
5. a test for satirical feeling
6. a general acting test for all-around acting ability
7. a personal interview for character, intelligence, and sympathy, and to supplement all other tests—this may well be given first; or it may be given in two parts, before and after the other tests

For the reading test the candidate may be asked to read at sight from several different scenes, taken perhaps from another play of Coward, such as *Blithe Spirit.* The material may be varied for different candidates, according to their apparent possibilities, but the attention should be upon speech habits rather than character interpretation. The director should

note any slovenliness of enunciation or any markedly un-English pronunciation, giving special attention to the long and short *o,* the *a* as in "laugh,"
"half," and "past," and medial and final *r,* and the more difficult labial and
dental consonants, especially *b, t,* and *d.* In the word "kitten," for example,
the Englishman explodes the *t* as if it were a *t,* whereas the American is
apt to swallow it with a slight cough through the nose. Failure to achieve
a perfect English pronunciation on the first reading should not necessarily
mean summary dismissal, for a candidate may be very distinctly American
in his ordinary speech and yet have the gift of learning dialects other than
his own. The director should criticize the first reading, allow a little time
for preparation, and then hear the same candidate again. If, after several
chances, with criticism and time for preparation, the candidate still displays extreme uncouthness of speech—bad grammar, slovenly enunciation, vulgar intonation, coarse voice, or roughness of any kind, matters that
are too serious to be corrected in a few weeks—he may be disqualified
promptly for anything but a supernumerary part.

The conversational test is a useful check on the reading test because
there are some people who can read fairly well in a schoolroom manner but
who revert to Brooklyn or Main Street English in conversation. Such persons are not usually to be trusted in sustained parts requiring cultivated
speech; they are apt to exaggerate the cultivation when they think of it
and forget all about it when the excitement of acting is upon them. The
director should draw the candidate out in conversation, putting him at
ease as much as possible, but noting carefully his speech habits. There
are matters of tempo, intonation, and sentence rhythm that are not revealed
in the reading test for the reason that reading has certain conventionalized
inflections of its own; but most of these come out in conversation. Some
candidates who can correct their pronunciation and clean up their enunciation are unable to catch the tune of English speech as distinct from American. And it is the sentence tune, even more than the vowel quality, that
conveys the best suggestion of a British atmosphere.

The improvisation test is hardly a fair test of speech if used alone because
of the added element of self-consciousness, but it does help to reveal the
relation of the candidate's speech habits to his manners and carriage. At
the same time it tests the imagination much more severely than an ordinary

acting test. The candidate may be asked to enter an imaginary drawing
room, acknowledge the greetings of guests, place a chair for a lady, retrieve
a lady's handkerchief and return it to her, perform an introduction, acknowledge an introduction, give an order to a servant, or what not, improvising his own lines as he goes. Or he may have a more definite and significant dramatic situation described to him, and be asked to enact his part
of it, again improvising the words. As a rule, it is best to apply this test to
several candidates at once, assigning them to the several parts involved.
After a group of candidates have floundered through an improvised scene
once or twice, they should be given a few moments to think it over and then
be heard again, for unless they are actors of considerable experience they
will seem a hopeless failure. After two or three trials and a little coaching
they will begin to loosen up enough to reveal to the director what he wants
to know about them.

The pantomime test is almost identical in method and purpose, except
that the emphasis is now on the action rather than the lines. The two tests
may, of course, be combined, but I have generally found that I can learn
more about a candidate's carriage, poise, manners, and action technique
by putting him through a few scenes entirely in pantomime. If he does not
have to search for words he can concentrate his imagination on the action.
The director may describe to him a simple situation: He enters a drawing
room; tea is being served; he sees Clara on a divan at stage left; he greets
her and expresses his pleasure at seeing her again; he asks if she has had
tea; she has not; he gets it for her; he asks permission to present a friend
who is in the next room, and goes in search of him; he brings his friend
on and introduces him to Clara. The scene may be done first in pantomime
and then repeated with improvised words. Either with or without words
the candidate will make an amusing grotesque of it on the first attempt,
but after two or three attempts he will begin to reveal some social poise if
he has any. When, after several rehearsals, he swaggers on with his hands
in his pockets and his chewing gum still in one cheek, stands almost on
Clara's feet, and says, "Hullo, Clarrer, wantcher ter meet m'fren' Jones,"
he can be set down as unavailable for any part in *Private Lives.*

For a play like *Private Lives,* the test for satirical feeling is especially
important. The candidate should be asked to read or recite a satirical poem

or prose sketch, or to act out a satirical passage from another play, and should be judged for his ability to convey the double meaning or the tongue-in-cheek attitude concealed behind the lines. Almost anybody can convey sharp, bitter irony, but with Coward the problem is to keep the whimsical light-comedy effect and the gentle good humor, and yet deliver the wallop. One candidate will fail utterly to detect any satirical meaning and will see only naïve romance; another will detect the satirical intent but exaggerate it and make it bitter; another will keep the comedy, but translate the satire into burlesque. The history of American literature is proof that Americans generally are not quite as keenly alive to high-comedy satire as the English, and it is not easy to find young American actors who can act Coward with just the right flavor. But a candidate who can read Sir Peter Teazle's famous monologue, or Dickens' description of Mr. Turvydrop, or Goldsmith's *Elegy on the Death of a Mad Dog*, or Gilbert's *Rhyme of the Nancy Belle,* or Kipling's *Pink Dominoes,* and do it in such a way as to bring out the humor and satire, is at least a possibility. The purpose of the general acting test is clear enough. As already suggested, it should consist of an opportunity to act a complete scene thoroughly prepared in advance. Several candidates may be tried together in a scene from *Blithe Spirit*, or perhaps a scene from some other author of high comedy, like Oscar Wilde. Costumes and scenery are not essential, but if time permits, there should be several repetitions so that the individual may do himself justice after the first self-consciousness has passed. Inexperienced directors do not always make sufficient allowance for the unusual strain attached to tryouts, a strain that is far greater and more artificial when individuals are competing against each other than when they are working as a group to perform the finished play.

The last test, that of a personal interview, is in many respects the most valuable of all, and yet one that many directors omit altogether. It will not, of course, serve by itself, for one wants to know how the candidate will look and act on the platform, viewed objectively; but, on the other hand, it will reveal quickly many things that will not appear at all in the platform tests until after weeks of rehearsal. The director may question the candidate as to his previous experience, his knowledge of technique, his knowledge of the drama in general, and the play to be performed in particular, his tastes and preferences, his admirations and ambitions; and, in a general way, discover his background and attitude. The candidate's preferences in reading will throw a great deal of light on his possible ability to appreciate satire, as well as on his understanding of literary and social values. Quite obviously, this test may be combined with the conversational test already discussed, and the candidate's speech habits tested at the same time; but the director must not be overly concerned with externals and fail to note those deeper things that cannot be taught.

All this is but a suggestion of method. The several tests may be combined in any convenient way, or still further subdivided, and not all of them will be needed with every candidate. The director who has confidence in his own snap judgment will regard the whole business as fantastic, of course. If he can get along with something simpler, that is his good luck. Personally, I want to know as much as I can find out about every candidate who applies, and I have found each of these tests helpful in one way or another, at one time or another.

the casting list

In a well-organized theatre group, all casting experience centers, of course, in a casting list, or catalogue of available talent. This should be carefully studied and kept up to date. The results of all tryouts should be reflected in filed entries, both for candidates who have been awarded parts, and for those who have been rejected as unsuitable for certain parts but who might be very useful in parts of a different kind. In addition, periodic or seasonal auditions may be held, without reference to any particular play, but solely for the purpose of building up the talent pool.

A good casting list is extremely helpful when plays are being considered for production, and often the principal parts of a play under consideration can be tentatively cast from the list without recourse to special tryouts.

Each entry in the list should include the player's sex, height, weight, complexion, date of birth (not the age, unless the entry itself is dated), and a dated photograph that is as recent as possible. The entry should list the parts played, with dates, together with any director's comments on the player's special abilities and limitations, including his mannerisms, peculiarities of voice, movement, and temperament, his possession or lack of a comedy sense, and the like. It might well include, also, his measurements, hat and wig sizes, and so on. Most important of all, it should include his record for attendance at rehearsals, ability to take direction, quickness and accuracy in learning lines, and general reliability. Naturally, the list should be kept under lock and key and made available only to directors and casting committees.

In the study of the play and the planning of the production the director is first of all an artist, and as an artist, he must continue to function until the finished performance leaves his hands. But with the assembling of the cast and the start of actual rehearsals he begins to function also as a teacher, and his ability as a teacher is so important an element in the success of the production, and the permanent success of the producing group, that it deserves rather more than the usual amount of emphasis.

the theatre as a school

In the European repertory theatre the *regisseur* is, as a rule, not only the managerial head of an organization but the headmaster of a permanent school as well. He is interested in the artistic presentation of each play and in the efficient conduct of the business of production; but he is also interested in the development and improvement of the actors and the building up of a strong ensemble. He does not go out and hire a ready-made cast for each new play; he adds new recruits to his company because they show promise, and he helps them, through years of training and experience, to develop that promise into achievement. The result is an *esprit de corps,* a group solidarity, and an artistic unity almost unknown today in the American professional theatre.

Now and then, of course, an American producer does succeed in establishing a somewhat analogous relationship. William Ball did this in founding the American Conservatory Theatre. Tyrone Guthrie started such a company at Minneapolis, and the Lincoln Center Company was planned basically as a repertory group. But perhaps the most successful repertory companies are those attached to some of the nation's major university theatres. The University Resident Theatre Association was founded in 1968 to promote these very principles.

But for the most part, the strictly commercial theatre in this country operates on an entirely different basis. A producer accepts a play, engages a director, and hires a cast. He does not hire learners if he can help it; he hires people who are already identified with the types of parts they are to play. The director starts with the assumption that his actors are finished artists who know their business thoroughly, and the actors generally start with the same assumption. The director tells them where to go and what to do rather than *how* to do it, or *why*. If the actors are good-humored and the director tactful, he may give them some hints on acting, or suggestions as to interpretation, but he cannot feel any deep obligation to teach them anything beyond the needs of the particular play. If they are not good-humored, they are likely to resent any instructions beyond the needs of the play. If they are underlings they do as they are told; if they are stars they sometimes do as they please. The combination of trade unionism, type casting, and temporary organization has made almost impossible the teaching relationship so necessary to a permanently fine theatre.

It is in the amateur semiprofessional theatre, the school or community theatre, that the teaching relationship can best exist. The director of amateurs, especially when he is himself a professional, has an obvious responsibility for the training of his actors that the hired director in the commercial theatre is under no obligation to feel; and if the actors happen to be earnest and eager to learn, the theatre soon begins to function as a school and the director as a teacher. It is, I believe, the existence of this relationship in our little theatres that has enabled so many of them to compete in popularity with the commercial theatres, and that has caused some of them, on their own merits, to turn into professional theatres of the repertory type. It has also caused a number of them to establish schools of their own, so-called, as was the Pasadena Playhouse, or in the numerous *summer stock* theatres; or to arrange cooperative educational programs with the colleges or universities, as in the Cleveland Playhouse and Western Reserve University.

What the American theatre — amateur and professional — most needs is the constant encouragement of its function as a school. Not, of course, as a school for the audience, and not as a school in the uplift or missionary sense; but as a school for its own development, a school of its own art. For the development of such a function, the director — or directors, if there are several — must establish, in relation to the actors, a true teaching attitude.

the teaching attitude

A true teaching attitude does not mean a didactic or dictatorial attitude, an assumption of omniscience or of superiority on the part of the teacher. Nobody is more painfully aware of how little he knows than the earnest teacher, for the very effort to teach somebody else reveals to him the gaps in his own knowledge. An effective teaching attitude is not, of course, inconsistent with dignity and self-respect, but it is characterized by modesty, sympathy, and tolerance. A good teacher aims to teach rather than to command. He does not pretend to know everything or to be right in all his opinions, and he expects to learn as much from his students as they learn from him. His function is to guide and assist them in their efforts to learn, and to serve as a sort of clearing house through which the experiences of others may be passed on to them.

Perhaps the most essential element of a good teaching attitude on the part of the stage director is a willingness to explain his directions; to give reasons; to teach the *why* as well as the *what*. Tell an actor what to do and it may serve for the needs of the play; tell him why and you have taught him a principle that he may be able to apply for himself on another occasion. Too often the director begrudges the time or effort involved in giving reasons; or he assumes that the actor is too stupid to understand them, or too indifferent to care; or—breathe it softly—he *has* no reasons to give. Sometimes he has a conscious conviction that the actors ought not to know why they do things, that they ought to be clay in the director's hands, mere brainless *übermarionettes*, expressing the director's art in their own.

It may be said in objection to the teaching of reasons that there is not sufficient time for the director to explain every direction he gives, or to teach elementary principles of acting; and this, unfortunately, is true. But no one contends that the director should turn his rehearsals into kindergarten classes and permit the work to be constantly interrupted by foolish or needless questions; and no one contends that he should put himself on the defensive and feel compelled to explain himself every time he makes a decision. What he should do is to meet halfway the actor who is seeking to improve himself, who is interested in the play as well as in the part, and who is willing and eager to give serious study to the whole problem of production. Sometimes it is necessary to require that questions and discussions be postponed until after rehearsals—but this is a matter of expediency and not of attitude. The important point is that the director shall take it for granted that the actor wants to learn and shall help him as much as possible.

what to teach

Given a teaching attitude on the part of the director, the question arises: What shall he teach?

Clearly he must teach meaning, lines, and business of the play in hand. Also, if he is to have any permanent success, he must teach the actors an attitude. But possibly the most obvious need, if we consider the little theatres of the country, is that he shall teach acting, for it is in the acting that our nonprofessional theatres are most conspicuously inferior.

That the acting in our college and community theatres has improved no one will dispute; nevertheless, it still is—and in the nature of things will always be—the point of greatest difficulty. My own observation indicates that the problem is more a lack of teamwork than of individual talent. Amateur actors often show flashes of brilliance or power, and a freshness, a spontaneity, that in itself is good; but they lack technical smoothness, poise, and group coordination.

The director should teach his actors to think in terms of plays, not parts; of scenes, not lines; of stage pictures and stage actions as seen by the audience, not individual movements and business. Such teaching will not confuse the actor, nor will it tempt him to neglect the movements and business prescribed. The better he understands the purpose of what he does and the more clearly he sees his own actions as a part of the general scheme, the easier it will be for him to accept the directions given and perform them with precision, and the greater will be his individual creative freedom within the natural limitations of the play. There is nothing so conducive to real artistic freedom as knowing just how far you can go.

The director should teach his actors how to analyze a play, to find the author's meaning, to catch the mood and rhythm of each act and scene, to visualize the background or period, and to discover the relation of each character to the play as a whole. He should explain the essentials of plot construction, the distinction between comedy and tragedy, and the characteristics of the principal styles and types of plays. He should stress particularly the importance of theme and the advisability of toning the acting according to the theme rather than the plot.

The director should teach his actors the essential principles of stage movement and business. He should encourage intelligent discussion and intelligent experiment. He should emphasize especially the element of compensation that so often appears—the necessity for one character to balance another, to give way for another's movement or fill in after it. He should teach them to feel the balance of the stage picture in their own bodies, to correct it, when imperfect, as unobtrusively as possible, by slight changes of position; but he should distinguish between an accidentally unbalanced picture and one purposely unbalanced to create suspense or anticipation. He should teach them to take and hold the attention at certain points and to yield it at others, according to the needs of the play. He should teach them how to remain in character and to act when not speaking, yet without distracting attention from the other characters; how to listen effectively to other characters; how to remain in repose when on the stage but out of the action.

He should teach them to maintain what is referred to as the *illusion of the first time*—the illusion that the character is uttering his words for the first time and not merely repeating memorized lines.

He should teach them the most important conventions and devices of acting, emphasizing always the principles and purposes rather than the mechanism, but bearing in mind that the stage is not real life and that acting is not just "being natural." He should teach them to play toward, but not to, the audience; to convey meaning without direct communication; to suppress meaningless movement; to cultivate repose; to keep out of emphasis what is not emphasized by the dramatist; to heighten effects a little beyond nature; and above all, to simplify—to select essentials and reject useless detail as every artist does.

The director should encourage his actors to train their bodies, to cultivate grace and poise and expressiveness. If they need more instruction than he can give them, he should try to have them get it elsewhere. Some will need courses in dancing, or fencing, or eurhythmics, or plain gymnastics. Others will need drill in gesture and in traditional stage movements, foot positions, turns, and the like—although stage drill is capable of abuse and should not be carried to excess. Others will need instruction in etiquette, poise, and carriage; for almost no young man today carries himself with the dignity of an earlier generation, and almost no young woman can walk across the stage gracefully. The actor can never tell when he may be called upon to play a drawing-room part or to dance, fence, box, or play the piano; the greater the number of such accomplishments he has at hand, and the greater his flexibility and adaptability, the better his chance of success.

The director should encourage his actors to practice pure pantomime. It may even be worthwhile for him to conduct such exercises himself. Numerous articles on pantomime may be found, most of them suggesting lists of subjects; or the director may draw his subjects from bits of pantomimic action in plays with which he is familiar—the poker game in *The Odd Couple,* for instance, the dart-throwing scene in *You Can't Take It With You,* or the scenes in which the inmates of Charenton act out their various forms of madness in Weiss's *Marat Sade.*

The director should impress upon his actors the importance of voice and should give them every possible help in voice training. Most young actors fail to realize the need of such training and can only be driven to it by constant urging.

He should teach his actors to observe the life that is about them, to be interested in the speech and the actions of all sorts of people. He should suggest that they carry notebooks in which to jot down interesting bits of action, traits of character, mannerisms, tricks, or peculiarities of speech, or what not, as observed on planes or buses, in the stores, or on the streets. He should, however, caution them against too literal a copy of life with consequent loss of aesthetic distance, and against the danger of dragging in good business for its own sake without regard to relevancy. He should encourage the study of human motives and the cultivation of sympathy and understanding. He should warn his actors against interpreting all human life in terms of their own motives, or the motives of their own age, race, nation, or social level, and should impress upon them the advantage of mixing with all classes of society, of knowing all quarters of the city or country, and of understanding the conditions of other countries and other historical periods.

He should urge them to read and study – to know something of history, philosophy, and literature, and perhaps even of science. He should encourage study and appreciation of the other fine arts and should emphasize the similarity of aim and principle in all of them. He should teach the leading theories of aesthetic appeal, especially the principles of empathy and aesthetic distance,and he should make every effort to relate these principles to actual practice. He should strive to make his actors artistically sensitive, that they may learn to avoid false notes in acting to spare themselves pains, as a musician avoids false notes in music.

To teach all of these things is, of course, a superhuman task. There is never any limit to the possibilities; the limits are found only in the equipment, the time available, the capabilities of the actors, and the ability of the director himself.

the teaching method

There are those who believe that a teaching attitude and something to teach make a teacher; there are others who consider the technique of teaching a science in itself, and an essential element of any educational process. The problem is too extensive to be considered here. There are, however, one or two controversial questions concerning the teaching method of the stage director that have disturbed the teachers of dramatics greatly and, even, the critics of the professional theatre. They therefore deserve some comment.

The first of these is the question of democracy versus dictatorship, already discussed in relation to the planning of stage movement and business. As applied to teaching method, the question is this: Should the director adopt a sort of *laissez-faire* policy in teaching, striving to inspire his students to learn for themselves, but leaving them to find the way; or should he assume definite control of their activities, guiding and shaping their

studies at every point? Stanislavsky, one of the greatest of teaching directors, suggested that the director should not generate an idea, but should
merely preside at its birth. Gordon Craig, on the other hand, would make
the actor an *übermarionette*, subservient to the director at every point.
David Belasco shaped and trained his actors by close personal instruction
until they were always recognizable as Belasco products; others sit quietly
at rehearsals, giving no sign until something goes wrong, and then merely
indicating that something is wrong and leaving it to the actors to find out
what, and to correct it.

Clearly the question of which is the better teaching method depends
somewhat upon the object to be attained. But it depends also upon the
director's own ability and upon the age and temperament of the actor who
is to be taught. The beginner may require more definite rule-of-thumb
teaching than the experienced actor. In so complex a problem generalization is futile; the director should understand and use both methods, according to circumstances.

Another and more important question is whether the director should
make use of demonstration in his teaching — whether he should show an actor how to do a thing and permit him to learn it by imitation. On this subject
there has been violent disagreement. Some amateur directors and teachers
of dramatics are so afraid of imitation that they will not permit the slightest
suggestion of it — not even when the actor is totally at a loss for what to do
and says, "Please show me." They seem to feel that it means the downfall
of the actor's creative freedom and the enslavement of his personality, if
not the loss of his immortal soul!

With the essence of their contention one must, of course, agree. Nobody
except Gordon Craig ever wanted the actor to be a mere puppet in the hands
of the director, and nobody at all wants him to be a pale copy of someone
else — a mere mechanical imitator of things he does not understand. But
when the extremists insist that imitation is necessarily ruinous to the
sincerity and individuality of the actor, one wonders whether their theory
is consistent with the psychology of the learning process. The psychologists
themselves are divided on this point. Some maintain that the impulse to
imitate is inherited and plays a large part in the learning process; others
insist that the learning process begins with random movements that are

gradually "conditioned" by experience, and that imitation is possible only in the case of activities already learned by accident. If the latter are correct, there can be little danger in imitation since it cannot take place until the thing to be imitated is already learned through experience. If the former are correct, and imitation is an essential part of the learning process, why be afraid to make use of it?

Our education is built up largely, if not wholly, out of our experiences. We do not create our thoughts out of nothing; we build them out of elements drawn from observation. If the necessary elements are lacking, we cannot create; we must first gain more experience, and it is here that demonstration comes in. When the director tells an actor that he ought to get a certain effect and the actor, after several attempts, says: "I can't do it; I don't know what you mean; please show me"—he is merely saying that he cannot create because he has not had the necessary experience. If, at that point, the director can show him what to do, or have someone else show him, the whole situation may be cleared up. If, after being shown, the actor still does not understand and falls back on slavish, hollow mimicry, it is a very dull director, indeed, who fails to detect the fault, and a very foolish one who allows it to go uncorrected. But if the effect of the demonstration is to give the actor just that fresh light that he needs—to make him say, "Oh, now I understand; that is a good idea; I wish I had thought of it myself"—I do not believe that he is likely to be ruined by the slight element of imitation that may creep into his playing.

There is still another question of method in teaching that every director must face, and that is the question of the actor's emotions and the extent to which the director is to appeal to them, to exercise them, and to teach the actor to depend upon them. But this is so bound up with the theory of acting, to be discussed in a later chapter, that I shall omit consideration of it at this point.

the teacher as director

The teaching relationship of the director to his actors is seen at its best, perhaps, in the school or college play. The person who is a teacher in the classroom naturally functions as teacher in directing a production by his own pupils, whether as part of a course or as an extracurricular activity. To be sure, he does not always preserve the classroom manner—which is a gain rather than a loss—but he assumes as a matter of course the task of training the individuals as well as the group. To this fact may be attributed the surprisingly high quality—all things considered—of the average school play.

I say "all things considered" because I happen to know some of the difficulties of the schoolteacher-director. In the first place, there is the inescapable youth and immaturity of the players, even among those of college age. In the second place, there is the fact that the boys and girls do not remain long enough under the director's charge to gain the necessary experience; about the time they begin to develop they take their diplomas and leave. In the third place, there is the almost total lack of persons to play old and middle-aged parts. In the fourth place, there is frequently the handicap of an unsuitable place to play and the difficulty of finding time for rehearsals. In the fifth place, there is the financial problem. And finally, there is the fact that in many cases the teacher, no matter how good a teacher or how well fitted temperamentally for the work, has had little practical training backstage; has, in many instances, never seen a first-class professional performance or been inside a real theatre. This is especially true today, for motion picture and television have driven the road companies out of the small towns, and first-rate companies visit only a very few of the larger cities. Under the circumstances, it is no wonder that many school performances are crude and unpolished and immature; the amazing thing is that they show as much intelligence and imagination and taste as they do. At least it may be said that, taking the country as a whole, the school play is a good two jumps ahead of the audience.

The teacher as director is, as a rule, more likely to have the right attitude toward his work than most other directors and, perhaps, more likely to pursue an effective teaching method. If he makes any mistake in his teaching, it is almost sure to be an overemphasis on the interpretative work of the individual and an underemphasis on the teamwork. School plays are often poorly organized and loosely directed, though excellently coached—if the distinction may be permitted. For that reason the teacher who is called upon to direct plays should lose no opportunity to learn of the technical side of the theatre and to cultivate the organizing ability so necessary to the director as executive.

educational theatre

Many schools and colleges now make theatre a part of the curriculum rather than an extracurricular activity. The educational influence of play production in teaching literary and artistic values, appreciation of the drama, sympathetic understanding of character, control of body, speech, and imagination, has very properly earned it a place in the curriculum. But its classroom values have led some teachers to take a somewhat distorted view of the whole purpose of educational theatre.

According to these teachers, theatre in an educational institution should exist for educational rather than artistic purposes. To this end, they say, there should be less attention paid to the excellence of the production as a whole than to the educational effect on those taking part; there should be no attempt to choose the cast for the good of the play by selecting actors according to their suitability for the parts; the students should, instead, be deliberately assigned to characters unlike themselves, in order to correct their faults of personality. Thus, a small, effeminate youth should be chosen for a heavy, masculine part in order to render him less effeminate; an ill-tempered, surly person should be chosen for a courteous, kindly part in order to improve his disposition. And above all, no attention should be paid to the matter of pleasing the audience, who should be suffered to attend at their own risk.

In this point of view there are really several propositions more or less distinct.

The first is that educational theatre should exist to educate the person taking part and not to please the audience. At first sight this seems reasonable enough, but the danger lies in the assumption of an irreconcilable alternative. To assume that such methods of production as will please the audience are probably not the best methods to educate the actor is to distort the problem. The truth is that the very sort of excellence in production that best pleases audiences is also the best educational influence upon the actor. It is true that pure type casting is bad for the actor—as well as for the production—and if students can be given varied experience without ruining the production, the effect is educational. Even deliberate miscasting may afford good practice to the student if confined to rehearsals without audience, or to classroom exercises. But the purpose of a play is to give aesthetic pleasure to an audience, and any indulgence before an audience in play production that deliberately ignores or sets aside this purpose is intellectually insincere and, therefore, vitiating to the educational purpose. Clarity of purpose, sincerity, and coordination of effort are far more important educationally than facility in interpretation, and to sacrifice the greater to the lesser is to falsify the emphasis in education. If the purpose of the fine arts is inconsistent with sound education, the fine arts ought to be bundled right out of our schools. If not, then the purpose should be given the main emphasis, and every effort should be made to accomplish it with the highest possible degree of excellence.

The second is that the student actor should, for his own sake, be cast for parts unlike himself. But is it a proper function of the educator to mold character in this sense? Is it right to subdue each individual bent or bias by the neutralizing force of an opposite? Or, if only the bad traits are to be subdued, who is to be the judge to decide which traits are bad and what models to follow in the molding process? The proponents of the plan would take a little, effeminate chap and make a man of him by having him play a masculine part. But would they take a husky, boisterous young athlete and make a mollycoddle out of him by having him play an effeminate part? And if their purpose is to mold character, what parent would want his son to be cast for Macbeth or Shylock or Iago in the school play? Or, are the unpleasant parts to be left out and educational theatre confined to the representation of saints and heros?

But educational theatre should not be justified as a therapeutic device. It must exist to give training in theatre arts to students and pleasure to an audience. It can and does provide a vehicle for interesting and exciting study of man in every age and environment and so can enliven literature, history, psychology, and virtually every other field.

Theatre, although it can be a useful extension of the audio-visual department of the school or college, must be justified on its own terms. A whole man in a civilized society needs an understanding of, and an involvement with, the arts. Educational theatre provides opportunities for those who would practice the art and for those who would simply appreciate it.

Time was when educational theatre was simply a pleasant and harmless way to pass some leisure hours. It is more and more becoming an area of study and specialization that is feeding the commercial theatre with the trained talent it needs and that is providing knowledgeable audiences with high standards of taste. This is the justification for educational theatre. We need only live up to a standard of excellence that will achieve these goals.

We come now to the director's most active personal responsibility: the conduct of rehearsals.

Rehearsals have at least three different purposes, and it is well to distinguish them at the start. The first is to give opportunity for experiment; the second is to teach the text and meaning of the play to the cast; and the third is to perfect and polish the performance. The division is arbitrary, but useful.

Most amateurs are too busy with other interests, too pressed for time, and too restless for very much indulgence in experimental rehearsal. The director working with such people must do most of his experimenting in advance or between rehearsals, and devote the rehearsals themselves to learning and to polishing. A certain amount of experiment is, to be sure, inevitable in the early rehearsals, for no matter how well a production has been planned, unexpected problems will arise during the *blocking-out* period, and changes will have to be made. But it is a common mistake of amateur directors to use so much time in the feeble, head-scratching kind of experiment that, when the date for the performance begins to draw near, it becomes necessary to concentrate on the learning process, and the polishing gets crowded out altogether. The director should realize that a production not learned in time to allow for thorough polishing cannot be otherwise than crude in performance, no matter how well worked out in the experimental stage; and if he values his reputation, he will sacrifice other things, including his own time, to provide for adequate polishing.

the schedule of rehearsals

To avoid the danger of neglecting some phase of production, it is a good plan to work out in advance a definite schedule of rehearsals. The shorter the time, the more important this becomes. If a complete schedule cannot be arranged before the first rehearsal, a tentative schedule may be posted, to be replaced after the play has been blocked out by a corrected schedule, showing the exact number of remaining rehearsals and the exact ground to be covered in each.

Different types of plays call, of course, for differently planned schedules. Some plays are so constructed that they must be rehearsed by acts; others by separate scenes. These scenes can be rehearsed separately and the whole play need not be put together until the last few rehearsals. Plays built around ensemble scenes require that most rehearsals be general ones with the whole cast present. Some plays are so dependent for their effects upon costume that they require a number of dress rehearsals; others depend upon lighting effects that must be rehearsed carefully, and others depend so completely upon the recital of the lines that much of the work may be in the nature of individual coaching.

In general, it is a good plan to break up the play into small scenes and to rehearse these separately in the early stages — partly to permit more intensive study, and partly to save the actors who appear in only a few scenes from sitting about all evening doing nothing. Difficult scenes involving only one, two, or three characters — soliloquies, love scenes, duels, fist fights, quarrels, dances, conspiracies — should be worked out in special rehearsals with as much individual instruction as possible. Most amateur directors other than teachers fail to realize the importance of individual consultation; they follow the professional method of issuing directions at rehearsal and expecting the actor to perfect himself at home, which is just what the inexperienced actor cannot do. A great deal of time is wasted by amateurs in poorly planned and ineffective general rehearsals.

It is well, also, to vary the emphasis of the general rehearsals, announcing one for detail, another for continuity, another for cues, another for tempo, and so on. This helps to insure that each important phase of preparation will be attended to; at the same time it gives the actors a clearer idea of what to work for, and promotes teamwork. During the last week or so it is especially desirable to alternate rehearsals for detail and for continuity; if you pull the play apart one night, put it together again the next.

It is not possible to lay out an ideal schedule of rehearsals that will do for every play, but a sample schedule may be helpful to the inexperienced director as indicating what he may do with the time available. Suppose, for instance, that he has eight weeks in which to rehearse a modern three-act comedy, and that most of the cast, except for the principals, can spare only two full evenings a week, with perhaps a little more time during the last two or three weeks. Suppose that only four of the principals are in all three acts, and that Act Two uses a different setting and a different group of supporting characters from Acts One and Three. Suppose, also, that only the last week of rehearsals can be held on the stage, and that the others must be held in private houses or borrowed rehearsal rooms. A tentative schedule might read somewhat as follows:

first week

| Tuesday, 8 P.M. | —Reading of play. Discussion. |
| Thursday, 8 P.M. | —Blocking out of Act I. |

second week

Tuesday, 8 P.M.	—Blocking out of Act II.
Thursday, 7 P.M.	—Review of Act I.
8:30 P.M.	—Blocking out of Act III.
Sunday, 3 P.M.	—Round-table conference; discussions of meanings and interpretations.

third week

Tuesday, 7 P.M.	—Review Acts I and III, for detail.
Thursday, 7 P.M.	—Review Act II, for detail.
Sunday, 3 P.M.	—Key scenes, principals only.

fourth week

Tuesday, 7 P.M.	—Act I, without books.
Thursday, 7 P.M.	—Act II, without books.
Sunday, 3 P.M.	—Act III, without books.

fifth week

| Tuesday, 7 P.M. | —Run-through, whole play, for lines. |
| Thursday, 7 P.M. | —Key scenes, for detail. |

Sunday, 3 P.M.	—Whole play, for detail.

sixth week

Tuesday, 8 P.M.	—Whole play at fast tempo, for continuity.
Thursday, 7 P.M.	—Act II, for detail.
Sunday, 3 P.M.	—Acts I and III, for detail.

seventh week

Monday, 8 P.M.	—Special rehearsals or consultations as needed.
Tuesday, 7 P.M.	—Rehearsal for mood and emphasis. Whole play.
Thursday, 7 P.M.	—Rehearsal for speed and polish. Whole play.
Friday, 8 P.M.	—Special rehearsal or individual coaching as needed.
Sunday, 3 P.M.	—Line rehearsal, while crew sets up stage.

eighth week

Monday, 7 P.M.	—Stage rehearsal with furniture and props. Whole play.
Tuesday, 8 P.M.	—Special rehearsals, individuals or key scenes.
Wednesday, 8 P.M.	—Rehearsal for speed and polish.
Thursday, 8 P.M.	—Technical rehearsal, all lighting and sound. Stop as needed.
Friday, 7 P.M.	—First dress rehearsal, makeup and costumes and all technical. Only critical interruptions.
Sunday, 3 P.M.	—Full dress rehearsal run as a performance, with invited audience and no interruptions.

ninth week

Monday, 8:30 P.M. sharp	—Performance (cast report at 7 P.M.).

Obviously, all this is subject to great variation. There may be objection to Sunday rehearsals; Monday, Wednesday, and Friday nights may turn out to be more suitable. Important players may have fixed engagements that interfere with certain dates. A different type of play may call for an entirely different distribution of emphasis. If all rehearsals can be held on the stage, the schedule may be simpler and perhaps shorter; if the set and props are available earlier, a more polished result can be expected.

If only six weeks are available, the proper procedure is not to omit the work of the seventh and eighth weeks, but to condense as far as possible the work of the first two weeks, and of the fourth, fifth, and sixth, as here given.

It will be seen that this schedule requires very few of the actors to attend more than two full evenings a week until the last week, but still gives them opportunity to come out for short additional periods now and then to rehearse special scenes or to join in consultations. The director, of course, must work every evening.

Some groups of experienced amateurs or semiprofessionals would, of course, regard an eight-week schedule as absurdly long and exacting. Sufficient, they think, to have genius, experience, ability to commit lines—and four or five rehearsals. The players of the Polish Laboratory Theatre, on the other hand, would regard it as inadequate and would prefer to labor over the play for up to two years. Doubtless there will always be these two extremes of opinion, with corresponding results.

the first reading

Many directors like to begin rehearsals with a reading of the play. Whether this is necessary or not depends upon circumstances.

If books are not available and the actors must learn their parts from *sides,* a reading is almost essential as a means of telling them what the play is about. It should not be conducted as a rehearsal; there should be no blocking out of the stage positions and no reading of parts by the actors. Instead, the reading should be done by some person who can read well and who is already familiar with the play—the author himself, if possible. Interruptions should be permitted only for necessary questions on the meaning, but at the end of the reading there should be a little time for informal discussion.

When printed books are available, they should be distributed several days before the first meeting of the cast, and each player should be instructed to read and analyze the play for himself, and to make note of any points he may care to have discussed. Some actors – even experienced professionals – have to be driven to do this, and some cannot be driven. There are actors who prefer not to know what the play is about, being interested only in their own parts. They are nuisances. The only really satisfactory actor is the one who wants to understand the play thoroughly in order that he may become a part of the whole rather than an exploiter of his own powers. The strongest argument for the use of printed books is that they emphasize the play rather than the parts, and so encourage the group attitude.

Whether a formal reading is necessary when the actors are supplied with books depends largely upon the nature of the play itself. If it is subtle or obscure in meaning, a reading may be advisable, particularly if the author can be present and can do the reading; the actors are bound to learn from him a little more about his meaning and intention than appears in the text. But if time is very short and the author not available, it is seldom wise to use up a whole evening in mere reading.

the first rehearsal

After the actors have read the play or had it read to them, the next step is the blocking-out process. If the director has done most of his planning in advance, this process will be greatly simplified. If not, it will consist largely of a trial and error method of working out positions, movement, and business, with many halts for head scratching, many false starts, and many corrections, and with everybody more or less at sea.

If the action has been carefully planned, the director will open the first rehearsal by explaining the arrangement of exits and entrances in the first scene, the positions of the furniture, and the terminology to be used in giving directions. Some directors like the actors to *walk through* their parts on the first rehearsal to fix the locations in their minds; others prefer to have them remain seated and take careful notes. Some like to show a chart of the stage and indicate the positions of the characters at each point in the text with movable push pins. If there is plenty of time and the actors are earnest, this plan is helpful; otherwise it does not work. In most cases, perhaps, the walking method is the best. But whether the actors walk through or remain seated, they should be instructed to take notes freely and, especially, to mark on their parts every position, movement, and action. It is surprising how many actors will not think of taking notes unless told to do so. The director should insist upon the importance of getting everything right in the first few rehearsals, and of learning the positions and actions with the lines.

If the actors are to walk through their parts, the furniture should be placed as accurately as possible, and the entrances indicated by extra chairs or by chalk lines on the floor. Hand properties are not needed at this stage, and would seriously interfere with the note taking; but anything that may help to establish spaces and distances should be included. The actors should read their own parts, moving to position as directed, and the director should interrupt freely to give instructions and should allow time for the actors to enter them in their notes. Continuity is no object at this stage; care and thoroughness in the preliminaries take time, but they mean smoother and better work later on. When the first rehearsal is held in the evening and the actors have been otherwise employed all day, it is best to block out only one act; some directors do this anyway, going over the act two or three times to make sure that the directions are properly understood. When the interval before the second rehearsal is to be long, this is undoubtedly the best plan.

The director should permit free discussion at the first rehearsal, and should welcome criticisms or suggestions from the actors if given in good faith and good humor. He should try especially to discover whether any of his directions conflict with the actor's understanding of his part, and to thrash out all such difficulties at the very start. However, when a knotty point arises involving only one or two actors, it is usually best not to delay the rehearsal too long, but to pass over the point, make a note of it, and call a special consultation of the persons concerned to meet, if possible, before the next regular rehearsal.

It should be understood that the chief purpose of the blocking-out rehearsals is to give the actors something clear and correct to study; whatever is not ready for study should be postponed until it can be made ready.

rehearsing the love scenes

The love scenes—and any other especially difficult or embarrassing scenes —are best worked out separately before being rehearsed in the presence of the whole cast. Inexperienced players are naturally self-conscious in the love scenes and afraid of being laughed at. They should be cautioned from the first that the surest way to get themselves laughed at is to look as if they expected it, and that the best way to avoid it is to act their parts boldly, sincerely, and convincingly. But they cannot be expected to do the latter before an audience until they know their parts well and are sure of every posture and movement; hence, the need for the separate rehearsal, and the sooner the better, for postponing work on scenes of this kind makes them harder and harder to do.

The tendency of amateur actors in a love scene is to keep too far apart and to be too stiff and rigid in posture; to be physically tense rather than imaginatively intense. Often they will attempt to embrace with their arms and shoulders while their feet are separated by a good eighteen inches; and instead of gazing fondly into each other's eyes—as it is said real lovers do— they stare vaguely at each other's hands, or coat collars, or at the walls or ceiling. The effect, of course, is ludicrous. The director must attack these and similar faults at the first rehearsal, and if necessary prescribe the exact posture for every minute of the scene. If the actors have had some experience and are known to be reliable, he may insist upon their looking into each other's eyes for a part of the time. This is a bit embarrassing, and can be done effectively only if well rehearsed, but properly done, it often marks the difference between a painfully amateurish love scene and one having professional finish. If the actors are too inexperienced or self-conscious to succeed with it, the attempt should be abandoned early and a more conventional plan substituted. The girl may rest her forehead against the man's breast, for example, while he looks down at her hair or off into the distant future. Such a device is less effective empathically than the direct gaze, but is reasonably convincing and more certain. A conventional posture of this sort should not be held too long.

Audiences seem especially sensitive to the element of beauty in a love scene, and it becomes necessary, therefore, for the director to give particular attention to the pictorial effect. The postures should be chosen not only for appropriateness and convincingness, but also for line, mass, and color. An awkward or ungainly posture or a clashing color scheme will just about ruin an otherwise beautiful love scene.

For the very reason that the love scene is usually the weak point of an amateur production, a well-played love scene will do much to make the whole production less amateurish. It will pay, therefore, to take pains with such scenes in the early rehearsals.

the first review

Ordinarily the first rough blocking out will extend to the second and third rehearsals, but a portion of the time at each rehearsal after the first week should be devoted to following up or reviewing what has already been blocked out. Otherwise it will grow cold. The director should be cautioned, however, against giving so much time to the first act in review that the other acts never get proper attention. This is one of the commonest faults in amateur production.

The chief purpose of the first review is to afford a check on the actors after they have had a chance to do a little studying. Ordinarily they should not be required to be letter perfect at this stage; they should be studying to understand their parts and especially to fit themselves into the teamwork, and not primarily to commit the lines.

It is in the first review rehearsals that tangles and misunderstandings are to be straightened out, questions answered, suggestions received, and broad problems of interpretation discussed. Details and fine shades of interpretation should be postponed, for the most part, until later, but essential questions of meaning should be settled and the major points of emphasis established. At this stage it is particularly important to remember the fundamental principles of good design: fidelity to the main thought and fidelity to the limitations of material. Irrelevancies should be suppressed, and the central idea of the play emphasized over subordinate ideas; and the slightest attempt to transcend the limitations of material should be restrained. The limitations in this connection would include those of space, setting, lighting, equipment, and ability; and the director should restrain his own tendency to attempt the impossible, as well as that of the actors. It will develop, perhaps, that some of the actors cannot do certain things assigned to them, and the director may have to modify his plans here and there to keep within their abilities. To know what changes must be made without making unnecessary ones is not so easy.

Useless or meaningless movements should be restrained in the early rehearsals before they get a chance to become habitual, and the actors should be cautioned against fidgeting. They should be instructed to make their movements simple, broad, and decisive so far as these qualities may be consistent with the meaning. When there is much fidgeting, the director should try to ascertain the cause. Sometimes he will find that the action he has planned does not articulate effectively with the lines, or does not allow a sufficient outlet for the expressive impulses of the actors. In the latter case, as in the case of fidgeting, it is futile to attempt repression; the only solution is to devise new and more significant movements or business through which the restless impulses may be discharged. Sometimes the director will find that the movements he has called for do not fit the stage spaces, and that the fidgeting is due to that fact. A very common instance of this occurs when an actor has been told to perform a certain movement on a certain line, and the line proves too long for the movement, so that the actor arrives at his destination too soon, or else slows down the movement until it becomes painfully hesitant and unconvincing. The smaller the stage, the greater this difficulty; an actor having to enter on a line finds himself halfway across the stage before the line is finished, stops suddenly, fidgets, and perhaps backs up a little and comes at it again. Another common fault is for those already on the stage to crowd the entrances, so that the new-comer has no chance to come fairly on. The director should take special pains in his planning and in the early rehearsals to clear the way for each entering character, and to see that the center of action at the moment is far enough away from the entrance to give the actor an adequate excuse for coming well into view. It can hardly be repeated too often that meaningless and irrelevant movements are the bane of amateur theatricals, and that they should be stamped out as far as possible the moment they become evident.

After the first round of review rehearsals, another effort should be made to check all doubtful matters and conclude all necessary experiments. A stage rehearsal at this point, if it can be arranged, is very helpful for trying out voices, movements, stage pictures, and the like. If possible the actual furniture and other properties should be used; chairs and sofas should be checked for height, width, and depth; the actors should try sitting down on them and getting up; chairs that are to be moved should be moved to see if they are light enough; hand props should be tried out to see if they can be managed; even costumes and makeup should be tried out if important or difficult effects are to depend upon them in any way—although it is not essential, of course, that all these things be done at the same rehearsal.

In short, it should be the object of the director in the first half-dozen rehearsals to make sure, first, that nothing is being learned wrong, and second, that no actor is left in doubt or uncertainty as to what he is to learn, especially in respect to the teamwork. The next step is the consideration of the meaning and interpretation of the play in detail.

rehearsing for meaning

Professional actors frequently jump to conclusions about the interpretation much too early, especially when they work from sides instead of books. From the sides each actor studies only his own part, and being eager to make the most of it he begins to feel for the mood of the part before he is at all sure of the mood of the play; and he begins to read meanings into his lines that may or may not have been intended by the author. Experienced amateurs occasionally display the same trait, and the director must be on his guard against it.

For the most part, however, the problem in amateur production is to get the actors to pay sufficient attention to the meaning early enough in the process, and to assimilate the meaning well enough for reasonable freedom of interpretation. Beginners are apt to feel a bit dazed at the first two or three rehearsals. Groping vaguely for their positions on the stage and striving to remember the instructions given them, they are in no mental condition to appreciate the fine shades of meaning. Even actors of some experience feel the confusion and uncertainty, and it is not uncommon to find them at the fourth or fifth rehearsal still speaking their lines with a dismal lack of understanding.

Before any errors of interpretation can become fixed, the director should begin an intensive study of meaning, quizzing and challenging the actors repeatedly at all doubtful points. When a line does not come easily he may ask the actor to explain it in his own words, or to substitute his own words, temporarily. Or he may ask specific and troublesome questions about the line: Is it a serious line? Is it humorous? Is it satirical? Has it a double meaning? Is it charged with emotion? If so, which emotion? Is it an essential line for the audience to get? Is it a laugh line? Does it call for an answer? If so, in what mood is the answer to be awaited? Is the wording especially typical of the character? If so, in what way? If the line is a long one, how can it be broken up? What changes of tempo can be used? What bits of business? How, in general, can the meaning be enriched without strain or false emphasis?

Every now and then a line that is completely baffling to the actor turns up; he seems utterly unable to grasp the meaning or to express it by his reading. In such cases the director faces a difficult question: Assuming that he understands the line himself, should he give the actor the correct reading and seek to have him imitate it? This is the question discussed at some length in the preceding chapter, and the answer would seem to be that the director should do all in his power to suggest the real meaning of the line to the actor, whether by demonstration or by discussion, but should rigidly check any tendency on the part of the actor to rely upon a mere echo of the director's reading. Now and then an actor will be found who cannot, or will not, learn in any other way; the best remedy in such cases is probably homicide, though if no understudy is available, it may be unwise to apply it until after the performance.

To illuminate a line for the actor's better comprehension, the director must sometimes resort to the device of *bridging* – that is, interpolating an explanatory passage in such a way that the meaning of the original line will become clear. The following examples illustrate how this may be done, and also show how many different meanings may be drawn from an apparently commonplace line:

1. We must not forget.

   We must not forget (though others may).
   (To forget would be suicidal;) we *must* not forget.
   (They count on our forgetting, but) we must *not* forget.
   (We may forgive, but) we must not *forget*.

2. How many?

   (I know you want some, but) *how many*?
   (There are many, of course, but) *how* many?
   (What's that you say?) *How* many?

3. I don't know how.

   (Why ask me?) *I* don't know how.
   (You say you know how, but) I *don't* know how.
   I don't *know* how (but I can learn).

   (I'd do it if I could, but) I don't know *how*.

It is, as a matter of fact, the apparently commonplace line that causes most of the trouble. The unusual line challenges attention and dictates its own inflections, whereas the commonplace line, which has several possible meanings, is as likely to get the wrong inflection as the right, and so to convey a wrong meaning or no meaning at all.

When bridging is used, the actor sometimes catches the meaning immediately, gives the line its proper inflection, and has no further trouble. More often, he must repeat the bridging with the line – either mentally or aloud – at a half-dozen rehearsals before it begins to sink in. In the latter case the device is of questionable value, especially if the actor shows a tendency to revert as soon as he drops the interpolated line, or to have difficulty in dropping it. On the whole it is best to avoid too much mechanism in rehearsal, and if bridging fails to bring almost instantaneous results, it is better to abandon it and try something else. In any case the director should make sure that all interpolated phrases not to be retained as part of the text are dropped out before the polishing rehearsals begin.

In all study of meaning the director should bear in mind the construction and theme of the play as a whole, and should guard against the actor's tendency to interpret individual lines irrelevantly. Very early in rehearsals he should begin to emphasize the varying moods of the different acts, and to point out that a line correctly interpreted one way in Act One might bear a very different interpretation in Act Three. This is a difficulty that amateurs find very hard to master; the constant rotation of acts in rehearsal confuses them, and they cannot remember what the characters they represent are supposed to know, or not to know, at each point in the action. Accurate study of the meaning and mood of each line in a play calls for an alertness of mind and an unceasing vigilance scarcely comprehensible to those who have not tried it.

memorization

At what point in the preparation of a play should memorization begin, and at what point should the director require his actors to be *letter perfect*?

To answer these questions properly, one must first understand that there are two distinct methods of memorization, and that the answer is not the same for both. By one method the act of memorizing is made a purely mechanical process having no relation to the study of meaning; the two things are, so to speak, carried on independently by two separate portions of the mind. By the other method, the words, actions, and meanings are memorized coordinately, and all associations are built up from the start.

The first method is employed by a great many professionals as a matter of choice, and is almost essential in stock-company work when a new play must be learned every week with only three or four rehearsals. It has one important advantage: The memorizing may be done early and quickly—

even before the first rehearsal—and the actor need not be hampered at rehearsal by the necessity of carrying a book and reading his part. But to use the method successfully the actor must be able to separate the memorization from the interpretation, and to refrain from forming any impressions during the memorization that he may have to unlearn later. No actor can do this without some experience, and many can never learn to do it. Moreover, those who succeed in memorizing mechanically are not always able to throw off the mechanical effect when they come to interpret. On the whole, the method is to be recommended only when circumstances necessitate a very hasty production, or when the actors happen to be fitted for it by temperament and experience.

The second is the better one for those who have time to learn a play slowly and thoroughly, and is the only one suitable for beginners. By it the interpretation precedes the memorization, and lines, business, and meaning are memorized together. The advantages lie in the fact that nothing is learned incorrectly or mechanically and that the elements of acting are coordinated from the start. The disadvantage lies in the impediment put upon the early rehearsals by the actors' dependence upon their books and the consequent delay in reaching the polishing stage. By this method it is obvious that memorization cannot even begin until the meaning and the action are understood.

To answer our questions, then, we may say that when the mechanical method is used, the memorization should begin with the distribution of parts, and that the actors should be letter perfect at the second or third rehearsal; but when the associative method is used, they should not begin to memorize until absolutely sure of meaning, movement, and business. They should be letter perfect as soon after that as possible.

Some actors have a good deal of trouble with memorization, and some make themselves a nuisance by pretending to know their parts before they do know them, thereby overworking the prompter and disrupting the rehearsals. Often, of course, the failure to memorize is traceable to mere laziness or procrastination, or to a lack of will power; but when an actor who really tries hard is unable to memorize, it is commonly because of a tendency to straddle between the two methods. Seeking to memorize the words, he allows himself to be distracted and delayed by considerations of meaning; or seeking to study the meaning he tries too hard to memorize at the same time, and the memory process interferes with the thinking process. It is better to do one thing or the other. If the mechanical method is to be used, he should rigorously shut out of his mind all thought of the meaning, all play of imagination, establishing visual or auditory images rather than ideas. Sides are better than books for this kind of study, which is why the old stock-trained professionals so often prefer them. But if the associative method is to be used, the actor should not hurry or force the process. He should get at the memorization through the understanding, assimilating the meaning and action so well as to remember them subconsciously and involuntarily. The mechanical method may be practiced in an armchair, or the actor may pace aimlessly up and down as he commits the lines; but the associative method is best practiced in actual rehearsal, and even when studying at home, the actor should speak the lines aloud with the proper expression and should move about as on the stage, rehearsing the actions with the lines. When lack of privacy makes this procedure impossible, he should try to do it in imagination.

In memorization, more than in any other phase of play production, the youngsters have the advantage. It is the older, and especially the elderly, men and women who find it hard to remember their lines and who forget them in actual performance—although with professionals the facility born of experience often compensates for the difficulties arising from increasing age. It seems especially hard for elderly amateurs to coordinate lines and movement and to remember them together, and the director must often devote hours of extra rehearsal to drilling such actors. It is usually best to rehearse them by short scenes, going over and over each scene until the coordination becomes subconscious. The greatest difficulty is ordinarily met with when the intervals between rehearsal are long, and when the actors in question have only occasional speeches as part of the ensemble. The poise of these older actors is often valuable to an amateur company, but to get the best out of them without making everybody else nervous at their uncertainty requires patience and skill on the part of the director.

All actors have more or less trouble with the memorization of parallel passages or passages having similar associations. For example, if Smith and Jones converse about Brown in Act One, with Smith standing at stage

R. and Jones sitting at stage L., and then converse in much the same way in Act Three, a single wrong line in Act One may start them off on the scene that belongs in Act Three. Many of the serious disasters in amateur performances result from such transposition of lines. The director should guard against this, first by arranging different movements and positions for parallel passages (except when symbolism requires similar movements and positions), and later by checking up such passages to see that the actors are keeping them straight. When the actors show any tendency to transpose lines, he should point out to them the differences rather than the similarities, and should try to establish contrasting associations in their minds as mnemonic aids. A little ingenuity will solve the problem if applied in time.

No single recipe or formula for successful memorization can be laid down, and actors of different temperaments will swear by different methods. But one general principle is always sound, and that is the principle of *kinesthetic coordination* — coordination in the sensations of activity involved in expression. The actor who acts all over remembers his lines more surely and with less conscious effort than the one who memorizes a page of print and then reads it off from a visual image alone. As indicated in an earlier chapter, he is also more convincing.

It is an unfortunate fact that most amateur productions never get any real polishing. The chief reason for this is that the learning process has a way of drawing itself out indefinitely; the play never seems quite ready for polishing, and the director postpones the latter until it is too late. There is only one way to overcome the difficulty, and that is to announce certain rehearsals as polishing rehearsals, and to carry them out as such no matter how many details of study and experiment have to be left unfinished.

A professional producer planning a New York opening often relies upon public performances out of town or *preview performances* in the city to do the necessary polishing for him, and there can be no doubt that actual performance before an audience brings, by compulsion, a kind of polish that cannot be attained in any other way. When a play opens with two performances in Wilmington or New Haven, plays another week in Baltimore, and two weeks in Philadelphia before going to Broadway, the so-called first-nighters can expect to see a fairly smooth performance. But as amateurs seldom give more than three or four performances of a play altogether, they cannot very well depend upon this sort of polishing. As a rule they must expect to be judged upon the merits of the very first performance — sometimes the only one. Any polishing that is to be done under these circumstances must be done in rehearsal.

The presence of an interested *gallery* at the polishing rehearsals is a fairly good substitute when trial performances are impossible. An invited audience at the final rehearsal is nearly always advisable. The designation of certain rehearsals as *speed rehearsals* or *continuity rehearsals* serves to concentrate energy upon the polishing, and the elimination of unnecessary interruptions and unnecessary prompting helps to keep the emphasis. Sometimes it is a good plan to banish the prompter altogether after a certain point in the rehearsal schedule. If the actors are aware from the first that they must rely entirely upon themselves, they will learn their lines faster and more carefully. Should an actor "blow" his lines, a thinking cast can recover the scene and pull the stumbler back in with little, if any, disruption of the play. Working without a prompter will keep the actors on their toes, and any device that will exert upon the actors some of the pressure of a public performance is likely to be an aid in polishing.

speeding the dialogue

One of the chief problems in polishing is the problem of speed. Amateur performances nearly always drag. The actual dialogue moves too slowly and the chief causes are inadequate memorization and tardiness in taking up cues.

Inadequate memorization may be a matter of incorrect method, as discussed in the last chapter, or of inability to articulate lines and business, or of pure neglect. The fact that amateurs really can memorize if they are put to it is well demonstrated whenever there happens to be a keen competition under the tryout system. But with the best of intentions many amateurs totally underestimate the degree of memorization required for freedom in acting. They suppose it sufficient to be able to recite the lines at home without marked hesitation or serious error. Experienced actors know that the real study just about begins at this point; and the less experience an actor has, the better he must know his lines to achieve an equal degree of freedom. Sometimes the best thing a director can do to make the polishing process effective is to scare, shame, or cajole the actors into studying their parts all over again.

Nearly all amateurs are slow about taking up their cues. First Brown speaks his line, pronounces the cue, and waits. There is a perceptible pause. Then Smith wakes up and answers. In real life we do not waste time in this way; we pause only when there is some uncertainty about the answer, or some need for special emphasis, or when action intervenes. In the ordinary run of real conversation we make our answers promptly, often slightly anticipating each other's conclusions, and sometimes frankly interrupting in our eagerness to get ahead with the thought. Stage dialogue should proceed in the same way; if anything, it should move more rapidly than in real life, since art is selective and does not attempt to represent all the clumsiness and accident and friction of reality.

Perhaps the chief reason why amateurs are slow about taking up cues — aside from insufficient study — is their tendency to literalness. The book gives a certain word or phrase as the cue, therefore the actor waits until he has heard the word or phrase before beginning his line. And since it takes him a perceptible fraction of a second to hear and recognize the cue and to respond—even when he knows his lines well—there is a hiatus in the dialogue, not very marked in itself, but serious enough when it is repeated several hundred times in one play.

An experienced actor, or an actor properly directed, overcomes this tendency by a slight overlapping of line and cue. Instead of waiting for the last word of the preceding speech, he takes as his cue the second or third word from the end, and so begins to speak almost at the instant his colleague ceases speaking—perhaps even a fraction of a second before. As a general rule this produces the effect of a smooth and continuous conversation. Of course it may be overdone, and snappy professionals sometimes reel off their dialogue with so much rapidity and so much overlapping as to make the whole performance mechanical and unconvincing. Moderation is the best rule; but moderation for most amateurs means more, not less speed.

The extent to which overlapping is permissible with any given line depends upon the meaning. When the meaning of the line is not complete until the last word is uttered, the actor who is to reply should wait for that word; but when the meaning becomes clear some time before the last word, he may safely anticipate a little and begin his line. Even in such cases, too much or too frequent overlapping suggests impatience and impoliteness on the part of the character, and should be avoided unless these qualities are to be portrayed. The actor should consider carefully the mood of the character and his relation to the other characters. A character in a thoughtful or absent mood will be slower in response than a wide-awake, eager, or impatient character, or one who is in a hurry to end the conversation or turn it into another channel. A polite or deferential character will make prompt replies, but will not anticipate or interrupt. A master may interrupt a servant, but a servant may not interrupt his master without suggesting impertinence; all differences in age, social position, or official responsibility call for similar variations.

broken lines

A very marked interruption is usually indicated by the dramatist with the aid of a broken line and a dash. The broken line, however, sometimes makes trouble for the amateur actor, and occasions a special type of delay. When Brown's line is broken and Smith is supposed to interrupt him, Brown stops abruptly at the dash and waits for the interruption that he too evidently knows – or hopes – is coming; Smith, on the other hand, waits until he hears Brown stop, and then opens his mouth to speak. Brown, of course, should be taught to speak as if he had every expectation of finishing the sentence – should in fact be taught to finish it unfalteringly in the event of Smith's failure to interrupt; while Smith should be taught to take his cue a word or two earlier and get started in time to interrupt at the exact point indicated by the dramatist. Even when the interruption takes place on schedule, Brown should be taught to think through the rest of his line, or at least a few words of it – a nice little point in acting that some professionals neglect. Broken lines cause no end of trouble and do much to make amateur acting unconvincing and, for that reason, they should be timed and rehearsed most carefully.

Another source of delay is to be found in the entrance and exit cues. Here again it is the tendency to literalness that causes most of the trouble. When Brown and Smith are talking and Jones is to join them, the dramatist usually finishes a speech by Smith or Brown and then writes, "Enter Jones." The literal-minded actor waits in the wings until he hears the last word of the cue speech and then starts on; but as it takes him a few seconds to cover the intervening fifteen or twenty feet, Smith and Brown have to stand around doing nothing until Jones arrives. The actor should determine by study the exact point in the dialogue at which he is to arrive at a certain spot on the stage and then take a cue sufficiently in advance of that to get him there in time. Amateurs rehearsing in parlors and living rooms are apt to forget the greater distances of the real stage, and especially the three or four steps that they must usually take offstage before coming into full view of the audience. All exits and entrances should be carefully timed by the director at the first stage rehearsal – which should be held as early as possible for this if for no other reason – and then carefully rechecked in the polishing rehearsals. In most instances they will need constant speeding up. Poorly timed entrances and exits will make an otherwise good performance seem very crude and unfinished.

cadence

Inexperienced actors should be cautioned frequently against depending for the timing upon the inspiration of the moment—even when they know their lines perfectly. Once the correct timing is determined for a given line it should be rehearsed again and again so that the actor will remember not only the words and meaning but the rhythm and cadence as well. Perfect cadence teaches a platoon of soldiers to respond automatically to orders, and helps a motorist to change gears or apply the brakes instinctively and accurately, even in an emergency. In the same way it helps the actor to remember his line through bodily coordination rather than through mental effort; it helps, in other words, to educate the motor responses and insure the actor against the effects of excitement. The conscious mind is too variable and too easily distracted to be entirely trustworthy, but the motor responses, properly trained, can be depended upon. Helpful though this use of cadence is, the actor must be careful that it does not lead to recitation. Complete control by the thinking, imaginative actor is always necessary when creating the *illusion of the first time.*

It is a good plan to memorize each cue as if it were part of the line, running the two together mentally until the cadence is established. Lines that have a strong natural cadence are more readily memorized and retained and less apt to get out of timing. Actors generally take up their cues more promptly in verse than in prose, for if the poet has been sufficiently skillful, the meter itself suggests the proper timing.

easing the dialogue

After the dialogue has been speeded up sufficiently, it is still apt to remain artificial and unconvincing. Amateurs are inclined to deliver their lines as if they were reading instead of speaking; there is no illusion because there is no conversational quality.

The conversational quality is hard to define, yet it is one of the most essential elements in good acting. It does not necessarily include naturalism or conversational style. A natural or commonplace style would just about ruin a poetic or symbolic play; the characters of classic drama are not everyday persons and their speech is a matter of poetic convention rather than reality. Yet even in poetic plays, the characters who address each other must seem to be *speaking,* rather than reading or reciting. The most heroic language can be made to sound convincing if the actors are able to speak it with directness and imagination.

A good conversational quality includes, of course, such physical matters as variation of tempo, promptness in taking up cues, articulation of speech with action and gesture, significant use of pauses, live facial expression, and active vocal tone. But the essential element is imagination.

The actor must have imagination in order to realize the feelings of the character he portrays, to grasp the implications of plot and situation, and to feel a sense of communication with the other characters. Moreover it must be the right sort of imagination. A good reader may have imagination and yet be unmistakably a reader rather than an actor. The reader's imagination is, in a sense, detached and objective. He preserves his aesthetic distance as one of the audience and is not part of the play. The actor is part of the play, and his imagination must be of the subjective kind, enabling him to believe in himself as a character in the play and to address the other characters as if he were speaking, not at, but to them.

How to stimulate the imagination is not so easily told. Questioning helps, especially when the characters are questioned about their thoughts and feelings: "Where are you going?" "What brought you here?" "What room did you come from?" "Which act is this?" "Has such-and-such an event happened yet?" "Have we passed the climax?" "Are you pleased about it? Annoyed? Alarmed? Puzzled? Surprised? Indignant?" Addressing the actors as *characters* rather than as actors also helps the imagination. Costume and makeup rehearsals help—or better, full-dress rehearsals with scenery, lights, and properties. But something depends also upon the will powers of the actors and no director can provide them with imagination if they lack the will to imagine.

The greatest difficulty in easing the dialogue appears, logically enough, in those passages that are inherently least natural. It is not hard to get natural delivery of colloquial dialogue, full of current slang and common-place informality. But the moment an actor is required to deliver an extra long speech, or one that is a bit literary in flavor—not to mention one that is stilted, or heroic, or poetic—the trouble begins. Anybody can speak a colloquial phrase in a colloquial way, and anybody can speak a stilted passage in a stilted way. But to speak a heroic or poetic passage with heroic or poetic effect and yet with naturalness and conviction is not so easy; and to speak a really stilted passage in such a way as to conceal the stiltedness and make the speech seem dignified and natural calls for positive genius—and much hard work!

opening out the long speeches

A good director can ease the dialogue for inexperienced actors considerably if he can help them to open out their long speeches, to vary the tempo, and to articulate lines and business.

To open out a long speech it is usually necessary to devise additional business, or at least to suggest some changes of gesture or facial expression; otherwise the pauses will seem artificial and meaningless. Variations of tempo within the sentence do much to break up a speech that is too long, and variations of tempo throughout a stretch of dialogue do much to ease the whole. The variations, however, should not be arbitrary; they should be in keeping with the meaning. Variations of pitch and force are occasionally necessary, but are of less general use than one might suppose. There is plenty of pitch variation in the very reading inflections we are trying to escape, and in the affected or elocutionary style of delivery—so much so that a positively monotonous delivery is sometimes a relief by contrast. Extreme variations of force, on the other hand, are open to the objection that they tax the ear of the listener and make it difficult for him to hear without strain. Variations of tempo, and of timbre, or quality, are better.

Another matter that sometimes requires attention is the laugh or cry that sounds strained and artificial. If the book says, "Ha, ha!" the actor thinks he has to say "Ha, ha!"—which for him may not be a natural way of laughing at all. Such words are merely a convention by which the dramatist indicates that the character is to laugh, and the director should see to it that the laugh is made natural and convincing in whatever way is best adapted to the capability of the actor and the needs of the characterization. Sometimes that will mean an attitude, a facial expression, or a bit of business instead of a loud laugh, or in addition to it. It is usually best to keep the laughter and the weeping well within the bounds of moderation; amateurs have a tendency to overdo both.

The problem of easing the dialogue calls for some rather heroic and intensive work, even in the last stages of rehearsal. In the case of particularly refractory passages it may be necessary to resort to bridging or paraphrasing of some sort, or to actual modifications of text. General rehearsals should not be too frequently interrupted for this sort of work; the result would be confusion rather than polish. Yet care must be taken to avoid making an actor "gun shy" of a particular word or phrase, a laugh, or a bit of business. When the problem is noted it should be considered and carefully dealt with as soon as possible in special rehearsals or private conferences. If it is simply noted several times without solution, the actor thinks it is something he is incapable of doing correctly. As many problems as possible should be worked out in the earlier rehearsals, but often the difficulties do not become apparent until polishing has begun.

pointing up

In spite of careful planning it will often be found that certain portions of the play fail to work up properly and seem, in the later rehearsals, to lack point. Significant lines are delivered too casually and escape notice; lines that should be theatrically effective seem to fall flat and humorous lines fail to get laughs. It is always difficult to know how much of this is due to the lack of a proper audience and will correct itself in performance; laugh lines, especially, often fail to amuse the director and the cast but succeed very well with the first audience. The presence of a few strangers at each rehearsal makes it easier to determine which lines need pointing up.

In general, lines that are highly dramatic or theatrical in effect, or that convey strong passion or emotion, are likely to come up very well in the mounting excitement of actual performance; while smart lines, farcical lines, and broad character lines — especially in dialect — are likely to need toning down. Lines that are subtle but significant, lines that *plant* ideas necessary to the plot, satirical lines, and high-comedy lines are the ones most likely to need pointing up. Lines that are to convey repressed emotion sometimes require a combined treatment — a somewhat excessive pointing up, followed by a careful toning down.

The method to be used in pointing up will vary according to the nature of the fault to be overcome. When a line is delivered too casually, it is sometimes because the actor himself has failed to realize its significance and the remedy may lie in pointing it out to him. When a line that ought to convey a great thought or feeling fails to strike fire, it may be the actor's imagination that is at fault; or it may be the teamwork, or the director's own work in planning movement or business for emphasis. The distribution of emphasis is supposed to be taken care of in the planning and the early rehearsals, and when it needs attention in the polishing stage, it is because something has gone wrong. The problem is to find out what, and how, and to correct it.

It is important to remember that the pointing up of a line does not always rest solely with the actor who delivers it. No matter how well a line is spoken, it may fall flat if the listening actors do not play up. It is always harder for amateurs to listen effectively than to speak effectively, harder to keep still than to move about. Yet the slightest irrelevant movement at the instant an important line is spoken may ruin its effectiveness; and the slightest tendency of the listening actor to drop out of character may spoil some other actor's best line — a fact that is occasionally turned to account by a jealous actor eager to take unfair advantage of a rival.

Too much pointing up is as bad as too little and results in what is generally called *playing to the gallery*. The deliberate attempt that some actors and directors make to evoke direct applause for a line is usually not good art because it is destructive of aesthetic distance. Any attempt to get a laugh that is recognized as such by the audience tends to defeat its own purpose and even to give pain instead of pleasure. Nevertheless, some pointing up is sure to be necessary, and when the dramatist's purpose is to give pleasure through laughter, it is the director's business to see that the actors get the laughs.

getting the laughs

When a laugh line misses fire, it is usually from one of two causes: lack of appreciation on the part of the actor, or faulty technique.

Lack of appreciation in this connection does not necessarily mean stupidity; nor does it mean absence of a sense of humor. Indeed, one often finds it among the most intelligent beginners, and those with the keenest sense of humor offstage. It is the *comedy sense* that is lacking—a very different thing from the sense of humor.

The comedy sense is easily recognizable in those who have it but very hard to define. The sense of humor is subjective. The comedy sense is *projective*. To appreciate humor subjectively one must possess a sense of values and must be quick to note relations and catch implications; at the same time he must preserve an attitude of detachment. To enact comedy one must arouse empathy in others while seemingly not implicated himself. He must preserve their aesthetic distance and his own as well, but the two must be different. The comedy sense, more than any other phase of the actor's art, implies a dual psychology.

As for technique, the most important point is to avoid killing the laugh at the moment of its inception. Too often the actor spoils a good laugh by dropping the voice just as the point is reached, or by turning away, or by executing a sudden movement that distracts attention, or by failing to give the audience time to laugh. Since the most effective humor is conveyed to the audience by half-concealed means, it is necessary as a rule for the actor to be well downstage and facing front when he speaks his line in order that the audience may see his face and detect that subtle something that reveals the comic element; also that they may witness his ostensible effort to conceal his own appreciation and remain in character. Laugh lines are seldom effective when the actor turns away from the audience. When Smith is talking to Jones, if Smith faces Jones and Jones faces front, Smith's funny line will fall flat—unless the humor lies in the *effect* of that line on Jones and Jones registers clearly. When the humor is in the line itself, Smith should face front to speak it while Jones faces him. This is a good general rule though it should not be applied too sweepingly or too mechanically.

The tendency of the inexperienced actor is to drop the emphasis too quickly at the end of a line, to turn away too quickly, or even to stop acting and drop out of character. He should be taught to "follow through," as the golfer puts it—that is, to keep up the tension at the end of each line and go on acting out the thought just as vividly after the last word as before. This allows the audience to discover the humor for themselves. The actor who appears by his actions and delivery to say, "Hey, listen to this, here it comes, are you ready? This is really funny," and follows through with something that says, "Did you get it?" will lose the laugh because he took away the surprise element on which laughs depend. At the same time, audiences are usually a little uncertain whether to laugh or not, but inclined to do what is expected of them; and if the actor speaks what would seem to be a funny line but turns away casually at the end, as if he did not expect a laugh, they are quite likely to restrain themselves and perhaps to suspect themselves of having misunderstood the thought. They are eager enough to laugh if given a chance, but the actor must give them the chance.

He must also give them the time. When he hurries on to the next line, the stupid listeners will not get the point and the clever ones will choke back the laugh in order to hear the next line. Now and then it may be good policy, with a succession of funny lines, to hurry the audience a little in order to pile up a cumulative effect, but this will only work when the humorous element is in crescendo. The listeners will not enjoy holding back a hearty laugh for the sake of a more moderate one. If the pace is just right so that every point is clear, and there is just time for the listener to begin a laugh and then catch his breath for a better one, the result is sometimes worth the risk. As a general rule, however, the actor should be taught to "hold everything" after a humorous line until the laughter subsides; and should be warned at rehearsals to be ready for unexpected laughter at the public performance.

The technique of getting laughs is thus largely negative—a matter of not doing the wrong thing. There is, however, one constructive element that deserves mention, and that is the skillful use of a pause just before the main point is reached. Mark Twain's famous essay on *How to Tell a Humorous Story* emphasizes this element, and much of what he says in that essay is valuable to the actor. The pause serves to some extent as a conventional symbol labeling the laugh line as such; but its chief function is that of intensifying the suspense. It creates a little element of surprise, and at the same time lessens the chance of confusion or misunderstanding; but it must be timed correctly and there is no rule for timing it. The timing of pauses, in this and other connections, should be given careful attention in the polishing rehearsals. The foregoing comments are naturally somewhat exaggerated and oversimplified, but treated reasonably, the young actor will find these basic truths effective. Planning the procedures for getting laughs is mechanical. Executing these procedures well is an art.

rehearsing for smoothness

While attention to detail is a necessary part of the polishing, too much of it at the expense of continuity will tend to make the performance ragged rather than smooth. To guard against this it is a good plan to devote some rehearsals entirely to the cultivation of smoothness. If time permits, it may pay to run several of them as regular performances, with no interruptions and no criticisms. If time is short, much the same result may be attained by omitting the interruptions but retaining the criticisms. These may be set down in writing and distributed between acts or between rehearsals; or they may be given after the manner of sideline coaching. For this the actors must be taught to go right on playing while the director shouts occasional comments at them—a difficult matter for beginners, who are easily distracted by criticisms and likely to forget their lines and stop. When the actors have learned the trick and can stay in character while making mental notes, the director can conduct his rehearsals as an orchestra leader conducts a concert, and can do a good deal of coaching without loss of smoothness.

In rehearsals for smoothness the more general problems of emphasis, tone, mood, and tempo should be given the major consideration and individual criticisms kept to a minimum, although individual actors may occasionally be reminded of points previously discussed with them. "Watch that turn!" the director may say to an actor who usually turns the wrong way on a certain line; or, "There you go again!" or "Better that time!" The favorite remark of one successful director, always spoken in cheerful tones, is "Rotten – go on!" The actor goes on, but he remembers that spot in the next rehearsal and tries to do better. Not all of the comments given in this rapid-fire way bear fruit, but if detailed rehearsals or special rehearsals of troublesome scenes are sandwiched in between the rehearsals for smoothness, the general plan will, as a rule, be effective.

In regulating the emphasis the director should see that the main climax is sufficiently vigorous and that no subclimax is confused with it and given too much emphasis. He should caution the actors who have heavy scenes late in the play not to outdo themselves in the first act, but to hold some of their powers in reserve. He should see that the relative emphasis of the several acts is properly preserved, and that the climactic effect within each act is properly worked up.

In regulating the tempo he should see that the casual moments are not allowed to drag and that impressive moments are not unduly hurried. At the same time he should see that expository passages are played deliberately enough to be clear, and that the rushes of action approaching the climaxes are sufficiently spirited. In some instances he will be able to discern characteristic rhythms in certain scenes and to adjust the tempo in such a way as to bring these out. Secondarily he should see that the tempo is varied enough to avoid monotony.

In regulating the tone and mood he should look for two things: the characteristic mood of each scene, and any contrast of mood that may exist between different characters in the same scene. Harmonization of these two things is not always easy. There may be one melancholy character in a rollicking scene; and to bring out both moods in contrast without destroying the unity of the larger requires a nice sense of balance. Toward the end of the rehearsal period the actors are apt to become a little weary of the play, and so to lose their sensitivity to mood; and the director will find that they need constant reminding on this point. The continuity rehearsal accompanied by coaching without interruption is much more effective in regulating the mood than is intensive rehearsal with frequent interruptions.

dress and technical rehearsals

The so-called *dress rehearsal* is one of the cherished traditions of the theatre, but as ordinarily conducted, it is pretty demoralizing. The trouble is that two quite different purposes are confused, with the result that neither is fully accomplished.

Theoretically, the dress rehearsal is a complete rehearsal with full equipment, run without interruption and intended to be as nearly like an actual performance as possible. In this sense it is the final step in the process of rehearsal and is naturally scheduled for the last available date before the public performance. Unfortunately, it is also, as a rule, the first tryout of scenery, properties, costumes, and makeup, and as such is anything but a polishing rehearsal; it is an experimental rehearsal of the most rudimentary sort, and it usually goes to pieces, leaving the actors with the feeling that the play is only half learned on the day before the opening. True, the fright sometimes induces them to work a little harder in the few remaining hours, and the performance turns out better than expected; but that is no defense of a bad system.

The logical procedure is to try out the scenery, lighting, costumes, and makeup in technical rehearsals — not necessarily all at once, but in plenty of time to make adjustments. If the equipment is hard for the actors to manage in any way, it should be used at a number of rehearsals, some early, some late, so that the "dress" part of the play gets its polishing gradually along with the lines and action. When this is done, a full-dress rehearsal at the end is no longer a mere experiment and can serve its proper purpose as a polishing rehearsal. Sometimes, to be sure, this arrangement is not entirely possible. The equipment, or part of it, may not be available until late in the rehearsal period, in which case a special technical rehearsal should be held prior to the dress rehearsals to rehearse only those portions of the play that involve the use of equipment and troublesome properties. This is essential and worth the time it takes, for it gives both actors and crew a sense of confidence in each other, which is necessary to a smooth-running production. In the long run much less time will be spent by taking the time to solve the technical problems fully in such a rehearsal, and a far more professional production will result.

The stage crew should be rehearsed in handling the scenery, properties, lights, and sound before the actors are asked to rehearse with them. The technical rehearsal can then concentrate on problems such as the timing of cues, the manipulation of properties, and the specific placement of people, lights, and furniture so that everyone involved knows exactly what he must do and when he must do it, and can then rehearse it with adequate time to learn his job. All too often when a single rehearsal is used to put all the elements of production together, there is such a sense of urgency that quality is sacrificed to just "get it done," and there is no guarantee that the thing can be carried off properly under the pressures of production. Technical jobs are just as important as the acting roles and must be considered as such. An actor is not asked to perform without adequate rehearsal and a sound man or light man should not be expected to do so either. Giving the proper understanding and respect to the technical areas of theatre will not only result in better-handled productions, but a growing core of technical artists who will take pride in doing their jobs well. If technicians are sluffed off as the *scutworkers* in the amateur theatre, no one will aspire to those positions and the work will always be done badly. Well-rehearsed technical problems will produce well-executed effects, leaving the actors free to concentrate on character. The final dress rehearsal should instill a sense of confidence and well-being in everyone. This can be achieved only by proper recognition and integration of all the elements of production.

studying the audience

As already suggested, the last stage of polishing is that of actual performance, with the audience as collaborator. In this stage all sorts of unexpected things happen. Audiences are not passive but active; they contribute their own imaginations as colored by their experiences. Sometimes they show real creative power and more than one dramatist has expressed the thought that a play is not finished until it has been properly "rewritten" by the audience. Audiences occasionally insist upon an interpretation of some episode, situation, or character entirely different from the one intended by the actor.

This raises the question of whether the actor, author, and director should aim to give the people what they want, or make them take what is good for them. Is the actor properly the "servant" of the public as it is so often put? The Elizabethan actor undoubtedly so regarded himself, and his point of view has been more or less the prevailing one ever since. "We aim to please and hope you will like us," is, and in a sense has to be, the motto of professional entertainers everywhere. On the other hand, some producers take the position that the actor, or the director working through the actor, should be an independent interpretative artist, catering to no one, and letting the audience pick up the pearls or leave them as they choose.

In this, as in so many other things, the truth lies somewhere in between the two extremes. The attitude of the Elizabethan actor was inherited from the strolling players and minstrels who preceded him—mere vagabond entertainers, living on the bounty of their occasional patrons, and proud to be retained from time to time as actual servants to this or that nobleman. Worse even than the menial attitude is the purely commercial attitude that too often replaces it, and which is seen in its most vicious form today in the producer who panders to the lowest public taste and the actor who "plays to the gallery." From an artistic point of view there can be no defense of such behavior.

But to suppose that the proper alternative is a lofty disregard of the audience is to ignore the psychological fact that the most sincere creative effort is meaningless except in terms of its effect upon others. A painting is but a mixture of chemicals on canvas; its effectiveness as an object of art is in the thought or emotion it engenders in the observer. A piece of music is but a vibration of the atmosphere; its beauty is in the ear of the listener. In the same way a play is not what is written on paper or what is done on the stage but what takes place in the imagination of the audience. It is right that the actor should try to guide that imagination to the appreciation of the best, but this can be done only through a sympathetic understanding of audience response. Your audience will act for you if you first bring what you have to offer within their experience and comprehension.

The study of the audience should begin, of course, long before the first performance. The director, like the dramatist, should learn to know the tendencies of audiences in general, and which tendencies are most subject to variation. He should determine, if possible, for what type of audience he is preparing his production and what limitations he must meet. He should prepare to meet the most probable emergencies and should have his actors prepare.

what audiences like

Nearly all audiences demand surprise, suspense, action, love interest, something to root for, something to hate, something to laugh at, something to sympathize with, some satisfaction of poetic justice, and a chance to feel that they have understood the dramatist with remarkable sagacity. These things are as much the director's concern as the dramatist's, since it is the director who is responsible for the final contact with the audience.

Surprise need not always be sharp or startling, but a little of it now and then is needed to freshen interest; it may come at almost any appropriate point in the play, early or late. Suspense, however, must begin early. Unless an audience is in some way made anxious before the conclusion of the first act, the succeeding acts are pretty sure to fall flat. Action is needed to freshen interest and also to act empathically as a relief valve for the motor activities of the audience.

Love interest is of many kinds, and romantic love is not the only kind that appeals to an audience; but very seldom does a play without any love interest at all prove satisfying. In working up the love interest the director must keep constantly in mind the probable empathic responses of his audience and must not ask them to empathize in impossible situations or impossible people.

The instinct to take sides is bred into the very nature of the human animal; it is part of his pugnacious disposition. Children always want to take sides, to root for some hero, or country, or idea; and grown people, despite their restraints, crave the same right. Audiences cannot comprehend neutrality or empathize in a neutral character—which is why some indeterminate problem plays fail in popular appeal. The director, as far as the dramatist permits him to do so, should leave his audience in no doubt as to where their sympathies and loyalties belong.

The appeal of alternate laughter and tears—of what Belasco called the *emotional alternating current*—is very well known, and some dramatists and producers make a fetish of it. This *soap opera* technique seems to be more at home in movies and television than in legitimate theatre today, although such plays as *Our Town* and *Who's Afraid of Virginia Woolf* might fit the form in its best sense. Many plays in the *absurdist* tradition use this device of extremes as well, and where transitions from one to the other are usually carefully prepared for and are neither too sudden nor too obvious, the absurdist often jumps from one to the other deliberately for the shock or humor which this abrupt change causes.

As for the community of understanding between the dramatist and the audience, some producers think it the most important appeal. People like to be taken into the confidence of the author. They do not mind being fooled now and then within the rules of the game—in a mystery play, for example—but for the most part they like to feel a sort of superior intelligence in understanding what the author means without being told, and in perceiving or foreseeing what the characters do *not* perceive or foresee. This involves the matter of dual personality in acting, to be considered in the next chapter.

There are limits to all things, and the director should see that these various appeals are not all made at once in too hectic a fashion. That master showman Dion Boucicault put a great deal of wisdom in two sentences when he said to actress Clara Morris almost one hundred years ago: "Never rack your audience. Touch 'em—thrill 'em—chill 'em—but never s-t-r-a-i-n 'em."

how audiences differ

In studying the particular audience for which he is preparing a production, the director should consider its probable social, racial, and national characteristics, creed, occupation, degree of intellectuality, education, sophisti-cation, and experience in playgoing. He should consider also whether it is likely to include an unusual proportion of men, or of women, or of children; whether it is likely to be familiar with the play in advance; and whether it is likely to be critical in its attitude. Audiences differ greatly in these and many other respects.

The legitimate theatre in America has become the entertainment only for those who have money and are well educated. Television and movies, which are more readily available, cheaper, and more likely to "cater to the twelve-year-old mentality" have taken the place of the theatre for millions of people. Serious theatre people are trying every avenue to woo this potential audience by offering tickets at lower rates, curtain times that are more convenient for the working patrons, and plays which appeal to the young people of today. In New York a number of new office buildings with theatres in them have been built, and enterprising producers are trying to entice the office workers into the theatre before they leave for home.

Yet the theatre and the time may be made convenient and the ticket prices within the budget, and there may be no appreciable change in attendance patterns unless the audiences thoroughly enjoy themselves. No "great" play is going to have a value unless the audience comes to see it and likes what it sees. The audience must be met where it is in terms of understand-ing and interest. Once it has the theatre habit, then it can be led to explore other kinds of plays. The wise play selection committee or the director, if it is he who picks the play, must consider its particular audience. This is not to say that a community theatre should not do classics or controversial current plays, but a play is only effective if people see it. The artistically satisfying play that is viewed by the director and ten of his friends is far less valuable in any situation than the rah-rah musical which was viewed and enjoyed by hundreds – people who will come back, will talk about what they saw, and no doubt will bring their friends to the next play. These people would enjoy a straight comedy the next time around and would prob-ably return again, happily, to a mystery-melodrama. After such a varied diet they might well have cultivated enough of a background to enable them to enjoy an offbeat play by Albee, Pinter, or even van Itallie. A steady diet of the latter three might drive them from the theatre again, but the point is that an audience must begin with the pleasant and the familiar before it can be expected to enjoy the intellectual exercises as well. Standards and tastes must be cultivated. Theatre should be educational, but it must be this only after being entertaining, or the second purpose will never have a chance to take place. In this matter audiences are all alike.

It is dangerous to generalize about the differences between audiences: cities versus small towns, men versus women, old versus young. The audiences from the small villages along the Ohio River would often weep over the trials of the heroine in the melodramas presented on Indiana University's Showboat *Majestic,* while the people in Louisville and Cincinnati, for example, would laugh uproariously at these *tear-jerkers.* The high-school audiences invited to the final dress rehearsals at the University of Colorado theatre productions laugh and wriggle self-consciously at love scenes that college students and adults find moving. Yet students who have attended these plays for several years develop a level of reception comparable with adults. A generalization about high-school audiences would not fit this group. Put in basic terms, we would have to say that audiences must be understood and respected if their tastes are to be enlarged. One cannot simply cater to his audience, but he must be aware of it and be able to walk the path that includes what an audience wants or is used to, and what it will accept and learn to appreciate. There are many empty theatres around the country that are monuments to organizations and directors who thought that they could "give audiences what they ought to like." Their failure to understand and respect their audiences made them "artistic" successes but financial and cultural flops.

The choice of plays is not the only factor governing an audience's response. Although few audience members know what causes them to react as they do, the answers are most often found with the actor. The actors, on the other hand, have a tendency to blame audiences for not reacting properly, but, as a general rule, the audience comes to the theatre expecting a stimulating evening, and when it does not come off, it is because the actors have not done their jobs. They anticipated a laugh which, because of this anticipation, they did not get. They punched the next situation to make sure that the audience got the point; the overemphasis gave away the joke and the emphasis slowed down the delivery so that the tempo of the scene dragged a bit and there was a letdown. The audience is disappointed and gets bored and does not give back to the actor what he anticipated, and so the actor plods on to the end, complaining about the lack of response from the audience when the trouble really started with him. The director should sense what has happened; then he will often be able to set things straight by getting to a key actor before his entrance and reminding him of the way the scene was to be played originally. With the original tempo and pattern restored, the show picks up immediately as the audience responds to the proper playing. Inexperienced actors often have problems such as the one mentioned above because of their eagerness. The seasoned director must be constantly on guard to prevent whole performances from suffering because of an early shift in emphasis or tempo, and not because of a wooden audience.

notes on polishing

So many elements need attention in the polishing of a play that anything like a complete discussion of them all is out of the question. A few practical hints in condensed form may, however, be useful, and I offer them as a sort of appendix to this chapter:

1. *Study your prompt book between rehearsals.* Note the points that have been missed or neglected; many of these can be written down and handed to the actors before the next rehearsal, at a great saving of rehearsal time.

2. *Direct the polishing rehearsals from the auditorium, not from the stage.* Move farther and farther back. Try the visibility and audibility from all parts of the house, including the balcony and gallery.

3. *Check up on the physical apparatus.* This includes settings, exits and entrances, sources of light, and arrangements of furniture, as seen from all angles.

4. *Test out the stage pictures from all angles.* Squint at them.

5. *Remember the time element in stage pictures.* (See Chapter Seven.) Polish the transitions.

6. *Remember the principle of grace.* This means economy of effort. Try to eliminate unnecessary effort, or the suggestion thereof. Check grace of plan from the balcony or gallery.

7. *Eliminate any detrimental empathies.* (See Chapter Two.) Rehearse carefully all scenes in which actors carry heavy weights. Teach the actors who are carried to relax. Watch all moving of furniture and all such actions as sitting, kneeling, or rising, to see that there is no unnecessary suggestion of effort.

8. *Check to see if any movements seem stiff or mechanical.* Keep in mind the charge that directions learned in advance inhibit the actor. If any such movements do exist, find out why. If necessary, allow the actor a little more freedom, or change the movements for him. As a rule he will need the change rather than the freedom.

9. *Seek out and remove all distractions.* Watch especially the actors who are not speaking. Eliminate fidgeting. When there is too much movement or business, select and reject, but retain that which is relevant rather than that which is clever. Check up constantly on the principle: "No movement without a purpose." Challenge any new movement or business introduced by the actors and accept it only when the purpose is sound.

10. *Aim constantly to simplify.* Work for strength rather than elaboration.

11. *Watch for violations of unity.* This applies to both the play as a whole and each act and scene. Watch especially for diffusion of interest, a very common fault in amateur production. Keep the balance between unity and variety.

12. *Break up "talky" plays with action.* When the play seems talky, introduce one or two significant bits of action at critical points rather than many unimportant ones. Consider whether some of the talk can be cut.

13. *Check up again and again to see that the most essential and significant lines are reaching the audience.*

14. *At the same time suppress any overemphasis, and any misplaced accent growing out of attempted emphasis.*

15. *See that the play as a whole is coming over the footlights.* See that the actors face the audience often enough and play far enough downstage, and speak with sufficient volume.

16. *See that the actors are creating the* illusion of the first time.

17. *Combat the tendency of some actors to shorten their movements, failing to use the full stage space.* Make the performance fill the eye. But guard against restlessness; work for bold broad movements, but not too many of them.

18. *Study the aesthetic distance.* Consider it from all parts of the house. Suppress any tendency on the part of the actors to establish communication with the audience, or to step out of the picture. Check excessive realism, especially unpleasant realism. (See Chapter Three.)

19. *Watch the acting at the points of strongest emotion.* Guard against false or exaggerated emotion and against painful empathies. But remember that the emotional phase is the hardest to judge correctly before the actual performance. When the emotional acting is false or unconvincing, consider the possibility of simplification, especially by substitution of significant business. (See Chapters Two and Five.)

20. *Remember the James-Lange theory.* (See Chapter Six.)

21. *Suppress any tendency of the actors to show consciousness of the "fourth wall."*

22. *Consider the tone and mood of the acting at all times.*

23. *In a comedy see that an optimistic tone prevails.* This should be done no matter how serious the play. The tone does not have to be a happy one all the time, but it should be one that foreshadows the ultimate triumph of the protagonist.

24. *In a tragedy, plant and maintain a sense of inevitability.* See that there is a crescendo effect as the tragic forces gather. Guard against any interruption or letdown that may break the climactic force.

25. *Do not let the actor strut or pose.* Stark Young defined this as the tragic "goose step," and it applies especially in poetic and heroic plays.

26. *Nurse the rhythms.* Make the most of them, at least as far as they express the moods correctly.

27. *Try to have the actors avoid the commonplace and give a touch of distinction to their parts.*

28. *Check the tempo constantly.* Guard against the tendency of the actors to slip out of tempo, especially the tendency of each actor to take the tempo of his line from that of the actor who speaks before him.

29. *Teach the actors to* hold the picture *and stay in character when interrupted by laughter or applause; also when taking curtain calls.*

30. *Inform everybody if curtain calls are ruled out as a matter of policy.* Also, see that a statement to that effect is printed in the program.

31. *If curtain calls are to be allowed, decide what actors or groups are to take them, and in what succession.* Rehearse the curtain calls as carefully as the acts. Insist, however, upon modesty and reserve, and see that the actors remain in character. It is always painful to see a group of amateurs take curtain calls in a stagy, ostentatious manner, with elaborate bows and smirks; but it is almost equally painful to see them caught unawares by the raising of the curtain and to see them running every which way and bumping into each other like a lot of frightened sheep.

32. *Finally, study the audience at the first performance.* Note the responses, especially the unexpected ones, and prepare immediately to make any necessary changes or readjustments.

In other words, be omniscient and omnipotent; let nothing escape you and perfect every detail. Outside of that there is very little to do.

Probably everyone who has ever appeared upon the stage has formulated his own theories of acting. Perhaps the best advice one can give to the new performer is, "If it works, keep it." But what is that ambiguous "it" and what do we mean by "works"? What is it that the actor is attempting to do?

William Gillette, a star of the American stage at the turn of the century, put it best when he referred to the actor's need to create "the illusion of the first time." Every audience must be made to feel that whatever is taking place on the stage is happening at that very moment before their eyes, that the actor has just thought of the words he says. This does not mean that the audience is fooled in any way into accepting the play as real, only that the audience is willing to suspend disbelief and enter into the world the actor offers them. Whether the play is quite realistic or highly unreal, if the actors create successfully the "first time" feeling, the audience will enter in.

Lee Strasberg, long-time great method acting teacher, says, "The conditions of acting demand that you know in advance what you are going to do, while the art of acting demands that you should seem not to know."[1] Here, again, is the illusion of the first time only phrased a bit differently.

Controversy has existed for hundreds of years regarding the best method to create such an illusion. Some of the greatest actors insist that they must *feel the role*. They must get inside the character and laugh and cry with him. If he flies into a jealous rage, they must work themselves into that state in order to project the emotion to the audience. Other actors, just as great, argue that to assume the emotions of the character does not allow them the control they must maintain and exercise as actors. They feel that they must constantly be able to observe the character objectively in order to manipulate him successfully for the audience. The great French actor, Constant Coquelin, said that acting is an art with certain natural limitations and conventions to distinguish it from reality; and that for effective creative work in that art, the actor must "remain master of himself throughout the most impassioned and violent action on the part of the character which he represents; in a word, remain unmoved himself, the more surely to move others. . . ." ("L'Art et le comédien," 1880–1881). He did not say that the actor should be insensible to emotion—merely that he should neither give way to it, nor depend upon it.

Since acting is such a subjective thing, there will always be a question regarding the degree of emotionalism or the degree of objectivity that any actor maintains, no matter what he says or thinks. We can be sure that no actor playing Othello, for instance, can get so far into the part that he will actually murder Desdemona in eight performances each week. Society would frown on this even if Desdemonas were so easily replaced. At the same time, the actor who is unsuccessful in his attempts to create the appearance of deadly rage in his Othello would be just as much a failure in the role as the emotional actor above, although the consequences might not be so great. The answer, of course, lies clearly between the two. One needs his emotions in order to create, through the use of his imagination, the illusion of jealous rage, but he must be able to control himself as well.

Constantin Stanislavsky, founder of the Moscow Art Theatre, was the leader in the attempt to develop a system whereby the imagination could be used to harness properly the emotions of the actor. He used the term *emotional memory* and taught the actor to delve into his own past experiences for the necessary emotional raw materials. For example, if the actor were called upon to show grief at the loss of a loved one, he would prepare for this scene by remembering a situation in his own past when a person close to him had died. His procedure would be to sit relaxed and then to attempt to recall all the physical circumstances of the time—who was there, what people wore, the surroundings, time and temperature, how things looked and smelled. The more completely the situation could be re-created in the imagination, the more likely the actor would then begin to reexperience the emotion of the time. The actor should not attempt to remember how he felt but he should let the emotion grow out of the recreation of the experience. Several repetitions of the exercise should allow the actor to slip into the emotional set appropriate for the scene he is to play. He then proceeds to enact the scene allowing the emotion he has created to feel the acting situation. Similarly, anyone who has ever felt anger at being awakened several times by a buzzing fly and then has leaped out of bed to smash it with a single, violent stroke has experienced the kind of emotion that an imaginative actor can recreate in order to play a provoked murderer. No matter what mechanics the actor may employ in such a scene, certainly some emotional stimulus is needed to drive him through the situation.

Stanislavsky arrived at this discovery because he was unhappy with his portrayal of Dr. Stockman in Ibsen's *An Enemy of the People*. The freshness and spontaneity had gone out of the role and, as he pondered, he realized that "I copied naïveté, but I was not naïve; I moved my feet quickly, but I did not perceive an inner hurry that might cause short quick steps."

This exercise and stimulation of the mind is an essential part of the actor's art, for he must understand fully what he is attempting to create before he can develop the needed emotional attitudes. Yet this understanding and feeling are not enough, for he must then be able to arouse in his audience the desired response. Audiences will react to what they see and hear, not to what the actor feels, and so he must have a superbly trained voice and body that will allow him to project the full range of his thoughts and actions clearly. Inspiration is no substitute for hard work.

the actor's approach

What has been said so far in this chapter is of a general nature and may be perceived more as a matter of philosophy than of technique. Only when one understands and accepts a philosophy — not necessarily this one — is he ready to consider the preparation of a particular role. Just as a carpenter does not begin to build a house without plans, the actor cannot build a role without *his* plans. He must know everything about the character he is to portray, and since the character exists within a special environment created by the playwright, he must understand as much as possible about the play.

If the play is a realistic one, the playwright will tell where and when the play takes place. He will describe, as much as is necessary, the economic and social conditions that affect the characters and the action. The wise actor will use all the signposts to help him understand not only what happens but why those things happen and how. In the case of a Restoration comedy, for example, he will know or shall learn that the late 1600s in England were times of wild excesses that were condoned as the "proper" methods of behavior. He will find that the forms of dress, as well as the forms of sitting, standing, walking, taking snuff, and so forth, were carefully prescribed for all who would be considered proper gentemen or ladies, and he will study this background in order to be able to place within it the character he is to play. When this understanding is complete, the actor can begin the deeper study of his own character and its special idiosyncrasies.

character analysis

When George C. Scott prepared for his screen role as General George Patton, he read everything about World War II and the general that he could get his hands on. He talked to people who knew and worked with the general, because Scott knew, as all actors must, that a character can be understood fully only by studying the character's actions, what he says about himself and others, and finally, what others say about him. Scott's phenomenal success in the role is a tribute not only to his talent but to his method of preparation as well.

In a play that contains purely fictional characters, the actor must gain all his knowledge from the play—from what the character says and does, what others say and do to him, and what they say about him. Clues as to conditions and the time of the play will help and will flesh out the character as well.

The young actor will be wise to write a character sketch about the person he is to portray. He should ask questions that will establish clearly in his mind such things as the age, social, educational, and economic background of the character. He should determine, as nearly as possible, the character's likes and dislikes. All of these things may not be stated obviously in the script, but if not, the actor, in consultation with the director, would do well to invent the information necessary to determine everything about the character. When the actor first steps on the stage, he begins to tell his audience about himself in everything he does and says. If he is to be successful, he must first of all know what he is trying to tell them. The study of the play and of the character must be the actor's first step in the process.

Suppose, for example, we consider the character of Eliza Doolittle from George Bernard Shaw's *Pygmalion*, later to be everyone's favorite, *My Fair Lady*. What must we know about Eliza to play her opening scene? The scene is set as late at night after the opera; it is raining and a crowd of people have taken shelter under the arches of St. Paul's Church in Covent Garden. Making a last attempt to sell her flowers is a young (perhaps eighteen), ragged, dirty street peddler. When we first see her, she is calling her wares in a distressing cockney accent. She drops a bunch of violets in the muddy street and sobs. We learn later, in the rest of the play, that she is bright, ambitious, self-sufficient, has had little or no education, and knows nothing about the social graces until she is taught by Pickering and Higgins. In spite of this background, she is a "good" girl who expects to pay her way.

Perhaps all of these traits cannot show in the opening scene, but most are at least hinted at. The costumer would, of course, supply the clothes, and the property master the flowers, but the actress would have to supply Eliza. That is the next step, showing Eliza as we have decided she is.

character development

Suppose Eliza is heard before she is seen. She shuffles through this impersonal crowd of strangers who are huddled closely together to avoid the rain but attempting to ignore each other. She is careful not to bump or offend anyone, but she takes pains to offer flowers to everyone she passes and those not in her immediate vicinity can certainly hear her cries. A quick smile, a bob of the head, perhaps a half-curtsy, is her thanks to these wealthy people who buy her flowers. She stops, snuffles, wipes her nose on her sleeve absently, and accidently drops a bunch of violets into the muddy street. She scrambles to pick them up and sees that they are ruined. The tragedy of the money she will lose as a result causes her to break into the loud sobs of a little child who has broken her favorite toy. Her very public suffering is embarrassing to others, perhaps, but Eliza thinks only of her personal tragedy. Is she really so upset, or is she playing for the sympathy and perhaps a coin or two from the well-to-do people around her? This Eliza, who has grown up on the streets, knows all the tricks, and perhaps it is her guilty conscience that makes her stop crying so quickly as she asks suspiciously what Higgins is writing down in his book. She is defensive immediately and wants to avoid any trouble as she says, "I ain't done nuffink! I'm a good girl I am!" Yet she does not retreat and is aware of the consequences, and later the possibilities for her, as she hears Higgins describe his abilities. All of these things that Eliza says and does show the audience the Eliza which the actress has earlier determined. How she moves, how she wears her clothes, and her hair, how she speaks, both accent and voice quality, all will contribute to the illusion. Both the analysis and the development of the character are essential to the actor's success.

Quite obviously there have been many successful and unsuccessful Elizas—as well as Higginses—over the last fifty years. The differences between success and failure lie, most likely, not in the actors' understanding of their characters, but in their abilities to create those characters through what they do and how they speak the lines. This is where the imagination of the actor must join with his industry and intelligence if he is to be anything but mediocre. The actor's best tool is his power of observation. What is special about the way an eighteen-year-old girl walks? How will she sit if she has not been taught manners? If her voice and language are only a rudimentary means of communication, how will they differ from the voice and language of a lady who has the voice and manners cultivated by generations of gracious living? In some roles the actor or actress can simply stand on street corners and observe real people of the right ages in order to answer these questions. In many other cases it is a matter of abstracting one trait here and another there and putting them all together into a believable character. A good imagination following the hard work of observation will do wonders for any actor.

But suppose the actor knows exactly how he wishes to move and to speak, to act and react, what guarantees has he that he can perform these functions accurately and successfully? He must learn to control fully his body and his voice. The serious actor must practice body movement so that he can show old age, drunkenness, fatigue, and the like, by the postures and techniques appropriate. Just as the pianist is able to press certain keys in a rhythmic order and with a certain degree of force as he presents a composition, the actor must be able to move his limbs and muscles on cue to create his effect. It does no good for the actor to determine that to show the physical characteristics of an eighty-year-old man in poor health, for example, he must droop at the shoulders, thrust his pelvis forward, shuffle his steps, and slow down his movements, if he is unable to put these things together as a believable character. He must be able to command his own body as the pianist does his hands.

Perhaps no one man has so aptly demonstrated this as the great French mime Marcel Marceau, who can create the illusion of walking upstairs while moving in place on a flat surface. Such abilities are the result of years of observation, analysis, and practice.

The same kind of work must be spent to develop an expressive voice, of which more will be said later. The actor would do well to study the traditional rules of stage movement mentioned in Chapter Seven. Although they are not engraved in stone, the exceptions to the rules are few in standard acting situations, and the actor who has this material as a part of his physical vocabulary will be able to concentrate on important things while those movements designed to make him appear at ease and graceful will be automatic.

After all, the actor's purpose is to create something not so much on the stage as in the imaginations of his hearers. He is there to give them aesthetic pleasure, and to do so he must give them something in which they can empathize — something into which they can feel themselves imitatively — but toward which at the same time they can maintain an attitude of personal detachment. The more realistically he portrays the bodily activities of the character he represents, the more completely will the audience feel those activities imitatively in themselves, and when the activities happen to be those that give rise to emotion, the more keenly will the audience (and, incidentally, the actor) feel the emotion. It is a part of our pleasure in the theatre, as in all fiction, to share empathically the emotions of the characters, but only when the balance of emotions in the play or book as a whole is satisfying, and only when we are able to maintain our aesthetic distance. If the actor portrays unpleasant scenes too vividly, too many unpleasant emotions are aroused in us, and the experience becomes too harrowing; and if his portrayal reminds us too painfully of ourselves and our real troubles, we lose our aesthetic distance.

Physical conditions, too, may affect the aesthetic balance. Empathic responses are harder to get in a large theatre than a small one, but aesthetic distance is easier to maintain. Makeup, to the extent that it disguises the actor, helps to maintain aesthetic distance; but when it becomes painfully obvious, it weakens empathic appeal. A platform stage, which is less realistic than a proscenium stage, is less likely to destroy aesthetic distance through excessive illusion of reality; on the other hand, it may destroy it through weakness of illusion or through establishment of direct communication between actor and audience. At its best the platform stage permits the strongest possible empathic appeal, but its technique is much more difficult than that of the picture frame stage, and the aesthetic balance is more precarious. The same is true of the *arena* or *penthouse* stage. On any type of stage the lighting effects play a very important part in maintaining the aesthetic attitude. But the management of the physical conditions is not our concern here; the point is that the actor must regulate the degree and nature of his empathic appeal in accordance with the conditions.

Good acting is neither wholly realistic nor wholly unrealistic. It is sufficiently realistic to be intelligible and suggestive and to arouse the necessary empathy; it is sufficiently consistent to be convincing; and it is sufficiently unreal to preserve aesthetic distance and to leave something to the imagination. Within these limitations of principle it is capable of great variation in style, from the painstaking yet spiritual realism of the Moscow Art Theatre to the pure make-believe of the Chinese.

The illusion that the actor wishes to create will be achieved only when he understands what it is he is trying to do and has cultivated his voice and body to respond accurately to his demands. Only then is the performer really acting. A good ballet dancer makes what he is doing look so easy that every member of his audience relaxes and enjoys the effortlessness with which he dances. A good actor so conceals his art that his audience accepts whatever illusion he creates as the "first time."

notes and references

1. Toby Cole and Helen Chinoy, *Actors on Acting* (N.Y.: Crown, 1970), p. 624.

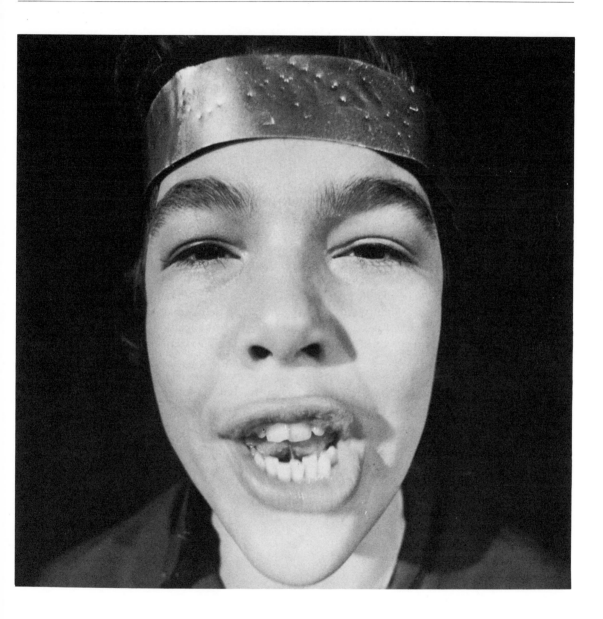

Not much can be done to improve the voice of an actor in the limited time devoted to any one production, but when the director and the group are to be together for several seasons, or even for several productions, some attention to voice and articulation is distinctly worthwhile.

The importance of voice to the actor hardly can be overstated. The great actors who have written of their art have, almost without exception, emphasized that point. "The voice is the most important of the actor's possessions," said Sarah Bernhardt. "By means of the voice the attention of the public is riveted; the voice it is which binds together actor and auditor. An actor's voice must run the whole gamut of harmonies—grave, plaintive, vibrating, metallic." Bernhardt's own voice was one of the greatest— "liquid music" people used to call it. Edwin Forrest's voice had such power and such depth of vibration that his outbursts of passion almost terrorized his audiences. Of James E. Murdoch, Professor T. C. Trueblood writes, "He had incomparably the finest voice I ever listened to. It was of wide range, powerful, a clear ringing baritone." Salvini's voice was, in the words of Bernhardt, "a whole orchestra." There have been fine voices, too, in our contemporary theatre—not so many great tragic voices, perhaps, as in the last century, but flexible, responsive voices, capable of force and variety in expression. There are fewer good voices in the American theatre since less opportunity exists for development than in the British system of training actors, yet the situation is improving. Richard Burton, Michael Redgrave, and Lawrence Olivier are examples of the kind of vocal development that is desirable.

For every good voice, however, there are many bad ones, and what with the prevalence of type casting and the lack of production of classic plays, the proportion of good voices is diminishing. The success of some stand-up comedians whose technique lies mainly in bad grammar and raucous, distorted voices may have contributed to the decline.

A good vocal equipment includes adequate volume, resistance to fatigue, good tone, good articulation, and flexibility. Practically all these qualities, and especially the first two, rest upon good breathing.

breathing

Teachers of voice disagree violently as to what constitutes correct breathing in voice production, and the problem is greatly complicated by confusion of terminology. Not all of those who advocate *abdominal breathing,* for example, mean the same thing by it. To avoid both the controversy and the confusion, I shall limit my discussion to the presentation, in nontechnical terms, of a few fundamentals about which there is little dispute.

The best authorities are generally agreed that correct breathing is natural breathing in the sense that it is free from physical constraint and conscious self-control like the breathing of a child. Such breathing involves a maximum of physical action but a minimum of physical strain. It is perfectly controlled in the sense that it is responsive to the demands of expression, but the control is subconscious, not studied. Most of us do not breathe naturally in this sense; our childhood freedom has been warped and restricted by training and habit, by poor ventilation, cramped posture, and tight clothing, so that very little freedom is left. Improvement of the breathing habits is, therefore, a matter of trying to restore a natural function.

Good breathing is not confined to the action of a few muscles or to one restricted area; it involves the coordinated activity of a large part of the body. Just which muscles participate, and in what proportion, I shall not attempt to state, since that is one of the matters in dispute. It is fairly safe, however, to assert that the diaphragm plays an important part and that any method of breathing which gives inadequate play to that muscle is probably wrong. The diaphragm is an internal muscle and its action is not easily felt, but since the external muscles about the upper abdomen are closely coordinated with it, an active diaphragm brings about a sensation of muscular activity at the center of the body — roughly, at the lower end of the breastbone. Good breathing is neither so high in the chest nor so low in the abdomen as to be grotesque; it is centered in what the pugilist calls the *midsection.* The strain is thus carried by some of the largest and strongest muscles of the body. At the same time, and most important of all, the throat is relaxed. A feeling of strain in a healthy throat during voice production is a sure sign of some fault — usually incorrect breathing.

Numerous exercises for the correction of faulty breathing may be found in the books on public speaking and on voice, and need not be repeated here. One of the best is the so-called *sipping and packing* exercise, by which the air is inhaled in small sips and packed away until the lungs are full. Another is the *panting* exercise that is just what the name implies. In general, those exercises that tend to develop the diaphragm and to encourage full open breathing are best; but no exercise should be employed which occasions the slightest strain or irritation in the throat. The actor should be cautioned to take his breathing exercises regularly at special drill periods and not to think of the breath or its control when actually speaking before an audience.

vocal quality

Many of the common faults in vocal quality are really faults in breathing and clear up satisfactorily when the breathing habits are corrected. Others are referable to poor resonance, poor tone placing, or poor selection of pitch; and the worst are referable to poor coordination of mind and voice.

Resonance has much to do with the carrying power of a voice as well as its quality. Poor resonance may result from malformation of the chest, throat, or head, or from a catarrhal or other obstruction; or it may result from faulty coordination of the parts involved. When it is due to malformation, or obstruction, the case is one for the physician or surgeon. When it is due to faulty coordination, it may sometimes be corrected by properly chosen exercises. Chest resonance[1] is usually improved by good breathing exercises that tend to increase the lung capacity and the responsiveness of the diaphragm. Head resonance may be improved by relaxing the throat and forwarding the tone so that the upper teeth and the hard palate vibrate; also by practice in singing *dans la masque,* that is, humming well forward in the nose with the lips very lightly closed and the whole front of the face tingling with the vibrations. Good resonance at any pitch requires instant adjustment of the soft or movable parts involved, and is greatly impaired by fatigue or irritation; a flat or wooden voice is often simply a tired voice, or a voice that has been strained or abused. The actor should never be allowed to shout or to force his voice in any way but should be encouraged to seek an easy, open, relaxed utterance. He should strive to decrease the effort and improve the quality without loss of volume rather than to increase the volume; if he succeeds in the former, the latter will take care of itself.

Poor resonance is often associated with poor tone placing. If the actor will pronounce in rotation the vowels *oo, oh, aw, ah, a* (the latter sound as in "at"), he will soon notice a sensation that the *oo* is very far back, the *oh* a little less so, the *aw* in the middle of the mouth, the *ah* just behind the teeth, and the *a* very far forward, almost out of the mouth. This statement refers not to the tongue position as recorded by the phonetician, but to the speaker's own feeling as to where the tone is placed. He will also notice that the mouth is opened wider as the sound comes forward. The resonance is usually poor on the *oo* because the mouth is nearly closed and any incipient resonance is smothered before it gets out. As the mouth opens and the tone comes forward, the resonance increases and the tone improves until it reaches its best on the *ah,* with the maximum vibration in the mouth, the nasal passages, and the front of the skull. Usually the *a* is not so good in quality; it is too far forward and the sound escapes into the air without having set up the proper head resonance. Constant practice on these vowels in rotation, with occasional variations of pitch within the natural range of the voice, will help the actor to acquire a sense of the relation between vowel quality, position, and resonance, and to form a concept of the sort of voice he wishes to cultivate.

In the effort to get volume with untrained voices, amateurs often strike too high a pitch. The higher the pitch, the greater the volume for a given amount of effort, but the greater the strain on the listener. Most voices are poorer in quality in the upper part of their range than in the lower and, therefore, less pleasant to the ear; moreover, a high pitch is emotionally associated with fear, desperation, impatience, or frazzled nerves, and is thus empathically disturbing. The actor should be taught to cultivate the lower middle tones of his voice, and to use them ordinarily in preference to the higher. Every individual has a single pitch level that can be used with the least amount of effort and which provides the greatest amount of resonance. This tone is called *optimum pitch,* and should be cultivated as the *home tone* for the individual's voice. The person who learns to place his voice here can achieve the greatest amount of flexibility possible with his instrument with the least strain and effort. The optimum pitch is approximately one third from the bottom of the total vocal range and is that point of greatest vibration of all the resonating chambers of the body. Everyone who has ever sung in the shower has noticed that one note he sings causes the whole bathroom to vibrate. That note is louder and richer than those on both sides of it. The same is true of the body's optimum pitch. One can find his own ideal note by humming down the scale from his highest note to his lowest, all the while with his hands on his chest, the *v*'s created by the thumb and forefinger resting on his throat. His hands should be on top of each other. As he hums down and back he will feel the greatest vibration on one particular note. That is his optimum pitch and should be used as the note around which to vary his speaking pitches. There will still be occasional need for the higher tones to express the states of mind mentioned, and the contrast will make them sound all the more effective. There will also be a need for the very lowest tones to express the deeper emotions. Both extremes of pitch express emotion, but the higher expresses excitement, weakness, and loss of self-control, while the lower expresses depth and sincerity coupled with a measure of restraint. Either may be effective in its place, but the average pitch level should probably be a little lower than most amateurs make it. Women especially are apt to pitch their voices too high, or, at any rate, to offend more by doing so—perhaps because their voices are a full octave higher anyhow. It is noteworthy that the great stage voices have nearly all been rich and flexible in the lower registers.

responsiveness

The most important quality of voice for the actor is not pure tone, but responsiveness—flexibility accompanied by perfect coordination of the voice with the mind. Nearly all voices are in some degree expressive of character or mood. A rough, hard voice, for instance, may reveal a tough character; or a high-pitched, frantic voice a nervous one. The actor's voice, however, must reveal, not his own chronic disposition, but the varying moods of all the different personalities he portrays. It must be a free and flexible instrument, responsive at all times to his imagination.

The actor should work for both variety and adaptability and should distinguish between them. Some voices are full of variety yet not adaptable to different parts. The actor playing Hamlet should be able to vary his voice in pitch, force, and tempo to express the many moods of the character, yet it should always be recognizable as the same voice — the voice of Hamlet. The same actor playing Shylock should have a different voice — the voice of Shylock — varying again within its own range, but always consistent with itself.

The sincere actor will attempt to establish a voice consistent with the character he is acting. The pitch range can be adjusted slightly, more or less nasality can be added, varying degrees of harshness can be used. These and other adjustments can provide special character voices within the actor's range of capabilities. The rhythms of the individual's speech can also be changed along with varying combinations of the above suggestions to give the versatile actor many voices. Most of the changes suggested here are easily accomplished with a little practice. The most difficult adjustment is change of timbre or quality that can be achieved only through a change of resonance. That means that the tone must be placed differently, or that different portions of the chest, throat, and head must be brought into play as resonators. Timbre is dependent upon the number and character of the overtones, and the overtones are determined by the resonance. There is only one way in which an actor can learn to control the timbre, and that is by experiment in variation of resonance followed by abundant practice, preferably under guidance and criticism. The use of a tape recorder is extremely helpful in this and other problems of voice and characterization.

One of the best possible exercises for the development of vocal responsiveness is the following: Choose a lyric poem embodying some strong emotion — love, grief, pathos, indignation, or mirth. Read it over to get the thought; then read it aloud to an imaginary audience, putting your whole soul into your voice, and a little more. Exaggerate the mood and its expression to the point of "slopping over"; if pathetic, sob over it; if humorous, chuckle over it; if enthusiastic, rave over it. Try to make your voice and body vibrate with the emotion. As soon as you have succeeded in expressing one selection with sufficient exaggeration, drop it and try another in an entirely different mood. Vary the mood four or five ways each time, and try, in the course of a week, to run the whole gamut of possible emotions. Do not concentrate on any one mood too long or mannerisms may develop. Remember that it is all mere exercise and that the exaggeration should not be carried into real life or into the theatre.

Not all actors, of course, need this exercise; some of them slop over quite sufficiently without any encouragement. But for the actor whose voice is inhibited and unresponsive it is really very helpful, especially when the inhibition has grown out of shyness or constraint.

Both variety and change of voice may — like everything else in the theatre — be overdone. Too much variety within the part weakens its consistency and gives the impression of straining for effect. Too much change for a new character that does not call for any special vocal quality likewise suggests strain. Straight parts require less adaptation of voice than character parts, and actors playing to a succession of strange audiences on the road have less need to change their voices than those playing in repertory, whose audiences know them too well. Several years ago, a clever, highly skilled nonprofessional actor in the Colorado Shakespeare Festival played three separate roles in *The Merry Wives of Windsor* and, aided by costume and makeup, along with excellent vocal variations, went undiscovered. On successive nights audiences were tested with new voices and vocal treatments as the same actor played the title role in *Coriolanus,* followed by the Prince of Morocco in *The Merchant of Venice.*

enunciation

No production can be effective unless the actors make themselves heard and understood, and in this connection, good enunciation is even more important than great volume. The two things, however, are not entirely independent; a certain amount of volume is a necessary part of the enunciation, and insufficient volume often induces mumbling. The latter fault is surprisingly common, even on the professional stage, and some of our best actors and actresses have been roundly scolded for it by the critics. The smaller, more intimate theatres of today have something to do with this; they encourage the actor to speak more quietly, and when he happens to find himself in a larger theatre, he cannot shake off the habit. Actors trained in movies and television, where all sound is electronically controlled, have not learned the need for clear enunciation and volume control. Amateurs speak in undertones because they do not know any better, or because they are obliged to rehearse in private houses where full stage volume would annoy the occupants. The director should know that habits formed in rehearsal are hard to break later, and that the only way to be sure of adequate volume in public performance is to have it learned with the lines and thoroughly rehearsed.

There should be enough volume from each player to make him audible, and, in addition, there should be a reasonable degree of uniformity. It is always distressing to hear one actor shout while another mumbles; the listener cannot adjust his ear to either and so misses many lines. Directors often fail to detect such variations in rehearsal because they remain too close to the stage; they should listen occasionally from the back row or the balcony; and they should insist continually that the actors place their voices for those regions.

An important element in good enunciation, especially when, for dramatic reasons, the volume must be subdued, is a forward placing of the voice. People marvel at the power of some actors to make themselves heard with no apparent effort and no perceptible raising of the voice. As a rule, these are the actors who speak well forward in the mouth with the maximum activity of lips, tongue, and teeth. Comedian Danny Kaye is an excellent example of this. Much of his material consists of very fast patter songs full of tongue twisters that he whips through without the slightest clouding of a single syllable. Some of our older actors and actresses still have this power, but it is rare enough among the younger American players.

Another essential of good enunciation is correct vowel quality. Some speakers blur the vowels, failing to distinguish one from another; all their vowels tend to become indeterminates. The several values of *o, a,* and *u* are almost reduced to a common *uh,* and the distinction between *e* and the short *i* is lost even in accented syllables. Contrasts of vowel sounds are a great aid to clarity of speech, and when a speaker levels his vowels, his syllables tend to become indistinguishable. "Uh wunna gutta Phulladulphia" is not the clearest way of saying "I want to go to Philadelphia," but it is about the way some people say it. American speakers are especially careless in this respect and also in respect to the duration of sounds; they shorten their vowels to such an extent that they frequently seem to be speaking in consonants only. Consonants are noises; vowels are tones; and since much of the beauty and expressiveness of a voice is in the tones, the actor should learn to give full value to his vowels, at least on the accented syllables. He will find that in so doing he also makes easier the enunciation of consonants.

The enunciation of consonants is, of course, the stumbling block for many actors. There are various reasons for this. One is poor breath control. Another is inadequate or excessive flow of saliva, usually induced by nervousness. Another is failure to sustain the vowel long enough for the muscles to get into position for the next consonant. But the worst and commonest cause is just plain *lip laziness,* or, more politely, lip sluggishness, especially sluggishness of the upper lip. Here again, the English usually have the better of us. Their habit of speaking forward in the mouth enables them to cultivate responsiveness and flexibility of lips and tongue, without the excessive mobility of countenance that so often accompanies a self-conscious attempt to enunciate distinctly. The actor who is badly troubled with lip sluggishness may profitably exercise his lips and jaws by practicing in rotation such widely divergent sounds as *ee, ah, oo,* or *ip, it, ik,* or *el, are, em,* or *fun, pun, shun;* but he should be warned against making faces and cultivating lack of repose. When the lips have been limbered up to a reasonable degree, such exercises should be followed by exercises in forwarding the tone. Although there are many exercises one may use to improve enunciation, my own favorite will quickly make the actor aware of his inadequacies and, well used, will help him achieve the needed flexibility. "She stood on the balcony inimitably mimicking him hiccuping and amicably welcoming him in."

pronunciation

The problem of correct stage pronunciation is a difficult one, involving both the choice of a standard and the practical task of training the actors to follow it. It has been said that the best English in America is heard on the stage, and there is some truth in the statement, but when it comes to explaining just why and in what respect it is best, complications arise.

Some plays, of course, do not call for standard English. Realistic plays with strong local color must be played in the dialect of the region depicted, or at least in a fairly suggestive approximation of it; and sometimes several different dialects must be spoken by different characters in the same play. But literary plays or plays of an abstract or universal character, not especially representative of locality or social class, must be played in a sort of English that is at least reasonably free from dialectal limitations and reasonably acceptable to all those who come to hear it.

Standards of pronunciation vary considerably, off the stage as well as on, and for that reason, the stage English of New York or London is not always necessary, or even desirable, in an isolated community. Although radio and television and films have done a great deal to acclimate our ears to high standards of speech, the very best Oxford English may still sound like an affectation to the ears of a small-town audience in Iowa or Utah, and so distract attention from the play. On the other hand, the small-town people do not expect even their local actors to play literary drama in the casual everyday speech and manner of the neighborhood. They expect some slight heightening of effect, some suggestion of universality in the artistic medium employed, including the language. How to get the universality without the affectation is the problem.

Since the American theatre derives historically from the English theatre, and English actors have been playing in this country on and off for 200 years, it is natural that the traditional standard in stage pronunciation should be slightly more English and less American than the standard of the streets. Up to a certain point this is a good thing, as it tends to preserve the unity of English and American dramatic literature; and up to a certain point it is not offensive. A tradition is mellowed in 200 years, and the pronunciation of our older actors, learned in the school of experience, does not sound affected in the ears of the Iowan or the Californian or the Philadelphian—much less in those of the Bostonian or New Yorker. What does sound affected is the pseudophonetic rule. The standard they follow is, for the most part, very distinctly British; but it is artificially so, lacking both the spontaneity of our native speech and the settled moderation that characterizes the traditional speech of the theatre.

The phoneticians who teach this standard—chiefly in Boston or New York—deny, it is true, any attempt to imitate the speech of England, and point out that every sound which they advocate is to be found native somewhere in the United States. The Italian *a*, for example, in words like "half," "laugh," and "master," is common in some parts of New England and elsewhere. The dropping of final *r* in words like "mother" or "father," and of medial *r* in words like "hardly" or "courthouse," is common all over New England and parts of the South. But the same New Englander who omits the *r* in "mother," "father," and "dear," supplies it gratuitously in "idea" and "law" ("idear" and "lore"), and the one who says, "It is hahf pahst two," often says, "Let's take the ca-a to Ha-a-vud"—using the so-called short *a* (as in "fat"), prolonged in duration, to which he objects when the Philadelphian uses it in "half" and "past." The Philadelphian, curiously enough, though he says "la-aff" for "laugh" and "ha-aff" for "half," reverses the New Englander on "cahr" and "Hahrvard." And while the phonetician is trying to persuade the Philadelphian to use an open o^2 in words like "not," "got," and "on," the Midwesterner is busy turning "daughter," "water," and "automobile" into "dotter," "wotter," and "ottomobile," and the Vermonter is turning "nought" into "naht."

The heightened conventions of the stage, however, demand a standard of pronunciation somewhat above the carelessness of ordinary speech, and one may well ask what standard, if not the standard of southern England, is to be accepted. The only safe standard, it seems to me, is that of normal English. Normal English is simply the kind of English that is reasonably acceptable wherever English is spoken. It differs from local speech chiefly in the omission of localisms. It is, in fact, a negative thing; its acceptability lies rather in what it leaves out than in what it includes. It leaves out the peculiarities that are familiar in one place but unknown in another, and, especially, those that are in some regions thought ugly or offensive. It is a kind of common denominator. It includes the elements that are uniform, or nearly so, everywhere; and when it must express what is expressed differently in different regions, it does so by compromise, choosing a middle ground.

Some such standard is exemplified in the speech of many actors and actresses who have traveled widely and acted in both England and America, and perhaps elsewhere, and who have been heard often on the radio and in the films. Some of them are English and some American, but it is difficult to tell by their speech which are which.

A similarly cosmopolitan standard is often heard from widely traveled authors, teachers, or statesmen, and from radio and television speakers who have proved acceptable to both British and American ears. It is the speech of such persons that the director should have in mind when training a group of amateurs, rather than a preconceived artificial standard.

Two qualities are essential to good speech: intelligibility and freedom from distraction. The trouble with localisms and other peculiarities is that they do distract; they call attention to the actor's limitations when the audience should be thinking of the play. But affectations distract attention quite as much as localisms and should be avoided for the same reason. Even beauty, in itself a desirable quality, is capable of becoming a source of distraction when overstressed. The problem of stage pronunciation is not ordinarily a problem of beautification. It is a problem of clarification. A maximum of intelligibility and suitability with a minimum of distraction is the proper goal.

notes on pronunciation

All this is perhaps too general to be of immediate practical assistance to the inexperienced director who will want to know just what types of pronunciation to encourage and what types to discourage. There is no room here for a pronouncing dictionary but certain fairly definite suggestions may be offered.

1. Suppress any marked individual peculiarity. An exception should be made if this kind of pronunciation is useful for character delineation.

2. Suppress or modify any ugly or unpleasant pronunciation. But be sure the ugliness is real and not merely a matter of personal distaste and that it is not unmistakably the preferred one, or only one, in common usage.

3. *Discourage any variant pronunciation based primarily on slovenliness.* Examples include the substitution of *oo* for long *u* (properly a diphthong *iu*) in words like "stoodent," or "institoot" (although in some words like "blue" and "true" this change is inevitable); the substitution of a cough through the nose for the true dental *t* before *n* in words like "Tren(t)'n" or "impor(t)'nt"; the practical elimination of medial *t* in other words like "men(t)al" or "in(t)eresting"; the substitution of *n* for *ng* in present participles and in words like "lenth" for "length" or "strenth" for "strength"; the substitution of shorter vowel sounds for longer ones as in "git" for "get" and "fer" for "for"; the transposition of sounds in words like "calvary" for "cavalry," or "irrevelant" for "irrelevant"; or the insertion of relief sounds in slightly difficult words like "stastistics" (for "statistics") or "athalete" (for "athlete").

4. *Discourage, on the other hand, any pseudolearned pronunciation.* This kind of pronunciation takes its authority from the spelling rather than from the speech of educated persons. This sort of *eye pronunciation* is very common in the present age of literacy without learning and has been widely fostered in this country by inadequately prepared teachers of English. Common examples include the reinsertion, under influence of the spelling, of sounds long omitted in good usage, like the *t* in "often," "fasten," "hasten," or "waistcoat," the *h* in "forehead," or the *th* in "clothes"; the substitution of a *t* sound for the well-established *ch* sound in words like "picture," "literature," or "fortune"; the unscrambling of *sh* into *s* in "passion" or "issue" ("iss-you" is bad enough, but "iss-oo" is worse); the punctilious separation of syllables in words like "uninteresting" or "extraordinary"; and the painfully artificial sounding of unaccented syllables in words like "lev-el" (for "lev'l") or "cap-tain" (for "capt'n").

5. *Discourage especially local pronunciation.* This is pronunciation so narrowly local that it identifies the user with a particular town or community, like the "boid" (for "bird") of the Bowery New Yorkers, or the "sitchyation" (for "situation") of the Pennsylvania Dutch.

6. *Discourage first those dialectal peculiarities that generally have incurred ridicule.* Examples are the prolonged diphthongal *a* of some Middle

Atlantic and Middle West regions ("la-aff," "ma-an," etc.); the somewhat exaggerated Italian *a* of Boston; the drawl of the South, especially when emphasized by diphthongization ("do-ah" for "door," etc.); the Hoosier twang; the Yankee palatal snarl; and the Bowery slur—which is by no means confined to New York.

7. *Discourage any American pronunciation commonly ridiculed in England.* These include "jun'lmen" for "gentlemen," "Amurrican" for "American," or "N'York" for "New York." Discourage equally any British pronunciation commonly ridiculed in America—though this is less likely to be a problem in training American actors.

8. *Suppress any dialectal peculiarity of recognizably foreign origin.* Examples include the Irish *oi* for long *i*, or *a* for *e* (as in "fate" for "feet"); the German confusion of *v* for *w;* the French *ee* for short *i* (as in "eet eez" for "it is"); the cockney English or Australian long *i* for long *a* (as in "lye-dy" for "lady"); the Swedish long *a* for long *i* (as in "Ay" for "I"); the Yiddish hard *g* in *ng* combinations; and the common Continental substitution of *t* or *d* for English *th*—very common in Brooklyn and South Philadelphia.

9. *Discourage any tendency to break single vowels into diphthongs.* For example "ha-and" should not be used for "hand," nor should "proo-un" for "prune," or "lowered" for "lord."

10. *Discourage also the opposite tendency to shorten diphthongs into single vowels.* Examples are the use of "ahr" for "our," or "om" for "I'm."

11. *Encourage any pronunciation that, though not universally employed, is universally admired.* In this respect so much depends upon association, intonation, and manner that it would be dangerous to cite specific examples. Some of the less extreme values of *o* and *a* in England and New England, some of the clarities of the Middle West, and some of the softnesses of the South are quite generally pleasing. But a pronunciation is not "universally admired" unless admired by all classes; if widely admired by purists or pedants on the one hand, or by gangsters and roughnecks on the other, but not by ordinary mortals, it should be discouraged.

12. *Encourage a moderate or middle sound of* a *in words like "laugh,"* *"class," "after," or "dance."* This is a sound between the *a* and the extreme Italian *a*. Such a sound is common in England as well as the United States and can be learned by most people without affectation, whereas a complete

shift from the nasal short *a* to the Italian *a* usually cannot. The phonetician may protest that this is a cowardly compromise; but the stage director's business is to avoid distraction, not to make or shape the language.

13. Encourage a general cleaning up of unaccented syllables. This does not call for, however, an artificial precision in the vowel sounds. Unaccented vowels are bound to weaken and become more or less obscure, as in "Trent(o)n," "cap(a)ble," or "c(o)mplete." The obscure vowel is usually a sound between English short *u* (as in "shut") and French *eu* (as in "peu" and it is usually brief in duration; sometimes the vowel practically disappears. In some cases the short *i* sound (as in "it") can be employed appropriately in the unaccented syllables; and as far as possible this should be encouraged because the short *i* is a clean-cut sound that carries well in the theatre, even when spoken very quickly. It is much less apt to sound muddy than the obscure vowel and less apt to induce poor enunciation of adjacent sounds. Thus "po-im" is better than "powum" (for "poem") and "pro-ibition" is better than "prow-ubition" (for "prohibition"); while "Trentin," "captin," "valit" (for "Trenton," "captain," "valet") are often heard from cultivated and clear speakers. More important than the exact shade of vowel sound in unaccented syllables is the clear enunciation of the consonants.

14. Encourage the young actor to lengthen the accented syllables rather more than is common in careless speech. He should give full duration and resonance to the accented vowels. This should not be carried to the point of suggesting a deliberate drawl or a consciously artful intonation; but within reason it is one of the most effective means of clarifying stage speech.

15. Encourage a reasonable modification rather than an abrupt dropping of the untrilled final r. This rule applies to those individuals who say "mother-r-," "father-r-," "dear-r-r." The sound is undoubtedly ugly when given full value, being little more than a growl, but it is so widely prevalent in this country that its complete elimination, even on the professional stage, is impracticable. Many persons who fully appreciate its ugliness cannot drop it suddenly from their speech without seeming affected and unconvincing. Moreover, the complete dropping of the final *r* is just as certainly a dialectal extreme as is the exaggeration of the final *r,* and has no greater sanction in usage — less sanction, in fact, from a numerical standpoint — for comparatively few people, even in England, eliminate the sound as completely as certain teachers of elocution would have us do. In Wiltshire, for example, sixty or seventy miles west of London, the *r* begins to be heard; and in Devonshire it is even more firmly pronounced than in Philadelphia. In Scotland it is a guttural trill. If the director can get his actors to bring the *r* forward in the mouth, shorten it, and limit it to a slight curl at the end of a clear vowel, he will be doing very well indeed.

These suggestions may be useful but they are no substitute for good taste and good scholarship on the part of the director. Any director who means business will want to know something more about standards of pronunciation than is set down here; for references on the subject he should consult the bibliography at the end of the book.

dialect plays

Plays in local or foreign dialect involve serious difficulties for inexperienced players. As a rule, the less an actor knows about a dialect, the thicker he tries to lay it on — often with distressing results. A certain degree of exaggeration is proper and necessary in the theatre, but, on the other hand, nothing is more painful to the audience than an obvious straining for effect. The more extreme dialects are usually easier to render than subtler ones; they sound so strange to the ear anyhow that inaccuracies pass unnoticed. Similarly, the dialects of comic or burlesque characters are ordinarily less troublesome than those of serious characters, for exaggeration is expected in burlesque, and laughter disarms criticism. It is the rendition of slight dialectal shadings in serious plays that presents the most difficult problem. The vast number of recordings by artists of many vocal backgrounds, as well as special materials on dialects, make it possible for the actors to hear the rhythms and intonations as well as the distortions that characterize a particular style of speech. The actor should take every opportunity to listen to the dialect he is learning, but he should avoid listening to another actor read his part. He must be able to make the language his own; if he presents only an imitation, the result will be dull and artificial and lack the full range of meaning needed.

Many of the plays produced in this country are English in subject matter and authorship, and the question naturally arises whether such plays should be rendered in full English dialect. When a play is universal in theme and character, and the choice of English names and an English setting seems arbitrary or accidental, it is often advisable to ignore the dialect and to render the play as if it were American; occasionally it is possible to change the locale and the names and to omit all English allusions. When, however, a significant element of plot, theme, or character is essentially English, some suggestion of an English dialect is almost imperative if the point is not to be lost. No indication of dialect appears, as a rule, in the text—except in the case of rural, cockney, or other type characters; and so must be supplied by the director or the actor.

In training a group of American actors to do an English play the first point is to suppress, more rigorously than usual, any Americanisms of speech—especially the excessive final *r,* the extremely nasal short *a,* the western *ah* for *aw,* and the neglect of medial *t.* The second point is to introduce the English values of long and short *o;* the long *o* is almost a diphthong consisting of short *e* (as in "get") followed by *oo* (as in "moon"), and the short *o* is a short *aw* ("not" being simply a quicker "naught")—though many British speakers now say "not" and "got" very much as we do. The third point is to work for a suggestion of the English sentence tune, which makes use of more rising inflections and fewer falling ones than the American. It is seldom wise to attempt any general changes beyond these three, though many individual words or phrases will require attention as they occur. The purpose is usually to suggest rather than to portray, and if there is no marked inconsistency to create distraction, a little positive suggestion will be sufficient. The director should not suppose that a complete representation of English speech as actually spoken in England is necessary before an American audience. Even English companies playing in America do not give us that; they find some modification almost necessary for intelligibility and for avoidance of distraction. However, the contacts between Britain and America through two world wars and the growth of international broadcasting have greatly lessened the unfamiliarity of British English to American ears, and there is likely to be an increasing demand for some degree of convincingness.

The director should, of course, remember that there are many British accents besides the London accent. In Shaw's *Pygmalion*, for example, contrasting characters display several quite different dialects which, if well handled, add considerably to the charm of the play.

Plays in Irish dialect involve a somewhat less troublesome problem, especially the plays of Synge, O'Casey, Yeats, and their followers. The tendency of the amateur actor in an Irish part is, of course, to assume the Irish brogue of the comic strip or the vaudeville stage, and this tendency must be suppressed. Some slight modification of long and short *a*, a slight suggestion of *th* on medial *t,* and an occasional trilled *r* may be permitted, but again, it is the sentence tune that is most important. Synge, especially, catches the flow of Gaelic rhythm in English words; the sentences are long and loose, with many participial constructions and many appended clauses. For this dialect the actor must have plenty of reserve breath and must conquer the temptation to hurry and to skimp the enunciation. But the beauty of the language at its best is a great incentive to mastery, and with sufficient practice, amateurs often do very well with it.

German and Yiddish dialects are among the easiest for most amateurs. The substitution of *v* for *w*, and *s* for *z*, and the pronunciation of *th* as *d* or *t* are the changes most needed. There is less modification of sentence tune in these dialects than in English or Irish, but a little more difference in manner. For the German, a more explosive utterance is usually desirable, together with a freer use of guttural sounds. For the Yiddish, more gesture is required, together with a husky or slightly nasal tone. The chief danger in these dialects, as in the Irish, is that of presenting vaudeville types instead of real people. The Pennsylvania Dutch dialect has some of the German consonant sounds but is mainly characterized by a peculiar rising inflection and by oddities of word order generally written into a play by the dramatist.

A French accent is usually suggested by an equalization of syllabic stress and by a squeezed quality of tone, accompanied by freer use of the lips (but not the jaws). The squeezing changes some of the vowel qualities, especially that of short *i* which becomes *ee*. Sometimes a slight suggestion of lisp (*th* for *s*) is helpful, though the *th* sound itself tends to become *t* or *d*.

Plays written in some of the local dialects of this country are more difficult than those involving foreign accents—except, of course, for actors native to the districts represented. This is partly because dialectal differences within our own country are apt to seem more strange and less convincing to most of us than those that are frankly exotic. We see nothing astonishing in the fact that a foreigner speaks a dialect unlike our own, but when an American does so, we are a little inclined to suspect exaggeration.

Many of the best American plays written in recent years depend so much upon local color as to require careful study of dialect. The Carolina Folk Plays and others of their type use both the negroid dialect of the South and the modified Elizabethan dialect of the mountain whites. The plays of Eugene O'Neill involve a number of dialects, including those of the Negro, the Bowery roughneck, the longshoreman, the tramp sailor, and the Yankee farmer. Other writers have found their material in the Ozarks, in Texas, in the corn belt, or on the prairies. Unfortunately, some of the most important writers are peculiarly amateurish in representing dialect on paper; no department of the dramatist's art requires more professional skill than this. The amateur actor can hardly be expected to deliver lines convincingly when they are not written convincingly; yet the director who is to produce these plays—those of O'Neill, for instance—must undertake to teach his actors to do just that thing. If he does not know the dialects thoroughly himself, he is almost sure to fail.

How shall he go about studying them? A few of the most characteristic local pronunciations have already been mentioned in this chapter, but a complete catalogue of dialectal variants would occupy a large dictionary. Actual sojourn in the region to be represented, with intelligent observation and analysis of the local speech habits, is obviously the best method of study. Often it is not possible and the director must depend upon the printed page or upon broadcasts and phonograph records. Broadcasting furnishes a disproportionate amount of certain dialects—"hillbilly" English, for example—and neglects others; and an army of second-rate radio and television actors give many false impressions of dialect, especially in the daily soap operas; nevertheless, radio and television, more than any other agency, have made dialectal variations familiar to our ears. Dialect dictionaries sometimes help, as do certain books using phonetic script. Many colleges offering phonetics courses now have large collections of dialect records available for study; many tapes have been published for sale.

The director should strive to pick out the most suggestive features of each dialect, but should be careful not to let his actors exaggerate them unduly. At the same time, he should check the probable tendency of each actor to revert to his own native speech between times; nothing is more certain to render the dialect unconvincing than excessive contrast between the points selected for emphasis and the rest of the language. Dialect plays add considerably to the director's task and so should be attempted only when plenty of time is available for study.

notes and references

1. Assuming that there is such a thing. The matter is in controversy.
2. The sound of *aw* as in "awful," but shortened. The phonetic symbol is (ɔ).

The preceding chapters have dealt primarily with the director and the actor, yet no production organization is complete without a technical staff. Although many plays are presented with the director and actors designing and executing the sets, lights, costumes, and makeup, these areas require special skills and knowledge, and it does not necessarily follow that a good director or actor possesses all the talents needed for technical theatre too! The theatre has become more and more an organization of specialists, and the caliber of all aspects of production has risen accordingly. There is no point in debating which elements are most important, since a good production can be ruined by incompetence either on or offstage. A crack stage crew cannot be made up of actors who were not cast, but must include skilled technicians who get the same satisfaction from a neat, fast, well-executed scene shift as actors do from a scene well played. This is not to say that actors should not work as technicians or technicians as actors. In fact, no better way exists for theatre people to learn mutual respect for each other's tasks. An actor who has built and rigged scenery will handle it more smoothly on stage and so look better as an actor. For example, opening and closing stage doors often causes the walls of the set to wiggle, even when those walls are well built and solidly braced, simply because the novice actor does not know how to handle the unit properly. If he has built and rigged a door, he knows that he must step over a sill iron and that slamming the door excessively hard, or pushing too hard before he turns the knob, will cause wiggles. Good actors can grab a door or a stair balustrade and apparently pull and twist it with great force with no ill effect on the units because they have learned how to move *themselves* to simulate the force required without disturbing the scenery. These are actors who respect the scenery and understand it. They have profited from time spent as technicians. On the other hand, terrible traps have been built into sets by designers or technicians who did not understand, for example, how much space was necessary for one actor to carry another up a run of stairs. The awkwardness was simply blamed on the actor, and bad feeling resulted. Mutual respect comes from understanding the contributions that both the onstage and offstage people make to the production. The wise director will make sure that this understanding occurs, and to do so, he must himself understand.

Although the director need not be skilled in all areas of technical theatre, he must be knowledgeable about them. He must be able to talk the technical language in order to make sure that he understands the problems and limitations under which the technical crews must work in particular theatres, with particular budgets, with particular equipment, and under particular time restrictions. Only then can the director make the final artistic decisions that affect all the areas of production. All too often a director agrees to a certain style of production, or, to use a more concrete example, to a certain size of stage playing space, only to find, when the set is mounted, that he has less room than he needs for stage business which he planned *after* the discussions regarding the space had been held. The director must be able to understand drawings also so that he knows what he will have to work with. They are a part of the language he must know in order to work successfully with the technical staff.

Likewise, the costumer who designs a lovely costume that takes longer to get into than the amount of time the actor has offstage, or in which an actor can walk but cannot sit when he is required to sit, has failed to understand the total problem. He has seen only the visual and not the practical considerations of the actor and the production.

Each theatre person has his pet peeves and biases, but the more he understands the total picture, the better he can do his own job. Since the director must work with all the artists and must integrate their efforts into the whole, he, more than any of the others, must understand the full range of stage production and its problems and possibilities if he is to succeed.

The complexity of his task will be more apparent when each of the six areas of production is described in some detail. Though in many small theatres the directors are also the designers, carpenters, seamstresses, and crew members, nevertheless, dividing the jobs into the various areas of responsibility will show the steps of the production process more clearly. The sooner specialists can be assigned their individualized tasks, the sooner the production can take on the finish and polish that will lift it from the ordinary to the exceptional level. No one person has time to do everything well. The director who can delegate some of the work and responsibility and still maintain artistic control will not only turn out a superior production but live to do another.

Designers and technicians argue among themselves about which area is most important, but that is really of no consequence here. A case may be made for each, depending on what play is being discussed, and the argument would change tomorrow. Suffice it to say that each is essential. When design is discussed in Chapter Eighteen, the interrelationships will be established, but the purpose here is simply to discuss and explain the makeup of the technical staff and their responsibilities.

Essential to the production is the designer who is responsible for carrying out the concept of the director. It is he who takes the director's statement, "I want to treat *Cyrano de Bergerac* as an historical romance," for instance, and determines that the play will be done in mid-seventeenth-century clothes with a bit more color and flamboyance of line than was really true of the period. Since the play calls for four settings, he may well suggest that the "romance" of the director's concept be interpreted as nonrealistic and that this romance will be carried through some exaggeration of line and simplification of actual details. Sketches to illustrate his interpretation of the director's concept would then be submitted for the director's approval. When a meeting of the minds had been achieved, then the actual construction would begin.

Whether a production is designed by one designer or whether the settings, costumes, lights, sound, properties, and makeup are designed by separate artists, the procedure remains the same. The designer and the director must achieve a unified approach to the production. Theatre requires an integration of many parts, and when any one is not in harmony with the others, the result is chaos. Often an artistic director serves as the design coordinator when there are several designers. He makes the decisions in order to bring the parts into balance.

For example, suppose the scenic designer has determined that the color combinations needed to achieve the effects the director wishes are blue and lavender, yet the costume designer insists that the only color which he can put the heroine in for that particular scene is bright yellow. Depending on the actual hues involved the results could be striking or awful. Next, the lighting designer comes along and says that since the scene is a night scene, he will need to use mostly blue light. If each went his way without coordination, the result could be a set that appeared, under lights, to be a combination of electric blue and gray with a heroine playing upon it in a dull brown dress. Truly, design coordination is essential and it must be done by a person who knows all of the aspects of production. But more about design later.

scenery

In most theatres the technical director, who is often a designer too, is responsible for seeing that the designs are turned into finished products. He does the working drawings for scenic construction, orders the lumber and other materials necessary, sets up the schedules for accomplishing the work, and finally supervises the painting and assembling and rigging of the sets. He is also responsible for the planning of scene shifts and often must train the stage crews as well. In his free time he keeps track of the expenses and makes sure that the budget is observed. He must be a good organizer and administrator, but he must be able to do practically everything. In many theatres, being technical director means doing everything but directing the play.

Once the scenic designs have been turned into working drawings, it is up to the carpenters to build the flats, platforms, steps, door and window units, and the like. The working drawings will show how these units are to be assembled as well, and the carpenters must finish the units to the point where they are ready for painting. Good stage carpenters know that scenery is built to be viewed from a distance and that it is temporary. They take many shortcuts that save time and money, but none which might affect the safety of the people involved.

When the scenic units are built and have been assembled temporarily to make sure that everything fits as planned, the scenic artists begin their work. Scene painting is divided into three categories. First is the layout work that consists of marking what areas receive what colors. In some cases the set might appear to be paneled to a chair-rail height and then plastered from there on up. The layout people would mark the line for the top of the paneling and mark the planking in the paneling as well as base boards and door facings if these were to be painted. Fillers would then base coat these areas according to the colors chosen and, usually, mixed by the designer. Finally detail painters would do the wood graining, put in the shadow and highlight lines, and texture the plaster above. The wise designer will constantly train new people in the art of scene painting or he will find that he must do all of the detail work himself. Top artists may seldom appear, but anyone who is interested can learn the mechanics of scene painting and turn out effective as well as attractive settings.

When the settings are complete and ready for the stage, the stage crew and the carpenters together should assemble them. It is essential for the stage crew to help with this operation so that if the need should arise for emergency repairs, or if some adjustment need be made in the rigging during an intermission, the crew will understand how things are assembled and will be able to make corrections or repairs quickly and safely.

Anyone who has ever had a hanging pipe, which was improperly weighted, come crashing to the floor carrying its scenic load to the top of the stage-house, there to smash and shatter, scattering pieces over the stage, will appreciate the need for full understanding and safe rigging of all scenic units. When rigging and hanging stage scenery, there is no place for carelessness or disinterest. Only the most capable and dedicated people should be allowed this responsibility, and even then the technical director should check all rigging. Then, and only then, is the scenery ready for technical rehearsal.

costumes

While the scenery is being prepared, the costume crews are doing a comparable job. The designer has done sketches that show each costume which will be needed. If the costumes are to be built, he has attached swatches of fabric to the sketch and done detail drawings of intricate pleatings, cuffs, collars, and anything else that the pattern maker might not understand from a single sketch. The pattern maker must take the sketch and turn it into patterns that are of the size needed for a particular actor. This means that seamstresses or beginning costumers have measured every performer carefully and recorded his measurements on a card which the pattern maker has access to. When the patterns are complete, the cutters lay out and cut the costumes from the patterns. Seamstresses then put the costumes together so that they may be fitted to the actors. Ideally, the designer will check the fittings to make sure that the costumes hang as he intended. When the fittings are done, the costumes are completed, fitted a second or even a third time, and buttons and trim, of whatever kind, are applied. The final step is the pressing of each garment, although in some cases, when the costume is that of a street urchin, the final step might be dragging it through dust and dirt and allowing it to lie crumpled in a corner for two days. Whatever the case, the final step consists of preparing the finished costume to match the character who wears it.

Just as the settings must be rigged and assembled for the technical rehearsal, the costumes must be organized. Earlier in the planning, a costume plot that shows exactly what is to be worn in every scene by every character is prepared. The wardrobe master and his crew is responsible for organizing the costumes so that the shoes, socks, shirt, tie, coat, cuff links, hat, and sometimes underwear that the actor wears in a given scene are all together, and so that the trousers are pressed and the shoes shined, if these things are necessary. Everything must be marked and checked after each use to make sure that all the parts are there, that they are in good repair and that they are cleaned and pressed as necessary before the next use. Actors should be taught to inform the wardrobe master when a button is loose, a rip occurs, or a shoestring breaks. The wardrobe master should always be available during the production for emergency repairs. His job is to keep the costumes day to day and to assist the actors in caring for them. He is not a valet and should instruct the actors in their responsibilities in caring for their own costumes. No one can do more to insure a smooth-running production with many costumes than an efficient wardrobe master.

makeup

No costume is complete without the makeup and hair styling for the actor. For this reason it is often taken for granted that the costumer is responsible for these elements. Certainly, careful coordination between costume and makeup designers is essential. Sketches should be completed for each actor showing what base, liner, rouge, and special features he is to use. Few beginning actors are accomplished in applying their own makeup but they should be taught to do so and supervised to see that the results they achieve are those the designer intended. Special sessions prior to a dress rehearsal will simplify the confusion and call for a smaller makeup crew. A large cast of inexperienced amateurs can best be handled with a makeup crew that mass produces results. Some people apply the base makeup; others follow this with rouge and liners. Still others do eye makeup. If powdering is required, still others specialize in this. Fifty people can be run through such a sequence with a crew of eight in about one hour. Such makeup is seldom subtle, but most shows calling for large choruses do not suffer from such treatment.

Stage makeup is a highly specialized area, and intricate makeup designs for old age or special prosthetics for scars, burns, or supernatural characters take much time and skill. Such work needs preparation and special materials that cannot be thought about only at the last minute. Designs should be done at the same time that the other production areas are making initial plans if top results are to be expected.

lighting

Stage lighting has become more and more a specialized area. Since lighting for the stage has ceased to be mere illumination and has taken on the characteristics of the other stage arts, it must be integrated into the production in the same way. The lighting designer cannot begin his work until the scenic designer has completed his sketches, but he can work with the scenic designer and remind him of the ways in which light may affect the settings. Once the scenic designs are completed, the lighting designer can begin his work. He must determine what effect his light is to achieve and then he can manipulate the position of the instruments, the amount of light, its distribution, and its color in order to accomplish his aims. Once his designs have been committed to paper, an electrician or an electric crew can follow the hanging plot to place the instruments, focus them, and place the proper color media over each light. The chief electrician will determine how the lights are to be hooked up in order to make the most efficient use of the lighting control system. The designer should supervise the finish focusing and then should set the light levels of each instrument when the scenery has been placed on the stage. Adjustments will be necessary during the technical rehearsal and the dress rehearsals, since no designer can predetermine how much light will be necessary to achieve a particular effect without seeing it. There always seems to be a disagreement between the director and the lighting designer regarding light levels. The director almost always wants more light so that the actors are better seen, while the lighting designer wants less in order to achieve atmosphere. The director wins most of the time.

Seldom does the designer run the control board for his own show. If he does, he is tempted to keep making "improvements" in his design by changing light levels, bringing in or taking out other instruments. Responsible electricians who have helped to hang the lights and know the setup are the best control board operators. They can follow the plot and cue sheets prepared by the designer, and they know how to make adjustments or minor repairs if something goes wrong. Budding designers can learn much about the effects of light by watching many performances of the same play and appreciating the importance of carefully executed cues as well as the actor who knows where to stand to take greatest advantage of his light.

properties

Properties are often considered along with scenery because many of the properties are really set dressing and must be chosen or designed by the scenic designer. Things like draperies, furniture, pictures, lamps, rugs, and the like all must be integrated into the stage setting. Although these things are called trim and set props and may ultimately be the responsibility of the property master, the scenic designer must pass on every item. The primary area of concern for the property master is in the design and selection of hand properties. He must coordinate closely with the scenic and costume designers to make sure that the weapon Cyrano carries matches the period of his costume, but its strength and practicality as a fighting weapon is his responsibility. The number and placement of the stools in the pastry shop he must determine with the director, but their style and coloring will be set by the scenic designer. The kind of pen and ink with which Cyrano writes his letters, the pastries in the bakery will be his to find, build, or buy. The clever property man who is well versed in period paraphernalia and who can find or build adequate substitutes is worth his weight in plastic, balsa wood, and flexible glue.

In addition to his skill in coordinating properties with sets and costumes, and making impossible items, the property man has to be a careful record keeper, for he must know exactly what is used by whom, whether the item is brought on by an actor, discovered on stage, and if so, where and in what position. It is his job to have everything placed in order for the actors to make proper and convenient use of the items. In addition, he must have a record showing whether an item was made, purchased, or borrowed. If purchased, the cost must be recorded for budgeting; if borrowed, the name and address of the lender should be listed and the date the item is to be returned. His record should show that the item was returned and have the signature of the lender indicating that the item was returned in good condition. Perhaps nothing is more important for a theatre than a good borrowing reputation. Many items of all types are too costly to buy and too complicated to build. If lenders know that things borrowed will be protected carefully and returned promptly and in good condition, they will be willing to lend things again and again, or stand as references to others. Such a reputation should be cultivated and carefully guarded. It will not only save hundreds of dollars but many hours of time as well. Complimentary tickets offered lenders cost the theatre nothing but help compensate lenders and encourage new theatre patrons. All these considerations carefully applied by conscientious property masters will make the job of securing properties easier and easier as well as more and more fun. Remember that it takes only one careless instance to ruin a reputation that has taken years to build. The property master should be chosen very carefully from the best people available. He, too, should begin his work as soon as the play is put into production, for his job is not done overnight.

sound

Sound is perhaps the newest of the areas of technical production, not because it is really new, but because it was, for many years, considered a part of the property man's responsibility. Rain was simulated by dropping dried peas on a drum, and wind was created by rotating a wooden cylinder over which was draped a piece of canvas. The rubbing of wood on cloth gave off a sound like wind, and the faster the cylinder was cranked, the louder howled the wind. Other effects were also created in some mechanical fashion. With the advent of recordings, both disk and then tape, much better sound could be created electronically, so sound passed into the hands of the lighting staff—not because light and sound necessarily went together, but because both were electrical. In recent years the sound specialist has developed, and a new area of specialization has been created. It is still most common for sound effects to be the direct responsibility of either the electrical staff or the property staff, depending on how the effect is to be created—electrically or mechanically. If there is no sound specialist, then the stage manager is responsible for making sure that all effects are assigned to one crew or the other. Otherwise, some cues may be overlooked. The stage manager will have all cues, lights and sound alike, marked in his master script and will prompt the appropriate crew to perform at his command.

Since most cues for sound are now handled electronically, it should be noted that there are essentially two jobs to be done in this area. The sound tape, the easiest and most foolproof way to handle electronic sound effects, should be prepared by a sound specialist working with the director. Only the director knows exactly how long a given cue should be and how loud certain music can be to create the background for actors' voices and yet not drown them out. Each cue should be recorded until the exact sound is achieved. After all cues are prepared, a master tape must be made by splicing each cue chosen in proper sequence and with leader tape between all cues. The wise technician will record a second tape from the first for emergency use. The sound operator who will run the tape for the performances must be familiar with the equipment and know exactly how to set up the tape for each cue so that it goes on time, at the right volume level, and over the proper channels. All sound cues should be rehearsed early so that they can be quickly integrated into the action with a minimum of confusion at the first technical rehearsal.

When everyone on every crew does his job correctly and on time, the technical rehearsal and the dress rehearsals can run smoothly and efficiently. The stage manager assumes responsibility for all aspects of the production at the first technical rehearsal. By this time he has worked with all the crews and the director so that he knows exactly what is to be done, when, and by whom. It is he who should go over all technical cues with the set, light, and sound crews so that every crew man knows what is expected of him and how the stage manager will cue him. When everyone is ready, the technical rehearsal can begin, followed by the dress rehearsals and performances. Details of each part of this preparation will be discussed in the appropriate chapter to follow, but the broad areas of concern and the responsibilities of the people do not change.

Although this chapter has dealt with many different jobs, the point should be made once again that in small theatres many of these jobs often are performed by the same people. This does not change the procedure or the areas of responsibility. Small theatres will become big theatres if they bring in new people, assign them specific jobs, and show them the order of the whole. An organized procedure will result in a well-prepared, orderly production, and the dismal picture of unrehearsed actors surrounded by frightened, confused stage crews so aptly drawn by George Kelly in the second act of *The Torch Bearers* will not be performed in real life.

But the business of theatre does not begin and end on the stage. What good would all the preparations and rehearsals be were there no audiences to view the performances? A crew every bit as specialized and essential must be working on the business and publicity related to the production.

Once again it must be said that all too often the director and the actors must perform these functions too, but the jobs that must be done are these: Once the play is selected, the business manager must secure the rights for performance. Most plays that are less than fifty-six years old or that have been translated or adapted within that time are usually protected by copyright. One cannot perform these plays without paying a fee to the person or company holding the copyright. In many cases a flat fee of perhaps $25 or $50 is listed for a performance with a discount for subsequent performances. In other cases the amount of the royalty fee is negotiated on the basis of the ticket price, the seating capacity of the auditorium, and the number of performances. This is particularly true of musicals. When the producing organization feels that a stated royalty is prohibitive, the business manager should write the holding company and offer a fee that the group could pay. Most companies would rather receive a smaller royalty than no royalty at all and so will make efforts, when possible, to compromise. Some theatres have performed musicals for a fee of perhaps $50, while comparable theatres have paid many times this amount simply because they did not attempt to secure some adjustment. "All the traffic will bear" seems to be the motto of some companies. A good business manager can often save the theatre money on royalties simply by trying for adjustments.

In no case should a theatre attempt to perform a play without paying the agreed-upon royalty. This is just as dishonest as stealing. Publishers and rights-holders have agents whose sole job is to report all plays performed in their areas so that proper royalties can be collected. Suits for royalties and damages are not uncommon when unscrupulous theatre groups try to cheat by not paying.

The business manager should have a contract for a given amount of royalty for a set number of performances. If a show is held over for additional performances, the company should be notified as soon as possible and the additional royalty paid.

But the business manager's job does not cease with handling royalty payments. He must also handle all monies related to the production and pay all bills. He must work with the technical director to determine that that part of the budget allotted to production is properly spent and recorded. He must either order tickets or see that the ticket manager does so and double-check to see that all information on the tickets is correct. Such things as seat location, time and date of performance, and title of play should be on each ticket. If there is a policy regarding refunds, this, too, should be stated on each ticket. Some means of recording income must be established and seating charts must be maintained so that prospective buyers can see what seats are available. If a separate ticket manager is in charge, he should work carefully with the business manager and is responsible to him. During performances a house manager is needed in addition to ticket sellers. He should see to the comfort of the patrons, solve any problems of seating or the like, and instruct his ushers in the handling of crowds. It is he who unlocks the house, turns on lights, checks the condition of lobby, house, and restrooms. He is in charge of the front of the house as the stage manager is backstage. The house manager should be clearly recognizable to the audience as the person in charge, and some means of identification should be employed on a continuing basis. A special jacket or a lapel carnation works well. It is the house manager who informs the stage manager when to start the show. He alerts patrons in the lobby before each act.

Ushers complete the house staff. They must be prompt and courteous. They should know the seating arrangement in the house, when the intermissions come, where the restrooms and telephones are, and any special house rules. When in doubt they should ask the house manager.

The other part of the *front of the house* organization is the publicity department. Pictures must be taken and stories must be written to publicize the production. Information about all members of the cast should be gathered and kept on file throughout the run of the show or as long as the same people are involved in productions. A standard form that should be filled out by every cast and crew member will supply the basic information. Personnel should be encouraged to suggest unusual things about themselves that can be turned into feature articles. Newspapers and broadcasting stations receive a vast amount of routine stories from many organizations and so must often be selective in what they choose to print. The clever or unusual feature will stand a much better chance of being used, and what is more, of being read once it appears. Pictures and stories of this nature are far more valuable than paid ads and cost nothing. The wise publicity director will attempt to place some paid advertising with the news media, however, for this public relations gesture is well remembered when the free stories are turned in.

Good pictures are really worth the "thousand words" when it comes to advertising a play. Good pictures are those that emphasize some action germane to the play and which show the performers in costume against the appropriate scenery. Unfortunately, the sets and costumes are seldom finished by the time publicity pictures must be taken. The good publicity director will anticipate this by requesting that certain costumes and scenic units be completed first so that they can be used. If this is impossible, he will attempt to find a location and partial costumes that will give the flavor of the play. In any case almost anything is better than having a number of people in street clothes standing in a line as a notice for the play. Such lack of imagination will no doubt appear in the production too and serve as a warning to stay away rather than as an invitation to attend.

The pictures that the publicity director arranges for must be taken by a photographer with imagination who can pose people well and incorporate the kind of excitement which the publicity for the play should generate. The pictures must be sharp and clear with lots of contrast if they are to reproduce well. Unless there is a good photographer within the group, this service should be paid for, because a professional quality picture is essential to the publicity effort.

Many radio and television stations will take public service announcements from schools and nonprofit organizations. Short, well-written spots of thirty seconds or less will add greatly to the total publicity effort. The journalism maxims should be incorporated in every spot—who, what, when, and where. A brainstorming session by half a dozen people who like to write may turn out enough short announcements for an entire publicity campaign. In any case, writers should be encouraged to do stories on all phases of the production. The publicity director can sort and screen these features as well as edit them so that all materials regarding the theatre group are channeled through one person. This is essential to maintain the quality of the publicity and the sanity of the media people who receive it.

Posters are still used by many theatres, although surveys show that they are the least effective means of publicizing a theatrical event. A good artist is essential, for the poster must be attractive, clear, and contain the necessary information. The most common error of poster-makers is that they try to put too much material on one poster. It must be easy and quick to read or passers-by will not bother. Finally, those posters must be put where they will be seen. People who distribute the posters must be attractive and personable people who represent the theatre well and who relate well with the managers of the places of business to which they take the posters. Ideally, a route can be established so that subsequent posters will appear in the same locations. In no case should a poster be put up without the permission of the proprietor of a given space.

The program is usually the responsibility of the publicity director, for he will have all of the information needed and he will have the artistic and technical expertise to do or secure the layout. All copy should be checked with the director and the technical director to be sure that all cast and crew are properly listed and that their names are spelled correctly. If possible, the corrected galley proofs should be copied and posted so that everyone concerned can check his own listing. If there are no complaints, then approval for printing can proceed.

Many programs contain advertising. The selling of these ads becomes the responsibility of the business manager, the publicity director, or better still, a new staff member aptly named the advertising manager. The advertising manager must work with the publicity director so that the number and size and location of the ads can be determined. Costs of the ads will depend on the amount of money that must be raised. The advertising manager can then proceed to solicit advertisers. He should examine the market to find those firms most likely to desire his ads. Restaurants, specialty shops, businesses that cater to the artists and intellectuals are good prospects. The advertising manager or his staff of salesmen should go armed with programs of earlier productions, if possible, to show the kind of service offered. He should have a facsimile of the current program and he should know costs, delivery dates, numbers of programs to be printed and distributed. Advertising should not be considered as a donation but as payment for services rendered. The ad salesman should know what he has to sell and offer it proudly.

It takes all these jobs well-performed to make a complete production. To be sure, some are more important than others, but each is necessary to the whole. If efforts are made to integrate all the workers into the production staff, each will take pride in doing his job. Ushers become house managers. Advertising managers become publicity and business managers. Carpenters become technical directors. Seamstresses become costumers. Actors become directors. Directors can begin to concentrate on directing because other specialists assume their rightful places of responsibility. Theatre has a place for everybody. It needs organization to take advantage of so many skills.

Although a fine theatre plant is no substitute for a strong group of dedicated actors and technicians, it is certainly something that every theatre person dreams of working in. But remember that the physical plant is the least important part of a producing theatre organization. Any place can be used for a theatre. Someone once said that "three boards and a passion" were all that is needed. Talented actors can exist without any more than a platform from which to perform, provided that there is an audience to watch. Audiences will go almost anywhere to see a good play that is well acted. They will sit on bleachers, straight chairs, or even on the floor if rewarded with a good performance.

At the same time there is more to good theatre than just actors performing well. Costumes, settings, lighting, as well as comfortable seats in a well-ventilated auditorium reached by passing through an attractive lobby and foyer, will contribute greatly to the total theatre experience.

It is important to remember that substitutes can be found for almost everything but the personnel who work in the theatre and the audiences who attend. Theatres, and good ones, exist in basements, surplus quonset huts, tents, geodesic domes, gymnasiums, and elsewhere. Yet none of these is ideal, and the people who work in them always have plans for improving their old quarters or finding new ones.

This chapter is devoted to the kinds of theatres and audience arrangements currently in use as well as a discussion of the support facilities necessary for a producing theatre organization. There is no such thing as an ideal theatre. Theatres designed and built for one kind of show are terrible for other kinds.

Stage shapes and sizes will vary depending on their relationship to the audience seating arrangements, so these areas must be considered together.

stages and auditoriums

There are only three basic ways of arranging actors and audiences: (1) The actor may be on one end facing all the audience who in turn face him. (2) The actor may be surrounded on three sides by his audience. (3) The actor may be completely surrounded by his audience.

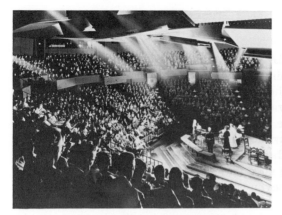

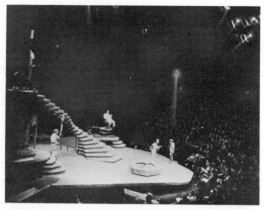

Tyrone Guthrie Theatre, Minneapolis, during a performance of *Three Sisters*. Note how the popular thrust stage provides intimacy with the audience and great spatial freedom. Scenery must be designed with visibility in mind. Note the variety of lighting positions.

Vivian Beaumont Theatre, Lincoln Center, New York City, during a performance of *Camino Real* (*Photo:* Martha Swope).

We call the first of these the proscenium or picture-frame stage. This form is used most frequently for realistic productions. Settings are often box sets with doors, windows, and furniture appropriate to the location established by the play. There is an attempt to create an illusion of the real thing. This form has often been called the *peephole* stage. The proscenium stage originated in Italy in the sixteenth century and has carried down to our time. The scenery has changed periodically in order to be more "realistic," as has the style of presentation that attempts to supply everything for the audience. Little is left to the imagination. For this reason the stage must be equipped for fast scene changes. A rigging system that allows scenery to fly as well as ample space into which scenic units can roll off and store is essential. The floors of proscenium stages are usually trapped in order to allow for additional kinds of entrances and exits. The proscenium stage requires the most involved equipment and is the most expensive to build.

The second staging arrangement is called, severally, the thrust stage, the apron stage, the open stage, and the three-quarter round. The name is not nearly so important as understanding what this kind of stage is for and

Playcrafters Theatre Barn, Quad Cities, Moline,
Illinois. This theatre is indeed a barnloft utilizing
a large thrust area with scenic background. Note
particularly the number of electric pipes used.
Seats and playing area are partially adjustable
(*Photo:* R. E. Sonneville, Barn Manager).

how to use it. Many stages built during the last twenty-five years are of this
type. Other more conventional proscenium stages have been adapted by
covering orchestra pits with forestages. These *modified thrust* stages have
the major advantages of the three-quarter round, for they get their actors
close to the audience and provide a large, unlocalized space on which to
play. They seldom have audiences on three sides but they retain the advantages of the proscenium stage as well and so can combine techniques
within a single play or switch techniques as occasions demand. No theatre
is ideal for all kinds of plays, and those that can make some physical adjustment are obviously more versatile. Some theatres, built at huge expense,
can be adapted mechanically to any form. Yet so many compromises are
necessary to accomplish this that such a *multitheatre* often results in many
mediocre theatres—and not one good one.

The true thrust establishes a close relationship between actors and audience. With audiences on three sides, no one need be more than fifty or sixty
feet from the playing area, even in very large houses. A sense of intimacy
is established between actors and audiences because of the physical close-

ness that is not possible in a conventional theatre of similar capacity, where some members of the audience might be 120 feet or more from the stage.

Since the usual kind of stage scenery would block the view of part of the audience in the three-quarter round theatre, the emphasis is shifted to costumes and furniture. Careful lighting is essential to separate actor from audience. (See illustrations from the Tyrone Guthrie and the Vivian Beaumont theatres.) Much more is left to the audience's imagination. Classical plays that require little or no actual scenery are ideal for the thrust stage. The lines of the author often contain all the description of the surroundings needed by the audience, and the speed of the production can be increased greatly if no scenery must be shifted nor time taken for breaks between scenes. Many period plays were written for such a stage and translate nicely to the modern version. (See photograph, p. 291, for a simple thrust stage.)

The third theatre form is the full round. In this arrangement the audience is seated on all four sides of the acting space. Any scenery which is used must be placed in such a way that the view of the stage is never obscured. Entrances are made through aisles, through trap doors, along special walks and stairs incorporated into the setting. Costumes, furniture, properties, and careful lighting do much to cover the absence of a full stage setting. An audience will accept any frame of reference given to it if that frame is clearly established and never violated in the production. Perhaps the primary problem with theatre in the round is the distraction an audience member finds in seeing his fellow viewer across the theatre looking back at the actors and intruding on the scene. Some theatres have solved this problem by elevating the stage so that it is above the audience. (See photograph of Casa Mañana in Fort Worth.) Others have gone the other way and have lowered the stage so that audiences on opposite sides of the stage need not gaze directly at each other. (See photograph of Theatre Three in Dallas.)

Each of these three arrangements has advantages and disadvantages, only a few of which have been suggested. The kinds of plays presented by a particular company and their method of production will be influenced greatly by the physical arrangement of the theatre. That is why the first consideration in theatre design must be the needs of the company and its style of working.

The round theatre is not always simple or small.
Interior and exterior views of Casa Mañana, a
musical theatre in Fort Worth, Texas. It seats
1832 and has been operating since 1958. The
geodesic dome is self-supporting, and no audience
member is more than 55 feet from the stage
(*Photos:* Lee Angle).

When the stage and auditorium arrangement has been determined, the
next most important question to be decided is one of size. How big should
the theatre be? How many people should it seat and how big should the
stage be? The best legitimate theatres are intimate theatres. Audiences
need to be close enough to feel involved and moved by the performance,
and the actors should not be dwarfed or lost in the space provided. At the
same time a theatre must be large enough to be practical financially. If
only thirty people can be seated, it will be difficult to generate enough income from the box office to keep the theatre running. In addition to the
financial consideration, each state has safety and fire laws that differ as the
size of the house increases. That is why many commercial houses seat 299
rather than 300 or 499 rather than 500. All these considerations, therefore,
must be weighed as one determines the house size – the artistic, the commercial, the practical. Most people feel that a straight play suffers if the
house is larger than about 500. This figure is great enough to allow a reasonable box office income for a noncommercial theatre, and the regulations
governing such a house are not too stringent. A commercial theatre can
seldom exist without a potential income of about $20,000 per week. At a
price of $4 per ticket (perhaps average) this would mean a 750-seat house

would generate $3000 per performance which, for an eight-performance week would be $24,000.

The size of the stage in relation to the house is important. If only straight plays are to be presented proscenium style, a stage opening of about 30 feet is best. Musicals fit better on a stage that has a proscenium opening of from 36 feet to 45 feet. A good rule of thumb is that the total width of the stage should be three times that of the proscenium opening and one and one half times the opening in depth.

The height of the proscenium should be half to two-thirds its width and the stage house height should be three times the proscenium opening height. Many educational and other organizations cannot be convinced that this amount of space is necessary, but any theatre person can quickly justify it in terms of shifting scenery and storing working units. Unfortunately, decisions governing buildings built with public funds are often made by nontheatre people, and this space is seen as an unnecessary luxury that can be cut easily. It is often better to scrap the whole idea of the proscenium theatre than it is to compromise too much in the above figures. Yet given the amount of floor space suggested above, one can cut a fly system and plan to shift all scenery by rolling methods. He must still have a provision for hanging curtains, masking borders and lights above the stage if his theatre is to be really functional. Under those circumstances a proscenium theatre could still work well. There is no question that equipping a proscenium theatre is basically more expensive than equipping any other kind. The counterweight system for flying scenery, lights, and curtains costs perhaps $500 per hanging batten, and the installation makes it even more expensive, not to mention the costs of masking curtains, cycloramas, scrims, and other equipment. Bigger, better-equipped shops are necessary to build scenery for the proscenium stage, which adds still another dimension to the total operation. Yet for the best treatment of the realistic play that is still our primary fare, there is no form as good as the proscenium theatre.

Few organizations are in a position to choose their theatres without making compromises due to cost, governmental regulations, or the like. This

Theatre Three—a Dallas, Texas, intimate theatre seating fewer than 300. Opposite corners are used for scenic units seldom employed in round theatres, which allows for the best of both theatre forms. This setting is for *Anything Goes* and was designed by Jac Adler (*Photo:* Steve Bromfield).

Wing and drop or wing and shutter scenery from the Renaissance provides period flavor and easy handling for Restoration and eighteenth-century plays. The false proscenium serves as a permanent frame for the scenic units. Note the detail photos of the top and bottom grooves in which the flats slide for *The Country Wife*, designed by John Kasarda, University of Iowa.

makes the thrust and round stages more attractive. The thrust stage need
not be as large as the proscenium stage, for there is seldom need for the
amount of offstage space or fly space that a scenery-oriented stage requires.
Such space is used primarily for storing scenery and properties until they
are needed. Then they are moved onto the main playing area. The thrust
stage, on the other hand, is almost entirely playing area. If any scenery
is used, it is usually a permanent structure against which, or upon which,
the stage action takes place, and it seldom needs to be shifted during the
course of the play. The size and shape of the playing area will vary with the
theatre, but 900 square feet arranged appropriately is adequate for most
thrust stages. The comparative simplicity of the thrust stage arrangement
and the lesser need for stage machinery make the thrust stage less expensive to build and to maintain. For these reasons it has achieved great
popularity. Realistic plays do not fare so well on this stage as on the proscenium stage, but the classics, most of which are presentational in nature,
suffer more at the hands of the proscenium stage. The thrust stage is an
excellent compromise to this author, but to many other theatre designers
and directors the thrust stage is the ideal form.

The full round theatre is perhaps the easiest form to achieve, since any
large room can be turned into a theatre in the round. All that is needed is
some means to raise the audience so that it can see the playing area or to
raise the acting area so that it can be seen from the audience on the floor
level. An area about 16 to 20 feet square is large enough for most theatres
of this kind. Audience accommodations are seldom greater than 300. The
advantages of this form of theatre are that scenery is virtually eliminated
in favor of furniture or simple set pieces arranged in a "natural" way. Costumes do not need the kind of exaggeration that distance requires in the
proscenium theatre, and, therefore, carefully chosen clothes can often be
gathered rather than designed and made for the occasion. Lighting must be
very carefully controlled and is, perhaps, the single most important technical element. All in all, theatre in the round is the least expensive to
produce. This is not to say that it is the easiest, however. Since audiences
surround the stage, actors must be arranged in a three-dimensional way

rather than in the old two-dimensional patterns of the proscenium style and the modified version of this required by the three-quarter round. Every member of the audience wants to see expressions, bits of business, and relationships between actors. The director must constantly check his blocking from all sides to insure some kind of balance, or part of his audience will look mostly at backs. Acting in the round takes a kind of subtlety which is not found in the other forms because the audience is often close enough to touch the actors, and every tremor, twist, and smirk carries to the assemblage. The kind of consistency and control required of the actor here is perhaps the most difficult of all the forms. He cannot even hint one thing with his voice while saying something different with his face and body.

It should be clear by this time that the size and shape of the auditorium and the stage is an integral part of the total production problem. For this reason the group planning a new theatre must decide its aims before committing itself to any form. By the same token the group that has a particular facility should reckon with it when planning a season or a single play. *Ben Hur*, with teams of charging horses, would be a bit difficult in the round, while *Two for the See-Saw*, or another two-character play, would suffer just as much in a theatre seating 3600 people with a 50-foot wide stage.

Assuming that the kind of theatre and its size and relation to a program has been established, what else is needed to support such a plant?

stage equipment

Looking first at the proscenium theatre, there must be provision for hanging masking draperies on the sides and across the top of the proscenium opening. To make the theatre truly flexible, these hanging positions should be pipe battens that can be raised and lowered in order to change the positions of the draperies easily and quickly. A stage with a counterweight system and pipe battens suspended across the stage on 1-foot centers from the proscenium arch to the back wall will provide hanging positions for draperies as well as any scenic or lighting units that need to be flown. Sky drops or cycloramas, scenic drops, set pieces, even entire sets, can be flown with such a system. It is a fast, efficient way to make scenery changes in the proscenium theatre. Special pipe battens with lots of electrical outlets placed every five or six feet within the same counterweight system provide the additional lighting positions necessary to light properly the whole of the proscenium stage not lighted from house positions. These house or beam positions will be discussed under lighting requirements.

The stage floor of the proscenium stage should be divided into sections, any or all of which can be removed in order to provide special entrances or exits from the stage. Dr. Faustus cannot descend to hell without such a trap, as these openings are called. A larger opening, made by removing several floor sections, can be a swimming pool or the East River or a grand staircase, while a small opening can be used for the brass pole for firemen, or an entrance to a bomb shelter, or a mine. If the entire stage floor cannot be trapped, then at least one large trap should be located down stage center where a clever designer can arrange his designs to take advantage of this single location. The fully trapped stage floor is one of the requirements for any fully flexible stage.

Many theatre people feel that a revolving stage and/or stage elevators are essential. These features are wonderful and useful. They are also luxuries less essential than a trapped stage. A temporary revolve can be built and assembled on top of the regular stage floor, but a "temporary" trap can seldom be cut. Perhaps the elevator that is also the adjustable floor of the orchestra pit is not so much of a luxury. It can be the means of transporting equipment to the stage level from the basement areas as well as the adjustable floor for different kinds of orchestral arrangements, and it can also be the modified thrust forestage, which makes a proscenium theatre even more flexible in its uses.

The thrust stage needs some form of rigging system to allow masking on the fourth side. A counterweight or winch system that will allow for some lighting positions and hanging positions for drapes or scenic pieces will prove most useful. There is seldom the need for the very high stage house of the proscenium theatre. The thrust stage will be somewhat more flexible if the fourth side does have some *backstage space* for storage, shifting, and scenic manipulation. A screen for projection and space to rear project from would add greatly to the stage equipment.

Most of all the thrust stage needs some kind of tunnel system so that the actors can make entrances and exits from other than the backstage side of the playing area. Such tunnels should allow for two actors to move abreast and with sufficient headroom to avoid ducking. Lighting is of special importance, but this will be discussed separately. Traps are as essential to the versatile thrust stage as they are to the proscenium stage. They should connect with the tunnel system so that actors can move freely from area to area.

The full round stage is perhaps the least demanding. Entrances from the aisles or through tunnels are important, and traps that allow entrances within the playing area would be excellent. Yet few round theatres are so constructed. Special rigging for flying is almost impossible, for there is no "standard" way in which pipes could be flown, but a series of spot lines that could be dropped anywhere on the stage from an overhead grid which was strong enough to support weight in addition to the lighting equipment would greatly aid the theatre in the round. Most round theatres are simply large rooms converted to theatres, and the round form was chosen because of the light demands. Planning with these considerations in mind, however, will provide many more opportunities for enterprising directors and designers.

lighting positions and equipment

In the proscenium theatre, the lighting designer is concerned only with the way the actors and the settings appear from the audience side and he lights accordingly. In thrust or full-round staging, he must worry about appearances from all four sides. The problems of lighting are much the same in any theatre form; the number of sides simply compound the problems.

Certain rules of thumb can be applied to stage lighting. For example, an actor usually looks best and most normal when he is lighted by at least two instruments that strike him from about 45° up and the same angle left and right. (See Chapter Twenty.) This necessitates hanging positions over the audience from which lights can be directed toward the stage. Additional

The interconnecting panel allows any circuit to be connected to any dimmer. The plugs come from the outlets to which the lights are connected. The sockets on the face of the panel are inputs into various dimmers. Plugs are counterweighted so that they return to their places when released. *Left,* A small panel for connecting 15 dimmers, 6 outlets each, with 132 circuits. Plugs are pulled up from the bottom (*Photo:* Kliegl Bros.). *Right,* A large panel for 200 dimmers and 704 circuits. Plugs are pulled down from the top on this unit (*Photo:* Century-Strand).

---

onstage positions are also essential. Lighting positions that allow for as many angles and directions as possible will simply make the arrangement that much more versatile – from the floor, from directly overhead, from left and right, and any combination of these. Thrust and round lighting must provide the same variety as proscenium lighting. The differences between the forms result from the fact that there are many more places for actors to be in thrust and arena staging, and, therefore, that many more locations are needed.

In addition to many hanging positions one must have lots of circuits into which instruments can be plugged. It is both time-consuming and dangerous to run many temporary cables about. The more circuits there are located in positions where instrument use is heavy, the more flexible the system. Most theatres being built today will have at least 150 circuits and many will have between 250 and 500.

Lighting control equipment should include a dimming system and an interconnecting panel. The interconnecting panel allows any circuit in the theatre to be connected to any dimmer. Several circuits can be grouped

on the same dimmer so that a number of instruments can be controlled together. This simplifies the running of the show and it also allows the electrician to load several small instruments on a single dimmer of large capacity. Fewer dimmers will be necessary with such a system. There are several kinds of interconnecting panels manufactured. Some are like telephone patch cords with plugs on flexible cables that are simply inserted in holes in a panel to complete the circuits. Others are like strips of copper running in opposite directions; the vertical strips represent the circuits and the horizontal ones the dimmers. Plugs like big clothespins are stuck in to connect a vertical to a horizontal strip completing the circuit. Still a third type is a rotary selector switch. One simply turns a dial to connect the dimmer to the circuit.

Dimmers are electricity control devices that allow the operator to regulate the degree of brightness of the stage lights. Autotransformers are perhaps the best and cheapest of the voltage regulator dimmers. Silicon controlled rectifiers are the best of the current regulators. Some dimmers are dial controlled and some have lever action. The lever action is easiest to use in the theatre, and it is possible to group several levers and control them with one hand, one foot, or other parts of the anatomy capable of manipulating a lever. More and more theatres are discovering the value of the remote controlled lighting system. The dimmers are located in any out-of-the-way place, but the dimmer controls are placed at the rear of the auditorium so that the control board operator can see the stage clearly. This way he can see what he is doing and better coordinate the lighting

---

The dimmer racks for remote-controlled systems may be placed far from the control console. Silicon controlled rectifier dimmers are small, quiet, and require minimal ventilation so that any out-of-the-way room near the stage can house them. *Top left*, A single 12,000-watt SCR dimmer is approximately 6 x 8 x 10 inches and weighs less than 10 pounds (*Photo:* Kliegl Bros.). *Top center*, An eighteen-dimmer rack with dimmers in place (*Photo:* Kliegl Bros.). *Top right*, Twenty-four dimmers arranged in a standard rack with space for sixteen more (*Photo:* Century-Strand). *Below left*, A portable combination dimmer rack and interconnecting panel. Two men can easily carry a unit capable of dimming over 7000 watts (*Photo:* Kliegl Bros.). *Below right*, A control console in a suitcase is this small two-scene preset board that hooks up in seconds to one or more of the combination units above (*Photo:* Kliegl Bros.).

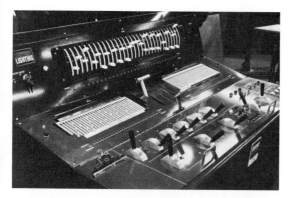

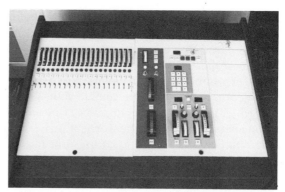

Remote control consoles of the most advanced types. Smaller, simpler units using the same components are within the financial reach of most schools and should be considered in new construction or remodeling. *Top left*, A control card system with submastering. The cards can be preset and inserted in the board when needed. Manual controls for the thirty-dimmer system are at the top (*Photo:* Century-Strand). *Top right*, The Memo-Q console made up especially for demonstration with only twenty dimmers. Such a console is not practical for less than forty-eight to sixty dimmers. The "memory" of this system is capable of storing hundreds of cues and playing any one immediately upon request. Direct control of any dimmer is possible at any time (*Photo:* Century-Strand). *Bottom left*, A sixty-dimmer control console with five presets and submastering in use at the State University of Iowa (*Photo:* Kliegl Bros.). *Bottom right*, A similar system shown in use at the Tyrone Guthrie in Minneapolis overlooking the set for *Three Sisters* shown on page 290 (*Photo:* Kliegl Bros.).

cues with the total show. Educational theatres used to oppose such systems because they could be operated by only one person, and they felt it necessary to give many people experience. They have since learned that there is far more learning with the new system and that eight people back in a darkened corner pulling handles at cues from someone else were not getting lighting experience for they could not even see what they were accomplishing.

The remote control systems are of varying complexity from simple direct controls with a master dimmer to systems that can store hundreds of cues in their memories and have the ability to jump from any cue in the show to any other. Such systems are designed individually from standard component parts, and the costs will vary from a few hundred to many thousands of dollars, depending on the complexity. Systems costing over $100,000 are not unusual.

For the best lighting for any theatre, then, there should be lots of hanging positions for instruments, enough circuits to handle all the instruments in these positions, an interconnecting panel so that any instrument can be plugged to any dimmer, enough dimmers of sufficient capacity to handle all of the instruments used, and a control board placed where the operator can see the stage, a board on which one or two people can operate fairly complex cues quickly and accurately.

Although every theatre is different, general guidelines for educational theatres should indicate at least 150 circuits and 36 dimmers, each of 4-kilowatt capacity, with a control board on which at least two full light cues can be set up at one time. Many theatres operate with considerably less, but this suggestion might well be taken as a standard for any new theatre planning.

lighting instruments

Lighting instruments must be chosen with great care, and the choice depends heavily on the theatre in which they are to be used. One must calculate the length of throw from the various hanging positions, and he must

An excellent working beam position with easy access to the lights and a continuous beam slot for easy focusing in the new Teatro Bellas Artes, Caracas, Venezuela (*Photo:* Century-Strand).

figure about how large an area will be illuminated from those positions. He must determine also whether the light should be sharply defined or soft and general. Only then can he choose among the various sizes and types of instruments. Generally speaking, ellipsoidal reflector spots with plano-convex lenses will throw the greatest amount of light the longest distances, while spherical reflector spots with fresnel lenses throw a softer light for shorter distances. Floodlights and strip lights, for lighting backdrops and for general fill light, are also necessary, but their choice also depends on the specific theatre. A theatre consultant and/or a lighting designer should make these choices. But more of this in the chapter on stage lighting.

sound equipment

There are two types of sound equipment that must be considered. First there is the intercommunications and telephone systems that theatres need. The stage manager must be able to maintain constant communications with the light and sound people, the flymen, the house manager, and any others to whom verbal cues must be given from a distance. A telephone system with headsets instead of handsets for these busy people is ideal. Signal lights should be used instead of bells in order to avoid distracting noises.

A system of speakers over which the play in progress can be programmed to dressing rooms, director's office, and green room areas will allow actors and others directly involved to listen to the show while waiting for cues without gathering in the wings to wait and without requiring calls to be made for them. A two-way talk system to all working areas of the theatre is very useful, and this same system can be set to program the play to all stations in such a way that talkbacks will not cut in and interrupt backstage. A ten-station system is available for under $300.

Sound reproduction and amplification equipment is the second type to be considered. There are a great many factors involved as well as personal preferences as to types and manufacturers, but several general comments can be made.

Two tape recorders and a turntable will allow the operator to record his own sound effects and make his own tapes. An amplifier will provide increased power to drive external speakers. Two will allow mixing of volumes and qualities of sound from several sources. Matched speakers properly mounted and baffled will give balanced, quality sound. Every sound input should be able to be plugged to any amplifier and, through it, to any speaker. Such combinations will greatly increase the possibilities of sounds the system is capable of producing. Permanent connections are very limiting.

Self-cueing cartridge tape players have been used for some years in radio stations, but they are just finding their way into the theatre. A cartridge tape has several advantages. It starts instantly on cue without the warm-up or speed-up noises heard on discs or tapes. When a cue is finished, the tape sets itself ready for the next cue. An operator of such a system need be concerned only with starting each cue. If all cues are recorded at their playing sound level, the operator need not set even a volume level. Such a system is as protected from human error as is possible. Anyone who can press a button at the right time can run it. Cartridge tape equipment of this type and quality is comparatively expensive but worthy of consideration in new theatres.

support spaces

No theatre is complete with simply a stage and an auditorium. There must be dressing rooms, scene and costume shops, storage rooms, and for the front of the house, a lobby, ticket booth, business office, and restrooms. Theatres that house touring shows only are called *janitor houses*, and these buildings do not need construction and storage facilities, but all the other spaces are necessary.

Dressing rooms should be large enough to house comfortably thirty people. Two such dressing rooms will take care of all but the largest casts. Makeup mirrors with lights on three sides are needed, and at least twenty such stations should be provided. Sinks with running water are needed in the makeup areas, and restroom facilities for cast and crew must be available and separate from the audience facilities. Costume storage racks are a necessity, and places for the actors to store their own clothes should be provided. A safety lock-up area is also needed, although people should be encouraged not to bring valuables to the theatre.

Although the same space must often be used for costume construction as is used for dressing rooms, this is not ideal, for it limits the number of activities that can go on concurrently. Costume shops must also have extra light, power, and water for sewing machines, electric irons, washers, driers, and dyeing equipment. The well-planned theatre will provide lots of costume storage space somewhere in the theatre, ideally on the same level with the costume shops and the dressing rooms. Most storage can be further away as long as some active storage space for the bulk of items currently in use is available. Being able to build, finish, and prepare costumes in one area and move them on rolling racks directly into adjacent dressing rooms will save hours of work and many strained backs. Those theatres that have the costume storage on the fifth floor, construction on the third, and the dressing rooms on the first are all too common, because no one planned for them when the building was constructed. Every little cubbyhole not used was later assigned to the costume people. Even now our consultants and architects very often overlook this vital area and its requirements.

Just as important and often just as abused is the scenic construction area. A good shop must be large, well ventilated, and have good light and enough height to allow for trial setup of scenery. There must be adequate electric power for power tools and, under the best of circumstances, gas and compressed air as well. A scene shop should be laid out to allow easy access from loading doors to lumber storage racks. A logical arrangement of tools and working spaces should allow for the normal construction sequence of scenery without lots of carrying back and forth. The closer a scene shop can approximate an assembly-line arrangement, the more efficient it will be. Rough cutting is first followed by basic assembly with covering and finishing next and painting last. There must be space for each of these activities to go on concurrently, and further, there must be adequate storage space for units that may be used again and again. Storage space is most often overlooked, but a good theatre, well designed, with space for proper storage, will enable that production organization to operate on half the budget and in half the time of other theatres, with no loss of quality in production.

No two designer-technicians will agree on the tools with which a shop must be equipped, but a radial arm saw, a table saw, a band saw, and a drill press would constitute a pretty good start. There are now so many small power tools that will substitute temporarily for even these that choosing the bulk of the shop equipment should be left to the discretion of the people who are to use it.

property rooms

A separate property construction and storage area may appear to be something of a luxury, but it too will pay for itself in time by allowing items to be properly stored and catalogued, so that properties will stay in good condition and ready for repeated uses. A property construction area with its own small tools, painting equipment, and plastics and foams for molding will allow construction of items that would otherwise have to be bought at exorbitant prices. The construction area must have forced ventilating because of the toxic nature of lacquers, varnishes, acrylics, and plastics currently in use in the theatre. The storage area needs lots of shelves and as much dust control as possible. With shelves and cabinets numbered and labeled, a card file for properties can be set up to enable anyone to find anything without the kind of searching that usually leaves the room a mess. Card files are very useful for scenery as well.

Finally, and just as important as the space and equipment discussed above, is the need for a person or group of persons who know how to make the equipment work to maximum capacity. Equipment is useless without people of imagination and creativity who can tax it fully.

The previous chapters have stressed that it is the director who has the final responsibility for the entire production in every theatre organization except the commercial. There, the producer, by virtue of the fact that he hires the director, sets the budget, and often hires the designers and the actors, exercises controls that do not exist in the educational or amateur theatre.

In these theatres it is the director who not only picks the play, but his actors and production staff as well. In many cases he is the production staff in addition to being director. In those theatres where he is fortunate enough to have designers, costumers, and technical directors, the director meets with the designers to explain his play concept. He does not appear with designs, of course, but he does come in prepared to discuss the many questions for which the designers must have answers before they can begin their work.

Suppose the director has decided to present the production of *Cyrano de Bergerac,* mentioned earlier. When he attends the first production, he indicates that he sees the play as "a psychological study of a handicapped man," or "an historical treatise of a seventeenth-century poet," or "a swashbuckling historical romance of a man almost larger than life." Whatever he ultimately decides will be the concept within which every member of the staff must work if the production is to be a unified one. It is perfectly appropriate for the designers to attempt to influence the director in establishing his concept. They may point out how much more attractive one style would be visually, how much more variety could be achieved with another, or, plainly, the fact that the budget cannot be stretched to achieve the spectacular grandeur required in authentic period costume—all of the things that their own degrees of expertise make them acutely conscious of. A good director will weigh these suggestions and comments before he makes a final determination of concept. In a repertory situation the demands on key actors may also be factors, as would the costs of scenery, costumes, and stage facilities. These items are major limitations that the designers face and as such will affect their abilities to carry out the director's concept. Whatever the case, once the director has established the concept, it must be the governing plan for everyone working with the production. Yet within this scheme there is still a great deal of leeway for the designers. The scene designer's case is typical.

Unlike the painter, who is limited only by the size of his canvas, the range of his paints, and his own abilities, the scenic designer has a number of other considerations that affect his work. After he knows the director's ideas concerning the play, he still has much to learn from the script before he puts pencil to sketchpad.

The designer should be able to answer the following questions when he finishes with the script.

1. Where does the play take place? Is it in America or China? Is it indoors or outside? Is the setting a restaurant or a family living room? Need it be anywhere in particular?

2. When does the play take place? Is it a contemporary or period piece? Is it winter or summer? Is it noon or midnight? Need it be any time in particular?

3. How do the characters relate to the setting? Is it their home? Are they visitors? Are they there by choice or by chance? Does the place reflect their tastes and interests? Need there be any particular relationship?

4. What kind of people are these characters in this environment? Are they warm, friendly people? Do they like each other? Are they natural or artificial? Are they poor or well-to-do? What is their social and economic status?

5. Does the setting change in any way? Do the people change? How is the setting affected by the action of the play?

6. What physical requirements must the set include?

Still other factors that the designer must consider include where the play is to be performed, how much money is allotted for scenery, how much time there is until production, how much help is available for building, and how skilled the people are. The availability of special materials is often an additional factor. With each of these answers the designer is better able to begin to shape his designs.

The description of the action tells him whether he needs doors, windows, fireplaces, stairs, trapdoors, or what. He knows if specific relationships are required of these various parts, and he knows if a specific description of some element is mentioned in the lines that he must incorporate. He knows, for instance, if the play calls for someone to jump out of a window, that the window must be built to open and must be of such size that one can indeed

Differing solutions to the problems created by multiset shows. *Top left, Peer Gynt,* San Jose State College. One part of the impressionistic setting designed for a revolving stage by Dale Dirks. Polyurethane foam sprayed over brown wrapping paper makes the rugged mountainside. *Top right, Peer Gynt,* University of California, Santa Barbara. A fluid platform stage provides nonlocalized areas for the play as designed by David Sackeroff. *Bottom left, The Man With the Oboe,* University of Illinois, Urbana. Shifting screens, small wagon units, and two levels allow for many fast changes in this broadly cartooned design by George Talbot. *Bottom right, Death of a Salesman,* University of Iowa. Arnold Gillette created this multilevel, interior, exterior setting that allows concentration on one or several areas through light control. Notice the scrim walls behind the living area so important kitchen business can be seen. *Opposite: Top left, Toys in the Attic.* University of Northern Colorado. This

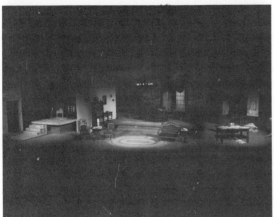

interior-exterior setting designed by Welby Wolfe is simpler and more skeletonized than the Gillette one for Death of a Salesman, yet the whole is clearly suggested to provide the flavor of period architecture. *Top right, Six Characters in Search of an Author,* Indiana University. A novel solution to the problem of play within the play arrived at by William Kinzer, who designed a curved architrave resting on slender pipe columns into which simple screens and cutouts could be inserted by the actor-stagehands. *Bottom left, An Enemy of the People,* Brigham Young University. Charles Henson designed three realistic sets and placed them side by side on this very wide proscenium stage. Light provided the necessary emphasis and control of attention. *Bottom right, Yes Is for a Very Young Man.* Hunter College, City University of New York. Robert Guerra shifts free-standing painted screens behind a permanent false proscenium arch that unifies his design scheme.

jump through it. He knows that if a body must be hidden in a window seat, that seat must be large enough to accommodate the actor playing the role. All of this specific information he garners from careful reading of the script.

His discussions with the director tell him the style in which the play is to be treated. *Historical romance* allows for more color and exaggeration than does a straight *historical treatise*. Special emphases of the director must be determined. If special bits of business are planned but not discernible from the script, the designer must be informed about them. The director might want the hero to sweep the heroine into his arms and carry her down the stairs. If the script indicates that the heroine is not even upstairs at the time, the designer might design a narrow run of stairs for only one person to descend unless the director has told the designer of his plan.

Until the designer knows where the play is to be presented, he will not know the stage facilities available to him nor will he know the arrangement between stage and audience. The theatre is of major concern to the designer. Without this knowledge he cannot determine the scale of his settings nor the amount of space they can occupy on the stage. In multiset shows the amount of storage space available is just as essential as the playing space. Every play has essential bits of business that everyone in the audience must see, and these must be located within absolute sightlines. The designer cannot determine the arrangement of the parts of the setting until he knows what parts of the stage are totally visible.

Another item of major concern is the means of shifting the scenery. If there is more than one setting, then it must be removed and replaced by others. Often the amount of time available for such a change is very short and the whole design of the setting is affected by the necessity for speed in shifting. When a stage is equipped with a flying system, revolving stage, or various kinds of stage elevators, or even if there is ample wing space to roll scenic units into, the number of sacrifices necessary in order to shift the set rapidly will be far less than those required on small, poorly equipped stages. This is not to say that the problem cannot be solved without costly equipment. The point is that the designer must know under what circumstances he is working in order to do the job to the best of his ability. The better he knows the stage and its limitations, the better his scenic designs will be.

A designer must be constantly aware of costs. He must work within a budget that fluctuates greatly due to constant changes in prices for lumber, fabric, scene paint, lamps, and color media. Even the play done in modern dress on a bare stage will have some expenses. Masking draperies must be cleaned occasionally. Lights must be burned and lamps replaced at costs of from $4 to $35 each. Color media will average about $.50 per instrument, and makeup is essential under almost all circumstances. Actors' clothes must be laundered or cleaned. Production costs may be hidden but they are always there. It is part of the designer's job to recognize these costs, establish them, and assign them in a realistic fashion within his budget.

A scenic designer must be able to turn out artistic, exciting settings, but he must be able to do this on a predetermined budget. A good designer uses this budgetary limitation as a challenge; he begins to plan his designs as though money were no object. Only after he has designed the ideal setting does he begin to eliminate, substitute, and rearrange his ideas as dictated by his budget and his ability to estimate costs. The resulting setting hopefully keeps the essence of the original but has been adapted to the budget. On occasion the trimming may require nothing more than substituting a different quality of fabric to reduce the costs. It might be a matter of changing a proportion in order to reuse door units in stock, or it could be something as major as using a single set in place of the specified two or three. Whatever the case, the designer must be a practical theatre man who knows how to estimate costs and make each dollar do the work of three.

Arnold Gillette, long the designer-technician at the University of Iowa, kept a card file of every flat in his theatre. Each card carried a notation stating when the flat was built, in what shows it had been used, and its current state of repair. It was not unusual to find units older than twenty years still being used regularly. Some of those flats had been used in far more than one show a year. If the original cost had been $15 each, then even twenty uses of a unit would make each use an average $.75 expense. If a standard box set required about thirty units of all kinds, then the initial expense would be only $24 with the rest of the show's budget available for furniture, draperies, or special items. An all new set would have cost $450 just for the basic shell. This kind of planning and organizing can reduce scenic costs by at least half, but it takes a considerable amount of storage

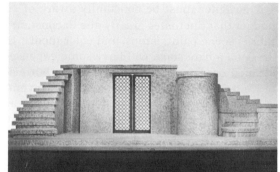

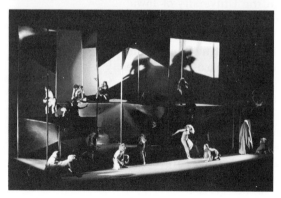

Varying design concepts for producing Shakespeare. *Opposite: Top left, Measure for Measure,* University of Northern Colorado. An architectural space designed by Welby Wolfe. The use of a revolving stage adds variety by revolving new forms for each scene. *Top right, Romeo and Juliet,* Eastern New Mexico University. A permanent architectural setting unchanged except by light designed by Larry LaGrave. *Center left, Troilus and Cressida,* University of Georgia. W. Joseph Stell designed a formal setting with primitive overtones that provides a wide variety of blocking opportunities (*Photo:* Gates Studio, Athens, Georgia). *Center right, Henry IV, Part 1,* Indiana University. A formal setting located within a proscenium arch that allows for continuous action. Designed by the director, William E. Kinzer. *Bottom left, Measure for Measure,* University of California, Berkeley. An exciting athletic, nontraditional approach designed by Henry May (*Photo:* Dennis Galloway). *Bottom right, Henry IV, Part 1,* University of California, Berkeley. A purely theatrical design by Henry May (*Photo:* Dennis Galloway). *Above: The Merchant of Venice,* University of Iowa, designed by Louis Lager as though staged by prisoners at Auschwitz concentration camp.

space and a designer who can see the variety of possibilities in his current stock of materials.

Even when the designer has the ideal plant, a huge budget, and his favorite play and director, he must consider time as he is working out his designs. Everything that is to be built, rigged, or painted will take a certain amount of time and the skillful designer must be able to estimate this, too. The curtain will rise at the appointed time and the set must be finished.

One does not walk out to face his audience on opening night with an apology for not being ready. Most designers have been in the unenviable position of painting the third act set while the first act was playing and from this experience have learned not to over-design. The designer must know how long it will take to execute his designs. Some shortcuts can be bought with additional funds—preformed plastic panels and glue-on mouldings, to mention only two. These items are expensive but save hours of preparation. On the other hand, rope, plastic hose, and papier-maché laboriously worked for hours by hand can be used to create wonderful hand-carved effects for next to nothing.

One of the best ways to make every minute count is by having complete working drawings for everything that is to be built. Skilled workers who can read these drawings can make an hour do the work of five if they do not have to stop to ask questions or puzzle over a poor sketch in an effort to guess what the designer had in mind. Examples of such drawings are shown in Chapter Nineteen.

Each of the above limiting factors is partially offset by the many skills of the designer, who must be able to do far more than draw pretty pictures. A top designer is not only an artist but a skilled draftsman, architect, efficiency expert, and, finally, a public relations man. For in addition to designing the settings, doing the working drawings, building and painting or supervising these phases of production, he must also manage to integrate his ideas with those of the director and the designers for lights and costumes. It is not unusual for the same person to handle all the technical chores, and this simplifies the communication problem and insures the integration of the various production elements. Just as often, though, there are three designers, each of whom feels that his contribution is the most important and must be adjusted to by the others. Who determines the choice of colors, the light level, even the placement of certain items of furniture?

In a production of *Dial "M" for Murder*, the scenic design incorporated a color scheme of ice-blue walls and cream-colored woodwork. The combination was chosen because the blue created a kind of cold sterility that reinforced the relationship between the husband and wife. Because of budgetary reasons, some champagne satin draperies from stock, which tied in nicely with the rest of the color scheme, were being used—at least until the lighting designer began to light the set. The lighting man insisted on using blue gels for the moonlight scene. When the lights were first turned on, the set appeared luminescent. The blue glowed and the satin drapes hung drab and dirty looking. The lighting man wanted to have the set repainted and the drapes changed so that he could keep his blue moonlight, which he insisted was essential to the plot, since the murder had to be committed by moonlight, which was apparently the only source of illumination. After much discussion, the lighting designer agreed to use a blue-green gel, which gave the moonlight quality but was less electric for the blue of the set and turned the drapes a handsome gold. Such compromises must be made frequently among the designers. The designer who understands the whole picture and who can adapt his designs for the good of the whole production is not only a talented designer but a joy to work with. Much has been made of the dedicated artist who places his vision and his genius above everything, but the solid, producing artists of the theatre are those who see more than their own efforts. Prima donnas are sometimes tolerated in the theatre, but they are never admired. Theatre is a team activity, and this is as true for the designers as it is for the actors.

Although the preceding paragraphs have dealt specifically with the scenic designer, the procedures for the other designers are essentially the same. A costume designer is concerned with the play for he must learn about the characters in order to dress them appropriately, be it satins or rags, hoop skirts or minis. In many respects we are what we wear and so the costumer must learn the personalities of the characters so that he can reflect this in their dress. His conversations with the director will indicate special relationships and special emphases that the director wishes to make more clear through visual means. Family relationships or political alliances might be subtly stated in a Shakespeare history play by having all those loyal to the crown wearing garments within the red color range from lavender on the one hand to orange on the other. The rebels might be dressed in greens from chartreuse to blue-green. The range of colors possible keeps the statement from being as obvious as opposing uniforms could be, but the allegiance of the dozens of nobles involved is clearly established.

The costume designer must be just as concerned with the bodies of his actors as the scenic designer is with his stage. The costumes must be designed to fit the character, but they must also fit the body of the actor playing that character. Seldom can a costumer design the costume until he knows the physical limitations of the actor assigned the role. He might need to use long lines to make the actor look taller, or he might need to pad a too-slim actor. He might want to emphasize the size of an already hefty body. All these physical considerations will affect the designs of the costumer.

The stage is a costume limitation too, for, depending on the distance the actors will be from the audience, costumes will have to have a greater or lesser degree of finish. An extra in a crowd scene placed 90 feet from the audience will not need to have clothes finished with the same meticulous care as those of the leading lady in a theatre in the round where no one is further than 25 feet from her.

Time and budget affect the costumer in exactly the same way as they do the scenic designer, and one additional factor should be mentioned—that of kind and availability of fabrics. Good costumers are constantly on the prowl for everything from carpet remnants (good for boots, if the scenic designer does not get it for platform padding first) through upholstery and drapery fabrics to the usual dress materials. If a yearly budget that allows him the flexibility to take advantage of sales and closeouts of discontinued merchandise can be set up, costume budgets can stretch much further.

The lighting designer is perhaps most affected by the work of the other designers, for he cannot begin his work until they have finished theirs. His job is to light the sets and costumes they put on the stage in such a way as to create the proper mood and atmosphere while enhancing their work. This means that he must consult with them during their own design stages in order to avoid such problems as those suggested earlier. Helping to determine color schemes and choices of fabric by explaining what he wants to do with light will make the entire design scheme more cohesive, and it

A striking use of skeletal structure in a traditional theatre is R. B. Chambers' setting for *Celebration* at the University of Texas, Austin, pictured on the next three pages. The entire set can be used as an "acting machine" while individual areas can be isolated by light and, with the addition of simple properties, become anything the action demands.

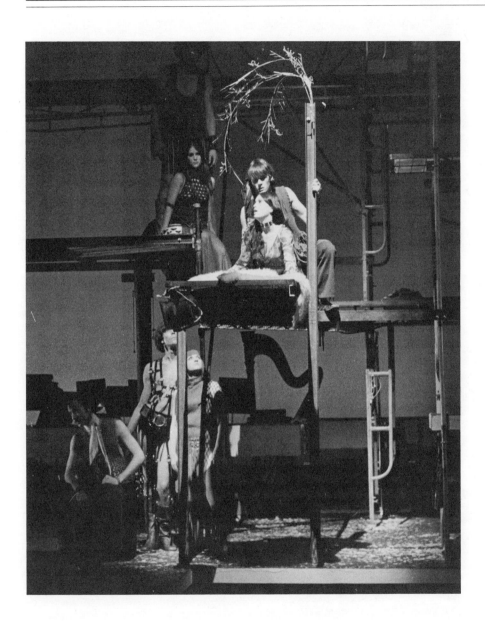

will actually give all of the designers more flexibility. Although the lighting designer would appear to be the most limited, he still has a great amount of freedom to accomplish his purpose. It has only been in recent years that the lighting artist has become a recognized specialist in the theatre. Most sets used to be lighted by the scenic designer or by an electrician who carried out vague directions from the scenic designer, the director, or even the stage manager. As long as the audience could see, lighting had accomplished its purpose.

With the great improvement in instruments and control systems in the mid-twentieth century, theatre lighting has become much more than mere illumination. There is so much variety possible that only a specialist can take full advantage of it. Lighting has become the newest of the design areas in the theatre.

The lighting designer is just as concerned as the others with the play and the director's concept. He is often the most concerned with the physical plant, for, since lighting is the newest of the theatre arts, it is often given little consideration in the building of new buildings. Inadequate circuitry, a lack of dimmers, poor hanging positions, and inadequate power supply are only some of the problems that theatres may cause for lighting designers. He must study a theatre carefully in order to learn what kind and what quantity of lighting is possible. The number and complexity of light cues will depend on the capabilities of the control board.

In addition to knowing the work of his colleagues in a given production, the lighting designer must know how to use his theatre and its equipment. Some years ago, a new theatre was opened in Canada. It was equipped with the finest, most advanced electronic lighting control equipment available. On opening night the performance had to be canceled because the "control system failed." A subsequent check showed that the personnel had simply not known how to operate its complex controls properly.

Few of us suffer from such riches, but just as much a problem is the theatre group that fails to attempt anything out of the ordinary because it feels it must have more lights and more dimmers. A clever lighting designer can distill the essence of his needs and, with imagination and ingenuity, make a little do a lot. Such situations seem to bring out the best in real designers.

The points that have been mentioned so far are normal parts of any designer's homework. These limitations establish bounds within which he must create artistic settings, costumes, or lighting.

Like any other artist, the scenic designer must arrange the elements of his setting in ways that are both pleasing and meaningful to his audience. Suppose the designer is to design the setting for Ibsen's *A Doll's House*. The director has stated that it is his intention to direct the play as a realistic problem drama treating women's rights in the late nineteenth century. The designer reads the play and finds that it takes place in a room identified only as "in Helmer's house." There is no indication that it is located in Norway or that the date should be 1879. Since the playwright was Norwegian and the play was first performed in 1879, the director or designer might logically make these determinations, however. The designer does learn from his reading of the script that the play calls for a room with four doors, a stove, and a grand piano, along with other items of furniture. He learns also that the man of the house is a banker, reasonably well-to-do, who treats his wife as a child. She goes along with this game to maintain a happy household but finally leaves home when she cannot make her husband understand that she is a reasonable, thinking, responsible adult.

With these details the designer is ready to go to work. He knows his theatre, his budget, and his other limitations. Now he must arrange the doors, windows, furniture, and wall hangings in such a way as to create an atmosphere appropriate to the play, and give the kind of emphasis to particular locations that will underscore the plot. He will choose architectural styles that fit the period of the play, and he will combine them with colors which reinforce the mood of the situation and fit with the total design scheme. He might use dark woodwork and medium blue walls with a darker wallpaper pattern. This combination could be lightened or darkened by the right lighting to help change the mood of the play, but it would also be essentially an accurate historical possibility for nineteenth-century Norway.

In this way the designer's element of line, form, and color have been used to create a setting both architecturally correct and dramatically expressive. But the designer must go further than this.

He might, for example, use a number of conflicting patterns to provide not only appropriate period flavor, but to create the feeling that there are inner struggles between the people who live there. He might use a formal furniture arrangement to show the rigid, ordered household that Helmer keeps. Those items of furniture might be a little bit ostentatious, too, to show how concerned Helmer is with appearances. The costumer might dress Nora in brightly colored frilly clothes during the first part of the play to show how Nora attempts to play the part assigned to her by her husband Helmer. Then, when Nora realizes that she must deal seriously with Helmer, she could be garbed in more severe, dark attire. These few examples illustrate the use of line and color and form to create atmosphere or to define character.

In order to emphasize the separation between Helmer and the rest of his household, the designer might place the door to Helmer's study alone on the D.L. wall. The other doors and furniture could be grouped variously, but away from that door. The door and its significance would loom larger and larger in the minds of the audience by virtue of its obvious separation.

Less symbolically, the designer might solve the problem created by an actor playing Dr. Rank who cannot play the piano, by placing the piano so that the keyboard cannot be seen from the audience. An item so large as a piano will change the balance on the stage if it is moved around, so the designer must, by other manipulations, make the piano seem at home in its location. Each adjustment causes a chain reaction of other adjustments, and so the designer must consider all these matters as a single problem to be solved. He cannot, for example, place a chair in a prominent location so that a particular actor can deliver an important speech from it without considering where other things must be placed in relation to that chair. If the chair's position is the most important concern, then he must build his whole design around it.

The designer uses line, form, and color to create interesting stage pictures, but as the preceding paragraphs show, he must also use these elements for dramatic purposes as well. In other words, the stage designer, whether he is concerned with scenery, lights, or costumes, must create work that speaks dramatically as well as aesthetically to the audience.

Good stage design does not just happen. The process is long and tedious. It consists of the analysis mentioned earlier and proceeds through sketches to the finished rendering and on to the completed set or costume that appears on stage. The designer usually begins with *thumbnail* sketches. These are small pencil sketches, hardly larger than a thumbnail, that allow the designer to test many arrangements and styles without taking a great deal of time. Those ideas that seem worthy of development are drawn again, this time larger and more completely. Furniture, decoration, even characters are often sketched in so that the idea may be examined more fully. Several sketches of the same idea may be done in order to test various color schemes. After consultation and approval by the director, the designer prepares his finished sketches in full color (Chapter Nineteen). The sketches are usually accompanied by a floor plan (*ground plan*) that shows to scale exactly how the scenery is arranged on the stage as viewed from directly overhead. (See Figure 14.) Additional drawings, called front and rear elevations (Figures 15 and 16) show the scenery as it appears from the audience side and from backstage. These drawings carry all the information necessary for the building, rigging, and painting of the units. In the case of complicated three-dimensional units, special drawings might be required. With this group of drawings the carpenters and painters should be able to complete the scenery.

There is no substitute for complete, careful drawings. Although they take time to prepare, they will save endless hours, for they make it possible for the building crews to proceed without having the designer there constantly to tell them what to do.

The parallel in costuming and lighting continues. Costuming requires sketches, followed by color sketches accompanied by fabric swatches, followed by patterns, and then finished garments. The lighting designer works from the scenic designer's sketch and floor plan. He develops his light plot that shows the choice of instruments, their locations, the area each is to light, and the color media to be used. He further determines how the instruments will be plugged and what dimmers will control them. When the setting has been mounted, the lighting designer executes his lighting design and sets the necessary cues and light levels.

Stage design is an integrated art. It requires that the various designers work closely with each other in order to create a total production. The suc-

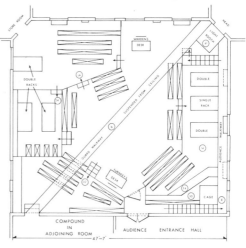

Some designers prefer to work with models rather than sketches. Multilevel, complex settings are often easier to understand as models than as sketches. *Opposite: Top, The Caretaker,* Southern Illinois University, Carbondale. Darwin R. Payne designs for the three-quarter round (*Photo:* Bob Jones). *Bottom, The Brig,* Northern Illinois University, DeKalb. Alexander Adducci executes his design first in a hardware cloth, wire, and wood model that leads to the scaled floor plan. *Above:* The completed set for *The Caretaker,* fully dressed.

cess of the production depends on the ability of these separate artists to achieve unity.

The major unifying factor that can bring together the work of different artists is style. In simplest terms "style" means the manner of doing. When we say that a play is to be done *realistically,* that is the style. To the director the realistic style implies that his actors will move, speak, and react in a manner approaching life. To the scenic designer this style means that the stage setting will give the appearance of what we would find in life. If the setting is to represent a kitchen, it would be furnished like a kitchen and appear to be a kitchen, although the sink would not be hooked up and the stove would not really work and the walls would be made of standard theatre flats. It is as "real" as it needs to be for the sake of appearance and practicality, but not more so. The costumes would look like real clothes, and the lighting would appear real, which would mean that there would have to be apparent sources for the light on the stage.

In each case we would be talking about the *appearance of life*, not real life. The "manner of doing" would be the creation of the appearance of reality, and the name applied to the style would be *realism*. Hence, realism would be the unifying factor for the production. This consideration would govern the work of all the designers, and whatever they did would have to fit within the bounds of realism.

There are a number of other styles called by such terms as *formalism, expressionism, impressionism,* and *symbolism,* to mention only a few. Descriptions of these terms can be found in almost any book on scenic design and so no definitions will be given here. The point must be made, however, that style must grow out of the play and the concept. One does not assign, arbitrarily, a style to a production. He finds the style within the play. It is great fun for designers to do exercises in style by picking plays and designing them a number of ways, but this is a game, it is not sound working theatre practice.

Whether a play is treated in a single, pure style for which there is a convenient label or whether it demands its own special style, there must be consistency in all elements of the production if the play is to stand as a whole. It is style that makes the difference. And it is designers, by their imaginative use of line, form, and color, who must enforce the style.

Stage settings come in all shapes, sizes, and colors. There are realistic box-set interiors; formal, nonrealistic, platform, stair, and ramp arrangements; draperies with set pieces; and many others. Some are extremely complicated and expensive; others may be as simple as two chairs placed on a bare stage. Whatever the set, it is important that it be arrived at by a designer who has analyzed the requirements of the play and, after careful discussion with the director, created this particular arrangement especially to serve this particular play.

No play can succeed because of the quality of its production alone, but the appearance of the setting will do a great deal to set the tone of the piece. Sets that are built, painted, and mounted according to standard methods of procedure will be strong, safe, attractive, and economical. Crew members who learn proper basic building techniques will be able to build any kind of scenic unit and will develop, along with their skill, a pride in doing their work well. Technical theatre demands the same degree of ability and talent as does performance. Only when this is recognized and expected does the technician become a collaborator *in*, rather than a worker *on*, the production.

A well-built stage set begins with complete, accurate working drawings. The designer should draw the floor plan for the stage setting on a master plan of the stage. This will show him exactly how the set will be placed on the stage, what the sight lines are from every part of the house, and how much space will be left for storage, entrances and exits, placement of property tables, and even some lighting stands. The floor plan should be drawn to a scale large enough to be easily readable but not so large as to make the drawing too big to handle conveniently. A scale of $\frac{1}{2}''$–$1'$ seems to work well in most cases. A single dark line represents set walls; a somewhat lighter line represents edges of platforms, stairs, and other stage areas and locations. The darkest line is always the set outline. A number of special symbols are used to stand for various openings in walls—different kinds of doors, windows, and fireplaces, for example. (See Figure 17.) Platformed areas are marked with x's from corner to corner; their heights are marked in feet and inches and then circled. Items of furniture are drawn in place and at the same scale as the rest of the plan. Everything is dimensioned so that the drawing can be transferred to the stage floor without the need for

The designer's color sketch must show clearly how the finished set will appear on stage. *Top*, This design for *Il Matrimonio Segreto* (*The Secret Marriage*) was prepared by W. Joseph Zender, University of Colorado. *Bottom*, A photograph of the finished setting. See Figures 14, 15, and 16 for the working drawings of this setting.

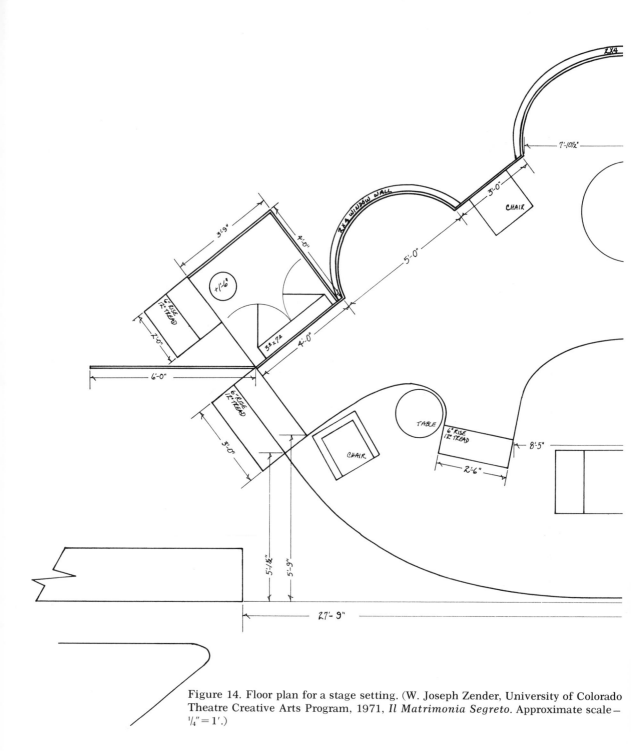

Figure 14. Floor plan for a stage setting. (W. Joseph Zender, University of Colorado Theatre Creative Arts Program, 1971, *Il Matrimonia Segreto*. Approximate scale — $^{1}/_{4}'' = 1'$.)

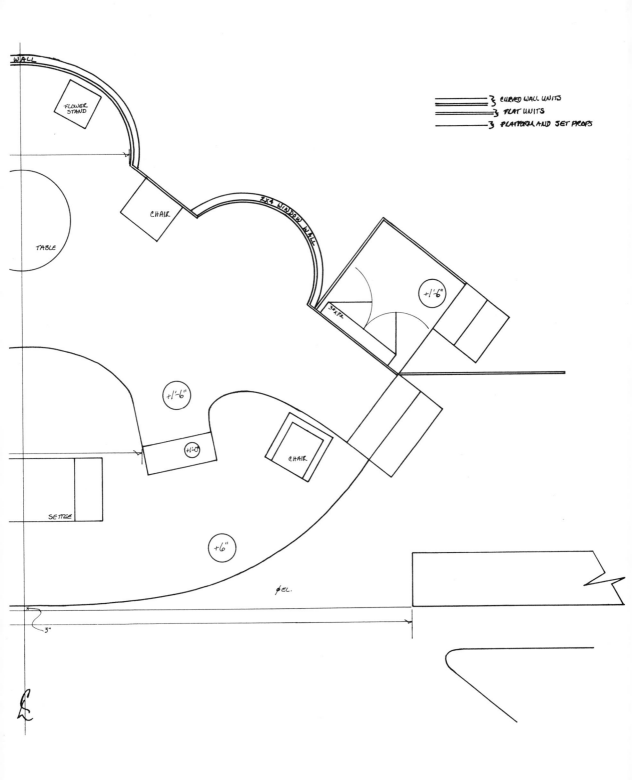

WALL

FLOWER
STAND

CHAIR

TABLE

2X4 WINDOW WALL

3X7½

+1'-6"

+1'-6"

+1'-0"

CHAIR

+1'-6"

SETTEE

+6"

∅EL.

3"

3 CURVED WALL UNITS
3 FLAT UNITS
3 PLATFORM AND SET PROPS

337

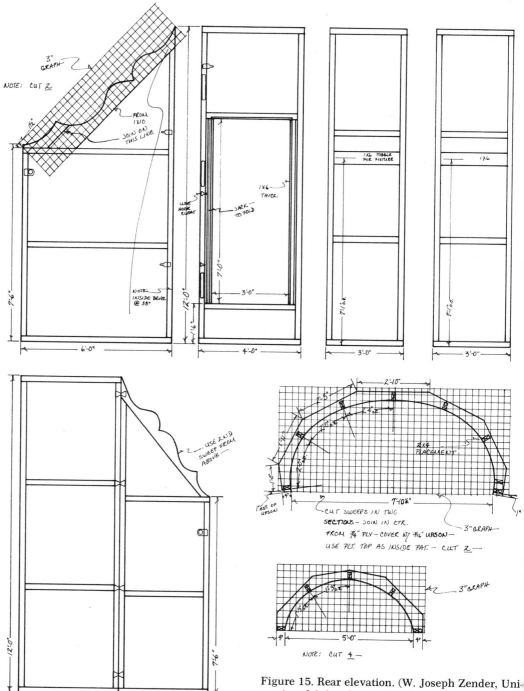

Figure 15. Rear elevation. (W. Joseph Zender, University of Colorado Theatre Creative Arts Program 1971, *Il Matrimonia Segreto*. Wall units, app. scale $-\frac{1}{4}'' = 1'$.)

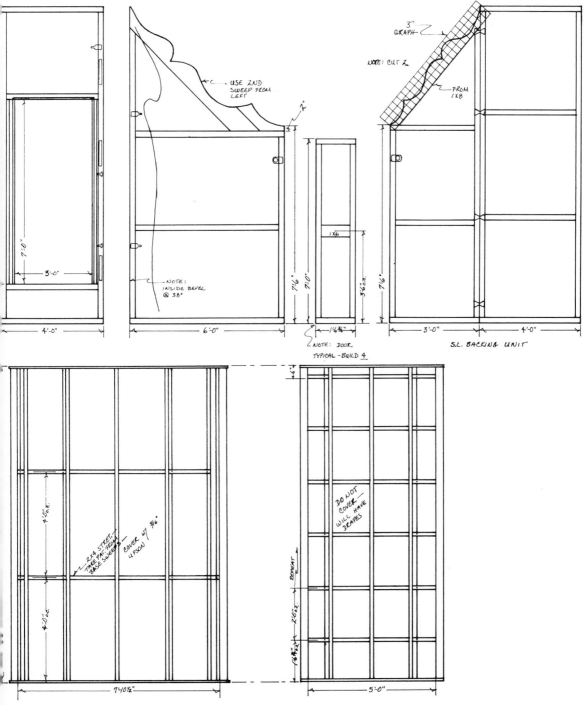

NOTE: BASE AND FRIEZE ON CURVED UNITS FROM ¼" PLY—

BASE — 8" — FRIEZE — 6" --

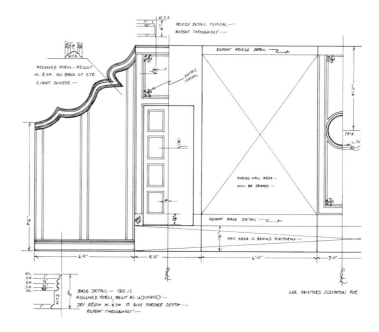

Figure 16. Front or painter's elevation. (W. Joseph Zender, University of Colorado Theatre Creative Arts Program, 1971, *Il Matrimonia Segreto*. Painting layout, app. scale $-\frac{1}{4}'' = 1'$.)

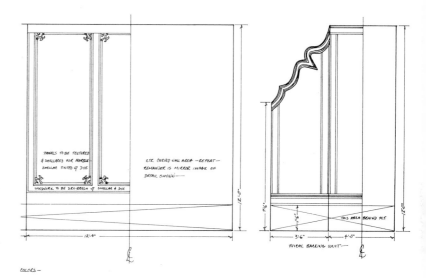

COLORS —

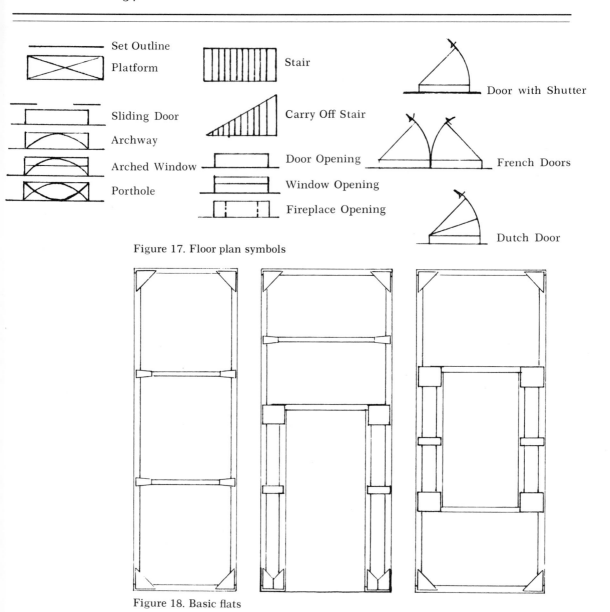

Figure 17. Floor plan symbols

Set Outline

Platform

Sliding Door

Archway

Arched Window

Porthole

Stair

Carry Off Stair

Door Opening

Window Opening

Fireplace Opening

Door with Shutter

French Doors

Dutch Door

Figure 18. Basic flats

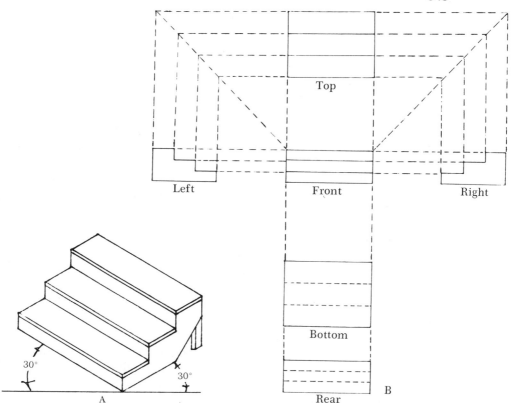

Figure 19. A, Isometric detail; B, Orthographic detail

additional measurements. A completed floor plan looks like Figure 14. It shows exactly where every part of the set is located and how much space it takes up.

The basic unit of stage scenery is a canvas-covered wood frame called a flat. Flats may be of many different shapes and sizes but they have only height and width. They have no depth except the thickness of the lumber from which they are built. Most theatres use flats of varying widths up to 6 feet. Height for standard flats will depend on the theatre and its proscenium opening, but 12 or 14 feet is average. The Metropolitan Opera uses units of 24 feet and often extends these to as much as 36. Flats are most commonly built of 1 × 3 clear white pine and covered either with unbleached muslin or lightweight scenic canvas. Standard flats of the most common types are shown in Figure 18.

Flats such as these can be put together in many ways to create rooms with widely differing floor plans. The numbers and types of units will determine the number of possibilities. When a designer decides on his floor plan, he must then draft a rear elevation drawing which shows the relative size, shape, and position of all the flats necessary to make up the set. (See Figure 15.) Since the view drawn is from the back, the flats are drawn in order from stage L. to stage R. The rear elevation shows what is to be built, how it is to be built, and what material it is to be built from. Each piece of lumber in the frame is drawn in place, and all height and width dimensions are included so that the carpenters can build the units as they are shown.

This drawing shows, too, how the flats are to be joined together. When several units are necessary to make up a single wall, permanent joining techniques are used. On the other hand, corner joints are often lashed or fastened by some other temporary means. Various devices used to keep straight walls aligned or supported when in position are also indicated on the rear elevation. Any information necessary to allow the carpenter to build, assemble, and erect the shell of the set must be included on the rear elevation drawing. (See Figure 15.)

The front or painter's elevation shows how the set is to be finished. It includes wallpaper patterns, paneling, door and window trim, and other woodwork. (See Figure 16.) Anything that is to be a part of the architectural trim of the set or the decoration should be shown on the front elevations. The dimensions necessary to allow a painter to transfer the patterns and trim to the finished flats must be marked on the front elevation drawings. All of a repetitive pattern need not be drawn, but enough must be shown to establish the sequence.

Occasionally special kinds of units must be built to complete the stage setting: window seats, bay windows, or special items of furniture that cannot be bought or borrowed. Units of this type must be drawn in three dimensions to be clearly understood by the carpenters. Either orthographic

Variations on the two-dimensional scenic approach. *Above:* A line drawing technique on a small screen is carried through to properties and costumes as well for Menotti's *The Telephone* by designer P. R. Hendren, State University College, Fredonia, New York. *Page 346: Top*, The full, painted drop for *She Stoops to Conquer*, designed by Paul Camp at the University of Georgia (*Photo:* Gates Studio, Athens, Georgia). *Bottom*, Exaggerated leaves with jointed stems, designed by Roger Klaiber, which made the entire forest for *Androcles and the Lion* at the University of Colorado. *Page 347: Top*, A broad, cartoon-like style lends itself well to the farcical treatment of Shakespeare's *Comedy of Errors* while forced perspective is used behind the false proscenium arch to create depth in the Renaissance manner, designed by Joseph Stell at the University of Georgia (*Photo:* Gates Studio, Athens, Georgia). *Bottom*, Cutouts of fence and trees spaced in front of the painted house façade used for *Man and Superman* at San Jose State by J. Wendell Johnson (the car is an antique Maxwell).

or isometric drawings are the best kinds, depending on the complexity of the items. (See Figure 19.) Again, the clarity and completeness of the drawings will allow for fast, error-free construction because the designer will have solved the construction problems through the preparation of his drawings.

Set construction is not a haphazard, hope and pray activity, but a highly specialized craft. The better trained the technicians are in technical theatre procedures, the cheaper, faster, and safer the set construction process will be. A. S. Gillette's book *Stage Scenery, Its Construction and Rigging,* is one of the best books on the subject. It treats in detail the operations listed here.

shop tools

An adequate scene shop is essential to a smoothly run technical program. Few theatres have the ideal arrangement, but in addition to the space and general layout arrangements mentioned in an earlier chapter, certain items of equipment will greatly facilitate construction. Few technicians will agree exactly on the order of importance of tools, but those that follow are high on most lists.

hand tools

   I. For Driving
      A. Rip hammer (16 ounces)
      B. Claw hammer (13 ounces)
      C. Screw driver
         1. Regular
         2. Offset
         3. Phillips
         4. Yankee
  II. For Cutting
      A. Crosscut saw (twelve teeth to the inch)
      B. Rip saw (eight teeth to the inch)

C. Matt knife
D. Hacksaw
E. Tin snips
F. Cold chisel
G. Wood rasp
H. Metal file
III. For Measuring and Marking
A. Framing square
B. Tri-square
C. Steel tape (at least 12 feet)
D. Sliding T-bevel
E. Chalkline
F. Spirit level
IV. For Miscellaneous Uses
A. Bit brace and assorted auger bits (including expansion bit)
B. Slipjoint pliers
C. Side-cutting pliers
D. Adjustable end wrench
E. Wrecking bar
F. Nail puller
G. Pipe wrench (always need two)

With the advent of small hand-operated power tools, a great many scene building jobs have been simplified. The ⅜-inch electric drill equipped with a wide variety of bits of all sizes—a screwdriving attachment, a sanding disc, and a polishing bonnet—has virtually eliminated the need for the bit brace, hand drill, and various rasps and paring tools. The sabre saw or hand jigsaw makes it possible to work without the more expensive jigsaw, the band saw, and, to some degree, the router. The circular saw does much of the work of the larger, more expensive table saw. Many small shops can do quite nicely without the larger power tools, but such equipment, along with the items mentioned above, will contribute to a safer, more efficient operation.

Even on a limited budget it is possible to accumulate gradually the above small power tools. Every one can be bought for $50 or less, although the stronger, heavy-duty models may cost a bit more. The cheaper lines often start at less than $10 for drills and sabre saws, and the circular saws begin at about $25. One additional hand-held power tool that is invaluable in a shop which does a great deal of bolting of legs to platforms is the electric impact wrench. This electric wrench with a full set of sockets will tighten or remove a nut with a single squeeze of the trigger.

The well-equipped shop needs as a minimum four major power tools. The *radial-arm saw* is used primarily for cutting lumber to length, but it can be adjusted and used for ripping as well. It will not cut anything wider than 15–18 inches, but theatre lumber is seldom wider than 12 inches.

For those special wide boards and large sheets of plywood that must be ripped, the *table saw* with rip fence is used. A dado attachment used for notching should be interchangeable between the radial-arm and table saws.

A considerable amount of hole-drilling in metal occurs in the average scene shop, as does the need for precise holes in wood. The portable hand-held electric drill may be powerful enough for most of these jobs, but the operator can seldom keep a heavy enough pressure on the tool or keep it perpendicular to the piece he is drilling. Loss of time and sloppy work are the results. A *drill press* solves both problems.

The fastest and neatest way to cut gentle curves such as sweeps for arches is with a *band saw*. The width of the blade limits the sharpness of the curves that can be turned, but varying widths are available and the blades can be interchanged.

Extra power tools for future consideration include a grinder for sharpening cutting tools and a wood-turning lathe for stair spindles, candlesticks, and other properties that must be carved from wood.

Of course the list can go on and on, but any scene shop equipped with all the tools listed above will be able to create anything of wood and fabric. Sooner or later an acetylene welding outfit will add the new dimension of metal working, but this is not a consideration for the first years of operation in amateur theatres.

Rather than listing prices here for the above items, which change constantly anyway, it is recommended that the scenic technician keep current catalogues in his shop. The major mail-order houses sell first-quality tools and their prices will serve as excellent estimates of current average prices. The bibliography includes, too, major sources for all kinds of theatrical equipment and materials.

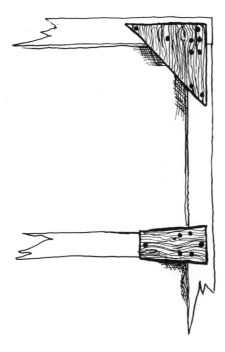

Figure 20. Joint construction
and nail patterns

With an equipped scene shop and completed working drawings, building
scenery is a fairly simple task. Most settings are made of flats of various
kinds fastened together to represent a room of some kind—a living room, a
kitchen, a hotel room, a restaurant. When the builders know how to build
plain door and window flats and put them together in various combinations,
they are well on the way to creating good stage scenery.

flat building

A flat is a canvas-covered wooden frame as has been mentioned previously.
The frame is built of clear white pine that is light, strong, and easily workable. It is relatively inexpensive. Framing material is usually 1 × 3 inches,

which means that it is 1 inch thick and 3 inches wide—or it was when it was rough sawn. Its actual finished dimensions are about ³/₄ × 2³/₄ inches. The pieces that make up the frame are called rails (the top and bottom pieces), stiles (the side pieces), and toggles (the cross pieces). Whether the flats are plain or have openings within them, the pieces go by the same names and the construction is basically the same. Note carefully the way the pieces butt together in Figure 20. The flat frame is joined together by means of ¹/₄-inch plywood pieces called cornerblocks (triangles) and keystones (rectangular pieces) that are nailed over the joints. A specific nail pattern is also indicated in Figure 20. Notice, too, that the visible grain in the plywood pieces runs perpendicular to the joints made by framing pieces. This provides the greatest possible strength for the joint. Three-penny resin-coated nails, clinched by driving them through the plywood and frame against a metal plate underneath, will lock the joints in place. The cornerblocks and keystones should be set back from the edges of the frame by the thickness of the framing lumber, usually ³/₄ of an inch. This allows the finished flats to be butted smoothly at right angles along their entire length. If the plywood extended to the edges of the flat, the spaces between the pieces would be visible.

When the frames have been assembled, they must be covered with canvas or muslin. Canvas is stronger but muslin is cheaper and a bit easier to work with. The fabric should be cut to a size slightly larger than the frame to be covered. A mixture of half white casein glue and water is then brushed over the stiles and rails of the flat frame. No glue is put on toggles or inner braces. Two workers lower the fabric onto the frame, making sure that the material is not stretched tightly but allowed to sag on the frame. The fabric should be rubbed briskly to press it against the frame. Scrap blocks of 1 × 3 work well for this purpose. There must be no wrinkles around the outside edge of the frame. When the glue has dried, the excess fabric should be trimmed off, leaving the finished, covered flat.

Next, a thin paint solution called size is brushed over the entire flat. Casein paint cut by 50 percent with water will also serve this purpose. It fills the pores of the fabric, providing a good painting surface, and it causes the canvas or muslin to shrink so that the fabric is stretched tightly over the frame. If the fabric has been stretched when it is glued to the frame, the shrinkage may cause it to pull loose, tear, or warp the frame. The bigger the flat, the more sag is necessary in the original attachment.

After the sizing operation, the flat is ready to have the necessary joining and/or bracing hardware attached to it.

joining and bracing hardware

Because flats are seldom built wider than 6 feet, it is often necessary to join two or more edge to edge to create a longer straight wall. If the wall must be moved from place to place, then the flats that make it up must be joined so that they can be folded into a smaller, more compact unit for storage or transport. A wall that is 15 feet long and 10 feet high will not go through a normal doorway, but a wall that can be folded into a unit only 5 feet wide and 10 feet high can be turned on edge and easily moved through a standard door.

The best way to join the flats for a straight wall is by means of hinges placed across each joint on the face or canvas side of the flats. If three or more units of approximately the same width are fastened together, two things must be remembered. (1) The narrowest flat of the group must not be in the middle or the units will not fold. (2) If the units are the same size, then a folding strip or tumbler must be placed between two of the flats. When the hinges are in place, a canvas strip only slightly narrower than the wooden members on either side of the joint (the stiles of the flats) is glued over the joint to hide the crack. When the wall is laid out straight, it appears to be a single surface rather than several separate units, yet, because of the hinges, it can be folded up into a size no larger than the largest flat within it. (See Figure 21.)

Stage corners where two flats meet are usually nailed in place (if the set does not have to be shifted) or lashed together using sash cord and lashline cleats. Two kinds of corners must be considered, the one that points away from the audience (Figure 22A) and the other (Figure 22B), which points on stage. The important thing to remember here is that the crack between the flats must run across rather than up- and downstage to make it as un-

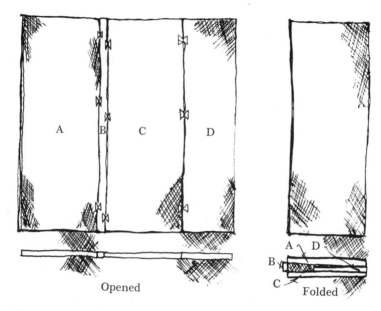

Figure 21. A three-fold flat assembly

obtrusive as possible. The sash cord or lashline is attached to the upper right-hand corner of the left-hand flat as one faces it from the rear. Lash cleats are spaced about every 4 feet on alternate sides of the joint with the exception of the first cleat, which is down only about 6 inches below the point of attachment of the lashline and on the other flat, and the bottom two cleats that are directly across from one another and about thirty inches up from the floor.

In order to keep lashed joints aligned, stop cleats are used on the offstage

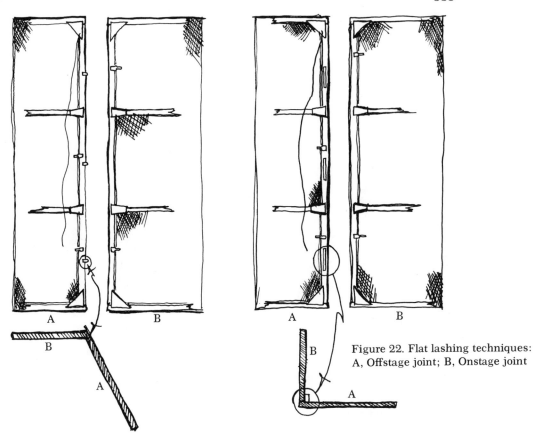

Figure 22. Flat lashing techniques:
A, Offstage joint; B, Onstage joint

joints. Stop blocks are attached to the back of the downstage flat in the onstage joint and are set back from the edge of the flat ³⁄₄ inch. (Note stop cleats in Figure 22A and stop blocks in Figure 22B.)

When joints are nailed together, they are placed in the same relative positions and three or four nails are spaced along the joint. Since this joint will be broken when the show is over, double-headed nails should be used so that one head will stick out conveniently for the wrecking hammer.

Sets that have a number of sharply angled walls will sit sturdily on a stage

Figure 23. Bracing with the stage brace

Figure 24. Bracing with the knee jack

with little additional bracing, but long, straight walls or working doors have a tendency to wobble at the least touch or movement of air. Special bracing techniques must be employed to solve this problem.

The standard method for bracing a piece of stage scenery is with a stage brace cleat that is screwed to the back of the flat about two thirds of the way up. To this is attached an adjustable stage brace whose other end is fastened to the stage floor with a stage screw. (See Figure 23.) The second method is by means of a knee jack that is a brace made of 1×3 lumber and hinged to the back of the flat. The jack is either fastened to the stage floor with a stage screw or weighted with a sandbag. (See Figure 24.)

When two or more flats have been hinged to form a wall, it is often difficult to keep them aligned so that the wall appears straight. A stiffening batten attached on edge to the backs of the flats will help to keep the wall

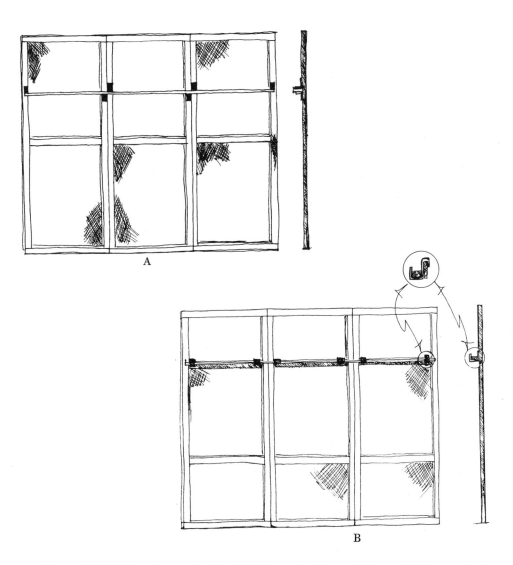

Figure 25. Stiffening long walls: *Top*, With loose pin hinges; *Bottom*, With keeper hooks

straight and secure. The batten may be hinged in place with loosepin hinges (Figure 25A) or it simply may be hung on the toggles of the adjoining flats with large S-hooks made especially for this task. (See Figure 25B.)

doors and windows

When the basic shell of the set is built and properly joined, braced, and stiffened, shutters must be added to the door openings and window trim to the window openings.

Door and window units are of two types: those that are built and attached permanently to the flat openings and those that are separate structures fitted into the flat openings. The latter method is best in the long run, for the same door units can be used again and again with little or no rebuilding except for a change of trim and a new paint job.

Such a door consists of a frame with a working shutter. The frame is made up of the facing, which is the "woodwork" surrounding the door opening, the thickness that helps to create the illusion that the wall is more than canvas flats, and the threshold, which is the bottom thickness that covers the sill iron and serves as the base for the entire unit. The shutter hangs from the thickness or jamb, and the latch attaches to the opposite side of the jamb. (See Figure 26A.)

It is important to remember that the door unit will be $1\frac{1}{2}$ inches wider and $\frac{3}{4}$ inch higher than the actual opening because of the thickness of the lumber. This means that the opening in the door flat must be 3 inches wider and $1\frac{1}{2}$ inches higher than the opening planned for the door unit if the unit is to slip into the flat easily. Since the facing of the door unit will cover any extra space between the two, the above dimensions will allow for ease of assembly and save hours of needless fitting.

Window construction is basically the same. It is not necessary to allow additional fitting space at the bottom of windows, since the bottom rests on the frame of the flat with no space between.

These door and window units may be locked into place by means of strap hinges. The size of the hinge depends upon the size and weight of the door

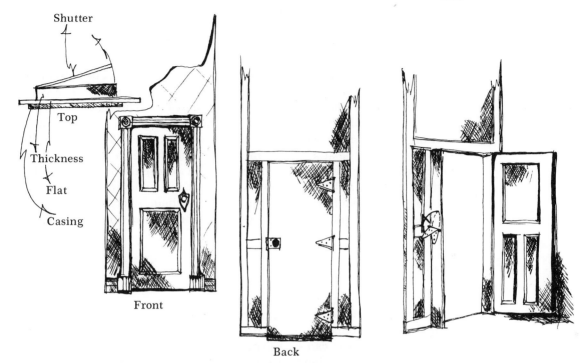

Figure 26. *Left*, The removable door unit; *Right*, The strap hinge locking device for removable doors and windows

or window, but hinges with six-inch long leaves would be usual. The hinges are attached with their joints placed against the outside of the thickness pieces on either side and about two thirds of the way up the frame. The hinge is about 15° out of vertical alignment with the bottom closest to the back of the facing. Only the bottom half of the hinge is attached. When the top flap is pulled down, it clamps the door flat between the flap and facing, locking the door unit in place. (See Figure 26B.) Door and window units rigged in this fashion may be inserted or removed rapidly with no additional construction needed.

It is seldom practical to spend the additional time and money for removable door or window units if they are apt to be used only once due to their odd size or shape. In those cases it is often wiser to fake the whole thing by tacking a 1 × 1 strip around the door opening, which is set back from the opening and appears to be a moulding on the edge of the facing. The space between opening and moulding is then painted to represent the facing. 1 × 3 or 1 × 4 lumber is nailed on edge to the back of the flat around the door opening. This creates the appearance of wall thickness. The lightweight shutter can then be attached by hinging it against the back of this thickness. Magnetic or friction catches can be used to keep the door closed. This method is fast, fairly light, and inexpensive for a one-time use. The removable door is still best for repeated use. Although harder to build and more expensive initially, it is the cheapest over the long run.

levels

Whenever possible, levels add greatly to the interest and practicality of sets. Actors can be grouped in more attractive pictures if they need not all be on a flat floor. Areas can be separated or emphasized by means of level. When levels are used, there must be platforms to create the levels and steps to allow actors to move from one to another.

Perhaps the most practical kind of level is the solid platform. It is made by placing a ³/₄-inch sheet of five-ply plywood on a 2 × 4 frame. Such a platform provides a raised level of 4¹/₄ inches. This same unit can be legged to whatever height is needed. The platform can be castered to provide a wagon for moving set pieces on and off stage. The 4 × 8 foot size is one that two people can carry easily; it will pass through any doorway on edge; and it can be built without having to cut the plywood, since 4 × 8 is the standard size of plywood sheets. Two notes should be made about the building techniques. Note that the end rails of the frame are the full 4 feet in length, while the center toggle will be shorter by the thickness of the stiles on either side, or approximately 3 feet 9 inches in length. The frame should be fastened together by ten- or twelve-penny nails that are resin-coated, or by screws. In both cases the platform will be stronger if triangular pieces of

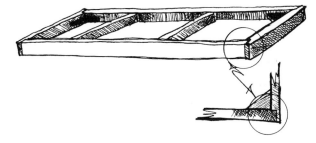

Figure 27.
Rigid platform framing

lumber are glued into the corners as well. These blocks will not only help to hold the corners securely but they will serve as bases for casters to be attached should the platforms be used as wagons. (See Figure 27.) There is often a need for platforms that are not rectangular in shape. The same procedure can be followed simply by framing whatever shape of top is called for. There is need, too, for platforms of different heights. Every theatre should standardize platform heights so that regular step intervals are established. Perhaps the most practical height is 6 inches. If a template is used to drill bolt holes in the platform frames and also in legs of 2 × 4s that are precut to provide heights of 6 inches, 1 foot, 1 foot 6 inches, and on up to 4 feet, most height demands can be met by simply changing the legs of the basic platform units.

With step units built in these same 6-inch increments, any step unit can be used with any platform combination. This is another great time and money saver for the designer who plans ahead.

The steps that are used with the above platform units would vary in height but would be in multiples of 6 inches. Step units consist of three basic parts (see Figure 28A): the rise, the tread, and the stringer. Architects use a standard formula to determine the relationship between tread and rise— $2R + T = 24$ inches. This means that if the rise is to be 6 inches, then the tread would be 12 inches to equal the 24 inches of the formula. Such dimensions work well for theatre step units because the height is easily negotiated by actors and the tread is deep enough that an actor can walk along such a step and it becomes, in effect, another acting area level.

Rises are usually faced with $\frac{1}{4}$-inch plywood, while the treads can usually

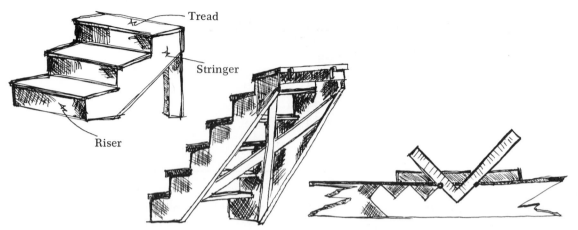

Figure 28. *Left*, An independent step unit; *Center*, A dependent step unit; *Right*, Marking the stair stringer

be made of standard stairtread material available at lumber yards at about the same cost, or often less, of good 1 × 12 pine. Stringers should be built of 1 × 12 clear pine for runs of up to 4 feet. Higher runs should be built from ⁵⁄₄ × 12 pine. Long runs of stairs should have diagonal braces attached to the underside of the stringers to keep the units from sideswaying (see Figure 28B).

The most difficult part of building step units is marking the stringers properly before cutting. This is actually very easy if one uses the proper equipment. A framing square, two small C-clamps, and a short, straight length of 1 × 3 lumber are all that is needed. The 1 × 3 should be clamped to the square so that the edge of the lumber touches the 6-inch mark on one arm of the square and the 12-inch mark on the other. The square is then moved along the edge of the stringer using the 1 × 3 as a guide and the angle of the square drawn each time it is moved. Whatever the rise and tread dimensions used, this method will insure exact marking every time. (See Figure 28C.) If the shop has powerful enough tools, two stringers can be clamped together and both can be cut at once.

The major rule to remember in step building is that the width of the step should not be greater than 30 inches without an additional stringer being added in the middle to avoid saggy treads.

Although there are many additional touches that will make a basic set appear more finished, chair rails, baseboards, and stair railings, to name but a few, a setting that has solid-appearing walls, well-built, working doors and windows, and useful levels contains all the essentials. When the set is well painted and well decorated, it will look very professional.

The foregoing pages refer to standard building techniques for "normal" kinds of realistic plays and platform settings. But what of the others? When one knows these basic techniques, he can use them as takeoff points to the creation of new things that defy the ordinary. He can experiment with erosion cloth and plastic sheeting, polyurethane foams and styrofoam sheets, materials that can be torn, draped, hung, twisted, and glued into forms which no standard building could accomplish. The main thing to remember is that *anything* can be used in stage building as long as it works, is safe to use, and is fire resistant. Wise technical directors will accumulate junk that can be turned into useful scenic items. Old plastic or rubber hose and rope make good trim materials. Insulation material, grass mats, and cardboard rug tubes are only a few of the weird and wonderful things that designers can create from, and best of all, lots of these items can be had for the asking. A big budget is nice, but old cardboard refrigerator boxes, some paint, and scraps of black plastic sheeting may do a better job when used by the imaginative designer-technician than all the flats and draperies money can buy.

basic scene painting

Painting materials and techniques vary widely today. Many scene painters prefer to use the modern latex paints, and they are satisfactory for this work provided the painter has a source for securing the intense, saturated reds, greens, blues, and yellows needed. Scene painting requires far more hues than the pastel tints of standard house-decorating colors. Several companies do manufacture these intense colors but they are quite expensive, running up to $10 per gallon. Most of these colors can be cut with water to double their volume, but they are still quite expensive when compared with the use of dry colors bought by the pound and mixed with a paint binder such as glue, mixing latex liquid, or Elvanol, a polyvinyl al-cohol resin. Most dry colors can be mixed up for from $.30 to $.75 per gallon.

Remember these three main rules when mixing paint.

1. The liquid should always be added to the dry color, not the reverse. The two will not combine properly otherwise.

2. When lightening or darkening a color, always add the dark to the light. Otherwise the result is often five times as much paint as necessary.

3. Paints made from dry colors always dry lighter than they appear when wet. Caseins and latexes, which come fully mixed, dry darker than they appear when wet.

There are no rules on how much liquid to add per pound of dry color, or how much paint a pound of dry color will make. This depends on the color and the consistency desired. There is no substitute for some trial and error experience. Experiments with earth colors are cheaper since most of them sell for about $.50 per pound. Turkey red lake, purple lake, and Prussian blue are three times that price with the other colors varying in between. Although every painter will have his own special colors and methods of mixing, a standard palette might include the following:

1. Danish whiting—used to lighten other colors
2. Hercules black—a black black, mixes easily
3. Turkey red lake—brilliant red on the scarlet side
4. Ultramarine blue—closest to primary blue
5. Light chrome yellow—bright lemon yellow
6. Medium chrome yellow—gold in color, closest to primary yellow
7. Light chrome green—a green apple green, closest to primary green
8. Dark chrome green—a very dark green with strong blue tones
9. Italian blue—a bright blue-green, excellent sky color

earth colors {
10. Raw sienna—a yellow buff
11. Burnt sienna—a rich red-brown
12. Raw Turkey umber—a grey-green
13. Burnt Turkey umber—a dark brown, somewhat red
14. Venetian red—old brick color, mixes well to warm up all earth colors
}

15. Permanent white—used when white white is needed
    NOTE: Danish whiting is used for mixing, and permanent white is for white paint.

Extra colors such as purple lake and French orange mineral cannot be mixed satisfactorily from the above pigments and should be ordered specially when such colors are necessary.

brushes

There are three types of brushes needed for scene painting. Large brushes that range from 4 to 6 inches in width, called priming brushes, are used for priming flats and covering large areas with a single color. Either nylon or pure bristle brushes are satisfactory. Nylon brushes are easiest to clean, but the pure bristle brushes will hold more paint without refilling. Brushes 2–3½ inches in width are called filling brushes. They offer the painter a bit more control than priming brushes for comparatively large areas that must be treated. Detail brushes are those from 2 inches on down to two hairs. Both flat and round brushes from 1 inch down to ¼ inch are necessary for fine lining and finish work. Nothing is more essential to good scene painting than good brushes of the proper size and type. Every artist has his own special styles and sizes, but the above description provides a basis for equipping the paint area.

Another vital tool to the scene painter is the straight edge. This should be about 5 feet in length with a smooth straight edge. Either wood or aluminum will work. The tool should be about 1 inch wide and about ¼ inch thick. A large handle that does not interfere with the working edge should be attached at the balance point. With the straight edge a painter should be able to draw a straight line as long as the straight edge with a single stroke of his brush.

painting techniques

1. Base coating. Base coating is done with the largest brush the painter can handle comfortably, either 4- or 6-inch. The brush is charged with paint and then applied in all directions with short choppy strokes so that no pattern is brushed into the coat. The purpose is to cover the surface completely and as rapidly as possible. Although this is not a difficult job, the beginner tends to leave brush marks on the flat along with puddles of paint. Care should be taken, too, to stir the paint every several brushfuls so that the color stays evenly distributed throughout the paint.

Many inexperienced designers and painters think that their work has been finished with the base coat. This is only the beginning. Every real wall has variety brought about by the texture of the surface, the variety of light and shade it reflects, even the differences in color that show due to the different colors of light which strike the surface. In order to make stage walls as interesting, artificial means must be used to texture the smooth canvas surfaces. Several different painting techniques may be used.

2. *Spattering.* Perhaps the most generally useful and also the fastest texturing technique is spattering. Small droplets of color are showered over the flats in order to break up the flat base coat. The spots are visible at close range but from the audience the droplets simply blend with the base coat, producing an appearance of depth similar to textured plaster, for example. When the purpose is purely to texture the wall and not to change its color, two spatters are necessary. A gallon or so of the base color is split into two containers. To one can is added some black, to the other, some white. The purpose is to provide a lighter and a darker value of the color already on the painted surface.

Starting with either color and with the flats arranged in the order of their assembly, the painter dips his brush into the paint. A 4-inch pure bristle brush is best for spattering, for it holds enough paint to allow the painter to cover a large area with each paint charge. Pure bristle assures that the paint will be retained on the brush until the painter directs it. Nylon bristles are so slick that much of the paint tends to sail off the brush with the first flip of the wrist.

The painter holds the charged brush bristle-up in one hand and strikes the ferrule of the brush against the heel of his other hand. The quick arrest of the brush's movement causes the bristles to bend and flip the paint forward onto the flat being spattered. The brush should be held about 30 inches from the flat and it should be kept in constant motion, redirecting the

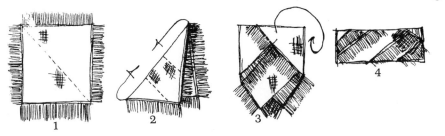

Figure 29. Folding the burlap paint roller

spray of droplets evenly over the surface. A little experimentation is necessary to learn how hard to strike the brush against the hand as well as to direct the paint onto the right spot. One soon learns that the bristles bend in both directions and a certain amount of paint seems to shower back on the painter as well as on the flat.

Some painters like to spatter flats standing upright and others prefer to spatter horizontally. This, too, is a matter of choice and experimentation. As soon as one coat of spatter is applied, the flats should be given a few minutes to dry and the contrasting value should be spattered over the first coat. The heavier the spatter, the better the texture.

Spatter of other hues may be used as well. Flats painted a neutral grey can be spattered with primary red, green, and blue so that lighting can change a unit set to any other color. The dots of color are sufficient to reflect the color of light directed at them. (See further comments in Chapter Twenty.)

3. Rolling. For simulating rough stone as well as general texturing, rolling is simple and fast. Different values of the same color may be prepared as with spattering paints suggested above. A 2-foot square of burlap is fringed on all four sides so that the fringe is about 3 inches long. It is folded according to the diagrams in Figure 29. Dip the roller into the paint and wring it partially dry. Then, holding the roller lightly, roll it in indiscriminate patterns over the base-coated surface. Be sure to hold the roller so that it does not unroll as it is turned. Care must be taken not to exert too much pressure on the roller when stiles and toggles are crossed, or the line of the wood will show.

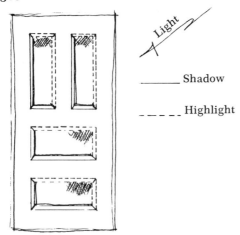

Shadow

Highlight

Figure 30. Placing highlight and shadow

4. *Sponging and stippling.* Natural sponges, crushed newspapers, or feather dusters may be used for further texturing. The feather duster is especially useful in creating foliage. Different values of the same hues or different hues may be used with these texturing devices. A little experimentation and imagination will go a long way. Simply dip the paint carrier, drain and pat onto the base surface. In creating foliage, a base coat of several shades of green should be blended over the surface as the base coat. The same colors, plus two more — yellow for highlight and purple for shadow — should then be added by feather duster. One dips the feather duster into the color, drains slightly, and then with a whirl and drop motion proceeds to flip the feathers into a jumbled pattern of color over the surface.

5. *Detail painting.* Indicating highlights and shadows in order to cause architectural areas to appear to stand out in relief is often done by lining. It is necessary for the painter to determine where the source of light that illuminates the area he is to paint supposedly comes from. Suppose the object is a paneled door in the stage R. wall. The light source is a large window high in the back wall. This means that the upstage edges as well as the top edges of the panels would catch the light and so would be highlighted. The downstage and bottom edges would be lowlighted or shadowed.

Again, two values of the base door color would be created. How dark and how light these are would depend on the amount of light that supposedly comes through the window. The extremes would be black and white. Usually something slightly in between is used, although beginning painters usually err on the side of too little contrast rather than too much. The thickness of the lines suggests the degree of relief of the panels. (See Figure 30.) Whether the object is rectangular or irregular, the principle of highlight and shadow is still the same.

cartooning

Producing painted drops or pictorial work that is nongeometric in nature is feared by nonartists, yet it is possible to create these large painted areas in much the same manner as the paint-by-number kits do. This process is called cartooning. The small color sketch is squared off into a graph paper appearance. The large area is then squared in the same way at the full scale being used. If ½ inch equals 1 foot in the small drawing and 6-inch squares are needed, then ¼-inch squares are drawn over the surface of the sketch to represent the 6-inch squares drawn on the full drop. Dots are marked on the full drop corresponding to those points at which lines of the small drawing cross the grid lines. When all points are marked, the dots are connected and a full-scale picture emerges on the drop with all the proportions exactly the same as those on the small drawing.

Next the paints are mixed to match those on the color sketch. Then the designer or head painter codes the various areas of the drop with the base colors and the helper-painters fill in the areas according to the code. The drop can then be finished by the designer, who adds the texturing, the highlights and shadows, and other detail work necessary for completion.

Of course there is considerably more to the art of scene painting. The reader is encouraged to consult sources listed in the bibliography and to experiment at every opportunity. Working with an experienced scene painter is, finally, the best way to master the skills required.

Two-dimensional set pieces treated in broad theatrical style solve the problems imposed by no fly space, no wing space, access through a 3-foot wide door only. *The Love of Three Oranges*, designed by A. S. Gillette, University of Iowa.

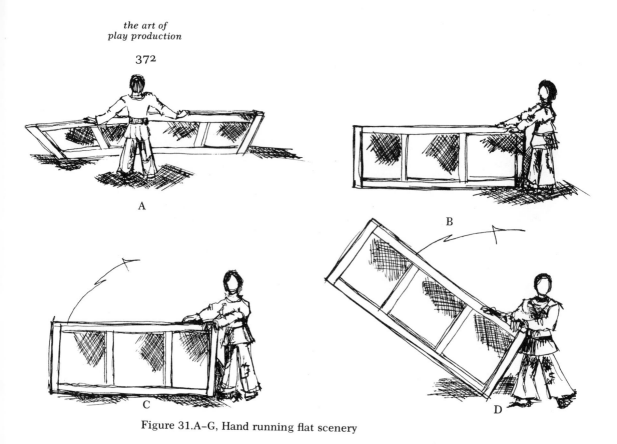

Figure 31.A–G, Hand running flat scenery

rigging the completed setting

When the set has been painted, it is ready to be placed on the stage. If the play being performed calls for only one set, then no provisions are necessary for shifting. Nevertheless, the good technician will normally plan his set so that it can be assembled and disassembled with a minimum of outright carpentry. Corners will be lashed or hinged; bracing and stiffening will be done with the hardware designed for the purpose so that nails or screws seldom will be needed to complete the assembly. Sets built in this fashion can be set up quickly and easily so that no time is lost for rehearsal. Such techniques are especially important when the stage must be shared with other groups and, therefore, is available for a limited time only.

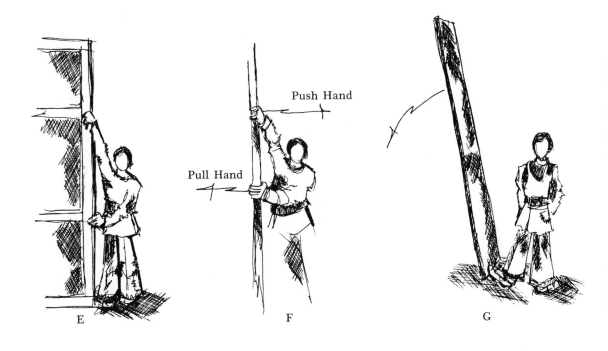

Push Hand

Pull Hand

E   F   G

When the shell of the set is in place, the doors and windows can be added and the room is ready to be dressed by the addition of draperies, pictures, furniture, rugs, and whatever other accoutrements the designer has planned. The wise designer will have found his set dressing before he decides finally on his set colors, for it is far easier to alter a paint color than to find draperies of a particular color or a sofa upholstered with the right tones. Planning ahead will save hours of anguish and searching.

A final word on dressing the set. Most beginning designers fail to finish the job. They place the necessary items of furniture, hang curtains on the windows, and even place a picture or two on the walls, but seldom is this sufficient. Living rooms often have some items of furniture that are just decoration. Pictures are hung in clusters, while windows often have draperies, glass curtains, or Venetian blinds, and sometimes even window-shades as well. Small tables and bookshelves are often loaded with various gimcracks that show the character of the particular family; books and newspapers, articles of wearing apparel, bouquets of flowers, and many other things are common additions. The designer should resolve not to quit dressing his set until it has a real lived-in look.

shifting multiset shows

Many directors shy away from plays that require more than one set be-cause of the problems created by having to shift from one to another. Sug-gestions were made earlier about the ways in which settings can be mini-mized and still be effective—in fact, even more so at times than the usual full sets. Yet the problem of getting scenes changed rapidly still remains. Changes that are slowly and awkwardly done may affect the pacing of the play and ruin its success. Shifting scenery quickly and well is almost a separate art but one that the designer-technician must understand if he is to support his director adequately.

Some years ago the University of Colorado Theatre presented *Three Men on a Horse*. This play calls for three complete, interior sets. Some changes were scene changes and not act breaks, making great speed essential. This requirement was the major one set for the designer. His work was done so well that a complete change from one set to another was finished in no more than thirty-five seconds. This figure becomes even more im-pressive when one realizes that a complete change of furniture was re-quired each time and that no set was handled as a complete unit. All units were built as large periaktoi and contained an essential part of each setting. Furniture was often attached to a wall and moved with it so that, on cue, the wall sections were pulled, spun about, and returned to new positions with a separate side facing the audience. It is interesting to note that this efficiency attracted as much surprise and delight from the audience as did anything about the play.

Such techniques are essential to any well-run multiset show. A few examples are suggested here to stimulate the imagination, for there are hundreds of ways to incorporate the basic devices of *hand-running, flying,* and *rolling* stage scenery.

The basic method of moving scenery is to carry or slide it. The latter is called hand-running, for no special devices are incorporated. Some years ago a crew was moving a portable Shakespearean stage. The flats were 18 feet high and about 6 feet wide. A little girl about 5 feet, 1 inch and weighing 100 pounds and I were running these units off the stage for storage. Helping us were two husky men of well over 6 feet and some 200-plus pounds. The young lady and I could move the units quickly and easily because we understood how to make the units work for themselves by letting the air through which they passed hold them up and having their weight serve to brake them into position. The huskies had never moved scenery and so were simply powering these units about with great difficulty, needing all their strength. Both were amazed at the ease with which Jeanie did the same job they were struggling with. The point is that hand-running flats is easy when one knows how. There are three operations one must master: picking up the flat, traveling with it, and floating it down.

Picking up the flat is done in the following manner. (See Figure 31.) With the unit lying flat on the floor the stagehand lifts it on its side by grasping it in the middle of the opposite side. (Figure 31A.) While holding it in this position, he walks along it to the bottom (Figure 31B). Next, he places one foot against the bottom rail where it touches the floor (Figure 31C). Grasping the top end of the bottom rail with both hands, he pulls backward with all his strength (Figure 31D). His foot against the flat is the pivot point and the unit rises. The stagehand continues to pull the unit upright by pulling hand over hand up the stile until the unit is standing on its bottom rail (Figure 31E). To keep the unit vertical requires the stagehand to hold it with both hands, one held high and the other about waist high. Slight pressure inward with both hands will hold the unit easily. If the hands are placed too closely together, the individual does not have the leverage necessary to hold the unit and it will tend to fall.

Moving the unit requires the stagehand (or grip, as he is called in the commercial theatre) to face the direction he wants to go as he stands next to the leading edge of the flat he is moving. He grasps the flat high with the hand closest to the flat and reaches across his body with the other hand. Using the bottom hand braced against his body to lift with, he raises the front edge of the flat just off the floor. While he balances the flat upright, using the top hand to push gently away from himself and the bottom hand to pull toward himself, he walks rapidly to where he wants to go (Figure 31F). The air pressures created by the movement will help to keep the flat upright and the back edge of the bottom of the flat slides on the floor, serving as a runner and as a brake to help keep the bottom from sliding left or right and falling over. It is essential to keep the hands apart, to move rapidly, and to keep the back edge of the flat on the floor. When two people move a single large flat, the front one lifts and balances while the one on the back edge provides the forward motion. The flat is still dragged on the back edge of the bottom rail—the flat is never lifted entirely off the floor.

To lay the flat down again, one simply makes sure that it is upright. Next, he lets it go entirely and walks quickly to the center and places his foot against the bottom (Figure 31G). The flat will fall gently to the floor on the cushion of air that it begins to compress as it falls, provided the flat bottom is kept from rising from the floor and letting out the air being compressed. The flat must be *footed* to keep this air underneath. The larger the surface of the flat the more gently it will fall, but it is essential to start the flat down evenly. If one side is held a brief instant longer than the other, the air will rush out and the flat will fall with a crash. A good crew can hand-run an entire set easily, quickly, and quietly. Nevertheless, the speed of such a change may not be sufficient for many shifts.

The ability to roll entire sets, or at least large sections of them, on- or offstage in one operation greatly speeds up shifting. The University of Iowa stage is equipped with small railroad tracks sunken into the floor on which a platform 36 feet wide and 18 feet deep can be rolled from a large offstage area. In this situation an entire setting can be erected on this wagon and rolled on- or offstage at will.

Smaller wagons can be equipped with swivel casters that allow rapid and completely flexible movement. Special scenic units can be equipped with their own wheels so that they are solid and stationary when in use but easily set on their casters for quick movement. Two such methods employ what are called *tip jacks* and *lift jacks* and are clearly illustrated in most basic stagecraft books.

If a single wagon or unit is to be moved on- and offstage many times along the same path, it is best to use rigid casters that will follow the same line each time and need not be reversed. When rigid casters are used, it is seldom necessary to use guide tracks on the floor, and minute spotting of the wagon is possible.

A recent production of *Pal Joey* used many small scenic units with an item or two of furniture with each one. The designer used small wagons with rigid casters pushed in from the left or the right or the rear. When a wagon was offstage, the scenic unit and furniture could be changed to prepare it for a later scene. Long push sticks were hinged to the offstage end of each wagon so the units could be shoved on- or pulled offstage without any stage crew members coming into view. Such a shifting scheme using these wagons helped to make the show very fast-paced, for one wagon was coming on as another was going off and the show was virtually continuous. No scene change took more than five seconds, and each could be accomplished in total blackout because the rigid casters determined the exact direction of the wagons and stops on the push sticks regulated how far onstage each should go. Commercial productions accomplish much this same operation by building up a false floor, leaving slots in which rudders under the wagons slide, allowing the wagon to follow any path the slots create. Steel cables under the false floor, powered by electric winches, move the wagons about easily, quietly, at an exact speed, and to exact points. Although such rigging is out of the reach of the average amateur budget, the clever employment of swivel and rigid casters, as well as cables, ropes, and pushsticks, will accomplish much the same results.

Many of the new theatres built after 1950 have followed the new trend of open stage. A large thrust area in front of the proscenium—assuming there is a proscenium at all—almost negates the use of flying as a scene-shifting technique. For those who are fortunate enough to have a stage equipped with some means of flying scenery, congratulations! You have a stage that offers you one additional way of manipulating scenic units. Anything can be flown if the proper equipment is used, a jeep, a full set, a simple cutout, or one or more actors.

It is essential to know the load limits of the equipment. Since the counterweight system is the most common fly system, the examples will be based on it. Figure 32 shows the principle parts of the system and how it operates.

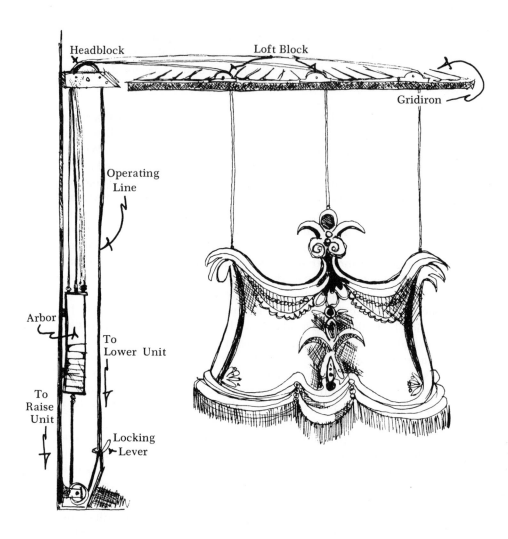

Figure 32. The counterweight system

This is one unit; most theatres that are equipped for flying will have twenty or more such units or *sets of lines* as they are termed.

The principle of the counterweight system is simple. The unit to be flown is attached to one or more pipe battens suspended from the gridiron at the top of the stagehouse by means of steel cables that extend over pulleys, called loft blocks, to a large multiple pulley, called the headblock, over it and down to the top of the arbor or counterweight carriage, where they are tied off. Sufficient weights are added to the arbor to counterbalance the weight of the unit being flown. When the two match, the scenic unit can be raised or lowered by means of the operating line, which is a continuous line running over the headblock, and the bottom or takeup block. When one pulls down on the back line, the arbor comes down and the scenic unit is raised. When the front line is pulled, the arbor goes up and the unit comes down.

Since the parts of the counterweight system are engineered to carry more weight than can be counterbalanced by a full arbor, there is no danger of failure in this part of the equipment. The hemp operating line should be replaced periodically, however, since it will weaken in time. The problems arise when the unit to be flown is not secured properly to the pipe batten, either due to lines that are too weak to carry the weight, or because of improper attachment. A good rule of thumb is to make sure that the breaking strength of the rope, wire, chain, or cable used for flying is capable of carrying five times as much weight as the unit actually possesses. A 300-pound unit would be supported by lines rated at 1500-pound capacity.

Finally, all units that are flown should be lifted from their bottoms, not pulled up from their tops. (See Figure 33.) Under this method there is no danger of the unit pulling apart due to its own weight. This is called flying *under compression,* and it means that the greater the weight, the greater the force pushing the pieces together, as opposed to having that same weight pulling against the joints of the unit.

Flying can be very dangerous unless the above rules are carefully observed.

Building and rigging scenery is a fascinating and an exacting theatrical art that is as rewarding for one group as acting or directing is for others.

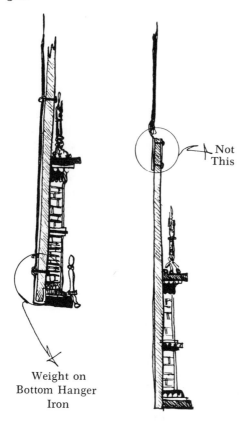

Not
This

Weight on
Bottom Hanger
Iron

Figure 33. Flying scenic units safely

Just as much talent is needed to do this job well as any other job in the theatre. Those persons with special interests in this area should use the bibliography of this book to help find more specialized sources for continuing their study.

Since the invention of the electric light in 1879, lighting has been a major part of theatre art. The first theatre to be electrified entirely was the Bijou in Boston in 1881. At first there was no way of controlling the brightness of the light, but it was not long before the resistance dimmer was introduced. Later, the spotlight that used a lens to concentrate the light rays into a smaller area was invented. Each of these inventions was developed to allow the lighting artist to do the same things he had been doing—controlling the quantity, the color, and the distribution of light available to him. In this respect things have not changed, for the same properties of light are still being manipulated to enhance the productions of today. Dimmers of advanced types, activated by computer technology, can be programmed to perform hundreds of complicated cues. Yet, in simplest terms, they only allow us control of the quantity of the light and, to some degree, the distribution. Instruments using new types of lamps are more efficient and easier to hang and focus, yet they are only new ways to affect the distribution of the light. Improved materials for color media and experiments with special lamp gases have affected and will affect the quality of color in lighting, yet they do not change our use of color control. Whatever the improvements in engineering and equipment, stage lighting depends and will continue to depend on the manipulation of color, quantity, and distribution, the controllable properties of light.

Lighting performs a number of functions for the production. Most obvious is that it illuminates the stage so that the audience can see what is going on. But a stage bathed in general light is seldom interesting, and the eye darts about, led only by the objects or action on the stage. Light can be used for emphasis, and through contrast, certain areas will attract and hold our attention far more than others. Imagine a dimly lit setting of a public house in Ireland. The room appears to be illuminated by a hanging lamp in the middle of the room and some light reflected by a glowing fire of peat in a stage R. fireplace. The corners are full of shadows and the only faces we can see are of a boy and girl sitting in front of the fire. Through the windows we are aware of bright sunlight, but it does not penetrate this gloomy room. Our attention is taken by the couple because they get the most light. The contrast between light and dark is strong, and the brightest light takes our eye. Suddenly, the door to the outside, which is in the back wall, is thrown open, and silhouetted against the strong sunlight is the figure of a man. Our attention is taken immediately to him, first of all by the noise and motion of the door, of course, but it is held and strengthened by the strong flood of light, contrasted with the dark figure of the man in the doorway.

A more subtle example is the case of twins sitting in identical chairs facing the audience. If neither moves or in any way reacts, the one in the greater intensity of light will be the one at whom we look. The difference in intensity may be so slight that we are not consciously aware of it, but our nerves are and our attention is directed there.

Lighting can also help to set, control, or change the mood of a scene. We associate dim lighting with serious or mysterious goings-on. We associate bright light with open, happy, friendly situations. Deep, saturated colors seem more serious in nature, while pink, blue, lavendar, and yellow tints seem less so. Deep shadows contrasted with areas of brightness contribute to the mood as well. No doubt as much intrigue and wickedness takes place in broad daylight as in darkness, but we enjoy and accept the convention of villains slinking in the shadows. Psychological associations may vary from society to society, but the lighting artist who understands his audience can create, through light, any mood required.

While establishing mood, creating emphasis, and illuminating the scene, lighting accomplishes some additional things. Good lighting will give depth to actors and setting by molding them with highlights and shadows. Things will appear more three-dimensional and, hence, more real.

Since what appears on the stage is not real, we often need to strengthen the illusion of reality. A play that takes place in a set representing a living room will have furniture, architectural features, and set dressing as "real" as we can make them, and to enhance these elements, and to harmonize with this style, the lighting must fit this same scheme. It must provide visibility, control attention, and create the proper mood, and at the same time, it must make this living room look like a living room looks. During the day it would be illuminated by the light that comes through its windows and is reflected from its walls. At night it must appear to be lighted by the lamps and other fixtures in the room. "Appear" is the key word here, for in the theatre the illusion and not the imitation of nature is the goal.

To achieve the desired effects requires an understanding of how quantity, color, and distribution can be controlled. The choice of instruments is the most important part of this, and the light designer must know exactly what the various instruments are capable of doing.

Although there are only two types of lighting instruments, there are many variations within these types. Spotlights include any instruments that have lenses. Floodlights have no lenses.

spotlights

Spotlights are identified by wattage, size, and reflector. Working stage terminology often shortcuts this description, however, as will be mentioned later. Wattage refers to the power of the lamp used in the instrument. Since some instruments will accommodate several sizes, the middle size is the common designation. Five hundred- and 1000-watt instruments are the most common, but those having 150 to 5000 watts are in frequent use and are readily available. The size of a spotlight refers to the diameter of its lens. Most common sizes are 6 inches and 8 inches, although instruments both smaller and larger are in use. Either the spherical or the ellipsoidal reflector is used in spotlights. The reflector is designed to gather up and re-direct some of the light rays emanating from the lamp in order to make the light output of the instrument greater. Because of its greater surface, the ellipsoidal does a more complete job, and ellipsoidal instruments are generally more efficient.

In order to specify a particular instrument, it would be necessary to include the three factors mentioned above. A 1000-watt 8-inch ellipsoidal tells us the essential characteristics of the instrument. A 500-watt 6-inch spherical reflector spot gives us the necessary information, yet one of the basic idiosyncrasies of the business should be mentioned here. Instruments that have spherical reflectors usually have *Fresnel* (franél) lenses, and electricians have nicknamed such instruments *Fresnels*. It is easier and faster to ask for a 500-watt Fresnel than for a 500-watt 6 inch spherical reflector spot with a Fresnel lens.

Years ago, Century Lighting Company developed an ellipsoidal spotlight that they named the Lekolight. Whether the instrument in question is manufactured by Century-Strand or not, an ellipsoidal spot is commonly referred to as *Leko*. So Lekos and Fresnels are nicknames used on stage. Exact designation for ordering instruments would require the fuller identification.

The Fresnel and the Leko have special characteristics that determine which should be used in a given circumstance. (See Figure 34.)

The Fresnel (Figure 34A) is generally smaller than the ellipsoidal with the same designation. It is lighter in weight and it is also about 50 percent cheaper, yet cost is not a factor in choosing between these instruments. The Fresnel has a shorter length of throw and is used most commonly for distances of from 15 to 30 feet. The Leko (Figure 34B) is used for longer throws and where tighter control needs to be exercised on the beam of light.

The catalogues of major manufacturers include performance charts to help in the selection of the proper instruments. The chart might show that a particular instrument would throw a 10-foot circle of light at a distance of 40 feet. It would also say how many foot-candles of light would be reflected there. The right instrument for the job can be determined by a comparison of charts from several manufacturers.

A further difference between the two spotlights is that the Fresnel generates a light that is soft and diffused. The area it illuminates is brighter in the center and then gently fades to darkness. The Leko throws a hard, concentrated light with a sharp-edged beam. Light from the Fresnel can be used on top of an already illuminated area to emphasize a smaller part of it without calling attention to itself. A Leko beam is far more obvious.

The beam of a Leko can be controlled better, however, for ellipsoidal instruments are usually equipped with framing shutters that allow the operator to shape the beam of light by thrusting four leaves of brass into slots at a specific point between the lens and the light source. An alternative device is the iris shutter similar to that used to adjust the light opening in a camera. Any size of light circle can be created by moving a single lever.

The beam of light from a Fresnel can be changed in size only by changing the focus of the instrument or by means of barn doors (hinged flaps inserted in the color frame holder of the instrument).

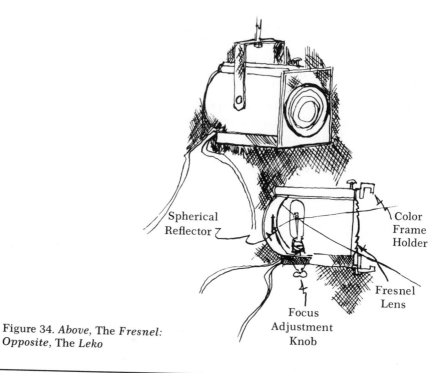

Spherical
Reflector

Color
Frame
Holder

Fresnel
Lens

Focus
Adjustment
Knob

Figure 34. *Above,* The *Fresnel:*
Opposite, The *Leko*

Both kinds of spotlights are needed to light properly the normal stage setting. These lights were designed to solve specific kinds of stage lighting problems, and the lighting artist must understand fully the capabilities of both if he is to take full advantage of them.

floodlights

The obvious difference between spotlights and floodlights is that floods

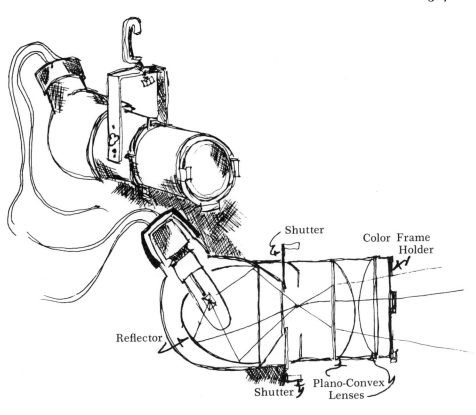

Shutter

Color Frame
Holder

Reflector

Plano-Convex
Lenses

Shutter

have no lenses. They throw a fairly soft, widely distributed light directed
only by the opening of the instrument and the reflector, if any. Early floodlights were simply large, flat boxes open on one side. The interior of the
instrument was painted white and there was no separate reflector. Improved models have reflectors to gather the light spilled within the instrument and to redirect it out the front. Both spherical and ellipsoidal reflectors are used, although the ellipsoidal is now the most popular because of
its increased efficiency. A third type of reflector is used in beam projectors,
or *sun tubs*, as they are often called. The parabolic reflector throws light
rays that are parallel, and so this light best substitutes for the sun's rays on

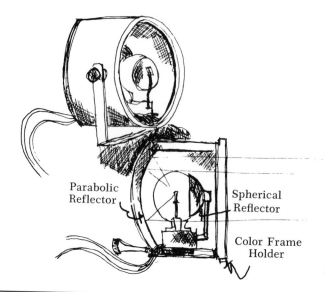

Parabolic
Reflector

Spherical
Reflector

Color Frame
Holder

Figure 35. The beam projector

stage. A black cap or reflector is placed in front of the lamp so that *only* reflected rays emanate from the instrument. Those rays that would go directly from the lamp must be trapped and absorbed or redirected, for they would not be parallel and so would destroy the special quality that this instrument can supply. (See Figure 35.)

Floodlights are designated by their wattage and by a size comparable to the width of their reflectors. Nine-, 14-, 16-, and 18-inch floods are common. Floodlights are often grouped together in rows of six to twelve and mounted in a single housing. Such units are then referred to as *striplights*. Modern striplights have individual reflectors for each light source, separate color frameholders for either glass or standard color media, and they are usually wired so that every third light in the row will be on the same circuit. When a row of striplights is so wired and the lights in each of the three circuits are equipped with red, blue, or green, the primary colors of light, the area flooded by these lights can be made to look like absolutely any color through the control of the amounts of each of the three colors used. When all three are on full, the light appears white. When only the red and blue circuits are on, the light will be magenta. When only the red and green circuits are on, the resulting light will be yellow. Slight adjustments will allow the lighting designer to create any color.

Striplights used in this manner add a nice variety to the color capabilities of a stage lighting system, but striplights are certainly the least essential of all of the lighting instruments, and the theatre on a limited budget should be sure that its stock of Fresnels, Lekos, and floods is adequate before investing in striplights.

footlights

Footlights are simply striplights used on the floor at the front of the stage. Much money can be spent designing disappearing footlights that could best be spent for other things. If money permits, then striplights that can be used anywhere on the stage can be purchased. It is foolish to build in permanent units in the average stage when the same lights could be used in a number of other places were they not permanently installed. Flexibility is the key word, and fixed, permanent installations, be they dimmers or instruments, are simply factors that limit the use of equipment and make the possibilities less and the costs in time and money greater.

costs and ordering

Although the costs of lighting equipment are subject to constant change, some general guidelines can be established. Floodlights are the least expensive instruments because they are the simplest in construction and materials. Ellipsoidal spots are more expensive than Fresnels, and the larger the instrument, the more it will cost. Instruments are usually sold without lamps and without any kind of electrical plug, and so these items must be ordered separately and added to the total cost. Finally, educational organizations, as well as certain others, are entitled to discounts on all purchases.

Since the major manufacturers supply materials that are comparable, price can often be the determining factor. It is wise to write an order for which bids from several manufacturers can be solicited. Their prices are "suggested" prices, and a bid may be considerably below the catalogue price. At the same time one should examine carefully the bargain-priced instruments on the market. They are often cheaply made and faulty optically so that they are no bargain at all. Others may be instruments bought in quantity during the off season from the best companies and resold on a narrow margin of profit and so are excellent buys.

Allow time to solicit bids and add in the costs of the extras. Companies are delighted to make their catalogues available, and technical theatre people should be sure that they are on the mailing lists of all theatre supply organizations.

The four basic instruments of stage lighting. The shapes and sizes may vary depending on requirements and manufacturer. *Opposite left,* Six-inch ellipsoidal. This instrument has a step lens (*Photo:* Kliegl Bros.). *Opposite right,* Six-inch spherical reflector spot with fresnel lens (*Photo:* Kliegl Bros.). *Above left,* The beam projector (*Photo:* Kliegl Bros.). *Above right,* A three-section striplight. This is the powerful punch strip that lights a cyclorama fully and evenly from either top or bottom. Note the abbreviated ellipsoidal reflectors. The lamp is quartz-iodine (*Photo:* Kliegl Bros.).

Perhaps no single catalogue is more valuable to the theatre person than *Simon's Directory of Theatrical Materials,* which lists all kinds of theatrical supplies by title and then includes a geographic list of sources with dealers, addresses, and phone numbers. These sources, along with the many general facts about the theatre, make the directory indispensable.

lighting design

Just as the stage designer and the director must analyze the play before beginning to plan their work, the lighting designer must begin with the play. He reads the play and makes notes of everything that might affect light. If the play takes place at night, he will note this and the consequent need for artificial lighting. If an outside door opens during a daytime scene, he will note the possible effect that this will have on the light. If a strong emotional effect is suggested in the play, he will note this so that he can learn the director's attitude about the situation. When he completes his work, he will know the play well and will be ready to meet with the scenic and costume designers and the director to integrate their ideas.

Until the concept conferences have taken place and the scenic designs are set, the lighting designer cannot complete his work. He must know what he is expected to light. The scenic designer will consult with the lighting and costume designers on color, but the lighting designer cannot, any more than the other designers, arbitrarily pick his own colors. Once the scheme is settled and the scene designer has supplied the lighting director with a floor plan of the set, the lighting designer can continue.

the light plot—instrument placement

The lighting designer needs two drawings with which to work. He must have the floor plan of the set superimposed upon the ground plan of the

Special uses of light and projection. *Opposite: Top, Narrow Road to the Deep North.* University of California, Berkeley. Henry May, designer, incorporated elements of the traditional Noh stage and created screens for shadow projection to picture action symbolically (*Photo:* Dennis Galloway). *Bottom, Juno and the Paycock,* Indiana University. Designer David Waggoner used scrim to create a transparent wall (*left*). The building silhouettes help to complete the cutdown, touring set (*right*). *Page 394, Abe Lincoln in Illinois,* Brigham Young University. Slides by Robert Marshall provided the only background, and minimal furniture completed the setting (*Photo:* Kent Davis). *Page 395, Another MacBeth,* University of Illinois, Urbana. Bernhard Works and James May designed the unusual platform arrangement backed by photograph slides that create an expressionistic quality due to their size. *Page 396: The Crucible,* San Jose State. Designer J. Wendell Johnson used minimal scenic units backed by powerful Linnebach projections for this multiset play, resulting in speed and ease of shifting as well as great economy. *Top,* The garret bedroom. *Bottom,* John Procter's house.

theatre. This plan needs to be of such size that all the lighting positions appear on it as well as the stage area. He needs, too, a cross-sectional diagram of the theatre with the setting drawn in place in order to determine what the angles to the stage will be from the various hanging positions. It is sometimes possible to eliminate the second drawing when the designer is thoroughly familiar with the theatre in which he is working, but the novice must have the information that only this drawing can give him.

There are two basic approaches to lighting design. The one works by dividing the stage into areas and lighting them with at least two instruments each. Additional specific requirements are supplied by other instruments called *specials*. The second method is to plan all the special requirements first and then add the necessary *fill* light to blend things together and to tone the areas sufficiently. Although the second may seem to be more free and flexible, it is also the most difficult for the inexperienced lighting artist to accomplish satisfactorily. The beginner will succeed best by using the system Stanley McCandless explains thoroughly in his book *A Method of Lighting the Stage*.

The floor plan on which the lighting designer works should show the setting complete with all items of furniture. Conferences with the director will help the designer learn the areas of major interest, heavy use, or special effect.

Then the lighting designer can divide the stage into areas that are approximately 10 feet square on the average. Most stage sets can be divided into six areas, three across and two deep. (See Figure 36A.) Extremely wide stages may require four areas wide, and deep ones may have to be three rows deep, but the designer will make these determinations on the basis of space as well as the instrument capabilities and the hanging positions available to him. No two theatres will be exactly alike. The two lights used to illuminate each of these areas should be hung so that the angle to the stage from the instruments is approximately 45° (Figure 36B) and the horizontal angle between the lights is approximately 90° or slightly less. (See Figure 36A.) Areas 1, 2, and 3 can best be lighted from positions above the auditorium in front of the stage, called *beam positions*. The length of throw is usually long enough, and the desire to control exactly the beam of light

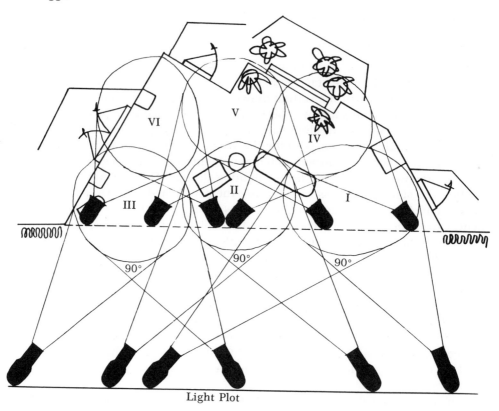

Light Plot

requires that these areas be lighted with ellipsoidal spots that have framing shutters.

A comparable number and arrangement of instruments is needed to light areas 4, 5, and 6. These lights are normally hung immediately behind the proscenium on the light bridge or first electric pipe. The angle from this position to the upstage areas is also about 45° and certainly not more than 55°. Fresnels are most commonly used here, for the areas need not be defined so sharply as the downstage ones and the feathered edges of the Fresnel beams blend smoothly with each other. The length of throw is

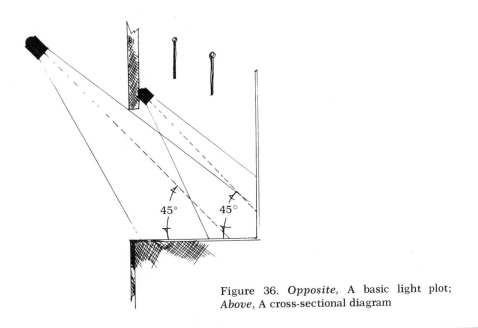

Figure 36. *Opposite,* A basic light plot;
Above, A cross-sectional diagram

shorter, too, and is more within the province of the Fresnel.

These twelve instruments, two for each area, provide the basic illumination, and because of the angles at which the pairs strike the stage, they create a three-dimensional quality that head-on light cannot. This *revelation of form* helps make things look "real" on stage and is essential to good stage lighting.

Area lighting is only a start toward the finished design. Next the designer must place light to emphasize particular positions on the stage. Perhaps an intense scene is played between two actors seated on opposite sides of a table. Although the area light covers them, it does not make them stand out in any way. Several light placements are possible. Additional light from the front might be used for broad, general emphasis. Lighting from the side, either one or both, would create strong highlights and deep shadows and might underscore the conflict between the two. A direct downlight would distort the features of the two and create strong highlights on the tops of their heads as well as their shoulders. This light is often somewhat grotesque but adds an air of mystery. A downlight from the back helps to make the actors stand out from the setting and further molds them. It is important to balance this against the front lighting. With backlighting only the figure appears as a silhouette. When the identity of the characters is already established and more than simple visibility is not required, backlighting or sidelighting, which is stronger than area lighting, will add greatly to the emotional qualities the scene is creating. All these additions might be desired in the same design and used at various times during the show. The same considerations would need to be made about other locations on the stage. An important phone call, a love scene, an argument—all might require specific lighting effects.

Another special consideration that governs the addition of more special instruments is the *illusion of nature*. If sunlight should flood in the windows, the instruments must be placed offstage at the proper height and direction to create this effect. If a room is to appear to be lighted with light from a lamp on a center table, then special instruments must be placed. The area lights for the place where the lamp is located might be placed at a higher level than those around, but a circle of light covering this area, which can boost the light level and also tone it with warm yellow light, will help to create the illusion. Wall brackets and chandeliers can be used as apparent sources for light to heighten the appearance of reality.

The number of instruments needed will vary with the design and the designer. Many theatres will use all the instruments they own for every show and still need more. Commercial productions, where equipment is not á limiting factor, may well use 200 or more. Forty to sixty may be a reasonable average figure for high school and college productions—if there is such a thing as average when so many variable factors must be considered.

the light plot — color

Although there are some lighting designers who do not use color in their lighting, most do. Color can create mood, help with the molding of the set and actors, and add to the illusion of nature.

Perhaps the most common use of color is that used in area lights. Those instruments that strike all the areas from the left are gelled with one color, while those from the right use another. One color is usually warm — a light pink, a straw, a light scarlet, while the other is cool — a lavendar, a light blue, a chocolate. Since these colors are pale, they appear more as degrees of white rather than as actual colors. For this reason warm and cool designations are more meaningful. The reason for choosing pink over straw might be because the pink is more flattering to the particular actor or his clothes or the setting than is the straw. In another situation the reverse might be true. Frequent combinations are pink and special lavendar, light straw and steel blue, light scarlet (bastard amber), and special chocolate.

Nonrealistic plays offer unusual opportunities for the use of saturated colors, and no justification for the choices need be made except that they are emotionally stimulating. The designer does need to realize the psychological effects of color if he is to use them successfully. Beyond the obvious connotations that society has placed on color — white for purity, green for fertility, and black for sterility, wickedness, or death, to mention only a few — certain other kinds of emotions are stirred by color. Blue is considered a cool, peaceful, tranquil color. Yellow is a bright, warm color. The lighting designer can reinforce the emotional quality of a scene to some degree by the color of the light he uses, and he can inadvertently negate an effect by choosing wrongly.

Certain physical things take place in working with color that the designer must understand. Colors are recognized because of the light rays they reflect. White objects reflect all colors in the visible spectrum. Black objects absorb all colors. A blue object appears blue because it absorbs all the light rays except blue and reflects only the blue ones. The same is true for each color. When we use a colored light onstage, we have already subtracted all the other hues from it. If we place a red filter in front of an instrument, we subtract both the blue and the green rays from the light. When the red rays, which are left, strike a stage, they will be reflected only by objects that have some red in them and thus have the property of reflecting red. If the stage is painted blue and the actors are dressed in blue or green and no red-reflecting surfaces are present, no light will be reflected and the stage will appear black. This process is explained as subtractive color theory.

Suppose a magenta or red-blue light is directed at the blue stage with actors dressed in blue or green. Since the filter will pass both red and blue rays, objects possessing either of these colors would reflect these rays and so be visible as red or blue. Green objects could not reflect either red or blue and would appear black.

Few hues of color media are so pure that they will not reflect somewhat more than their own narrow wavelengths and so the above examples are theory only, but to a great degree this theory is applicable and must govern the color choices of the designer. A lady should never wear a yellow dress if she is to appear in stage moonlight, which is usually blue. The dress will appear a dirty brown and the costumer will insist that a new light color be found.

It is easy to see that a thorough understanding of the effects of color is essential to the lighting artist.

instrument scheduling

Lighting is not all artistry. Some of it is simple bookkeeping. The latter is also essential to good theatre practice. It saves time, money, and equipment.

Once the lighting designer has planned the light plot and drawn his design and section, he must record the information on an instrument scheduling form. This form must list every instrument, its hanging location, its focusing location, its size, color, plugging location, and dimmer number. No one can be expected to remember where each instrument is focused or how it may be paired or controlled. The instrument scheduling form provides all this information at a glance. Except for circuit numbers and dimmer designations, all the information should be recorded on the light plot, but no one carries this plot with him constantly, nor can it be read at a glance. Figure 37 shows a sample page of such a form. No lighting design is complete without it. Connecting all the circuitry is quick and easy with this form, and no dimmer will be overloaded, since capacities of dimmers must be reckoned with as plugging patterns are established. Locating the circuit of a given instrument may take hours if one has not recorded this information properly. It takes a short time to plan and prepare the form, but it is the most important time the lighting designer spends.

Instrument Scheduling Form

Production _Man of La Mancha_   Rehearsal Dates _Sept. 1 - Nov. 3_
Supervisor _Zender_   Operator(s) _Anderson_   Production Dates _Nov. 4 -9_

Type	Mfr	Lens Refl	Watts	Hanging position	Outlet	Dmr	Color	Scene	Focusing location
Fresnel	Century	6"	500	Bridge Left	18	6	Flesh Pink	All	R-6 area
Leko	Kliegl	8"	1000	Beam Right	64	3	Spec. Lav.	All	L-1 area

Figure 37. A stage lighting recording form

intensity level and variation

Setting light levels on paper before instruments are hung, gelled, and focused is next to impossible even for the most experienced designers. They must see actual conditions and then adjust their lights accordingly.

They may well know what they want when they see it, but few, if any, designers can visualize the difference between a level of two and one of three on a ten-point scale. They can say they want it "dim," or "contrasty," or "strongly flooding the stage L. wall," but putting numerical designations on these descriptions ahead of time cannot be done. The next best thing is for the designer and the operator to work in the theatre alone, setting tentative levels for each change required. Then, during the technical rehearsals, they can quietly make the adjustments required by the movements or costumes of the actors or the desires of the director.

Light designers work to create a particular mood with light, but it is seldom that the directors will agree with them on levels of illumination. Directors almost always want more light on the stage than will the designers, and the compromise that follows is usually in the direction of more light. Sneaky designers will often begin a bit lower with their levels in order to have some point, which they still consider artistically satisfactory, at which to compromise. As long as the audience is the winner, perhaps the methods of both director and designer should not be examined too closely.

Lighting cues must be planned carefully and rehearsed and then recorded so that they can be accomplished without error or question. Every lighting control system has its idiosyncrasies and so every theatre must have its own recording system for cues. Whatever the case, the operators should have a script of the play clearly marked with WARN and CUE indications so that each lighting change will be anticipated and carried out. Additional sheets that show the setups to be made on the board to prepare for the cues should be carefully filled out in order to eliminate potential human errors. Good lighting design does not just happen, nor does its execution. Thorough planning and careful recording and rehearsal is the only way to do the job.

theatre sound

When theatre sound is mentioned, one normally thinks of sound effects— howling wind, speeding trains, and all the things that playwrights ask us to imagine as taking place offstage. Important as these things are, too little attention has been paid to the use of music as a mood-setting device. Motion pictures, from their preelectronic sound days, used piano players in the pit to accompany the action and to heighten its effect. In today's movie theatre, the accompanying score often is written especially by a major composer, for the movies have learned that well-chosen music integrated into a production contributes greatly to its success. Psychologists have demonstrated that martial music may increase the heart beat and pump adrenalin into the bloodstream. Lethargic, funereal music has the opposite effect. Creative theatre artists should use sound as well as light and color to develop the total theatre experience.

This is not to suggest that every play should have a score of its own accompanying every line, but consideration should be given to music used as transitional bridges from scene to scene, as well as for other special effects.

Dried peas dropped or rolled on a drum head accompanied by a wind machine cranked at a feverish pace used to be acceptable for the offstage storm. Yet in our day, the great advances in electronic sound equipment make it possible for us to use recordings of every variety of storm sound to provide exactly the right accompaniment for the actors. Whether the sound required be a storm, a diving airplane, a noisy traffic tie-up, or waves pounding a rocky coast, recorded sounds are far better than the mechanical effects of old. Some of the devices were ingenious—machine guns, marching feet, thunder—but nothing is as good as the real thing. Any sound effect, in order to be accepted by the audience, must come at the right time, be of the proper degree of loudness, come from the appropriate direction, and contain no clue as to its electronic origin.

Timing is essential to theatre, whether it is in spoken lines or technical cues. Nothing is more ridiculous than for actors to stand on stage waiting for a telephone bell to ring. The whole scene may hinge on the phone call's interruption of the dialogue at a critical moment. Perhaps the heroine is saying, "Of course, Alphonse, the final digit of the combination to the safe is—" and the bell does not ring. What can poor Gwendolyn do but stop, listen, and weakly ad lib something about thinking she heard the phone. Just as she picks it up and says, "Father, is that you?" the sound person wakes up and rings the bell. The audience collapses with laughter and the play is ruined. Nothing could attract and hold their attention again with the possible exception of the murder of the sound man by Gwendolyn.

The volume of the sound needs some special consideration. A barking dog far in the distance must be loud enough to be heard but it should be faint enough to convey the feeling of distance. If the level of sound is set in an empty theatre while nothing else is happening, two things may occur. Some theatres reverberate when empty and the dog bark may seem much too loud, particularly when the technicians are listening for it. Yet, when the theatre is full of people and the sound is soaked up by this audience, which is not expecting a distant dog bark, it may go completely unnoticed. Such factors must be compensated for if the sound is to be right for audience acceptance. Invited audiences for dress rehearsals can help to solve such problems before the paying customers arrive.

The source of the sound may be critical. An explosion in the kitchen stage R. must have the sound originating from that area. A single speaker above the stage or speakers at the back of the house can hardly give the proper effect, and no amount of dust and carrying-on onstage right will be as effective as these things coupled with properly placed sound. Similarly, a telephone bell rung at the stage manager's desk stage R. is a poor substitute for the onstage bell of the phone the actor uses. These inconsistencies take the attention of the audience from their willing suspension of disbelief and bring them right back to the artifice of theatre. Make-believe is fine and right in the theatre, but it must be within the framework of acceptability. It is a simple matter to keep some sound speakers portable so that they can be placed in locations matching the requirements of the sound effects.

Many of the most modern theatres have sound systems that allow for locating the sound at any position around the audience, and a speeding train can seem to originate from the house left rear, run down the side aisle, across the stage, and up the right-hand aisle. Although most of our theatres are not so well equipped, it is usually possible to provide a minimum of six speakers that can be located left and right at the house rear, left and right at the proscenium, and two onstage that can be moved to any desired stage location. These six speakers will provide for the sound requirements of almost all shows.

Most of the sound effects that are required in the theatre have been professionally produced and can be purchased on discs or tapes. The exact requirements of each play will vary, however, so it is wise to make up rehearsal and show tapes that have the order, volume and duration needed for each specific instance. In this way there will be less wear and tear on the master copies, and the handling of all the effects for a given show can be simplified as much as possible. The more opportunities for error that can be eliminated, the better the chance of flawless performances.

It is of major importance that there be no sound reproduced either by the recording or by the equipment other than that needed for the effect. The better the quality of the equipment, especially the microphones, the better. Whenever it is possible to record directly from machine to machine without the use of a mike, any outside sounds will be eliminated and the original fidelity will be maintained. Some determinations should be made before the recordings are made as to the sound levels of the individual cues. If each cue can be recorded at its approximate playing volume, there will be less need for further amplification and, hence, less chance for sound distortion.

After all the cues have been recorded, the tape should be spliced with leader tape placed just ahead of the beginning of each sound cue. With these visual markers in the tape, the operator can set up the cue without turning on the machine. In many systems there will be monitoring earphones so that the operator can double-check the cue exactly. Some cartridge tape machines will cue themselves, and the process with leader tape, described above, can be eliminated entirely. Most small theatres will be using the visual means for some time to come and a well-prepared reel tape can provide the same high quality sound effects as the cartridges; it simply takes a bit more work on the part of the technicians.

Assuming that the rehearsal tape has been prepared by careful recording and splicing, each sound effect should be in proper order on the tape and at its approximate volume. Any volume adjustment for an individual cue can be made with a single control on the amplifier, and each of these changes can be recorded on the sound cue sheet. To set up a cue, the operator can turn up the tape to the end of the leader, set the volume level, and wait for the go signal.

Good sound effects must be virtually instantaneous. Nothing is more ludicrous or disconcerting than a turntable, held with needle in place, gradually working its way up to speed upon release. A spliced tape cut at the exact place where the sound should begin eliminates this problem— almost! Tape decks, too, take a fraction of a second, but this can be anticipated and the leader tape set so that it absorbs this takeoff time before the sound begins.

The cartridge machines begin at full speed, and since they automatically set themselves in readiness for the next cue, the operator need only hit his start button at the right time. When the effect is completed, the cartridge will run until the next cue is ready and then it will stop until the operator begins the sequence again. A chimpanzee can operate the sound with a cartridge machine, but people will have far more fun and excitement taking the responsibilities necessary with standard tape decks and amplifiers.

The basic equipment necessary for good sound reproduction should include two stereo tape decks, two amplifiers, a turntable, a microphone, and at least six matched speakers. Ideally, the tape decks should be identical as should be the amplifiers and speakers. This eliminates electronic problems in matching and simplifies the problems of the operator. All equipment should be of sufficient size and capability to provide adequate sound without the need to run at full volume levels. Some means should be provided for switching from channel to channel and from speaker to speaker for greatest versatility.

The above equipment will provide the opportunity for recording and re-recording sounds. Overrecording effects, reverberation, combinations of inputs from turntable and one tape will allow the creation of many kinds of sounds that a single amplifier and tape recorder could not accommodate.

The above equipment of good quality can be purchased for less than $800. Bids requested for the entire package will save money, but if a theatre plans to build up such a system over a period of time, it would be important to make sure that compatible equipment would be available at a later date.

The impression should not be given that all sound effects should be recorded. Bells, gunshots, and similar effects can best be done onstage by the actors. The kind of perfect timing such effects require makes it almost impossible for these sounds to be generated by a second person. Since the idea

in theatre is to simplify problems, it seems needlessly complicated to have
an actor point a gun and pull the trigger while the sound operator tries to
match the squeeze of the trigger with his electronic "bang." Besides,
where would one put the speaker? How would the smoke from the pistol
be generated without a sound, not to mention a squirt of flame? Electronic
sound effects can solve most problems nicely, but there are still some noises
that should be reproduced mechanically.

The two most common effects are ringing bells and gunshots. Whenever
possible real bells of the type required should be placed appropriately and
wired so that they can be rung by the stage manager or a property person.
Telephone bells have a special sound of their own and a real telephone can
be wired easily to ring. It is worth the effort. A special battery-powered bell
box with a number of different bells in it should be in every prop room. It
can be used as a back-up for a bell which does not ring on cue, or it can be
hung just off the set where the bell sound must originate. In the case of a
door bell it can be rung by the actor who is arriving on the set. These electric bells are far easier to handle than recorded sounds would be.

Gunshots are always very loud in a closed theatre and tend to jar an audience adversely. Twenty-two caliber blanks are large enough to substitute
for any handgun sounds. If the gun must be shot onstage, a variety of styles
of twenty-two caliber guns is available. The pistols used by starters of athletic events are often satisfactory and may sometimes be borrowed. More
important than the appearance of the gun is the way that it is handled onstage. Let the villain be menacing, but make sure that when he fires, he is
in a position to aim slightly upstage of his target. The direction in which he
points will not be discernible to the audience, and the wadding and sparks
from the blank will not harm his "victim." The killer should be kept at least
6 feet from his target in order to avoid any danger. Finally, guns, even
blanks, should be considered dangerous and treated with every precaution.
The stage manager should be charged with the responsibility of checking
the gun before every use and it should be returned to him after the scene
in which it is used. One gun is never enough in the theatre, however, and a
second one, kept in readiness by the property master, must be available and
fired by him should the onstage gun misfire. Nothing is more ridiculous
than having the victim clutch his chest and collapse after the tiny click of

a misfire. The killer should fire a second shot immediately if the gun fails to go off the first time. If it again fails, he should maintain his aim until the property man covers for him with the offstage shot. Although it is seldom that anyone is fooled by this device, it is the most satisfactory solution to the situation. Like the bell that does not ring, the shot which does not fire is part of the nightmares that cause actors to wake in terror. Careful preparation and maintenance of bells and guns can lessen such malfunctions.

Perhaps sound effects have never been responsible for the success of a production, but they have been responsible for the failure of many a performance. They deserve as much care and consideration as does the preparation of any other phase of technical performance.

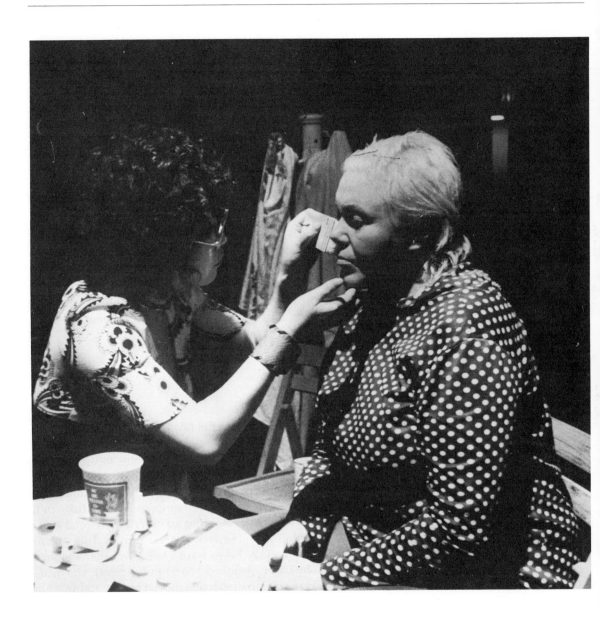

Costuming, like lighting and scenery, is a major area of theatre production. The same expertise and care are essential in the design and building of costumes as in the preparation of scenery. The same need for integration with the other design areas is prevalent, and certain special limitations, under which the costumer must work, exist here, too. Where the scenic designer works with the limitations of a particular stage, the costume designer works with the limitations of specific human bodies. He must make one actor look taller and another heavier by the way he attires the figure. Knowledge of color and line and fabric, of historical styles, and of the ways in which clothes of all kinds should be worn are essential to his craft. In addition, he must understand construction if the costumes he designs are to be built.

The costumer must be able to shop well in order to make his budget go as far as possible. He should be acquainted with every fabric source, notion shop, and thrift store for miles around. He must know fabrics well enough to recognize bargains, and he must be able to plan ahead so as to shop in the off-seasons, to pick up mill ends, remnants, discontinued lines and colors. In short, the costumer, like every other theatre technician, needs to be 50 percent human and 50 percent wizard.

wearing the costume

Costumes are made to be worn, and their effect can be complete only then. A well-trained actor must learn in the course of his study how to move in period costumes. He must know how to handle a cloak, how to walk gracefully in high heels, how to gesture with ragged sleeves that drag the ground. He must know how to bow using a tricorn hat or a lace handkerchief, and how to run while wearing spurs. He must be able to sit successfully in a short chiton, or to control a crowd while wearing an himatian. A good actor must be prepared for the clothes a costumer will dress him in. In a recent production of *Romeo and Juliet* a tiny Juliet wore a ball gown that weighed over 40 pounds. Although she barely weighed 100 pounds herself, she made the dress attractive by the way she handled it and moved in it. A young actor performing in *The Misanthrope* spent many extra hours rehearsing with a lace handkerchief practicing his bows and the taking of snuff in order that he would appear at home with these costume accoutrements. No matter how well the costumer does his work, he will be successful only insofar as the actors are able to make his clothes work well for the play.

A costumer may on occasion design clothes that are too much for the occasion. They may be too ostentatious or too stiff to move in, or any of many other things. Like good scenery, good costumes are simply "right," and because they are so, tend to go unnoticed by most audience members. Other theatre people, and certainly the actors, recognize and appreciate the artistry of the well-executed costumes. The beauty in any art is in the fact that it does not call attention to itself. Actors who wear and use good costumes well will do much to help the costumer go unnoticed. One actress who appears frequently in Shakespearean roles handles capes with such grace that the costumer with whom she works adds as much as ten extra feet of fabric to her trains. The flair with which she swirls them about compliments her role and position in the play, and adds to the grace and beauty of the scene. Another actress of lesser size and accomplishment would be lost with such a garment, and both she and the costumer would look bad were she to attempt a similar costume. A good costumer must study the capabilities of his actors as well as their physical qualities if his work is to enhance and not hinder the play.

understanding the costume

Costumes have a definite role to play in the total stage production. If the play is a period piece, the need for costumes is fairly obvious, for they will help to establish the time and place of the action. Costumes for contemporary plays may seem less contributory but they are just as essential.

The clothes one wears tell those who see him a great deal about his character and personality. Such clues for the audience help the actor establish his role identity more quickly and easily. Suppose an actor walks onto the stage in a contemporary play. His black and white checked suit is slightly

Top, Cardinal Wolsey for *Henry VIII*, designed by Thomas W. Schmunk.
Bottom, King Lear for *King Lear*, designed by Thomas W. Schmunk.

The costume designer provides color renderings, often with fabric swatches attached. Two different styles of rendering are illustrated here with photos of the finished costumes next to the designs. All designs were done for the Colorado Shakespeare Festival of 1971.

Top, Jaquenetta for *Love's Labor's Lost,* designed by Robert S. Morgan, Jr.
Bottom, Katherine for *Love's Labor's Lost,* designed by Robert S. Morgan, Jr.

too big for him and appears to have been slept in for some nights. His red tie, although tied, is loosened, and his collar is unbuttoned. His shoes are badly scuffed, and his red socks droop. He takes off a jaunty white straw hat as he enters. Suppose the stage is empty and a party is going on just off stage R. Upon hearing the gaiety, he puts down his hat, buttons his collar, and snugs up his tie. He buttons his jacket and brushes himself off; fluffs a red handkerchief, which he puts into his breast pocket; pulls up his socks; squares his shoulders; rubs his shoes on the backs of his trouser legs; and exits to the party. Although he has said nothing, he has told a good deal about himself.

He didn't know about the party or he would have been neater to begin with. Appearances are important to him, and he is out to salvage a good impression.

He is obviously down on his luck but trying to conceal it.

His gaudy clothes are an indication of better days and they also show his flashy tastes. He was either a used-car salesman or a con man, if the stereotype holds true.

He is a good bluffer and confident of his abilities.

Take a second actor in the same situation. He is wearing a dinner jacket that is beautifully cut, and he is turned out with everything, including black patent leather shoes, pearl studs, and a red carnation in his buttonhole. He enters casually and does a slow turn around the room, meanwhile taking out a cigarette from a gold case, tapping it, placing it carefully in a holder, and lighting it with a gold lighter. What has he said?

He knew about the party and planned to be there as (or at least be recognized as) a guest.

He is used to fine clothes and accessories, and either is, or gives the appearance of being, well-to-do.

He is a guest or expects to pass as a guest should he be interrupted.

Since a dinner jacket is almost the same thing as a uniform, there is much less chance for one's personality to show through here. Yet one's dress does provide major clues to the individual, his character, his social position, his economic status, as well as his nationality and his period in history.

Although each actor must be considered separately for costuming purposes, he is not just an individual, but a member of a cast that will make up numerous stage pictures. He may be expected to blend in with certain actors, and he may be expected to contrast strongly with still others. Color, line, or fabric are all means that the costumer may use. Mentioned earlier was the use of color to establish sides of warring factions in Shakespeare's history plays. The costumer's job is not only to dress each character appropriately, but to make the entire costuming scheme a whole that not only tells us about the individuals, but also establishes relationships or emphasizes the lack of them. A man dressed in white, surrounded by others dressed in dark colors, will attract our attention. A barefoot actor in a toga with others in business suits, or a man in a black and white checked suit surrounded by men in dinner jackets establishes an immediate difference between them. When a man in a gray flannel suit, white shirt, and black tie walks into a room where ten other men dressed in similar fashion are waiting, they are obviously members of the same firm with common interests, backgrounds, and goals. Whatever conflict there may be among them is not obvious visually. Were the same actor to walk into the same room, at a later time in the play, dressed in a green plaid suit with red shirt and white tie, it would be logical for the audience to assume that he had made some decisions to break with the company or, were he the boss, to change its image.

Costuming cues are not always so obvious as these examples, but whatever the degree of subtlety, these principles hold true. Many designers can create interesting clothes; the top costume designer is the one who can speak clearly through the clothes in which he dresses his actors.

When the play being costumed is a four-character, one-costume play, the costumer's job is considerably simplified, no matter how complicated these four garments may be. When the play is a big-cast, many-change show, the sheer organization that must take place before any designing begins is tremendous.

the scene block

The costumer must know, in addition to the number of characters, who is onstage with whom, what changes in garments each requires, when these

KING LEAR

KING LEAR	INSIDE LEAR'S PALACE 11	INSIDE GLOUCESTER'S PALACE 12	INSIDE ALBANY'S PALACE 13	INSIDE ALBANY'S PALACE 14	COURTYARD—ALBANY'S PALACE 15	COURTYARD—GLOUCESTER'S PALACE 21	AT THE GATE—GLOUCESTER'S PALACE 22	FIELD—GLOUCESTER'S PALACE 23	AT THE GATE—GLOUCESTER'S PALACE 24	HEATH 31	ANOTHER PART OF HEATH 32	INSIDE GLOUCESTER'S PALACE 33
LEAR	I			I	I				I		II	
KING OF FRANCE	▲											
BURGUNDY	▲											
CORNWALL	▲						NO CAPE		▲			
ALBANY	▲			NO HOOD								
KENT	I			I	I		II		II	II	II	
GLOUCESTER	I	I		I		II	II		II			II
EDGAR		I				I		I				
EDMUND	▲	▲					▲					▲
CURAN						NO HOOD						
OLD MAN												
DOCTOR												
FOOL				▲					▲		NO CONCOMB	
OSWALD			▲	▲			▲					
CAPTAIN												
GENTLEMEN					▲				▲	▲		
HERALD				▲								
CORNWALL'S SERVANT							▲		▲			
LEAR'S KNIGHTS	▲	▲		▲	▲							
OFFICERS	▲			▲	▲							
MESSENGERS				▲								
SOLDIERS	LEAR'S			CORNWALL	LEAR'S							
ATTENDANTS	▲			▲		▲						
GONERIL	▲		NO HOOD	▲					▲			
REGAN	▲					▲	▲		▲			
CORDELIA	▲											

Figure 38. A combination scene block and costume plot. I, first costume for each character; II, second costume; III, third costume. If there is no Roman numeral, the same

	A HOVEL – HEATH	INSIDE GLOUCESTER'S PALACE	AN OUTBUILDING GLOUCESTER'S PALACE	INSIDE GLOUCESTER'S PALACE	HEATH	OUTSIDE ALBANY'S PALACE	FRENCH CAMP – NEAR DOVER	FRENCH CAMP – NEAR DOVER	INSIDE GLOUCESTER'S PALACE	OPEN COUNTRY – NEAR DOVER	A TENT – FRENCH CAMP	BRITISH CAMP NEAR DOVER	A FIELD – BETWEEN TWO CAMPS	BRITISH CAMP NEAR DOVER
	34	35	36	37	41	42	43	44	45	46	47	51	52	53
	II		II							III	III			III
		NO CAPE		◣										
					◣							NO HOOD		◣
	II		II				II				II			II
	II		II	III	III					III			III	
	II		II		III					III		III	III	III + HOOD
	◣		◣		◣									◣
								◣		NO HOOD				
					OVER FRANCE									
								OVER BURGUNDY			OVER BURGUNDY			
	◣		NO CONCOMB	◣					◣	◣				
														◣
						◣	◣			◣				◣
														◣
				◣										
														◣
														◣
								LEAR'S				CORNWALL		LEAR'S
								LEAR'S		◣		CORNWALL		LEAR'S
				NO HOOD		◣								
				◣				◣						
								ADD HOOD			ADD HOOD			ADD HOOD

costume is worn throughout with only noted minor changes. (Colorado Shakespeare Festival, 1971, *King Lear*.)

changes take place, and how much time is allowed for the change before the character must be back onstage.

This process can be accomplished by creating a large chart on which each character's name is listed. When the play begins, an X is placed by the character's name, in a column marked with Scene 1 and the page number. When an actor enters or leaves the stage, X's are placed in the second column for those now on the stage, and so the process continues for the entire play. (See Figure 38.) At a glance it is easy to see who appears with whom and how long he remains on the stage. If there are questions, the page numbers for the "scenes" allow a quick and accurate check of the script. With this kind of reference chart, the costumer can quickly answer the questions posed above.

the costume plot

Once the costumer learns what costumes are required through his play analysis and with the scene block above, he can begin the process of designing the individual costumes. He must always be aware of what the other actors will be wearing and never lose sight of the total effect. The costume plot both helps him keep the individual actor's accoutrements scheduled and constantly shows the actor in relation to his fellow players. Figure 38 serves both purposes by means of notes inserted. When one reads across the costume plot, he sees each change or addition to the individual actor's costume. When he reads vertically on the plot, he sees the combinations that appear onstage at any time. Color combinations can be checked quickly to insure the proper total effect before the actual costumes are built. Sketches can be altered at this point, should problems arise; it is far easier to do so at this stage than to rebuild finished costumes after viewing the problem at first dress rehearsal.

The costume plot also provides a means of organizing the costumes in the dressing rooms. All the accessories that make up a full costume should be listed on the plot. The costume assistants can use the plot as a check sheet to make sure that all the parts of each costume are ready and laid out for the actor. Hats, gloves, purses, or special jewelry will not be overlooked if the plot is carefully followed.

When these mechanical processes are completed, the costumer, having consulted with the director and the other designers, is ready to complete his designs. He must often begin before the actors are chosen. In this case he has no choice but to design the ideal costume for the ideal actor. If he is lucky, his designs can be translated into costumes that are appropriate. All too often his Juliet may be short and chubby while his Romeo is tall and skinny—or worse still, the reverse. If the costumer is aware of casting, he can help to minimize the physical problems of the actor. When the costumes must be designed and built from scratch, it is wise to cast somewhat early in order to give the costume designer the advantage of knowing his actors.

In addition to being an artist and a good tailor, the costumer must be an historian and researcher. He must have in his own library, or easy access to, drawings, photographs, and paintings of clothes from all the periods of history. If he is to costume a play in the dress of the Italian Renaissance, he must know what the clothes were like and what fabrics and colors were used so that he can create costumes appropriate to the period. Fortunately for the nonprofessional costumer whose library probably will be comparatively small, there are a number of excellent costume books that cover not only period dress but hair styles and accessories as well. Several of these are listed in the bibliography. Many modern seamstresses are lost when they first face a period costume, but if provided with proper patterns, they can build these garments quite satisfactorily. Books that contain patterns are also listed, and the patterns can be adapted easily for size. Some period patterns have been created by the major U.S. pattern-makers and are available wherever patterns are sold. A little digging will usually turn up the necessary styles.

Other excellent sources for research materials about clothes of the last 100 years or so are the periodicals available in the libraries. *Harper's* began publishing in 1867, *Life* in 1936, and *Vogue* in 1892. *Godey's Ladies Book* was the rage during the nineteenth century. Mail-order houses, such as Sears and Roebuck and Montgomery Ward, have been distributing catalogues for many years. These and others are often available for research purposes.

The actual process of costume design cannot be covered here, but perhaps the considerations which the costumer must treat have been sufficiently stressed to explain what happens. How the designer answers the questions that have been posed is the real artistry of costume design. No two costumers will answer these questions in exactly the same way, but the skill of each will be judged on how successfully he helps to create a particular character, how fast he is able to make a full-costume change, how clearly one character is differentiated from another, and how integrated the entire show is.

costume measurement

Once the designs have been done and approved by the director, the construction can be begun. Even before the designs are finished, just as soon as casting is complete, the measurements for every actor must be taken carefully and recorded. Even when actors appear in several plays in a given season, many costumers will insist on remeasuring them every time, for even small fluctuations in their weight can cause costumes to fit poorly. One costumer takes new measurements after holidays like Thanksgiving and Christmas because student actors in particular have a tendency to gain weight when allowed to eat mother's cooking for even a few days.

Although every measurement indicated on the measurement chart (see Figure 39) may not be used for all costumes, it is wise to get all the information in case changes necessitate adding a hat or special gloves. With the figures on this chart, the costumer is ready to turn the design into a pattern that will fit the actor properly. Accuracy in taking measurement is important. Costume people should follow a standard procedure so that, regardless of who has done the measuring, the figures always mean the same thing.

Figure 39. An actor measurement form

Colorado University Theatre
Costume Shop

Name _____ Address _____ Phone _____

Production _____ Role _____ Date _____

Height _____ Weight _____ Shoe Size _____ Shoe Width _____

Bust or Chest _____ Wrist _____

Under Bust _____ Arm, Upper _____

Waist _____ Arm, Lower _____

Hip _____ Waist/Hip, Back _____

Neck _____ Waist/Hip, Side _____

Shoulder Width _____ Waist/Hip, Front _____

Back Width _____ Waist/Floor, Front _____

Chest Width _____ Waist/Floor, Back _____

Neck/Waist, Front _____ Waist/Knee, Front _____

Neck/Waist, Back _____ Knee, Around _____

Underarm/Waist _____ Inseam, Crotch/Ankle _____

Armseye _____ Outseam, Waist/Ankle _____

Sleeve, Shoulder/Elbow _____ Head, Around _____

Sleeve, Shoulder/Wrist _____ Head, Forehead/Nape of Neck _____

Sleeve, Back/Wrist _____ Head, Ear/Ear, Back _____

Sleeve, Inside Underarm/Wrist _____ Head, Ear/Ear, Top _____

Shirt Size _____ Neck, Floor/Back _____

Suit/Dress _____ Girth _____

Notes: _____

_____

costume sources

Only period shows will require the building or renting of all the costumes. In many cases the personal wardrobes of the actors may supply the garments necessary. Often things may be borrowed on a *cleaned and pressed and full responsibility* basis. If this is the case, then it is essential that clothes be very carefully protected, and that they be examined with the owner both before and after borrowing.

Excellent sources for clothes from the past thirty years are the thrift shops of Good Will Industries, the Salvation Army, and those maintained by other charitable organizations. Fur coats in all stages of condition are often available for considerably less than $5 each. Those that can stand examination from 20 feet will do a great deal to add an air of wealth and style to a scene, while the others can be used to add fur trimming to ordinary clothes. A collar, a muff, a hat, or cuffs — or all four — can change a simple suit into a smashing outfit at practically no cost.

Older clothes from the first part of the century often can be found by advertising for them or, better still, through a feature story which describes the needs, explains a bit about the play, and serves as publicity for the play at the same time. Notes in the programs, which offer to collect the results of attic and basement cleanings, will often net a variety of items useful for the theatre. In addition to clothes, old-fashioned furniture, picture frames, and draperies are often available for the hauling.

A note of caution is needed lest the costumer count too heavily on finding all his period costumes by the above methods. Since people have grown considerably in the twentieth century, due to good nutrition and vitamins, the clothes in the attic that fitted grandma and grandpa may fit few of today's teenagers and adults. In some cases these clothes can be reworked, but often only the accessories can be used. A beaded cloak, which is part of a handsome, rich, and authentic 1890s costume in the Colorado Costume Shop, has been worn or carried in at least ten plays in the last five years. The costume continues to hang, waiting for a tiny girl of 4 feet, 10 inches, or so, who weighs about 90 pounds. It is too perfect to salvage and too small to be of real use. The cape is used and the dress serves as an inspiration to designers of turn-of-the-century clothes.

Many theatres have neither the staff nor the space to develop costume-building and storage facilities. Although this is understandable, efforts should be made to establish this essential production area. Not only is the construction experience necessary for the students of theatre, but a considerable amount of money can be saved by having a stock of costumes that can be pulled, reworked, and used again. As is true with scenery, a unit used twice has cost only half as much in the long-range budget. A $15 garment that appears on the stage ten times may cost an average of $1.50. Yet that same garment rented ten times will cost $15 each time, or $150 all together. Large-cast shows may easily cost from $500 to $800 or even more to rent. The ideal costuming arrangement includes a shop and personnel for building, a stock from which costumes can be pulled, and rental sources when this is necessary and advisable.

costume rental

With the above figures indicating the vast savings in building and storing as opposed to renting, it would seem that no other arrangement should ever be considered. This is not true, however. Some shows have such specialized needs that if the costumes *were* built, they would probably never be used again. The musical, *Kismet*, for instance, requires three sets of exotic harem-type clothes for three princesses. When, in the history of show business, could these three sets of three outfits be used again? Although the rental cost might be high, it would not be as great as the combined cost of materials, design, and construction time, and storage for umpteen years with little hope of reusing the costumes. Such costumes require careful engineering because they are so skimpy and, for the same reason, there is little fabric that could be salvaged and put back in stock. It is easier to rent things that offer little or no future possibility for use.

What and when to rent must be carefully thought out along with a second consideration—what and how long to keep things, for storage space is a constant problem for most theatres. A costumer friend at a major midwestern university plays a *name three plays* game each spring during clean-up and fix-up time. Unless she can name three plays in which the garment can be worn, she sells it, salvages it, or throws it away. Such a game is a good one for the theatre's property and scene storage rooms as well.

The costumer must plan at least three months ahead if he wishes to rent a show for certain show costumes are in great demand, and few costume houses can do the same show at the same time for several theatres without the quality suffering. Once again, *Simon's Directory of Theatrical Materials* will tell the costumer where costumes are most readily available. Only experience will tell the quality and reliability of the firm. Other theatre people in the area may know about them, however, so the experience need not be always first-hand.

Major costume rental houses will supply forms to help the costumer prepare his order. With more popular shows a costume plot that indicates exactly what each character needs may be sent along with the blanks for recording measurements for each cast member. Such firms will alter to your specification every garment ordered. The better the preparation for the order, the better the results from the company will be.

There are a number of considerations in renting costumes, and the most important one is value. Value is the result of multiplying quality times cost. Since no figure can be established for value, such a judgment must be made by eye. Cheaply rented costumes are often cheap costumes, and the result is a cheap, shoddy-looking show. Cost should be considered carefully, but it should not be the only factor considered. The costumes chosen for rental should be well made, right for the show, properly color coordinated, well fitted according to the measurements submitted, finished in appearance, with the necessary trim and so on, clean, and in good repair. They should arrive on time and the cost should be "reasonable." An average figure of $15 per costume would fall in the reasonable range. With so many variables, a good deal of investigation needs to be done about the firm. It is worth the time it takes to plan so carefully.

A factor often overlooked is that the costumes will be sent and returned at the expense of the theatre renting them. Large shows that must be shipped by air across the country may increase the rental cost by as much as $200. If costumes are to be imported, even on a rental basis, U.S. Customs may be a major factor. The University of Colorado once paid almost the same price to Customs as it paid in rental to a Canadian costume house!

costume construction

To the person truly interested in costuming there is nothing so exciting as the design and construction of period costumes. With the machines, fabrics, and patterns now available, it is not difficult to create excellent period costumes.

The building of a period *costume* is somewhat different from building a period *dress*. The dress was fashioned to be worn for close inspection; the costume seldom is viewed from closer than 20 feet. Inside seams of dresses were usually bound; costume seams seldom are. The dress lines were dictated by the period style; the costume often exaggerates or simplifies certain features for dramatic effect. Intricate details may have been essential to the period gown; the costume treats only those that affect its total impact. A costume is usually a simplification of the dress, but it may be complicated by special problems stemming from the play. It may need to have concealed zippers for fast changes although only buttons or hooks and eyes were historically correct. It might need a pull-away skirt for a dance routine or any one of many other special features which the costumer must take into account. Making period costumes is not the same thing as making period clothes. The stage is not a museum; it is a theatre that must treat its own special problems, whether they are clothes, scenery, or people.

No attempt will be made here to treat costume construction in detail, because it has been treated well by authors listed in the bibliography, but some further comment must be made about space and equipment as they affect the process of costume construction.

Once sketches are completed, these must be turned into patterns that are sized to the actors playing the roles. Contemporary patterns can be bought in sizes, and fitting will take care of the individual deviations, but when no patterns are available, they must be created as well as sized. A drafting table that is about 4 × 8 feet and covered with a padded top is ideal. It should be of sufficient height that the pattern drafter can stand comfortably to work with no back strain. The table top must be marked off with a 1-inch grid system to facilitate transferring patterns from books to full size. A second table like the first allows the same work to go on when necessary but it serves, too, as a cutting table where fabric can be cut to the patterns drafted. Standing tables are easier to work at and allow faster work than low tables, and if the height is adjusted to the persons who do this work, fatigue can be kept to a minimum. The tops of these tables must be kept clean, clear of any snags, and soft enough to accept pins without effort. Muslin covers over celotex are excellent, for they are reasonably nonskid and cheap to replace.

Any sewing machine that will sew has a use in a costume shop, but the most versatile are the open-arm machines that allow more flexibility in handling sleeves, legs, and other awkward problems.

Tailoring dummies of standard sizes are excellent and save much fitting time on the individual actors. Space must be available for this fitting as well as for basting and other handsewing if the costume shop is to be used efficiently.

The costume crew should be broken down like an assembly line. Pattern drafting and cutting are highly specialized skills and require the most expert of the staff. Good seamstresses and tailors may wish to attempt the above jobs and should be encouraged to learn under the watchful eye of those already accomplished. Beginning sewers who can sew only straight seams on machines should, under guidance of the seamstresses, try to master more sophisticated sewing skills. No one wishes to spend his life sewing on hooks and eyes and buttons, but he who starts there – as everyone must – will object less if he sees opportunities for more interesting jobs in the future. Even the pattern makers and cutters may desire to create designs, and such progression lends a feeling of constant growth and advancement to what might otherwise be tiresome repetition.

Some method of organization should be set up in the shop so that the state of each costume can be charted. In an educational theatre, where several people may work on the same garment, a shop foreman must continually check progress and assign jobs. A chart system where the person leaving a job marks off what he has completed allows the next crew person to pick up the job with a minimum of confusion. No shop where people work less than two hours at a time can function efficiently. When one person can be assigned to sew, fit, and complete a single garment, less time will be lost, but this is not always possible. The costumer who can do everything and be everywhere at once to assign tasks or to answer questions is needed here to make the best use of everyone. This process must be a learning experience for the crew, and this will be true only if there is time and organization to make it so. As costumes are finished, they should be pressed carefully and hung up in the appropriate dressing room along with their accessories. The actor's name should be pinned to every costume along with any special instructions on how and when the costume is to be worn. Then, and only then, is the costumer ready for the first dress rehearsal.

makeup

Makeup is worn for the same reasons costumes are worn. It must assist the actor in creating his character and must be an integral part of that character. Whenever a makeup looks "fakey," it interferes with the total effect by calling attention to itself. A badly applied beard or one of a color that does not match the character's other physical characteristics becomes a comic feature and does far more harm than good. Well-done makeup is as subtle and as simple as the situation allows.

The makeup artist or the actor who does his own makeup must plan according to the lighting of the theatre and the distance he will be from his audience. Since the lighting will have been planned far ahead of the production, the actor will know the kind, the color, and the intensity of the light that will strike him, and he should be able to simulate this in the dressing room as he plans his makeup. The distance depends on the depth of the house. The actor plans his makeup for the audience about halfway back in the theatre. To those who sit at the front, his makeup may seem a bit too heavy, and to those who sit at the rear, his makeup may hardly show, but to the average group in the house, he will look just right.

Makeup is used to establish age and character or to enhance the actor's own features. The *straight* makeups seldom require more than an attractive skin tone, a heightened color of health and youth, and emphasis of the eyes and bone structure so that the actor will look natural from the middle of the audience. Bright lights tend to wash out skin tones, and these must be put back with the use of makeup. The straight makeups can be accomplished most easily by using a pancake base, a bit of dry rouge, a lip rouge, and an eyebrow pencil. Although theatrical supply houses sell such materials, they can be purchased at any cosmetic counter and often at considerably less cost.

Character makeups that require changing of the actor's appearance because of advanced age, ravages of disease or dissipation, race, nationality, or other causes must be treated with far more involved means. Seldom will a bit of hair whitener or a penciled wrinkle serve convincingly. Such makeups require a careful preparation from the base upwards with materials far more flexible than pancake base and dry rouge. This is where the need for greasepaint is essential. Grease can be mixed, blended, and actually painted with so that subtle highlights and shadows present a believable imitation of the real thing. With the addition of putty for structural changes that cannot be painted, crepe hair, and various colorants, the transformations can be completely convincing.

straight makeup

The simplest makeup can be done by the actor on himself. Pancake makeup colors should be chosen to approximate natural, healthy skin tones. Since actors will be viewed from some distance, the colors used should be slightly darker than one would first imagine. A little experimentation will determine the best colors for healthy juveniles and for those slightly older. Women will usually wear slightly lighter colors than men. Stage makeup companies have charts with colors whose names indicate their normal uses.

Pancake is applied with a damp sponge to faces completely bare of other makeup. Men should be clean-shaven to make the process easiest. Pancake is simply wiped on, covering the eyelids, the ears, the neck, or whatever can show to the audience. It provides a smooth, uniform skin tone. As soon as the pancake has dried, dry rouge is added. Young people are generally rosier than adults and so just a blush of rouge should be applied to the chin, the bones above the eyes, and a slightly heavier treatment to the cheekbones. When applying cheek rouge, the rouge should start at the point of the cheekbone and blend out and up slightly from there. Care should be taken that cheek rouge for men never be apparent as rouge, but appear simply as the sign of robust health. This is true also of lip rouge for men. It should be dark in color and lightly applied so that the appearance is one of no lip rouge at all. It is used only to make the lips blend with the darker skin tones of the base and dry rouge. Nothing is more ridiculous than men with great circles of red on their cheeks and bright red lips. Better to err on the side of too little color than too much.

Eye treatment is the final step in straight makeup. For women it is simply an emphasis of eye makeup for street wear. The brow must be emphasized as well as the lashes—usually with pencil or a liner. Artificial lashes are excellent for this purpose. Shadow color may be used, but care must be taken that the eye treatment does not overcome the rest of the makeup.

Eye treatment for men is necessary, but once again it must appear as no makeup. Except in the case of very dark complected people, a brown pencil works best. The natural eyebrows are simply darkened slightly while the upper eyelid is lined entirely with the pencil and the lower lid is lined from the middle out. Normal movements of the eye are emphasized in this way, and the actor's face will appear more readable and expressive to his audience.

A little practice will show any actor the necessary amounts and degrees of makeup he needs to appear natural on stage. He can appear slightly older by using a lighter base and less rouge. A touch of gray to his sideburns should be all that is necessary to carry him into the early-forty age range. Certainly pancake makeup is the simple, easy, and effective way for most basic makeup problems.

character makeup

The actor talented in makeup or the makeup artist enjoys the challenge of character makeup, yet the procedures are long and difficult. Hal Holbrook, whose one-man show, *Mark Twain Tonight,* required him to make the transformation from his own youthful features to the craggy age of Samuel Clemens, spent four hours making up to present his two-hour show.

Mask-wig showing construction and makeup detail for the Indiana University production of *Prometheus Bound,* designed by Richard Scammon

The materials needed for character makeup are quite extensive. Grease-paint, which comes in either sticks or tubes, is used because it can be mixed and blended directly on the face. Colors for the base are chosen to approximate the basic skin tone of the character. A dot of makeup applied to the chin, each cheek, the forehead, and the bridge of the nose is usually enough to cover the entire face when it is smoothed out in all directions. Next, shadow colors are added. They are much darker base tones and are placed in the areas that appear to recede—cheek hollows, temples, and eye sockets, for example. The shadows are blended out from the darker center until they mix with and flow into the base color. The deeper the hollow, the darker the color and the less subtle the blending.

After the shadows have been placed and blended, highlights are added. They are lighter base tones—often straight white—which are placed on areas that are to protrude. Bone structure to be emphasized should be highlighted. Overhanging folds of skin, as in wrinkles or bags under the eyes, are emphasized by highlights. Facial lines are drawn where these lines occur naturally. The actor should wrinkle his forehead to find out where the lines should be drawn. He should smile and frown in order to locate all his lines and draw in those appropriate to his age and character. The deeper the wrinkles are to be, the darker the liner and the whiter the highlight line that is drawn just above it. This use of highlight and shadow will make the face's natural lines deeper and deeper, simulating most convincingly advancing age. Lines painted on which do not match natural facial contours will move strangely or not at all when the actor's facial expressions change, and this artificiality will stand out to the audience. Well-placed lines will compliment the facial movement of the actor and give him one more means of convincing acting technique.

Once the highlights and shadows have been painted on the face, the eyes lined, and necessary rouging done (with moist rouge, of course, to mix with the greasepaint), the entire makeup must be set with powder. The powder color must be chosen carefully so as not to negate the makeup colors. A large powder puff fully charged with powder is patted liberally over the face, taking great care not to wipe with it so as to streak the greasepaint. Far more powder should be applied than is needed, since it is the powder that kills the shine of the grease and is absorbed into it, making the mask permanent. Only after the face is thoroughly powdered is the excess powder brushed away with a soft-bristled powder brush.

Some slight touching up can still be done with liners and pencils, but this should be kept to a minimum. Powder should be the final step of the character makeup. Additional powdering may be necessary from time to time for those who perspire heavily. Without such treatment, the greasepaint will begin to run and the age will literally melt away.

special effects

Some makeups cannot be accomplished with greasepaint alone because the features of the actor may be much too different from those needed by the character. Under these circumstances prosthetic treatment is needed. Nose putty and mortician's wax are fairly easy to work with and can be molded directly on the actor's face. Great care should be taken to do this building before any makeup is applied or the materials may not stick well. An astringent should be used for actors with very oily skin immediately before adding the wax or putty.

If a massive buildup is needed, then large amounts of the above materials would be too heavy for practical use. Cotton dipped in flexible collodion makes a light yet strong material from which whole great ears or noses may be built. Such pieces may be reused by gluing them on with spirit gum or latex. When building a large piece, care should be taken to build it up gradually so that each layer can dry fully before the next is added. This process is especially useful when creating animals for *Winnie the Pooh* or the grotesque dwarfs for *Snow White*. Many other uses will quickly suggest themselves.

Another special material is liquid latex. It comes in bottles and already is tinted to approximate skin color. It may be used as an adhesive as well as a base for masks or partial facial treatments. Burns, scars, and wrinkles can be simulated wonderfully with latex. It has the property of moving with the skin, and so can be applied over areas of the face that must still move and change expression. Latex can be brushed on and dries quickly so that a strong, reusable prosthesis can be created.

A final aid to the character actor is crepe hair. It comes in braided ropes and is sold by the yard. Many colors are available. Crepe hair is easy to use when it is properly prepared. As much as is needed should be dampened and stretched and allowed to dry. A fast substitute to this procedure is ironing it with a steam iron. Most beards and mustaches look tacked on because of two things. Too much hair is used and it is usually too dark in color to match the actor's hair. A mustache should be built in two sections and attached with spirit gum or latex. The hairs in the mustache should be set in the same direction and line as the natural hairline. Then it should be trimmed to the proper shape. A mustache built on several layers of latex can be reused many times.

The beard, too, should be built in sections from hair that has been stretched and combed. The first section is applied to the point of the chin, and then additional sections, about 2 inches in width, should be added and blended to each side. The natural beard line should be followed until the full beard is completed. Remember especially that hair also grows under the chin, and so the beard should continue onto the neck. In this way the profile of the actor will not show a wisp of hair attached along his jaw line only. Where the beard meets the sideburns some attempt should be made to match and blend the hair so that the effect will be one of hair continuing down the face. No man has a beard that matches his hair exactly, but neither is there an abrupt line of demarcation.

Such a beard, built in sections, can be used and reused after being trimmed to fit. In every case, far more hair should be used than is necessary so that the combing and trimming will leave the desired effect.

A wide variety of inexpensive wigs and hairpieces can be purchased today, along with many colors of hair spray. Any actor can be anyone he chooses with careful application of makeup.

The best book on the art and application of stage makeup is that of Richard Corson. Careful study of his techniques and much experimentation with materials will build the skills of those wishing to specialize in makeup. At the same time any good actor must understand and be able to execute all but the most involved makeup forms.

CHAPTER TWENTY-TWO

When the director and the various designers have worked carefully with the technical director throughout the preparation time for the play, each will know what the other is planning and the ideas of all will be integrated fully into a single whole. The acting style will be appropriate for the set and the costumes, and the use of line and color of set, costumes, and lights will compliment each other. All elements of the production scheme must then come together for the first time during the technical and dress rehearsals of the play.

It is at this time that one more theatre specialist, the stage manager, becomes the major figure in the production picture. This is not to imply that the stage manager does not begin his work until technical rehearsals. On the contrary, he will have been working with the director, learning the play. He will know who is onstage at any time in the play, what props he needs, what sound effects occur when, and the pacing of the various scenes so that he can anticipate trouble spots and be prepared to handle them. Above all, he will be getting acquainted with the actors and gaining their confidence, for when the technical rehearsals begin, as well as on through the run of the show, the stage manager is in full charge of the production when it is onstage. To be sure, he works carefully with the director and the various crew heads, but he is the boss in every sense of the word and the show is fully his responsibility. A good stage manager understands this and takes charge.

At the same time that he is learning the play from the point of view of the director and the actors, the stage manager is getting acquainted with the technical problems and requirements. He learns what light cues are to be used and where they occur in the script. He marks these along with the sound effects so that all cues that must be executed during the show are indicated in his master script. From the scenic designer he learns the placement of all the furniture and properties so that he can check before every curtain to make certain that everything is in its proper location. If scene shifts take place during the play, he works out with the head stagehand exactly what is to happen and who is to carry out each part of the operation.

Only when the stage manager knows exactly the assignments of everyone on the stage and the crews is he ready for the first technical rehearsal.

While the stage manager is making his preparations, other crew chiefs are also getting ready. They, too, must begin long before the technical rehearsal in order to be ready.

The wardrobe master has been mentioned before. He must have every costume with all of its parts hung and ready in the dressing rooms. If some changes must be made so fast that it is impossible for the actor to leave the stage, then the wardrobe master must arrange for an onstage dressing room where the new costume is placed. Often he will have to have a dresser to help the actor, and each part of the change may be virtually choreographed so that no time is lost. It is the wardrobe master's job to set up and execute such changes as well as to see that the costumes are maintained during the run of the show. This is not to imply that he is the actor's valet, for every actor should assume the responsibility for organizing his costumes after the first night of use. But rips and pulled-off buttons and other accidents must be set to rights daily, and shirts and socks and underwear must be laundered daily if the costumes are to look nice and be pleasant to wear.

A daily check for the parts of all the costumes usually will be run by the costume staff, but this does not relieve the actor from the responsibility of caring for and checking his own equipment.

The property master must determine which properties are needed for the play. He will go over his list with the director to make sure that it is complete and that he understands how each prop is to be used. In this way he will be sure that the items he makes or gathers will be right for the play. He will check next with the costumer to decide which items are considered costumes and which are properties. Because things such as purses, parasols, and often hats and coats must be coordinated with costumes, the costumer will often elect to provide these items. In other cases, when these things are only left hanging on the set or carried on or off, the costumer may not be concerned and the property master must consider them his responsibility. Unless the property master takes the initiative in finding out who is to gather the item, it often is overlooked. For this reason, all properties should be considered the property master's responsibility until he makes other arrangements. The prop master then talks with the scenic designer for the same reasons. Some items on the set the designer may consider set dressing, but others, which are necessary to the play—a bowl of fruit that someone must eat—he might not be interested in. Other designers would want to choose the bowl and even to arrange the fruit because of the effect of the item on the whole stage picture. In every case, the responsibility remains with the property master until he releases it.

Since the property master must gather so many items and know the exact use and placement of each, as well as who is responsible for each, he must keep careful records. Nothing is more important to a successful theatre operation than good borrowing credit. If the property master must have a doctor's bag, he may need to borrow it from a doctor. If previous experience with this theatre has taught a local doctor that things lent by him are returned in top condition and at the time arranged, he will not hesitate to lend things again. If things have not been returned in good condition, or if he has had to call to get his equipment brought back because it was not returned according to agreement, then he is not about to lend anything else. This same thing is true with furniture stores and other places of business as well as private individuals. People talk to each other also, and one bad experience takes years to overcome. The property master can make or break a theatre's borrowing ability.

A form that allows the property master to do his job with the least possible confusion is shown in Figure 40. Notice that it begins with the location of the prop in the script and ends with the return of the item at the end of the performance run. When this form is used and fully filled in, it becomes not only a record of the show's requirements, but a source record for every item procured. The initial in the returned column becomes a receipt for the theatre as well and indicates the strong likelihood of future borrowing possibilities.

In addition to gathering and recording his props, the prop man must prepare for the use of his props during the show. Under normal circumstances, he will set up prop tables both stage L. and stage R. so that actors can pick up and return needed props from central locations. He will often have an assistant at each table to keep things in order and to take a prop to an actor who does not have time to get it himself. These assistants also may be expected to dress the set with required properties at intermission or remove others as the case may be. These assistants are agents of the property master, and it is his responsibility to train them and supervise their work.

University of Colorado Theatre

Production *Charley Brown*   Tech. Rehearsal *Apr. 2*
Director *R.K. Knaub*   Play Dates *Apr. 5, 6, 7, 8, 9, 14*
                                              Property Master *Debbie Uty*

Prop	Page	Character	Use	Source	Returned date	Initial
Whistle	2	Lucy	C.B. March	Buy	Apr. 15	D.U.
Brown bag & sandwich	4	Charley	Opens bag, gets sand., puts bag on head.	Bruce will bring	—	—
Jump rope	7	Patty	always with her	Buy	Apr. 15	D.U.
Blanket	7	Linus	always with him	Borrowed / R.A.F. Lopez / 1350 - 20th / 443 - 6535	Apr. 15	R.L.

Figure 40. A Property scheduling form

They may need to keep records of their own assignments, but it is the prop master who keeps the master records. Again it should be stressed that property people are not servants to the actors and that no actor is absolved of the responsibility of checking nightly to see that each of his props is properly located and in good working condition.

The lighting control-board operators work carefully with the lighting designer. They should be familiar with the placement of all of the instruments and know how to check out minor electrical problems, replace lamps, and so forth. They should have a script for the play that has all light cues marked. The best procedure is to mark WARN in large letters at the top of the page preceding the one on which the cue occurs. CUE #6 or whatever its number should be marked at the top of the page on which the cue occurs and a dark line should be drawn down the margin and then into the script to the exact point at which the cue occurs. In this way the operator can follow the play and have these markings to insure his readiness.

What he is to do when the marked CUE #6 is reached will depend on what he has recorded on his CUE #6 card. Every action that requires some change of the lights must be numbered and the information recorded in whatever fashion the operator can best follow. CUE #1 will almost always be to dim the house lights. CUE #2 will normally be to bring up stage lights of some kind and number. Of course, these cues will vary from play to play, but the point is that every single change of even one lighting instrument is called a cue and the method of accomplishing it must be recorded. Recording will depend on the arrangement of the controls for the dimmers. In most cases a cue sheet, which is a drawing of the control board with spaces in which the level of each dimmer can be recorded, will show pictorially what changes are to be made. When only one or two dimmers are to be changed a point or two, the cue may say only, "Move dimmer 2 to six and dimmer 4 to nine." Whatever the simplest means of recording the cue so that it can be executed with no chance for error is the best method for recording cues. Since every board is different, every theatre will develop its own system for recording cues, but the main thing is that *every single operation must be recorded*. Memories are notoriously bad when called upon during the pressure of a fast lighting change. Recording the moves and checking them off methodically is the only way to avoid error.

The sound control operator works much like the lighting man. He should have WARN and CUE marks in his script and a set of cue sheets that indicate the effect, the sound level, and the speakers being used. Whatever switches or dials can be manipulated should show on his cue sheet with the proper positioning for each indicated. He then has only to check his cue sheet against the control panel to be sure that his cue will be performed properly.

The stage crew works under the direction of the head carpenter or head grip. Various crews may be broken down into the fly crew, the shift crew, the setup crew, or whatever is needed. It is the crew chief's job to work with the stage manager in planning every part of any shift operation. Exactly who moves what on and off the stage and the order of each move can mean the difference in many seconds of shifting time.

The crew heads and the stage manager talk through the entire shift. Then the heads explain to their individual crews the responsibilities of each man and the timing for the execution of his jobs. Next the shift is made at a slow speed with the heads and the stage manager watching the operation for problems that slow the shift or cause any safety problems.

When the stage crew, the property crew, and the light and sound crews have rehearsed and integrated their cues with each other, the group is ready for the technical rehearsal with the actors.

Again it should be stressed that the stage manager is in charge. The actors are informed that the technical rehearsal is designed to teach both actors and crew how to coordinate their efforts. Both should be aware that the rehearsal is a learning rehearsal and one in which technical problems are to be solved. Actors should be urged to try all actions that require them to manipulate any part of the set and to get acquainted with their props *before* they bring them to the stage for the first time.

There are two ways of running a technical rehearsal. One is called a *stop-cue-tech,* and only those parts of the play that have cues in them are rehearsed. For example, the opening of the show would be rehearsed by lowering the houselights, opening the curtain, and bringing up stage lights. If the action of the play consisted merely of two people sitting and talking for ten pages of dialogue, this would be skipped and the action would begin again just before a door was opened or a light level was changed or a prop was used. As soon as the action was accomplished properly—it might be done several times if this seemed necessary to set it—the players would skip through the dialogue until another place of technical action occurred.

Such a scheme has merit for getting many items of technical problems rehearsed in a minimum of time, but the disadvantage is that no feeling of continuity is created. Often the time elapsing in a given scene is crucial to allow a costume change. Without running the whole scene, the actor does not know if he can make the change in the allotted time.

If all the crews have been rehearsed and prepared as the early part of this chapter has suggested, then a technical rehearsal which is a *run-through,* with stops only at the points where major problems occur, is the best solution. Everyone gets more acquainted with the whole show and all of its parts, yet the stage manager can stop at any time there is a problem that needs immediate attention. Often minor problems can be solved by a note to the person in charge. Any problems that are still evident at the second technical rehearsal can then be handled directly with a minimum of time being lost.

Time spent during the technical rehearsals will insure that problems are solved and that the cast and crew develop confidence in each other. Nothing is more terrifying than to face an audience with doubts that the phone will ring on time, that the explosion will go off properly, or that the door will stick on an important entrance. This kind of situation results in bad feeling, sloppy timing, and lack of concentration. It is rank amatuerism at its worst.

The second technical rehearsal is often the first dress rehearsal, and there is much to be said for not introducing all the technical elements of production at the same time. Concentrating on lights, sound, scenery, and props is quite enough for one evening. When the major problems are solved and the actors appear in costume and makeup, there is an added feeling that progress toward opening night is that much further along. A kind of momentum develops, which adds greatly to the morale of cast and crew.

During this rehearsal any costume and makeup problems can be spotted while there is still time to adjust a hem or change an accessory. The lighting designer can set final light levels and make any color adjustment needed on the basis of costumes and makeup, and everyone still has time for the final finishing touches.

A technical and dress rehearsal week, whenever possible, which allows for one day between the first and second technical rehearsals and then provides three dress rehearsals (at least one with an invited audience), insures that everyone will be secure, confident, and ready for his audience.

Running the show properly takes a stage manager who prepares carefully in order to know and understand every part of the operation. He must be able to delegate authority to his crew heads and he must be able to check constantly on everyone without suggesting any lack of confidence in his crews.

Much of this can be accomplished by setting up a series of check sheets for others to initial when various jobs are done. There should be a check-in sheet for all members of cast and crew so that as each enters the theatre at his appointed time, he initials the appropriate date and time. Phone numbers should be listed on the board as well, so that in case of emergency, persons can be contacted.

When the light crew has completed its preshow check to make sure that everything is functioning properly, they should report this to the stage manager, who can check it off on his preshow sheet. The same would be true of the sound and prop people. Each simply checks in verbally with the stage manager. It is a reminder to each of them and is a guarantee to the stage manager that everyone has done his assigned tasks and is ready.

Whenever an audience attends the theatre, it must be able to expect the best efforts from the entire cast and crew. Only the careful preparation that a technical week provides can insure those efforts. Some idiot once said that a bad dress rehearsal meant a good performance. All that a bad dress rehearsal means is that people are not ready. If they do well on opening night, it is in spite of themselves. Good shows are a result of long and careful preparation. There are no shortcuts nor any magic. Theatre people know that the magic the audience finds in the theatre is the result of rehearsals and teamwork and the joy of creation.

This bibliography has been selected carefully to contain only a few special works in each major category of play production. Most of the books listed will have bibliographies of their own containing exhaustive lists of specialized sources. The purpose of this bibliography is to provide those sources which, in the author's best judgment, will give solutions to the most common problems faced by producers of plays.

source books

Simon, Bernard. *Simon's Directory of Theatrical Materials, Services, and Information.* New York: Package Publicity Service, 1970.
　(*Simon's Directory* lists play-leasing services, sources for everything to dress the actor and the stage, administrative and publicity materials, and general information about the theatre and theatre people; all are indexed by subject as well as geographically by dealers.) The University of Colorado keeps five copies in constant use.

aesthetic background

Blau, Herbert. *The Impossible Theater.* New York: Macmillan, 1964.
Brook, Peter. *The Empty Space.* New York: Atheneum, 1968.
Butcher, S. H. *Aristotle on Music and Poetry.* New York: Liberal Arts Press, 1956.
Clark, Barrett H. *European Theories of the Drama.* Newly revised by Henry Popkin. New York: Crown, 1965.
Corrigan, Robert and James Rosenberg (eds.). *The Context and Craft of Drama.* San Francisco: Chandler, 1964.
Craig, Edward Gordon. *On the Art of the Theatre.* London: Mercury Books, 1962.
Fergusson, Francis. *The Idea of a Theatre.* Princeton, N.J.: Princeton University Press, 1949.
Grotowski, Jerzy. *Towards a Poor Theatre.* New York: Simon & Schuster, 1969.
Jones, Robert Edmund. *The Dramatic Imagination.* New York: Duell, Sloan and Pearce, 1941.
Kerr, Walter. *Thirty Plays Hath November.* New York: Simon & Schuster, 1969.

445

Langfeld, Herbert S. *The Aesthetic Attitude*. New York: Harcourt
Brace Jovanovich, 1920.
Puffer, Ethel. *The Psychology of Beauty*. Boston: Houghton Mifflin, 1905.
Seltzer, Daniel. *The Modern Theatre: Readings and Documents*.
Boston: Little, Brown, 1967.

theatre history

Brockett, Oscar G. *History of the Theatre*. Boston: Allyn & Bacon, 1968.
Cheney, Sheldon. *The Theatre: 3000 Years of Drama, Acting, and
Stagecraft*. London: Longmans, 1961.
Gassner, John. *Masters of the Drama*. New York: Dover, 1954.
Gassner, John and Edward Quinn. *The Reader's Encyclopedia of World
Drama*. New York: T. Y. Crowell, 1969.
Gorelik, Mordecai. *New Theatres for Old*. New York: Dutton, 1962.
Hartnoll, Phyllis. *The Oxford Companion to the Theatre*. London:
Oxford University Press, 1967.
Macgowan, Kenneth and William Melnitz. *The Living Stage*. Englewood
Cliffs, N.J.: Prentice-Hall, 1955.
Nagler, Alois M. *A Sourcebook of Theatrical History*. New York:
Dover, 1954.
Nicoll, Allardice. *The Development of the Theatre*. New York: Harcourt
Brace Jovanovich, 1927; 5th ed., London, Harrap, 1966.
Simonson, Lee. *The Stage Is Set*. New York: Duell, Sloan and Pearce,
1943.

acting

Benedetti, Robert. *The Actor at Work*. Englewood Cliffs, N.J.: Prentice-
Hall, 1969.
Boleslavsky, Richard. *Acting: The First Six Lessons*. New York: Theatre
Arts Books, 1966.
Blunt, Jerry. *The Composite Art of Acting*. New York: Macmillan, 1966.
Chekhov, Michael. *To the Actor*. New York: Harper & Row, 1953.
Cole, Toby and Helen Chinoy. *Actors on Acting*. New York: Crown, 1970.
Diderot, Denis and William Archer. *The Paradox of Acting* and *Masks or
Faces?* New York: Hill & Wang, 1967.
Duerr, Edwin. *The Length and Depth of Acting*. New York: Holt,
Rinehart & Winston, 1962.

McDowell, John H. (ed.). *A Selected Bibliography and Critical Comment on the Art, Theory and Technique of Acting.* Ann Arbor, Mich.: University of Michigan Press, 1948.

McGraw, Charles. *Acting Is Believing.* New York: Holt, Rinehart & Winston, 1955.

Rockwood, Jerome. *The Craftsmen of Dionysus.* Glenview, Ill.: Scott, Foresman, 1966.

voice and dialects

Anderson, Virgil. *Training the Speaking Voice.* New York: Oxford University Press, 1961.

Blunt, Jerry. *Stage Dialects.* San Francisco: Chandler, 1967.

Herman, Lewis and Marguerite Herman. *Manual of Foreign Dialects for Radio, Stage and Screen.* New York: Ziff-Davis, 1943.

directing

Canfield, Curtis. *The Craft of Play Directing.* New York: Holt, Rinehart & Winston, 1963.

Cole, Toby and Helen Chinoy. *Directors on Directing.* Indianapolis: Bobbs-Merrill, 1963.

Dean, Alexander. *Fundamentals of Play Directing.* Revised by Lawrence Carra. New York: Holt, Rinehart & Winston, 1965.

Hodge, Francis. *Play Directing: Analysis, Communication, and Style.* Englewood Cliffs, N.J.: Prentice-Hall, 1971.

Sievers, W. David. *Directing for the Theatre.* Dubuque, Iowa: Wm. C. Brown, 1965.

Welker, David. *Theatrical Direction, The Basic Techniques.* Boston: Allyn & Bacon, 1971.

stage scenery and lighting

These areas have been combined because so many books treat both together.

Bellman, Willard. *Lighting the Stage: Art and Practice.* San Francisco: Chandler, 1967.

Burris-Meyer, Harold and Edward Cole. *Scenery for the Theatre*. Boston: Little, Brown, 1972.

Clark, Frank P. *Special Effects in Motion Pictures*. New York: Society of Motion Picture and Television Engineers, 1966.

Friederich, Willard and John Fraser. *Scenery Design for the Amateur Stage*. New York: Macmillan, 1950.

Fuchs, Theodore. *Stage Lighting*. New York: Benjamin Blom, 1963. (A reissue of the book first published in 1929.)

Gillette, A. S. *Stage Scenery: Its Construction and Rigging*, 2nd ed. New York: Harper & Row, 1972.

Gillette, A. S. *An Introduction to Scenic Design*. New York: Harper & Row, 1967.

Hainaux, Rene (ed.). *Stage Design Throughout the World Since 1935*. New York: Theatre Arts Books, 1956.

————. *Stage Design Throughout the World Since 1950*. New York: Theatre Arts Books, 1969.

Heffner, Hubert, Samuel Seldon, and Hunton Sellman. *Modern Theatre Practice*. New York: Appleton-Century-Crofts, 1959.

McCandless, Stanley. *A Method of Lighting the Stage*. New York: Theatre Arts Books, 1947.

————. *A Syllabus of Stage Lighting*. New Haven: Published by the author, 1949.

Mielziner, Jo. *Designing for the Theatre*. New York: Atheneum, 1965.

————. *The Shapes of Our Theatre*. New York: Crown, 1970.

Parker, Oren and Harvey Smith. *Scene Design and Stage Lighting*. New York: Holt, Rinehart & Winston, 1963.

Phillippi, Herbert. *Stagecraft and Scene Design*. Boston: Houghton Mifflin, 1953.

Seldon, Samuel and Hunton Sellman. *Stage Scenery and Lighting*. New York: Appleton-Century-Crofts, 1958.

Simonson, Lee. *The Art of Scenic Design*. New York: Harper & Row, 1950.

————. *Part of a Lifetime*. New York: Duell, Sloan and Pearce, 1943.

Welker, David. *Theatrical Set Design*. Boston: Allyn & Bacon, 1969.

costume

Barton, Lucy. *Historic Costume for the Stage*. Boston: W. H. Baker, 1961.

Fernald, Mary. *Costume Design and Making: A Practical Handbook.*
New York: Theatre Arts Books, 1967.

Hill, Margot and Peter Bucknell. *Evolution of Period Fashion, Pattern and Cut from 1066–1930.* London: B. T. Batsford, 1967; New York: Reinhold, 1967.

Kopp, Ernestine, Vittorino Rolfo, and Beatrice Zelin. *Designing Apparel Through the Flat Pattern.* New York: Fairchild, 1969.

Norris, Herbert. *Costume and Fashion.* 4 vols. New York: Dutton, 1947.

Payne, Blanche. *History of Costume.* New York: Harper & Row, 1965.

Waugh, Nora. *Corsets and Crinolines.* New York: Theatre Arts Books, 1970.

———. *The Cut of Men's Clothes, 1600–1900.* New York: Theatre Arts Books, 1964.

———. *The Cut of Women's Clothes, 1600–1900.* New York: Theatre Arts Books, 1968.

makeup

Corson, Richard. *Stage Make-Up.* New York: Appleton-Century-Crofts, 1960.

Strenkovsky, Serge. *The Art of Make-Up.* New York: Dutton, 1937.

theatre building

American Theatre Planning Board. *Theatre Checklist: A Guide to the Planning and Construction of Proscenium and Open-Stage Theatres.* Middletown, Conn.: Wesleyan University Press, 1969.

Burris-Meyer, Harold and Edward Cole. *Theatres and Auditoriums.* New York: Reinhold, 1964.

miscellaneous

Ewen, David. *American Musical Theatre.* New York: Holt, Rinehart & Winston, 1959.

Goodman, Randolph. *Drama on Stage.* New York: Holt, Rinehart & Winston, 1961.

Gruver, Bert. *The Stage Manager's Handbook.* New York: Harper & Row, 1953.

Kernodle, George. *Invitation to the Theatre*. New York: Harcourt
Brace Jonanovich, 1967.

Plummer, Gail. *The Business of Show Business*. New York: Harper &
Row, 1961.

Shank, Theodore. *A Digest of 500 Plays*. New York: Crowell Collier
Macmillan, 1963.

Whiting, Frank. *An Introduction to the Theatre,* 3rd ed. New York:
Harper & Row, 1969.

dramatic houses

Baker's Plays, 100 Summer, Boston, Mass. 02110. Telephone 617–482–1280.

Dramatic Publishing Co., 86 E. Randolph, Chicago, Ill. 60601. Telephone 312–726–5814.

Dramatists Play Service, 440 Park Ave. S., New York, N.Y. 10016. Telephone 212–683–8960.

Samuel French, Inc., 25 W. 45th St., New York, N.Y. 10036. Telephone 212–582–4700.

musical houses

Metromedia-On-Stage, 1700 Broadway, New York, N.Y. 10036. Telephone 212–757–8387.

Music Theatre International, 119 W. 57th St., New York, N.Y. 10019. Telephone 212–265–3600.

Rodgers & Hammerstein Repertory, 120 E. 56th St., New York, N.Y. 10022. Telephone 212–682–1860.

Tams-Witmark Music Library, 757 Third Ave., New York, N.Y. 10017. Telephone 212–688–2525.